D1210267

NATION INTO STATE ★ ★ ★ ★

NATION INTO STATE

THE SHIFTING SYMBOLIC ★ ★ ★

FOUNDATIONS OF AMERICAN ★ ★

NATIONALISM ★ ★ ★ ★ ★ ★

WILBUR ZELINSKY

THE UNIVERSITY OF
NORTH CAROLINA PRESS
CHAPEL HILL & LONDON

The paper in this book meets the guidelines for
permanence and durability of the Committee on
Production Guidelines for Book Longevity of the
Council on Library Resources.

92 91 90 89 88   5 4 3 2 1

Library of Congress Cataloging-in-Publication Data
Zelinsky, Wilbur, 1921–
    Nation into state: the shifting symbolic
foundations of American nationalism /
Wilbur Zelinsky.
        p. cm.
    Bibliography: p.
    Includes index.
    ISBN 0-8078-6750-0 (alk. paper)
    1. Nationalism—United States—History.
2. Patriotism—United States—History.
3. Signs and symbols—United States.
4. United States—Civilization. I. Title.
E169.1.Z39   1988   88-4211
973—dc19   CIP

TO
_____

Wilma Fairchild

Harvey Goldberg

Rhoda Gould

Bob Johnsrud

David Sopher

Joseph Spencer

John K. Wright

in payment for
the brightest of memories

CONTENTS ★ ★ ★ ★ ★ ★

TABLES ★ ★ ★ ★ ★ ★ ★

FIGURES ★ ★ ★ ★ ★ ★ ★

When I began this project six years ago, I had no clear idea of its outcome. The root cause is a lifelong, insatiable curiosity about all aspects of the American scene, but, more recently and particularly, the conviction that it is essential to know as much as possible about nationalism and its symbols if one is to make the maximum amount of sense out of the past or present United States.

The initial intention was to examine a large number of countries, comparing their nationalistic practices with those of my native land. But it quickly became apparent that such an ambitious work plan far exceeded my grasp. The relevant literature is spotty, and the effort to fill in the gaps in field and library would have been prohibitively expensive in terms of time and money and well beyond my finite linguistic capabilities. Realistically, then, what I had thought of doing may be very much worth doing, but is actually a lifelong program for some obstinate young scholar. At this stage in my career I was obliged to limit scrutiny to the United States—and to Canada, the only other country where my ignorance is not totally scandalous. For reasons of internal coherence in the final product, a chapter in the first draft that dealt with Canada does not appear in this volume, but may eventually see the light of day elsewhere.

The initial approach to the data was naive. I had no idea where they would lead or what sort of grand scheme, if any, might materialize. As the evidence accumulated, I began to be deeply troubled by contradictory trends in the historical development of certain nationalistic items. Only after much painful cogitation did I hit upon the rather obvious formula that strikes me as the only possible way to interpret the life history of nationalism in the United States. The title of this work telegraphs my discovery, one that is spelled out in greatest detail toward the end of chapter 5.

Many of the inadequacies in a volume conceived in a fit of foolrushery can be ascribed to my mere smattering of knowledge and lack of technical skills in the various scholarly disciplines that must be involved in any definitive treatment of nationalism. It is indeed a phenomenon that straddles a multitude of conventional academic areas, including history, geography, social psychology, theology, semiotics, political science, sociology, landscape architecture, and all of the humanities, among other items. I bring to it only my professional background as a human geographer, a fact that will be obvious to any attentive reader.

Because of the sheer immensity and diversity of subject matter, I have relied mainly on secondary sources. But in a few instances, notably in the treatment of flag, eagle, nationalistic place-names, and visits to nationalistic sites, I have been able to carry out field observations or exploit primary sources. Unfortunately, for many of the topics which I hoped to discuss in detail, the literature and statistics are either nonexistent or deficient in quantity or quality. I have flagged these deficiencies at the appropriate points in the hope that others will take up the challenge.

I lay down my pen (or, to be less anachronistic, switch off this electric typewriter) with the nagging sense of having only nicked the surface of an enormous subject. Even though I may not have succeeded more than very partially in attaining my goal, there is the likelihood that others will improve upon this effort, and that, in the meantime, I have suggested some of the ways in which an understanding of nationalism and its symbols can illuminate the much larger issues of societal change.

The fun part of this apologia is to acknowledge gratefully the special assistance received along the way from the following generous individuals: Richard Ahlborn, George F. Cahill, Daniel G. Connors, Michael Frisch, Alan Gowans, Helen A. Harrison, Deryck Holdsworth, J. B. Jackson, Michael Kammen, Victor Konrad, Peirce Lewis, David Lowenthal, Donald Meinig, Hugh Prince, Alan Rayburn, Carl Scheele, Beatriz Schiller, Thomas Schlereth, Daniel Walden, and Gladys and Hollis Zelinsky. A courtly bow to June Irvin, the most cheerful and sympathetic of typists. I owe a special debt of gratitude to the John Simon Guggenheim Memorial Foundation and the Earhart Foundation for grants that helped make this endeavor possible.

Wilbur Zelinsky
University Park, Pennsylvania

NATION INTO STATE ★ ★ ★ ★

ONE ★ ★ ★ ★ ★ ★ ★ ★

SETTING THE STAGE ★ ★ ★ ★

Nationalism is the reigning passion of our times. Here is what breeds the energy that drives the nation-state. And unless we probe the intense emotions at the core of nationalism, we cannot hope to comprehend the world order of nation-states governing us today.

Such assertions carry us well beyond the truism that all but the most remote or primitive (and cosmopolitan?) members of humankind today regard themselves as citizens of some 150-odd more or less sovereign states or nation-states, or that their lives and conduct are controlled in decisive fashion by the rulers of these entities. They ratify the elemental fact that such well-nigh universal acquiescence, even joyous acceptance of the nation-state system, would be utterly unthinkable in lieu of some powerful emotional commitment. Perhaps no one has stated the matter more pungently than George Orwell. "One cannot see the modern world as it is unless one recognizes the overwhelming strength of patriotism, national loyalty . . . Christianity and international socialism are as weak as straw in comparison with it" (Orwell, 1953:192). Indeed, the allusion to religion may be more than a figure of speech because, as Carlton Hayes has noted, "nationalism of the present age has an ever growing number of jealous and quarrelsome sects. It is also, as a whole, the latest and nearest approach to a world religion. Its cult is now universal, and is accompanied as well by African tom-tom as by European or American fife and drum" (Hayes, 1960: 172).

In any case, it follows, quite logically, that if we are to have any luck in coping with the many crises that bedevil human societies along that entire worrisome continuum from the local to the global, it is not enough to consider the economic, military, and political aspects of domestic and international affairs. We must know as much as possible about the spirit or faith, that remarkable obsession we call nationalism, that fuels the system, for there is nothing more powerful, outside the realm of inanimate forces, than a triumphant idea.

Despite an imposing mass of literature on the topic, there is still much to be learned about nationalism. However germane economic and political phenomena may be in explaining its origin or the evolution of nation-states, it is self-evident that social psychology is also a crucial item, that something ideational lives close to the core of nationalism, and that this attitudinal essence is still dimly understood. The central thesis of this study is that by scrutinizing the symbolic aspects of this complicated, socially shared mental construct as it has evolved over time and space in a particularly important country we can gain valuable insights into the general phenomenon.

In many ways, this is a peculiarly agonizing exercise, analogous to expecting a fish to describe what it feels like to swim in the ocean. Both author and readers have been so thoroughly immersed since infancy in the axioms of nationalism that viewing it objectively, or imagining alternatives to the present-day nation-state system, strains the imagination past its limits. We know, of course, that this system is historically recent, that it originated within the past five hundred years and attained maturity only during the past century, and that our ancestors thought and behaved politically in ways that now seem utterly strange to us (A. D. Smith, 1977:1). We must also acknowledge, however implausible such a development may seem at the moment, that nationalism and its associated world order are really transient affairs, like any other set of social arrangements, and that they must eventually yield to something else. What that something else may turn out to be is absolutely beyond our capacity to envision, just as it would have been impossible for even the brightest visionary of thirteenth-century Europe to foresee the shape of today's sociopolitical world.

It is arguable, however, that the transition to whatever sequel lies in store for us may be, in significant measure, deliberate and self-conscious, in contrast to the spontaneous, unpremeditated emergence of the current world order. If such social engineering should indeed come to pass, an intimate understanding of nationalism would certainly help lubricate the process. There will be both time and need for many more essays, like the present example, to explore the symbolic heart of our pervasive nationalistic syndrome, since any meaningful transformation lies far in the future. In the meantime, as Anthony Smith has so ably stated, "the fact is, that we have arrived at the point where nationalism appears to be a self-reproducing phenomenon, given the persistence of the world state system in any form. Hence, cosmopolitan hopes for an early withering-away of nationalism are doomed to disappointment, for they are based on a failure to grasp the importance today of the conjunction of ethnic sentiments, secular ideals and changing elements of modernization and its social concomitants" (A. D. Smith, 1979:x).

It is also useless to dabble in counterfactual history and speculate whether the nation-state was the only appropriate vehicle for the modernization of the world.[1] It is equally pointless either to praise or damn nationalism as, on the one hand, conferring the priceless, multiple blessings of advanced societies that can far outweigh its darker effects, or, on the other, as being an unmitigated disaster, or as being a boon in certain times and places but a curse in others (Sulzbach, 1943). There is probably no one who has indicted nationalism more forcefully than George Steiner: "From being a nineteenth-century dream, nationalism has grown to a present nightmare. In two world wars it has all but ruined Western culture" (Steiner, 1967:59).[2] But despite the varied perspectives we entertain as we view different instances from the lofty perch of our own national virtue, nationalism is really much the same creature everywhere, and from an ethical standpoint it is inherently ambiguous. Tom Nairn has set forth the situation in eloquent terms.

> As the most elementary comparative analysis will show, all nationalism is both healthy and morbid. Both progress and retrogression are inscribed in its genetic code from the start . . . it is an exact (not a rhetorical) statement about nationalism to say that it is by nature ambivalent. . . . [T]he huge family of nationalisms cannot be divided into the black cats, with a few half-breeds in between. The whole family is spotted, without exception. Forms of "irrationality" (prejudice, sentimentality, collective egoism, aggression, etc.) stain the lot of them.
>
> In short, the substance of national*ism* as such is always morally, politically, humanly ambiguous. This is why moralizing perspectives on the phenomenon always fail, whether they praise or berate it. They simply seize upon one face or another of the creature, and will not admit that there is a common head conjoining them. [Nairn, 1977:347–49]

But if nationalism is an ambivalent something we must coexist with for many years to come, an emotional blanket the thoughtful person dare neither hug without restraint nor thrust out of sight, it is nonetheless imperative that we try to arrive at a critical under-

standing of this fabric of feelings and symbols in which our lives
are so deeply enmeshed.

KEY TERMS AND CONCEPTS

We cannot enter the substance of this study until certain key terms
and concepts, including *nationalism*, have been defined as precisely
as possible. Such an exercise is particularly important since I shall
be adopting quite specific meanings for some relatively common
words, meanings that may depart somewhat from ordinary usage or
the rather loose and variable terminology in the scholarly literature.

Although it appears frequently in writings on nationalism, I shall
use the term *patriotism* most sparingly since, strictly speaking, it
signifies a sentiment only distantly related to nationalism. "Patriotism . . . is . . . naturally and readily associated with a small community in a restricted area much more than with a large nationality
in a broad expanse of territory" (Hayes, 1960:10). Therefore it is
an emotion experienced as love of, or loyalty toward, one's immediate environs, the personally perceived action-space an individual
encounters in his or her everyday life, something closely akin to
"topophilia" (Tuan, 1974). Thus "conceptually, nationalism is distinct from both patriotism or local attachment and xenophobia or
distrust of others" (Berry, 1981:75). The contrast between patriotism and nationalism becomes clearer if we take note of the situation in France, where "distinction is usefully made between *patrie*
(one's whole nation or 'fatherland') and *pays* (one's immediate homeland). Everybody, besides having a *patrie*, has a *pays*" (Hayes, 1960:
9). I shall give *xenophobia* even shorter shrift than patriotism since
it clearly materializes on the other side of the same coin. Since they
have abounded since paleolithic times, xenophobes are of limited
historical or geographic interest.

State is a term with considerable import for this inquiry and,
fortunately, one with a simple definition: a political apparatus that
claims or exerts absolute sovereignty over a given territory and its
inhabitants. States have existed in all shapes and sizes from such
enormities as the Roman, Persian, and Chinese empires of ancient
times down to such miniature curiosities as Liechtenstein, Singa-
pore, or the Vatican City. Forms of governance and ideology can
vary even more widely. But the essence of statehood, as exclusive
jurisdiction over land, persons, and resources, or the serious effort
to exert such control, remains invariant. So defined, the state has
manifested itself for several millennia in certain regions of the Old

and New Worlds. Only in recent times, however, has it become the universal mode of social organization and the object of powerful affection, even worship, and closely identified with nationalism—and *statism*.

The concept of the *nation* offers much greater difficulty. Indeed "no two students today will agree in detail on a definition of a nation" (Shafer, 1972:15). But Boyd Shafer's skeleton formula provides a useful start:

> The word nation describes a group of some size of people united, usually, by (1) residence in a common land (the *patrie* becomes the national land), (2) a common heritage and culture, (3) common interests in the present and common hopes to live together in the future, and (4) a common desire to have and maintain their own state. [Shafer, 1960:15]

Certain other definitions, including Anthony Smith's, are in essential agreement.

> A nation ... may be defined as any social group with a common and distinctive history and culture, a definite territory, common sentiments of solidarity, a single economy and equal citizenship rights for all members. [A. D. Smith, 1979:87]

For the purposes of this study, it is crucial to note that, although nationhood *may* imply aspirations toward statehood, nation and state are far from being synonymous concepts. If we distill the notion of nationhood, or peoplehood, to its essence, it is the shared belief among a sizeable group of individuals (too large a number for personal contact to be feasible among all) that they are united in the possession of a unique and cherished social and cultural personality. As enunciated by Herder, Hegel, and Grimm in the early nineteenth century, such a doctrine envisions all the peoples of the world as being clustered into a multitude of unique cells rather than sharing a common humanity (Kedourie, 1961:9). So specified, nation and ethnic group, or *ethnie*, are virtually synonymous, the only appreciable distinction being that an ethnic group may not always harbor a yearning after statehood.

It should be clear by now how impossible it is to define the nation without simultaneously defining nationalism, for belief in the existence of the former automatically breeds some level of allegiance, or even passion, for that rather mystical, romantic concept. In its fully ripened form, nationalism is a force that supersedes and crushes all competing loyalties (Silvert, 1963:19).

Nationalism holds that power emanates only from a "people" who form a seamless whole, an indivisible brotherhood which abolishes all existing ties, whether of family, neighborhood or occupation. The only genuine identity is a national one, and every man, be he peasant or worker, merchant or intellectual, can only rediscover self and freedom through that new collective identity. [A. D. Smith, 1977:7]

However spontaneous or natural it may seem nowadays, nationalism is not at all instinctive in character. Careful psychological experimentation with juveniles has disclosed the fact that "the feeling and the very idea of the homeland . . . are a relatively late development in the normal child who does not appear to be drawn inevitably towards patriotic sociocentricity" (Piaget and Weil, 1951: 562). Thus instead of being a genetically encoded entity, nationalism is a doctrine that must be drilled into the minds and hearts of its adherents. The fact that members of the "imagined community" we call a nation are normally far too numerous for more than limited face-to-face contact implies that nationalism can only flourish during an era when print and other advanced media of communication and tutelage are available (Anderson, 1983).

The essential attributes of the nation and nationalism are significant enough to merit brief recapitulation. Both entities are forms of social consciousness, and the nation is born only when enough people begin to believe in its existence. Nationalism means intense devotion to the nation, that real or supposed community of individuals who are convinced they share a common set of traditions, beliefs, and cultural characteristics so precious that no sacrifice is too great for its preservation or advancement. This bundle of shared traits and values is the peculiar property of the group, and sets it apart from all other nations. The sense of nationhood must appear to be the natural upwelling of sentiments based upon a mutual discovery of commonalities rather than something imposed from above. In actuality, however, the nation and nationalism are artifacts, whether crafted consciously or not, and, for technical and other reasons, could not have arisen until modern times.

The *nation-state* is even more emphatically a creature of our own historical epoch. As the word itself suggests, the nation-state is a novel form of statehood: the hybridization or intimate fusion of nation with state. Given the vastly enhanced instruments of indoctrination and control now at its disposal, the successful state can commandeer all the more desirable attributes of the nation(s) within its borders; and, if no well-defined, ready-made nation is immediately available, the state can endeavor, sometimes with signal success, to fabricate one.

In the simplest instance, a preexisting nation has managed to achieve statehood and a nearly total coupling of the new state with the parental nation. Classic examples of such transformations can be seen in the history of Poland, Eire, Israel, or Bangladesh. The reverse process, an antecedent state wittingly forcing its inhabitants into a contrived nationhood, has occurred in such countries as France (Weber, 1976), Italy, Mexico, and Germany, and is being tried in virtually all the newly independent states of Africa, Latin America, Asia, and the Pacific, with a full range of outcomes from abject failure to the promise of success. The easiest, least painful cases are those in which the modern state and a sense of peoplehood have matured simultaneously, as in Japan, Sweden, the Netherlands, or Greece. And, of course, we are still vexed with many cases of frustrated stateless nations; the Palestinians, Kurds, Bretons, Basques, and Macedonians are perhaps the best publicized.

In psychological and other terms, the perfected nation-state is radically different from the premodern state. In times past, the rulers of a state expected, at most, the obedience of their subjects (not to be confused with citizens) in return for the dubious privilege of being protected from the equally rapacious, possibly murderous rulers of neighboring states and the opportunity to extract taxes, loot, and labor from them. Under optimal conditions, these subjects might reciprocate with indifference or grudging respect for the remote person of the monarch or god-king who literally embodied the state, but more often they regarded him with fear and loathing. (Nowadays, of course, the sovereign is treated more deferentially in such constitutional monarchies as Great Britain, Spain, Japan, or Thailand, where pale vestiges of the past linger on.)

The modern state can no longer operate in that fashion. The nature of its economy, the need for a citizen army, the elaborate structure of the polity all demand some measure of enthusiasm, of volunteered participation and sharing in the complexities of modern society. Thus even such accidental states as Jordan, Malawi, or Guyana find themselves obliged to begin inventing some semblance of nationhood, and thus nation-state status. Moreover, such miscellaneous grab bags of nations as Nigeria, the Soviet Union, India, Spain, Indonesia, or Yugoslavia have taken some pains to discover or create common myths to bond together their disparate populations. If we substitute the term nation-state for nation, Clinton Rossiter is correct in claiming that "the nation has emerged, for better or worse, as the critical community of the world in which we live, the largest viable and also the smallest effective aggregate of sovereignty over the activities of men" (Rossiter, 1971:6).

The fully successful functioning of the nation-state demands, and receives, the wholehearted support of its citizens (not to be confused with subjects), indeed an incandescent level of adoration. This set of emotions, which amounts to the creed of the nation-state, we can designate as statism, and the condition of the citizens as *statefulness*.[3] The most extreme expression of this mind-set may be labelled *jingoism*, but, for the purposes of this study, the terms *statism* and *statefulness* will do. The devotees of statism, who now comprise a considerable majority of the world's population, worship the state-idea (precisely as adherents of nationalism revere the nation-idea). It is really a lofty abstraction that they look up to, mighty, faceless, suprahuman, stern but benevolent, and far grander than its transient acolytes. Its outward manifestations, the elected or (self-) appointed officials, the legislature, judiciary, army and police, a swarming bureaucracy, the local deputies, and all the inconvenient laws and regulations, are tolerated virtuously as necessary evils. It is not these instruments of the state that are loved, but the glorious essence they serve. The state (not the government) is perceived as the ultimate social reality, the repository of all that is fine and uplifting in life. Indeed it is more precious than life itself when other wicked states menace its safety or well-being. We are clearly in the presence of the sacred (Tuan, 1978:95–96)—an argument to be elaborated in a later chapter—and so firm is our faith that citizens can swallow the paradox that their state can commit the most ghastly of slaughters, for such transcendentally godlike institutions are obviously incapable of sin.

If nationalism is the coursing upward of a self-conscious peoplehood, essentially of "folk" attributes that have come to be familiar and deeply, communally cherished, the state maintains a much higher altitude. It is absolute, flawless, and olympian in its majesty, and works its magic through a downward dispensing of ordinances, of material and symbolic largess and emotional security into the cheerfully subservient masses. Such a sacred status is the explanation for the fact that citizens can accept the paradox that "a modern state, the organizer of the good, of the great society, of progress, should at the same time express itself through the most horrible butchery" (Ellul, 1975:83). It is worth noting in passing that while the sociocultural distinctions among nations can be striking and unbridgeable, the conditions of statehood are becoming more and more alike among the nation-states of our contemporary world.

It is evident enough that nationalism and statism share a great deal in common. In fact, we frequently see the former term used to cover both concepts, as I have been compelled to do in the subtitle of this work and also, in order to avoid clumsy locutions, at various points hereafter. At such junctures, I hope the context will indicate that the extended meaning of nationalism (i.e., nationalism strictly defined plus statism) is intended. Nevertheless it is essential to keep in mind that, despite their recent merger in so many places, nation and state, as well as nationalism and statism, are inherently different in character and origin. To reiterate, the basic distinction lies in the level and direction of the flow of grace and power. While the nation may be a freemasonry of brothers and sisters, a more or less democratic confederacy, conjoined through blood, soil, "the mystic chords of memory," or some other web of cultural sentiment, the state floats far above the reach or understanding of the common herd, stern and austere though nurturing: majesty rather than fraternity; compulsion replacing mutuality. An immigrant who is willing and able to endure the red tape can eventually become a citizen of almost any state; to become a full-fledged member of another nation is a much more trying, sometimes impossible feat.

STATE, NATION, AND NATION-STATE IN HISTORICAL AND SCHOLARLY PERSPECTIVE

I am hardly alone in the conviction that nations and nation-states, and indeed ethnicity, and their attendant ideologies are time dependent, historical phenomena that were socially and psychologically unworkable until recent times. Such is the consensus, with only minor reservations, among those scholars who have surveyed the evidence. The availability of several fine narratives and analyses of the evolution of nationalism renders superfluous any detailed review of these facts.[4] However, the essential findings bear repetition. We have a reasonably clear picture of the early history and prehistory of the state (M. Fried, 1967); and, even though there were scattered intimations of ethnicity in the ancient world and medieval Europe (Huizinga, 1959; A. D. Smith, 1981:85–86), nationalism (sans statism) does not materialize in anything like its present form

until the mid-eighteenth century, when it was unmistakably burgeoning in England, France, and, as I shall maintain below, the pre-
natal United States.[5] "The word *patrie* was not common before
1750. . . . The change came when after 1740 the *patrie* began to be
heard of in normal conversation, entering, along with the *nation*,
into the vocabulary of civilian life and public affairs" (Palmer,
1940:98). Subsequently, the nationalist movement spread into what
was to become Germany, the Scandinavian countries, the remainder of Europe, and, in due course, during the present century, to the
lands of the Third World.

The advent of the nation and nationalism was obviously related
to the social and intellectual upheavals of early modern times and
perhaps most directly to the spiritual crisis brought about by the
loosening grip of traditional Christianity on the hearts and minds of
its parishioners. (We need concern ourselves only with Christendom for the genesis of the nation.)

> It may well be that during and since the eighteenth century the
> rise of skepticism concerning historic supernatural religion, es-
> pecially among the intellectual and middle classes, has created
> an unnatural void for religious emotion and worship, a void
> which it has seemed preferable to supply with near-by nation-
> alistic gods and fervent nationalist cults rather than with far-
> off cosmopolitan deities and vague humanitarianism. [Hayes,
> 1931:299]

> Nationalism more and more offered what religion once had,
> a vision of a heaven, though this time an earthly heaven.
> . . . Through their nation, their community, individuals could
> eventually hope to achieve personally meaningful and creative
> lives. [Shafer, 1972:224]

Until the dawn of this epoch of truly profound transformation in
all aspects of human existence, social and political organization
bore little resemblance to the familiar patterns of today. During the
prenational era, in the words of Hume, "a nation [for which read
"state"] is nothing but a collection of individuals" (Berry, 1981:77),
that is to say, an arbitrary or accidental assemblage of often diverse
persons inhabiting a poorly defined, frequently fragmented territory. In these earlier times, a universalistic view of humankind prevailed. Since "all men are in Adam and are sinners . . . variety is to
be accounted for in terms of the normatively superior universal,"
and "the normative basis of political life was not located spatio·

temporally and no political prescription was premised on such particulars" (Berry, 1981:76–77). Political fealty, usually quite grudging, was extended only to the local lord and, possibly through him, to a vague and distant monarch. Reality was structured much more meaningfully in a heavenward direction, in unquestioning devotion to the Lord God, his local deputies and saints, and the eternal verities of the scriptures. With the crackup of this system of belief, the nation became both possible and necessary.

The formation of nation-states followed the appearance of nations in Western Europe (and North America) by approximately a century, and is still in its early stages in the "less developed" portions of the world. This is a development that has enjoyed relatively little scholarly attention (but see Arieli, 1964:321; Hayes, 1960:93; Karsten, 1978:11–12). Since this subject is dealt with later on, further discussion can be deferred for the time being. The crucial point to remember is that, whether it was the state or nation that engineered the transformation, or whether it was the two acting in concert, the nation-state arrives at a significantly later date in the biography of societies than its progenitors.

Although the modern state, statism, and nationalism are all inextricably enmeshed with one another, writers on the theory of nationalism (e.g., Boehm, 1933) and the authors of the even more extensive literature on the theory of the state (e.g., Clark and Dear, 1984; Held and Krieger, 1984) seem scarcely aware of the others' existence. The same comment applies, perhaps even more forcefully, to the rapidly swelling literature on modernization and socioeconomic development, which generally pays only the most casual attention to the issues of nationalism/statism. Especially disappointing has been the failure of Marxist scholars to come fully to grips with such matters and their rather indifferent success in dealing with the theory of the state (Blaut, 1980, 1982; Jessop, 1982; Koch, 1980; Miliband, 1969; Nairn, 1977).[6] "What is clear from reading Marxist literature is a complete lack of consensus about what ideology is and what function it plays in society" (A. Cohen, 1979:90).

As I have already indicated, the literature on nationalism is rich and informative, but it is also incomplete. In addition to the weaknesses of its connections with other bodies of scholarly work, there are certain internal gaps and inadequacies within its own domain in coverage of vital issues. One of the most serious of these—and a deficiency this study is meant to begin remedying—is the tacit assumption that nationalism is an absolute, universal phenomenon, that having once manifested itself, it is pretty much the same everywhere and in all periods. I must partially exempt Boyd Shafer from this allegation, since he does briefly note the mutable nature of nationalism and the wide range of its intensity (Shafer, 1972:7, 12–13), but he fails to explore the implications of these facts adequately in the remainder of his valuable treatise. The reality, I maintain, differs markedly from any such static condition; and my working hypothesis is that nationalism varies significantly in character and level from place to place and with the passage of time. This is not to deny intrinsic, congenital family resemblances among all its many expressions. In parallel fashion, we can recognize striking place-to-place contrasts in socialism, capitalism, Buddhism, or Roman Catholicism, for example, and their significant modifications over time without ignoring or minimizing the essential similarities.

This shortcoming, that is, an inadequate sensitivity to the sequential unfolding of nationalism and statism, and other historical subtleties, their uneven development at both the national and global scales, might be overcome through serious comparative study and the availability of a series of intensive explorations of individual cases. The potentialities of the comparative approach are well illustrated by Merriam's (1931) study of "methods of civic training" in the United States, United Kingdom, France, Germany, Italy, Russia, Switzerland, and Austria-Hungary; Bellah and Hammond's (1980) examination of civil religion in the United States, Mexico, and Japan; and, less successfully, in Snyder (1976) and King's (1935) dissertation.

Case studies of substance have been regrettably rare. For the United States, we have Merle Curti's (1946) detailed examination in *The Roots of American Loyalty*, which summarizes, in competent fashion, the historical and social underpinnings of nationalism, with some attention to its symbolic elements, and Hans Kohn's (1957) interpretative essay on the same subject, which is basically a tract oriented toward support of American foreign policy during the Cold War period. Briefer, but still valuable, is Daniel Boorstin's (1965:325–90) treatment of the American quest for nationalistic symbols. Quite admirable is Liebman and Don-Yehiya's (1983) study of civil religion in Israel. Elsewhere there is Weber's (1976) splendid work on the cultural and other forms of nationalization in rural France during the pre–World War I generations and Ginsburg's (1933) and Mosse's (1975) essays on the symbolic manipulations that heated up recent German nationalism. But until we have a much wider array of such publications covering a broad collection of countries, our understanding of nationalism will necessarily remain rather truncated.

One motif is pervasive throughout the literature on the state, though more often implicit than not: the preeminence of economic and political (and perhaps technological) factors in the origin and maintenance of the state (e.g., Hayes, 1931:252–87 passim). Cultural and ideological forces, if mentioned at all, are usually regarded as epiphenomena, mere froth on the mighty torrent of history. Students of nationalism have not fully succeeded in revising that dominant mode of thought; in fact, they have not seriously tried. If Lionel Rubinoff may have gone too far in arguing that "we do not become nationalistic in order to protect economic and political interests; we pursue economic and political interests in order to be nationalistic, and nationalism is primarily a mode of communion" (Rubinoff, 1975:1), surely a plausible view of social history is that cultural elements have been indispensable in the rise of modern states and nations, and that we ignore them at our intellectual peril.[7] Although I am sometimes tempted to believe that it is the cultural system and its mysterious dynamics that are the principal engines of societal change, including the economic and political aspects, in my soberer moments I know better. Culture, that is, that quintessentially human realm of myth and symbol, is only one of that complex tangle of items embracing economics, technology, politics, and the habitat that interact one with another to shape human destinies; but culture is no less potent than any of the others.

There is ample evidence to defend the contention that modern states could neither exist nor operate effectively without an adequate body of symbol and myth, whatever other excuses they may have for their creation (A. Cohen, 1979; Gabriel, 1956:441–52; Lasswell, 1966; Liebman and Don-Yehiya, 1983; Merriam, 1931:145–54; Sebba, 1962; Tudor, 1972).

Since *symbols* are so central to this inquiry, it would be foolhardy to proceed without author and reader reaching some sort of agreement as to the definition of this exceedingly slippery concept. Indeed the axiom upon which this entire study is built is that all aspects of human life, not just the political, are symbolically conditioned (the decisive fact that sets us apart from all other members of the animal kingdom), that indeed "we live by symbols," and that whoever or whatever controls them thereby controls our lives (Reiff, 1940:99). As it happens, anthropologists, semiologists, and other social scientists have wrestled with the explication of symbols in book-length writings without attaining final closure. However, nearly all students would accept Raymond Firth's succinct statement:[8]

> *Symbol*—where a sign has a complex series of associations, often of an emotional kind, and difficult (some would say, impossible) to describe in terms other than partial representation. [Firth, 1973:75]

Symbols exist in many forms—words, colors, graphic designs, gestures, facial expressions, structures, musical and other sounds, clothing, and other artifacts of every description, and even, inter alia, odors—but, whatever the medium, they operate, often quite subconsciously, in those multidimensional chambers of the human imagination far removed from the level of mere prosaic signs. Thus, for example, one might train a chimpanzee to recognize the swastika, or the Star of David, but how could the creature ever be beguiled to grasp their symbolic aura, or register the appropriate agitation? Virtually every moment, awake or dreaming, of our existence as human beings is saturated with symbols so numerous or subtle as to be uncountable; but, fortunately, we need be concerned here with only that relatively small subset of items that have something to do with nationalism.

This family of symbols is not a loose jumble of isolated bits; instead it is organized, after a fashion, into a sort of system we can call a *myth* or *mythology*. Although we often utter these terms in belittling fashion, confounding them with *legends* or *fables*, they belong to a separate order of reality. Myths, at least in the sense applicable here, are seldom narrative in form, nor need they correspond to the cold facts of history. What our larger myths do accomplish is to provide their clients with a cohesive, if often subliminal, depiction of the nature and meaning of the world and one's place in it: "At its deepest level—that collectively created thing which crystallizes the great, central values of a culture" (Ellul, 1975:102). (The reader will realize that *ideologies* can be one of the more comprehensible components of myths.) Their absolute truth or falsehood may be quite untestable (unlike the case of many legends or fables, such as the dubious tales about William Tell or Betsy Ross) and even irrelevant since nearly all of us are uncomplaining prisoners of mythologies. Possibly the most illuminating exploration of the nature of latter-day myths is that by Roland Barthes, and especially his account of the "bourgeois myth," veritably a supermyth transcending international boundaries and one in which individual national myths may be imbedded (Barthes, 1972:109–59). In any event, as Michael Walzer quite rightly claims, "the state is invisible; it must be personified before it can be seen, symbolized before it can be loved, imagined before it can be conceived. . . . Thus the image provides a starting point for political thinking" (Walzer, 1967:194).

WHY THE UNITED STATES?

My purpose is to document this notion and explore its ramifications through close examination of the American case. But why the United States? Isn't it a fact that this country holds an inconspicuous place in the standard accounts of nationalism? Indeed, the general practice in these Eurocentric treatises is to accord the United States only a passing glance. The rationale for such an approach is plain enough: one must turn to Western Europe to find the roots of the modern state and trace the earliest emergence of nationalism; and today it is in the countries of the Third World that we see nationalism catching so much attention and much of the blame for their all too conspicuous political and social turmoil.

The issue is not one of wounded parochial pride. I wish to argue instead that the American experience may tell us more about the essential nature of nationalism and statism than any other example, even though "no one has yet turned a full shaft of light on American nationalism" (Van Alstyne, 1958:426), a statement that has lost little of its relevance after three decades. Furthermore, I intend to prove that we can document the transition from nation to state in the United States with a clarity that would be difficult to duplicate in other instances.

One of the principal reasons for selecting the United States and chronicling its symbolic biography is the extraordinary character of its inception. The evolution of state and nation in England, France, and indeed every European country before or after 1776 has been clouded by the gradualness of the process and the baffling complexity of their social, cultural, and territorial ingredients. For example, who can put a date on the unwritten British constitution or say just when the bulk of the English first became aware of their common peoplehood? Or how and when did the Dutch, the Serbs, the Portuguese, or the Welsh first discover whatever it is they believe themselves to be? In the American case, we can pinpoint most watershed events with precision, sometimes down to the very day and street address (e.g., July 2, 1776, 550 Chestnut St., Philadelphia, Pa.). This was the first such self-creation of a state and synthesis of a nation, and arguably also the most influential. It may be significant that the American Revolution was "the first great war in which [propaganda] played its full part" (Humphrey, 1924:426). Indeed, we have here as close a simulation to a controlled laboratory experiment as the vagaries of history will permit us if our charge is to anatomize the workings of state- and nation-formation without the complications of extraneous factors. The American genesis was abrupt; it was voluminously and minutely documented; it occurred in relative physical isolation amidst a population who had barely begun to discern their peculiar ethnicity; and it happened without benefit of clear precedent. (The examples of the Italian and other city-states, the Swiss Confederation, or the republics of the ancient world were of limited utility.)

Later movements toward national independence among other overseas offshoots of Europe, as in Canada, Australia, South Africa, Argentina, and the remainder of Latin America, and in all the many twentieth-century instances in the Third World, were affected to a greater or lesser degree, but always significantly, by the two great exemplars: the United States and France (Anderson, 1983:144–47; Morris, 1970; Palmer, 1976). Although the French Revolution did spawn some original concepts in national ideologies and the structuring of states, it was also, in turn, decisively influenced by the American model, standing, as the latter was, in the vanguard of a worldwide bourgeois revolution. (The linkages between the two revolutions have yet to receive the detailed scholarly treatment they merit.) Along with Sidney Ahlstrom, I can respond affirmatively to the query "Is not 'the first new nation' the birthplace of modern nationalism?" (Ahlstrom, 1975:496). Not only is the American national consciousness remarkable in being "based upon the conviction of being different from other nations . . . in realizing . . . the greatest possible approximation to perfection" (Kohn, 1944: 291), but also in its transnational appeal as being "shaped by social and political values which claimed universal validity and which were nevertheless the American way of life" (Arieli, 1964:23).[9]

As a nation, the young United States differed strikingly from the emerging nations of eighteenth- and early nineteenth-century Europe (revolutionary France partially excepted) (Beard, 1934:49–50). It was not a folk-nation, or even a confederation of such nations rooted in autochthonous elements, but rather an ideological construct, the materialization of novel ideas that had been smouldering among the intellectually and religiously disaffected far and wide within the Atlantic community, but were first to reach criticality and burst into flames in such places as Boston and Philadelphia in the 1770s.

Missing were most of the standard building blocks for nation-building (Commager, 1975:170–71). Any sense of a general American ethnicity was, at best, embryonic when Lexington and Concord leapt into the news. Although transplanted Englishmen and women accounted for a majority of the inhabitants, conspicuous among the immigrants were the many distinctly non-English Scots, Welsh, Scotch-Irish, Cornish, Irish, Dutch, and the numerous folk from the Rhineland, not to mention the large, voiceless mass of Afro-Americans and interesting sprinklings of Swedes, Finns, French Huguenots, Spaniards, and Jews. If a lively American ethnicity (as distinct in this instance from nationhood) did eventually take shape a generation or more after political independence, it was more of an aftereffect than a governing factor in instigating the divorce from the homeland.[10] Similarly, the thirteen British colonies lacked any semblance of religious uniformity, even at the provincial level—Pennsylvania, New York, and New Jersey being only the most extreme examples. And, in Colonial times at least, the many creeds had all been imports from Europe. Both oral and written history languished at a quite rudimentary level, and what little existed was parochial or provincial in coverage. Before 1776, the new nation was symbolically impoverished, lacking its own music, literature, art, native costume or cuisine, and homegrown heroes. Furthermore, the English language, though already undergoing Americanization, was an illogical incitement toward political autonomy. There was no capital city as yet, no well-entrenched ruling class, nor any conventional military caste or even a name for the country that carried much emotional force.

One might even question the relevance of that most nearly universal and hallowed foundation of national consciousness: a cherished territory of one's own.[11] Although it may be generally true that, as Robert Sack and most political geographers would agree, "in order to make the social order and its power real and tangible, civilizations employ the most basic and powerful tool of reification, that of location and extension in physical space. Area and power become fused and allegiance to the territorial state becomes essential" (Sack, 1978:183), the American case seems to be something of an exception. There can be little doubt that the location, size, shape, and other physical qualities of the territory occupied by the

insurgent colonists and, subsequently, by a greatly expanded American state have been of considerable consequence in molding the
national character as well as in economic and geopolitical affairs
(Burns, 1975:61–71; Gifford, 1980; Marienstras, 1976:72–76; Somkin, 1967:91–130). Nonetheless, the heart of the matter is that
"American nationalism has always been connected not to place but
to principles" (Nye, 1966:47), and "America was not a territorial
definition (except in the vague sense of 'New World'), but the symbol of an ideological consensus" (Bercovitch, 1978:161). And could
it be otherwise for a people suddenly pledging themselves to the
contrivance of a novel earthly Eden in a land not yet adequately
explored and one they had had but scant opportunity to meet and
love, a country whose borders yesterday and today are so patently
arbitrary and artificial, unstained by those centuries of conflict or
celebration inscribed on the maps of Europe?

The idiosyncrasies of American nationalism are many,[12] but the
same objection could be lodged against any other nation-state one
might nominate as a likely proving ground for a deeper general understanding of nationalism. Every country is unique in its own way,
and for present purposes it would be wasted effort to rehearse the
arguments for and against American exceptionalism (Bell, 1975;
Veysey, 1979). Instead, I simply stake my claim that there is no
better strategy for the student intent upon penetrating the mysteries of the contemporary nation-state and learning how it came to
pass than to put the United States of America on the examination
table. Leaving aside the intrinsic importance of the country to natives and foreigners alike and the relative abundance and accessibil-
ity of evidence, we have here the purest instance of state and nation
formation uncorrupted by older mentors or irrelevant complexities,
and also one whose image and example have been so pervasive and
profoundly generative for the past two centuries that no program of
nation-building anywhere else has been untouched by the American experience.

But just how can one best diagnose or describe nationalism and
chart its fortunes and modulations? We are dealing with an elusive
quarry, an essentially intangible aspect of social psychology. Psychologists realize full well how difficult it is to plumb the mind,
moods, and subliminal impulses of even a single individual; and
students of public opinion find all too often that even their most
sophisticated devices fail to trap the temper of the collective psyche
of the here and now. How much more quixotic an exercise it is to
set about retrieving the shifting mind-sets of generations past!

I have operated on the premise that the most effective strategy is to evaluate the outward symptoms of American nationalism. And indeed the evidence amassed for this study does seem to confirm the notion that symbols, whether material or nonmaterial in form, whether expressed in terms of behavior or otherwise, serve the analyst in two ways. They can be influential, very likely essential, in begetting and later maintaining nationalism; they can also serve as rather subtle gauges to record its amplitude and temperature; and, in some instances, they can operate in both ways, as cause and symptom. Symbols may not be able to swing wide the gates into the dark inner chambers of our communal spirit, but they do open them a crack, far enough for us to peer into the murk and make some sensible guesses as to what may be crouching inside.

A simple sketch map of what lies ahead may be helpful to the reader. I march along two levels, the upper and more transparent of which is suggested by the chapter titles. Thus each of the next four sections examines a group of topics: first—easily the most interior and least material—the varied personifications of the nation or state and its ideals, those potent mental images that float within the minds of Americans singly and collectively; next, moving outward into the full light of day, two chapters on a large assemblage of observable deeds, the acting out in public of nationalistic sentiments; and, finally, the most overt and solid of evidence, those relatively durable nationalistic objects that have been installed in the American landscape. Such segmentation of evidence is, of course, a matter of artifice. To avoid being tiresome, let me say for the first and last time that, in actuality, every manifestation of peoplehood and statehood is entwined closely with every other one.

In any event, my ordering of themes is only a device for delving downward into the more meaningful dimensions of the phenomena in question: their demonstrable evolution and transformation over time and—less clearly given the spottiness of accessible data—their territorial diffusion. In the closing paragraphs of chapter 5 and throughout the concluding chapter, I distill the lessons legible within these two strata of evidence—the topical and spatiotemporal—to articulate some broad and, I trust, thought-provoking notions about the essential character of the American polity and its dynamics. In addition, I also brood briefly over our murky future, but with ample trepidation. Closely tied to the grander task is some elucidation of the common faith that still binds us all together in the United States and within other modern nation-states: our civil religion.

TWO ★ ★ ★ ★ ★ ★ ★ ★

PUBLIC EIDOLONS ★ ★ ★ ★

*"Through our heroes we announce to one
another who and what we really are."*
—Chaim Potok

A less puzzling title for this chapter might have been "National Heroes," but the terms *hero* and *heroism* are, paradoxically, both too confining and too varied in their connotations to cover the phenomena under discussion. We are not concerned here with deeds of physical valor or the protagonists in works of drama or fiction. Instead, the topic is that set of personalized images, of certain special perceptions, that are important, perhaps essential, in nurturing a sense of national community. For that purpose, the term *eidolon*, in the lexical sense of "an ideal figure," serves better than any other available word; but I limit the eidolons treated here to those with some semblance of human form—and those with mythic properties.

Such public eidolons embody the central meanings, values, and aspirations of a large population. They constitute a large, varied host of real and imagined personages, in the broadest sense of that term. Included are the standard national and regional heroes; those founders, explorers, statesmen, warriors, political thinkers, and legendary culture heroes who are believed to have wrought mighty deeds and to be responsible for the shaping or very existence of the nation. No less meaningful, however, are other symbolic figures in human shape: gods and devils, demigods, prophets, saints, martyrs, and various villains and scapegoats. Certain eminent scientists, scholars, inventors, and creative artists and performers may also qualify, but celebrities, dignitaries, and antiheroes are only marginal members of this collectivity.

Eidolons of nationalistic import may derive from living, flesh-and-blood persons or, at the other extreme, from legendary figures of dubious historicity in the remote past, supernatural beings, or the fabrications of poets and cartoonists. They range in character from the real, tangible, and intensely personal to highly abstract figures barely recognizable as human. At a further remove, the eidolons treated here shade into total abstractions: emblems and large, general ideas and emotions, sometimes inchoate or else expressed in slogans and catchphrases. But even when the eidolon is based on an actual, well-documented human being, the image may bear only a slight resemblance to the original person. In order to be effective, public eidolons require simplification, purification, and idealization.

There is also the matter of scale. Most of us carry a special, private set of eidolons in our heads, personalized abstractions or persons known to us directly or via public information media, whom we admire or loathe and who help lend direction and purpose to our existences. But we also partake of larger pools of eidolons that extend from the neighborhood community up to and far past national frontiers. Indeed, for much of the world's population, a key factor in defining their common humanity may be reverence for, or detestation of, a well-nigh universal corps of heroes and villains. For residents of the "Western," or greater European community, its members include, among others, Joan of Arc, St. Francis, Gandhi, Robin Hood, William Tell, the Little Dutch Boy, Florence Nightingale, Galileo, Pasteur, Saladin, Don Juan, Dr. Faustus, Attila, Quisling, Hitler, Beethoven, Chaplin, Dr. Schweitzer, Marx, and Napoleon. In this discussion, I restrict attention to those public eidolons that have enacted a meaningful role in helping create or sustain the American nation and in the subsequent passage to the nation-state.

The basic contention is that a robust complement of nationalistic eidolons, along with other mythic elements, is an essential ingredient in the nation-building enterprise, particularly in nations created in recent times. Obviously, some political states, normally with aspirations toward becoming full-fledged nation-states, can and do exist today without benefit of adequate kits of such eidolons. But one may doubt their inner coherence or even whether they qualify as genuine nations rather than administrative apparatuses foisted upon an inert populace; most especially, one may question their durability. Perhaps better than any other instance in modern times, the history of the United States illustrates just how vital to the forging of a nation it is to have a lively set of eidolons.

THE NATION PERSONIFIED

A number of countries symbolize their nationhood or statehood by means of a particular idealized human figure or totemic beast. Obvious examples of the former are France's Marianne and Britain's John Bull, while the lion, bear, dragon, and eagle often do duty for England, Russia, China, and the United States, respectively.[1]

In the case of the United States, the succession of personalized emblems has been especially interesting and pregnant with larger implications. Long before there were any stirrings of nationalism in the British North American colonies, indeed as far back as the sixteenth century, European artists and cartographers depicted the various continents in the guise of mythological maidens, and America specifically as a dusky, partially clad Indian Princess. This rather charming figure would seem to have been a "noble savage," a blood sister of the shepherdesses of Arcadia (Fleming, 1968:1). But by 1765, the Indian princess had become the dominant iconic symbol for British North America and achieved widespread notoriety in cartoons, book and magazine illustrations, newspaper mastheads, statuary, ceramic figurines and utensils, printed textiles and wallpaper, needlework, and government medals; but she shared the stage, during this period of political agitation, with the rattlesnake (Horwitz, 1976:26), pine tree, and representations of the Sons of Liberty (Fleming, 1968:1–9). In any case, throughout the 1760s and well into the early republican years, the visual symbolization of the incipient, then actual, United States was vague, uncertain, and changeable (Cresswell, 1975:239–406), although "the evidence . . . suggests that the identification of an American community distinct from the British had taken place by 1755 and was widely accepted by 1766" (Fleming, 1968:4).

Rather gradually, during the middle and late eighteenth century, the Indian Princess became a plumed neoclassical goddess in her feathered headdress and tobacco miniskirt, then either evolved into, or was replaced by, a thoroughly Caucasian young lady (Cresswell, 1975:xv; L. C. Jones, 1975). "Eventually the Indian Princess lost her symbolic meaning and while the female Indian remains a constant in America, she has appeared mostly in cartouches and in the engravings of stock certificates. With the mass production of cigar store figures during the nineteenth century, she no longer had any particular symbolic significance" (L. C. Jones, 1975:4).

As of the beginning of the nineteenth century, the goddess figure still reigned supreme as the embodiment of the United States and its ideals. According to Michael Kammen (1986b:177), "the obsession with Miss Liberty . . . reached its peak in American imagery between 1800 and 1815." Clad in long, flowing white robes, usually brandishing any of several patriotic devices, and often wearing the Liberty, or Phrygian, Cap, this lovely creature was, inter alia, another manifestation of the young republic's rapturous love affair with all things Greek and Roman. It was, of course, an infatuation shared with other Western European countries of the era. Marianne, who came so vividly to life during the French Revolution and has survived vigorously ever since in the collective French mind, is obviously a close sibling. There is also a family relationship with the often amazonian figures of Britannia, her Teutonic counterpart, and similar maidenly personifications of European states that we see so often in popular and propagandistic art. Although Fleming (1968) gives this American eidolon several names, including American Liberty, Columbia, or simply America, and draws some iconographic and literary distinctions among them, it is plain enough that we are dealing here with essentially one single being or concept.

In any event, we find Miss Liberty appearing ubiquitously in every medium of folk art during the past century, in the works of professional sculptors and painters, and, decoratively, on almost every conceivable manufactured object including "bank notes, letterheads, certificates, weathervanes, ship figureheads, circus wagons" (Fleming, 1968:18), official medals (Loubat, 1878), and cigar boxes (Horwitz, 1976:15–16). She achieved the peak of symbolic eminence, quite literally, in Thomas Crawford's 19-foot statue atop the national Capitol.

But, beyond any question, the most important, not to mention spectacular, materialization of Miss Liberty is Bartholdi's titanic monument in New York Harbor, a project requiring heroic engineering and financial exploits by citizens of two nations. This remarkable structure has acquired a life of its own, as witnessed by countless reproductions in figurines, drawings, photographs, cartoons, and folk art. The bacchanalian festivities that marked its centenary in 1986 provided vivid testimony as to its continuing, even growing vitality. The history and impact of the Statue of Liberty upon the American imagination demand, and have received, detailed treatment (Handlin, 1971; Higham, 1984; Pauli and Ashton, 1969; Trachtenberg, 1976), even though we have not yet arrived close to a full understanding of the monument's significance. The Statue of Liberty means many things apart from its unflagging

appeal to viewers foreign and domestic. One might argue that, in
addition to delivering its message of America's promise and loftiest
ideals to the newcomer and returning traveler, this artifact epito-
mizes the essence of our ethos or nationhood more eloquently than
any other single object. Yet perhaps the object has come to be more
ardently celebrated than the principles it was intended to represent. Although every citizen from childhood onward is aware of the
Statue of Liberty, how many would identify it, or rather Miss Liberty, as *the* visual personification of the nation? That honor belongs
to one of her successors.

The first significant masculine image of America, or, more likely
the prototypical American, was Brother Jonathan. This sobriquet
apparently originated during the Revolution, but remained rare before 1800. It may have been a derisive epithet (of British origin?),
as was the case also with Yankee Doodle, meant to designate a
country bumpkin; but, as occasionally happens with such ethnic
slurs, it was defiantly adopted by some of the objects of scorn,
yet without ever achieving much general acceptance or popularity
(Ketchum, 1959:27–33; A. Mathews, 1901). Brother Jonathan enjoyed some currency among journalists and cartoonists of the early
nineteenth century, though without attaining a fully standardized
appearance; but once Uncle Sam entered the scene, his predecessor
vanished leaving scarcely a trace. "With the Civil War and the final
assertion of the power of the central government Jonathan went
into total eclipse in America" (Ketchum, 1959:71). But perhaps he
has enjoyed a certain reincarnation in a succession of latter-day
homespun figures in the worlds of entertainment and cartooning:
modest but virtuous, unsophisticated but shrewd characters such
as John Q. Public and those played by Will Rogers, Gary Cooper,
James Stewart, and Henry Fonda.

It seems fairly certain that the name "Uncle Sam" originated during the War of 1812 deriving from "Uncle" Samuel Wilson, a successful merchant of Troy, N.Y., who was then supplying the American military with casks of meat stamped with the initials U.S.
(Ketchum 1959:34–44; Krythe, 1968). In any case, the term quickly
achieved general currency by means of the popular press, the first
citation appearing in a local newspaper on September 7, 1813 (A.
Mathews, 1908:33), then shortly thereafter throughout New York
and Vermont (A. Mathews, 1908:39).

It was only quite gradually that Uncle Sam acquired the definitive form and costume now so familiar throughout the world (Ketchum, 1959:59–119). Indeed it was not until the Civil War period that

we finally greet the tall, lanky, bearded elderly gent sporting red-white-and-blue top hat, tails, and gaiters and a shrewd twinkle in his eye—and, significantly enough, cast in the general mold of the New England Yankee.[2] Through a strange, but marvelous, quirk of history, the Lincoln visage deeply, permanently affected post-1865 delineations of Uncle Sam, adding further strength and durability to both mythic beings (Ketchum, 1959:86). In contrast to Miss Liberty and kindred characters, who were artifacts of the literate elite and sophisticated artists, Uncle Sam was a relatively spontaneous folk creation. It was the general public that begat him, in response, evidently, to some deep inner hunger for an earthy, paternal, or rather avuncular, figure who would better flesh out the American collectivity than the relatively ethereal and virginal Miss Liberty. It is interesting to speculate about the reasons for France having a female figure as its present-day national image while Americans have settled for a masculine character. Agulhon (1979a:233) suggests Catholicism as a factor and the deeply imbedded Mariolatry of Mediterranean lands.

For well over a century Americans have displayed warm affection toward Uncle Sam. They have even established a joking relationship with him, subjecting the old gentleman to some overly familiar buffeting at times. He continues to enjoy the liveliest of careers in cartoons and posters in the United States and other lands, and manufacturers and advertisers beyond counting have exploited the chap in ads and labels (Horwitz, 1976:16). As symptomatic as anything of Uncle Sam's place in the hearts of the community is his persistent popularity among folk artists and craftsmen (Horwitz, 1976:92–106).

But precisely what message does Uncle Sam convey? Who is he, and what does he stand for? Clearly this figure is no mere stand-in for a Miss Liberty who symbolizes the spirit of American nationhood in the purest, most sublimated of terms. Ketchum (1959:63) suggests that he represents the Government, although he tempers the claim with the statement that "it may be indicative of the American attitude toward government that the symbol for it is an uncle, and as such, an oblique rather than a direct connection" (Ketchum, 1959:59). But this is an unconvincing argument. From the very outset to the present, Americans have been disrespectful, indeed downright antagonistic toward government, whether national, local, or in between. With the exception perhaps of the persons occupying the sanctified offices of the presidency and the Supreme Court, appointed and elected officials have normally been objects of suspicion, dread, and derision; at best they are tolerated. Indeed "politician" is one of the more venomous epithets in the American lexicon.

I would venture an alternate interpretation: that Uncle Sam is the visible embodiment of the American *state*, an entity distinct from, though necessarily overlapping, the governmental apparatus, and also a concept not to be confused with the nation, whose epiphany has been Miss Liberty. This argument has been more elaborately developed earlier in this study. For the moment, it will suffice to say that the state is a great overarching, nonideological abstraction, the "we-ness" of a complex, centralized, deracinated modern society. As such, as a new form of mass identity, it transcends individuals, bureaucracies, legislatures, laws, courts, corporations, or testable propositions to become something uncontestable and holy unto itself. Uncle Sam is the human face of the state. The parallel course of the rise of Uncle Sam and American statism is thus more than coincidental; and the Lincolnesque visage of our favorite uncle also speaks volumes, for, more than any other single individual, our sixteenth president was both the savior and formulator of the modern American state.

Viewed from such a perspective, the near-eclipse of Miss Liberty by Uncle Sam since the Civil War (Hess and Kaplan, 1975:33; Horwitz, 1976:75–91; Weitenkampf, 1952:377) takes on added meaning. The earlier figure does preserve a ghostlike presence on coins, certificates, the occasional pageant or poster, and, of course, in gigantic amplitude as the Statue of Liberty. Her commercial exploitation in advertisements or, journalistically, in cartoons was much less frequent than was the case for Uncle Sam (Cobb, 1978:44–50, 74). We can concur with the notion "that Uncle Sam replaced Columbia, or that the American Colonies grew from helpless infants to sturdy youths almost out of their time, bespeaks a concomitant transformation in the personal identity of significant masses of people which is practically impossible to grasp from any other angle" (Burrows and Wallace, 1972:273–74).

The eidolons discussed above are comprehensive national icons in the sense of somehow representing the entire core or generality of the country. But we dare not ignore a related set of idealized entities, fractional figures or types who nobly signify a single facet of the presumed national character. Many of them are military in character. The Minute Man, immortalized in verse, marble, and bronze, sheds luster on our collective self-image. So too do the legions of eternal, anonymous Union and Confederate warriors of spotless repute gazing out at us from atop their pedestals in town centers throughout the land. Less visible, but still cherished, is the memory of the World War I doughboy and the GI Joe of the following generation. As the ultimate canonization of the sacrificial defender of the national faith, we have, of course, the Unknown Soldier(s) who, since 1921, have been entombed in Arlington National Cemetery (Wecter, 1941:410–14).

Another persistent set of heroic figures owe their origin to the early taking of the land: the Pilgrim Fathers, the pioneer frontiersman, and the Pioneer Mother (an earthier version of Miss Liberty?). And, distilled from the mass of individual western heroes, we have the idealized cowboys and outlaws who, in highly romanticized form, still haunt the American mind (Steckmesser, 1965; Wilbur, 1973). American business enterprise and technology have also given rise to ideal types, for example, the Horatio Alger hero (Hartz, 1964: 104–10) and our intrepid astronauts, who once gave us a comforting edge in the second most expensive of international competitions (Lott and Lott, 1963).

PREHISTORY OF THE NATIONAL HERO

Interesting and suggestive though such iconically realized abstractions as Miss Liberty, Uncle Sam, or certain idealized types may be, there is much more to learn by looking at flesh-and-blood heroes and fictional facsimiles thereof if we wish to appreciate the role of public eidolons in creating and sustaining American nationalism. In doing so, we are constrained by the truly surprising paucity of theoretical, or even comprehensive empirical, work on the general phenomenon of heroes and hero-worship. The most celebrated of extended treatments, those by Lord Raglan (1949) and Joseph Campbell (1949), take a narrow view of the subject, defining as heroes only mythical, usually religious, figures, or strongly mythologized historic personages drawn from the premodern past (Salomon, 1932). In the case of Sidney Hook's *The Hero in History* (1943), the author deals solely with the "Great Man in History" rather than the general subject of heroes and hero-worship. The few essays striving for a broader perspective are too brief or casual to fill a lamentable gap in the scholarly literature (Meadows, 1945; Nisbet, 1975:102–10; Potok, 1973). On the other hand, students of American hero-worship are richly blessed in having Dixon Wecter's (1941) admirable study, whose only major flaw is that it now demands updating.[3]

A reasonably safe generalization is that the roster of public eidolons linked to identifiable individuals has changed greatly, even radically, in character during the transition from premodern to modern times; and, as we shall see, it has not stopped changing during recent generations. Before the eighteenth century, when the nation was still largely a latent rather than a fully matured entity and the state was not yet warmly imbedded in the hearts and minds of its inhabitants, I believe we can distinguish two classes of personal eidolons. First we have the localized rulers, gods, saints, martyrs, larger-than-life rascals, and culture heroes, whether real or mythological in origin, but, in any case, the products of traditional folk communities. Beyond the locality, it was the exceptional king or emperor that was able to win general admiration and heroic status (Karsten, 1978:11–12).

Such a class of individuals could be regarded as heroes in the generic meaning of embodying the dearest values and aspirations of the society, "the perfect expression of the ideal of a group in whom all human virtues unite" (Karsten, 1978:1). One would be proud to reside in a locality that could generate such remarkable beings and to have some vicarious connection with them. And, conversely, of course, it was useful to have some despicable villains available to provide inverted images of virtue, and thus reinforce the community's sense of self-esteem. The great majority of such parochial stars or rogues left little or no documentary trail, and if their memory survives at all, it does so via oral tradition. But, occasionally, a local luminary might so brilliantly personify archetypal virtues or vices that his or her renown would spread upward and outward to attain universal currency. Robin Hood, King Arthur, Don Juan, William Tell, and Dr. Faustus would seem to be interesting examples, and the case of Pocahontas is especially instructive (P. Young, 1962).

The second category of premodern heroes consists of real or imagined persons celebrated throughout the world, or at least the Western world, who are the creations of elite society and who have also inspired a rich literature. As products of the state, church, and literati, they did not ascend from folk society but rather enjoyed a popularity that filtered downward from the educated classes. Their ranks include major figures of the Bible, the gods and demigods of ancient Greece and Rome, and the more notorious soldiers and rulers of earlier ages, for example, Caesar, Alexander, Nero, Hannibal, Roland, El Cid, Cleopatra, Charlemagne, and Barbarossa. Perhaps we might also list some of Rabelais's and Shakespeare's more memorable characters, because certain popular heroes and heroines of early fiction belong to this company. Although, for the most part, the nationalistic import of both groups of heroic figures was slight or nil, either initially or later, many of their representatives have survived into our nationalistic era, and coexist with a newer, quite different cast of characters.

As a colonial society, early America automatically inherited the British and Pan-European stock of heroic personages. We can also assume the creation of some localized heroes, despite a mobile population and the relatively brief period available for generating folk cultures. But of genuine national heroes there were none before 1775 in North America, or anywhere else for that matter (Karsten, 1978:53). The succession of British monarchs from Elizabeth I to George III, various prime ministers, and other leading statesmen might inspire awe, deference, loathing, or indifference, but never the uncritical veneration, the feverish enthusiasm accorded full-fledged national heroes. The closest approximations, and perhaps intimations of things to come, were three individuals prominent in the political convulsions of seventeenth-century England: Hampden, Sydney, and Cromwell (Karsten, 1978). But they engaged the imaginations of rather minute fractions of the British and American populace, and rarely roused truly strong feelings, pro or con.

Americans have remained curiously unexcited about the qualifications of early explorers for heroic apotheosis. Such worthy candidates as Cabot, de Soto, Coronado, Drake, Ponce de Leon, La Salle, Cook, Lewis and Clark, and Pike may have been duly honored by historians, but only casually noted by the general public. The one great exception, of course, has been Christopher Columbus, who, curiously enough, never set eyes on the territory of the United States and whom we share with many other Western Hemisphere countries. Although we lack a serious analysis of the history of Columbus's reputation (and of Columbus Day), it seems clear enough that Americans regard the great Genoese navigator as the ultimate founding father, and, like all other peoples, we impute sacred significance to our origins (B. Schwartz, 1982:376–77, 390, 399).

In accord with this principle, the former British colonies and the later American states have come to celebrate their own founders as well as other eminent local citizens. But this has been a hesitant, belated development, one that materialized long after the sanctification of the heroes and events of the American Revolution (Craven, 1956:61). Indeed it was not until the late nineteenth century, for example, that the veneration of the *Mayflower* reached full bloom (Craven, 1956:128). Moreover, a persistent sectionalism has nearly always confined the glorification of founding figures to their original turf. Thus John Winthrop, Thomas Hooker, Roger Williams, Nathaniel Bacon, Virginia Dare, James Oglethorpe, Stephen Austin, Sam Houston, and Brigham Young may have national reputations of sorts, but receive full honors only within their respective states (Wecter, 1941:32–34). The only two members of this group who seem to have transcended parochial status may be Captain John Smith and William Penn (Craven, 1956:76–77).

ENTER THE NATIONAL HERO

Thus, on the eve of the Revolution, the situation with respect to heroes as well as other public eidolons in the future United States closely resembled that in the United Kingdom and other Western European countries. The American colonists shared with other lands the same cosmopolitan pool of archetypal figures (saints, gods, monarchs, warriors, devils, protagonists of legend, epic verse, drama, etc.), and, like older communities elsewhere, they had anointed their own local worthies. But then, in a breathtaking rush of events, a profound change came to pass, with large consequences for both America and the rest of the world. If it is correct to say that the political and military turmoil of the Revolution endowed the American community with a radically novel cluster of heroes and symbols, it is equally fair to claim that this new symbolic vitality was indispensable to the triumph of the Revolution.

The most remarkable symbolic feat of the Revolution was the invention virtually instantaneously, and evidently for the first time anywhere, of a full-blown national hero. Arguably, this is the single most powerful device for fabricating a strong sense of nationhood in a hurry. This modern eidolon does have his antecedents, for virtually every society has its creation myth safely sequestered in a misty, prehistoric past. Thus China and Japan credit the founding of their nations to the first dynasty of emperor-gods; Augustan Rome and Britain share the legend of Aeneas; Ireland has its St. Patrick; Israel its Moses; and countless so-called primitive tribes cherish the memory of some hazy father-figure. But there is a critical difference between such legendary beings and their dazzling modern counterparts. The former are antiquarian entities that generate only casual concern; the latter individuals are actual or near-contemporaries and command extraordinarily intense devotion and celebration expressed in any number of ways. Whether such adulation is spontaneous amongst the citizenry at large or manufactured by the state, it ultimately involves all the many stratagems available to a technologically advanced society. The person so beatified is credited with establishing the nation or having transformed it through bold ideological and military means from the benighted misery of the past to the glories and promise of the present. Most importantly, this maximum hero is perceived as representing the very soul of the nation, or nation-state, as being the finest incarnation of its ideals and culture.[4]

For the United States, this charismatic figure was, of course, none other than George Washington, that single godlike individual standing so far aloft a veritable pantheon of contemporary heroes. The literature recounting Washington's career and, of special pertinence to the present argument, his political and symbolic significance is vast indeed (e.g., T. Bailey, 1966:3–4; Boorstin, 1965:337–56; Cunliffe, 1958; Curti, 1946:57–60; Forgie, 1979:22–28; Friedman, 1975:44–78; L. C. Jones, 1975; Lipset, 1963:18–23; Mayo, 1959:25–48; Melder, 1976:16–20; Nagel, 1964:225–30; Rabinowitz, 1978; Van Alstyne, 1970; Wills, 1984; J. F. Wilson, 1979:35–38). In fact, these writings have so exhaustively examined the Washington phenomenon I need do no more than summarize their principal points.

First, it is difficult to imagine how the American Republic could have come into being without the military and political guidance of some such powerful leader, or how it could have weathered its turbulent early decades without the unifying symbolic presence of a Washington during and after his lifetime. Quite fortuitously, by one of those seemingly miraculous strokes of fate, the right man appeared at just the right time. George Washington, whatever his intellectual limitations, was equipped with those precise qualities of personality, character, and mind prescribed for the maker of the first new nation, and he exercised them most judiciously (Walker, 1895:392). His physical bearing, comportment, moral attributes, and basic soundness of judgment were such as to inspire devotion among associates of every persuasion and to overcome the divisive tendencies of thirteen strong-willed states despite several military defeats and the tribulations and partisan sniping attending his presidency.

"Surely no one else has been so thoroughly venerated, and so completely frozen into legend" (Cunliffe, 1958:22). The process whereby Washington was institutionalized and marmorealized into *the* national hero seems to have begun immediately upon his appointment as Commander-in-Chief of the Continental Army. It was an event both spontaneous and unprecedented, the mysterious product of mass psychology, not the calculated plotting of some cabal, as the great unspoken yearnings of the gestating nation welled to the surface. "Washington did not create the republic. The republic created him. It called for him, asked him to live up to its expectations" (Wills, 1984:130). Washington was well aware of his canonization, and, although he did not actively lubricate the process, out of a deep sense of duty he fulfilled his assignment as graciously as possible. In fact, so effectively did he act out the role of "Father of His Country" that no scholar has yet succeeded in divorcing the man from the myth, or transmuting the marble back into flesh.

As has happened with several other mechanisms of nation formation, America showed the rest of the world how it could be done by offering the first good working model of the national hero in the person of Washington. It was an example many other countries were to emulate, consciously or otherwise. One can only speculate, but perhaps in lieu of the Washington precedent the galaxy of nineteenth- and twentieth-century national heroes might have assumed a rather different configuration. In any event, we can detect elements of the American experience in such disparate subsequent cases as Kossuth, Father Hidalgo, Bolívar, Garibaldi, Kemal Ataturk, Sun Yat-Sen, Lenin, Ben-Gurion, Nkrumah, Masaryk, Tito, Gandhi, Nehru, De Valera, Castro, and Ho Chi Minh. The enshrinement of national heroes has proved to be so effective that many countries have adopted them posthumously, for example, William Tell, Montezuma, Peter the Great, King Alfred, Joan of Arc, and Frederick the Great.

The glorification of George Washington took place via every possible medium from 1775 onward. At an early date, his countenance became ubiquitous, and has remained so to this day (Boorstin, 1965:353–55; Bush, 1977:28–39; Kammen, 1978:83, 103–4; Melder, 1976:50; J. C. Taylor, 1976:29–33). It may be something of an exaggeration to claim that "no man in history has ever been so frequently portrayed from life" (Horwitz, 1976:16); but certainly a multitude of paintings, engravings, busts, and sculptures of Washington materialized during his lifetime and in countless profusion thereafter (Eisen, 1932). "As early as 1811 a Russian diplomat noted that every American . . . 'considered it his sacred duty to have a likeness of Washington in his home just as we [Russians have in our homes our icons or] images of God's saints'" (Mayo, 1959:31). Writing in 1932, Gustavus Eisen noted that "there is hardly an association, community, village or city in the United States which does not possess one or more sculptured images intended to represent Washington" (Eisen, 1932: vol. 3, 745). His physiognomy adorns the walls of schoolrooms and other public buildings; we see it on paper currency and coins, all manner of business certificates, and, in the many billions, on postage stamps (Skaggs, 1978:98). In the era of sailing vessels, it was a popular choice for figureheads (Pinckney, 1940: Plate 16); Washington appears in many newspaper and magazine advertisements (Cobb, 1978:54–55); and he has been an especially important motif in folk artifacts for the home, including fabrics, furniture, glassware, crockery, and china (Klamkin, 1973:60–69). In short, his image is inescapable.

The names "Washington" and, less frequently, "Mount Vernon" have been applied to places and objects beyond counting, including counties, cities, and other political jurisdictions, male infants, mountains, streams, lakes, parks, forests, hospitals, schools, and other institutions, business enterprises, and commercial products (Boorstin, 1965:355–58; Fishwick, 1954:14; Wecter, 1941:136–37). Americans have preserved and revered all articles and places identified with Washington, most notably Mount Vernon and Valley Forge, but many other sites and buildings as well, and no inconsiderable stock of furniture and other memorabilia. Within the realm of literature, there has been no shortage of oratory, fiction, verse, and drama extolling Washington's deeds (Bryan, 1952); and perhaps there is special significance in the juvenile fiction celebrating the "Father of His Country" (MacLeod, 1975:98; Randall, 1969:20–22).

It is hardly surprising to discover a bountiful quantity of song proclaiming Washington's virtues (Lawrence, 1975:96). The utterances attributed to him were worshiped by many as sacred writ. "To nineteenth-century Americans, the Farewell Address stood almost with the Declaration of Independence and the Constitution as an important founding document" (Forgie, 1979:25). Perhaps as symptomatic as anything of Washington's powerful hold on the early American psyche is the fervor with which his birthday was observed from the Revolutionary years until the 1850s (Boorstin, 1965: 351–53; Melder, 1976:16–20). This may well be the earliest instance of such a commemorative holiday honoring anyone other than a religious figure or monarch.

In evaluating Washington's role in the genesis of the American nation, we can only conclude that both his actual deeds and, perhaps even more to the point, his numinous symbolic presence were absolutely central elements in the success of this unprecedented project. In describing Washington's symbolic import, the only appropriate term is deification, not as a mere figure of speech but as a soberly realistic assessment. The majority of his contemporaries and early nineteenth-century Americans looked upon him as an agent of providence (Berens, 1978:92–93). Although some of Washington's admirers and the artists who rendered him on canvas or in stone perceived him as the American Moses (Hay, 1969a), many more saw him as the American Cincinnatus, as someone reviving the heroism of early republican Rome (Wills, 1984). If this was a process in which the clergymen of the young republic participated actively (J. H. Smylie, 1976), it was also a broadly based phenomenon. Rank and file citizens were ready and eager to find in George Washington "the flawless American, at the very least a semi-divine emissary placed upon this earth to execute the sacred mission of the new nation" (Friedman, 1975:44–78).

Although the apotheosis of Washington had been well under way during the final quarter century of his earthly span, the cult began to reach its climax only after his death in 1799. Instantaneously, all the rancor that had embittered Washington's generalship and presidency totally disappeared, and his memory shone forth pure and undefiled. Undoubtedly, the many editions of Mason Locke Weems's best-selling biography, "a pioneering work in mass culture" (Forgie, 1979:25), broadened and raised the level of idolatry, as did the writings of more scholarly historians, but the canny parson was simply capitalizing on a pent-up demand, not creating it.

The futher trajectory of Washington's reputation tells us a great deal about the evolution of American ideals and sentiments. "Some men are symbols for an age. Washington was far more: he was a mirror reflecting the beliefs of generation after generation of Americans. Indeed in their remembrances of the Father of his Country is registered in large measure the entire ideological development of the American people" (Hay, 1969a:781). It seems clear that the Washington cult waxed in strength throughout the first half of the past century, reaching its peak in the 1850s (Forgie, 1979:185–89). Thereafter the brightness of Washington's image was eclipsed somewhat by Lincoln's rising star and by the changing character of American society.

The resurgence of interest just before and during the 1932 Bicentennial celebration (Wecter, 1941:143–45) was transient in character as Washington continued to recede into the cooler reaches of the nation's consciousness and began to mean different things to different constituencies. Elinor Horwitz comments on a decline of folk art interest in Washington after the Civil War (Horwitz, 1976:130). Karsten has discussed in some detail the rise and gradual decline of Washington's eminence since the late 1700s (Karsten, 1978:89–95, 104–9). He has also provided some useful statistical evidence for the process by tabulating the incidence, over a series of five-year periods, of "Washington" and "George Washington" as first names occurring in various biographical directories. The relative popularity of such nomenclature was greatest in the antebellum period, attaining its maximum during the 1820s, then becoming rather weak after the Civil War (figure 2.1). Gallup polls and responses by schoolchildren to questionnaires soliciting choices of public figures as exemplars administered from 1902 through 1958 (table 2.1) also suggest that the luster of Washington's name has dimmed (Karsten, 1978:93, 95, 104–5). Nevertheless, even though George Washington no longer commands the frantic adoration he once did, his place in the American firmament is fixed and eternal. His feats and larger-than-life virtues still radiate throughout the symbolic cosmos of the United States, steadily and brightly, if not with quite their former incandescence.

AND ALL THOSE OTHER EARLY DEMIGODS

Washington was only the first among many. The American Revolution and its immediate aftermath, when the new polity was fashioned, spawned a goodly throng of heroes, heroines, and villains, indeed by far the largest, most brilliant such group the country has ever known. They fall into two clusters: the many who won fame and glory, or disrepute, during or just after their careers; and a smaller, but fascinating, handful whose renown is posthumous and retroactive. The honor roll of the former is long and illustrious, but, of necessity contains only persons active in the political and military realms, or both. The following roster is far from complete: John Adams, Samuel Adams, Ethan Allen, George Rogers Clark, Benjamin Franklin, Horatio Gates, Nathanael Greene, Alexander Hamilton, John Hancock, Jasper and Newton, Thomas Jefferson, John Paul Jones, Tadeusz Kościuszko, the Marquis de Lafayette, Richard Henry Lee, Benjamin Lincoln, James Madison, Francis Marion, James Monroe, Richard Montgomery, Daniel Morgan, James Otis, Thomas Paine, Molly Pitcher, Kazimierz Pulaski, Israel Putnam, John Stark, John Sullivan, Baron von Steuben, Joseph Warren, Mercy Warren, and Anthony Wayne. By way of contrast and flooding this noble troop with an even more dazzling light, as they

Figure 2.1. *Relative Popularity of the Use of Washington's Name(s) as a First Name for Eminent Persons in America*

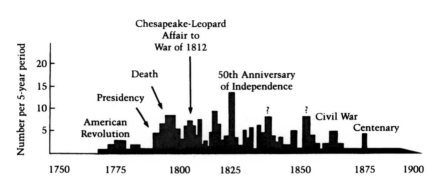

Source: Karsten, 1978:91.

wallow in the depths of infamy, we find Benedict Arnold, George III, and, possibly, Aaron Burr.

Historians may have amply documented the deeds and thoughts of all of the above, except perhaps for the folkloristic Sergeants Newton and Jasper, whose existences and exploits may have been fictitious, but whose paired names have been conferred upon many localities (Everett, 1958). However, the recollection of only a few still resonates strongly in the minds of present-day Americans; others only occasionally rise to the surface of our collective awareness; and still more are forgotten except by scholars and local patriots. It is possible that our historical attention span is too short or that the finite capacity for reverence must concentrate on just a few notables. What we sorely need for a study such as this are accounts of the changing symbolic implications of all those demigods of the Revolutionary era who have not slipped into obscurity. As it happens, definitive analyses are available for only two, Jefferson and Lafayette, while we have incomplete treatments for two others, Hamilton and Allen. Sadly lacking are discussions of such major figures as John Adams, Benjamin Franklin, or James Madison.

It is especially unfortunate that, aside from Wecter's brief comments (Wecter, 1941:77–80), no one has ventured a chronicle of Franklin's impact upon the mind and soul of America during and after his long lifetime, voluminous though the writings on other aspects of the man may be. Self-made Poor Richard was, perhaps more than any other famous individual, the quintessential Ameri-

Table 2.1. Children's and Adolescents' Choice of Public Figures as Exemplars, 1902–1958

Exemplars	Place, approximate date of field work, and investigator				
	1902 New Castle, Pa. (Chambers)	1910 Nashville, Tenn. (Hill)	1928 Birmingham, Montgomery, Mobile, Ala. (Hill)	1944 Springfield, Mass. (Stoughton, Ray)	1958 New Haven, Conn. (Greenstein)
Entertainment	4.7%	4.4%	15.5%	8.1%	37.9%
"Serious"	4.1	4.1	5.1	—	1.8
"Non-serious"	.6	.3	10.4	8.1	36.1
Business	1.6	1.0	1.0	—	.6
Contemporary political	12.5	2.3	2.4	3.1	6.3
Incumbent president	3.3	.9	.2	2.7	3.3
Other	9.2	1.4	2.2	.4	3.0
National hero	35.6	32.2	27.4	11.0	10.4
Washington	29.2	22.0	19.9	4.9	3.2
Lincoln	3.4	.6	2.4	1.5	3.6
Other	3.0	9.6	5.1	4.6	3.6
Miscellaneous figures from wider environment	17.2	20.6	15.6	33.4	14.8
Immediate environment figures	22.4	39.5	33.8	44.4	2.0
No response or invalid response	6.0	—	4.3	—	28.0
Total	100.0%	100.0%	100.0%	100.0%	100.0%
Ages included in present tabulation	7–16 yrs.	7–15 yrs.	6–20 yrs.	9 and 11 yrs.	9–15 yrs.
Number of cases	2333	1531	8813	259	659

Source: Greenstein, 1965:388–89.

can, earthier, less stratospheric in his attributes than Washington, but surpassingly clever, highly articulate, and, like Jefferson, an accomplished performer in an unbelievable number of roles. His popularity has been great and enduring. This claim is confirmed by the frequency with which American parents have chosen the name Franklin for their sons. In a sampling of 896 notables with "patriot-hero first names" appearing in major biographical directories and whose birth dates span the period 1760 to 1920, the number of "Benjamin Franklins" and "Franklins" (102) is second only to the Washingtons (Karsten, 1978:85). Two presidents (Pierce and Roosevelt) are among that throng; no other early American hero has earned such an accolade among our thirty-odd presidents. One might argue that, in essence, latter-day America is the playing out of Franklin's thoughts and dreams, that his spirit still permeates the land, and that by examining our changing attitudes toward him we can divine much concerning our evolving national character that might otherwise lie hidden. For many in France and England, during his long sojourns abroad, Franklin epitomized the young nation, and he was well aware of his role playing. In their subtle way, his many portraits, but, specifically, those featuring the famous fur cap, did their part in molding the emerging image of America (Sellers, 1962:97–100).[5]

If Franklin's writings and dealings were such as to ensure his immortality without any unseemly resort to self-promotion, that was not the case with a much lesser figure, Ethan Allen. He may well have been the earliest in that long procession of American celebrities who have gained notoriety through puffery. Despite some outrageous flaws in character and conduct, Allen managed to win an apparently permanent rating as a standard American hero almost entirely through his own self-serving publications (Beck, 1971; Rosenberg, 1974:115).

Like Franklin and Thomas Jefferson, his ideological sparring partner, Alexander Hamilton has been another of those looming presences inhabiting our collective psyche; but, unfortunately, his symbolic legacy has received only relatively brief notice (Kammen, 1978:64–65; Peterson, 1960:222–26, 333–47). It is obvious enough that Hamilton's stock has risen during those periods when the business oligarchy has been most firmly in the saddle; but since one may view the entire development of twentieth-century America as being so much in accord with the Hamiltonian philosophy, the enduring impress of the man certainly merits much careful analysis.

Thomas Jefferson has fared much better. In addition to some brief discussions of his symbolic significance and how later generations have regarded him (T. Bailey, 1966:4–5; Mayo, 1959:49–71; Wecter, 1941:178–79), we are fortunate in having two extended treatises of considerable substance. In *Patriot-Heroes in England and America*, Peter Karsten has dealt with Jefferson in highly productive fashion, in addition to his handling of Hampden, Sydney, Cromwell, Washington, and Lincoln (Karsten, 1978). But it is Merrill Peterson's lengthy, perceptive *The Jefferson Image in the American Mind* that furnishes the definitive statement (Peterson, 1960). Indeed, this superb volume is as close to the ideal example of the genre as one could hope to find. Peterson amply documents the fact that esteem for Jefferson, as well as his symbolic status, has undergone many a vicissitude over the years. In part this is because of changing currents of political and social thought, but perhaps even more because of the extraordinarily rich, complex, sometimes contradictory nature of the polymath of Monticello. Jefferson simply defies simplification. Although "Jeffersonian" has become a standard term in the political lexicon of the United States, no one has yet written a lucid definition. What does appear certain, though, is that he gradually evolved from the highly controversial figure he once was to someone who is now a universally revered patriot-saint, perhaps the closest approximation yet to a general American culture hero.

"Americans, it has been said, venerate Washington, love Lincoln, and remember Jefferson" (Peterson, 1960:457). The nadir of Jefferson's standing occurred during the period 1870–1920, when, significantly enough, the forces of industrialization and centralization were in their ascendancy (Mayo, 1959:60). The process of enshrinement reached its climax during the New Deal era and the 1943 Bicentennial when FDR went to some pains to exalt his predecessor and bask in some reflected glory, despite the fact that his political program was more Hamiltonian than Jeffersonian in its thrust. Karsten reaches a rather different conclusion than does Peterson using different types of evidence. Treating Jefferson, Hampden, and Sydney as exemplars of whiggish, antistatist individualism and localism as contrasted with the centralizing, cosmopolitan, statist proclivities of Cromwell and Lincoln, or freedom vs. efficiency, he discerns a recent swing away from Jefferson's camp (Karsten, 1978:164–69).

Amidst the hallowed troop of Revolutionary heroes, only one other name can be uttered in the same breath as Washington, Franklin, Hamilton, and Jefferson: that of Lafayette. His was a career and reputation without parallel in the annals of national he-

roes in any country. Again, as in the case of Jefferson, we have a
commendable account of the dynamics of his image over time in
Anne Loveland's *Emblem of Liberty* (Loveland, 1971). The Marquis
de Lafayette was the most acclaimed member of a corps of ideologically motivated French, German, and Polish army officers who
rallied to the rebel cause. As a foreign volunteer, "he was the one
prominent figure of the Revolution who had no loyalty to a particular state or region" (Loveland, 1971:16). More remarkable is the fact
that "Lafayette was, and still is, the only hero honored continu-
ously by this country and without reserve, without a murmur of
criticism, without the slightest taint of jealousy" (MacIntire, 1967:5).

Almost immediately after the arrival of the callow young French
aristocrat in the early stages of the struggle for independence, he
was transformed into a symbol in the popular mind (Van Alstyne,
1970:104–10). Lafayette's close association with the Washington
family certainly did little to weaken that perception, and his symbolic luster brightened with the years. Perhaps more acutely than is
the case with any of the other public eidolons, the ways in which
we have assessed Lafayette offer clear insights into two major aspects of American nationalism, as spelled out by Anne Loveland.
"On the one hand, since Lafayette was identified with the Revolution and the founding of the nation, his image reveals much about
American concern for the republican experiment. On the other
hand, as an emissary of liberty, Lafayette was identified in many
Americans' mind with their mission to spread republican principles
throughout the world. . . . Lafayette served as a focus for discussion
of these two concerns, the republican experiment and the American
mission" (Loveland, 1971:5).

As was also the case with Washington, Lafayette quickly became
aware of the persona that fate had assigned him, even if, unlike his
mentor, he had stumbled into it without adequate preparation. In
an intriguing essay, in which he draws an analogy with John Reed's
encounter with the Bolshevik Revolution, Louis Gottschalk argues
that Lafayette was an accidental symbol, but had the inner moral
resources to grow into the role. "Upon returning from his revolutionary activity, whether he liked it or not (though he would like
it), he would find it impossible to destroy the symbol and to resume
the old life as a dissatisfied son-in-law of an elite family. What he
said and wrote would be, probably without his knowing it, in the
new role rather than in that of the character he had once been. The
symbol would slowly become the reality" (Gottschalk, 1935:ix).

Ultimately, of course, after a lapse of more than forty years,

Lafayette returned to America fully prepared to enact his mythic mission. Never before or after has there been such a triumphal procession as his thirteen-month tour of all the states in 1824–25 (Brandon, 1950–57; Gottschalk, 1935; MacIntire, 1967; Somkin, 1967:131–74). In terms of sheer outpouring of emotion and involvement of onlookers, the only comparable event may be Lincoln's funeral journey. "This redramatization of the Revolution which Lafayette's visit accomplished was credited with causing a remarkable upsurge of republican fervor throughout the United States" (Loveland, 1971:45).

The brilliance of Lafayette's image scarcely lessened during the ensuing years, and actually increased during World War I with the second Franco-American alliance. But, as Loveland has noted, the Lafayette cult has lost most of its vigor over the past several decades. "Since 1919 the appeal of the Lafayette image has been gradually narrowing. As Americans became more sophisticated and less inclined to the demonstrative patriotism of their grandparents, the inspirational appeal of the 'patriot exemplar' declined. As the radical concept of mission lost influence, so did its chief symbol. By midcentury, invocation of Lafayette's name and example was confined primarily to children's literature and patriotic and Francophile organizations, Lafayette no longer served as a national hero-symbol" (Loveland, 1971:160). But if Lafayette has been relegated to a less prestigious corner within the American pantheon, he can still claim a perpetual lease on that site. In any event, it is well to remember that for the first generations of Americans he held a place in the hearts of our citizens only slightly lower than that of Washington, and indeed shared in whatever measure of divinity was accorded the elder statesman. In symbolic terms, Lafayette stood in a kind of filial relationship with Washington, at least until that position may have been captured by Lincoln.

Some of the more interesting heroes associated with the Revolution achieved notoriety long after the fact. In certain cases, such as Crispus Attucks or Haym Salomon, such belated recognition came about because of lobbying by previously impotent ethnic groups. In other instances, we can ascribe the phenomenon to the zeitgeist or the vagaries of literary fashion. Thus Paul Revere may have been a solid citizen and craftsman of some local eminence in his time, but it was only with Longfellow's popular poem that he attained heroic stature at the national scale (Wecter, 1941:86–87). Much the same pattern of delayed glorification through print may account for the eventual fame of Barbara Fritchie, Molly Pitcher, and Nathan Hale

(Potter, 1954; Wecter, 1941:88–89); but more research would be welcome, especially concerning the genesis and growth of the Hale mythology. Equally intriguing is the case of Patrick Henry (Meade, 1957). Although this enigmatic character won considerable notice during his troubled career, his lofty perch in the American firmament was mainly the result of nineteenth-century promotion (Boorstin, 1965:357–59; Mayo, 1959:1–23; Wecter, 1941:86–87).

Rather unexpectedly, the most significant of the posthumous additions to the ranks of American heroes has proved to be Betsy Ross. The fable that has her creating the first American flag and doing so at the personal behest of General Washington has long since been thoroughly debunked (Quaife, 1943:185–89; Wecter, 1941:476–77). But historical veracity may have little to do with the vitality of myths, and fables can readily outshine humdrum facts. It is easy enough to explain the timing of the Betsy Ross boom, which began in the mid-nineteenth century, when the national flag first began to claim the attention and emotions of the general population. Much less obvious are the reasons for the persistent, probably growing renown of Betsy Ross or the central meaning of the phenomenon.

In analyzing the surprising results of a questionnaire administered to several hundred college students at SUNY-Buffalo over the period 1975–83, Michael Frisch has advanced an interpretation with some broad and provocative implications. When asked, on each of five occasions, to "List up to ten names—*excluding* major public officers and military leaders—that you think of when I say 'American History from its beginning through the Civil War,'" the name most frequently cited by all five classes was that of Betsy Ross (Frisch, 1983).[6] Frisch suggests that "she represents this most inclusive of symbols of national identity [the flag], an identity perhaps more fragile and in need of shoring up, because of its uniquely political character, than is often recognized" (Frisch, 1983:10). But he goes much further:

> It is . . . hard to avoid the speculation that the virtual invention of the mythic Betsy Ross—and her immediate public enshrinement—came as a kind of needed supplement to the revolutionary myth, a final step in the "humano-centric" articulation of essentially religious beliefs and experiences. If George is the Father of country—of the nation, of all of us sons and daughters—then surely Betsy Ross exists symbolically as the Mother, who gives birth to our collective symbol.

One can go further. If Washington is, indeed, God the Father, the iconography of Betsy Ross is unmistakable: she is the Blessed Virgin Mary of our civil religion, the plain woman visited by the Father, and commanded to be the vehicle, through their immaculate union, of a divine creation. [Frisch, 1983:12]

Martha Washington, who has never attained much symbolic eminence, is excluded from the Holy Trinity, while, according to Frisch's speculations, George and Betsy are joined by Lafayette, Washington's "beloved and adopted" son (Frisch, 1983:11). The empirical evidence is suggestive enough, but clearly we need much more study and thought before fully accepting so radical a doctrine.

A SECOND GENERATION OF HEROES

During the three-quarters of a century between the Constitutional Convention and the outbreak of the Civil War a good many more heroic figures entered the American scene. If none of them rivalled in stature the greatest of the Founders, we can still deduce a good deal about the character of the rising nation from their identities and their followings. As might be expected, the various military conflicts, major and minor, yielded their quota of celebrities and genuine heroes. Among them we find Stephen Decatur, Oliver Hazard Perry, William Henry Harrison, Winfield Scott, Zachary Taylor, and other stars of the Mexican War. Several statesmen were also obvious candidates for the American pantheon, notably Daniel Webster, Henry Clay, John Calhoun, Thomas Hart Benton, Albert Gallatin, John Marshall, and, preeminently, Andrew Jackson.

Cast in a quite different mold is a new breed of idol, for whom there is no clear precedent in the Old World or Colonial America: the frontier hero. The earliest representative, and the one whose renown is strongest and most enduring, is clearly Daniel Boone. He appeared at just the right time in just the right places and was credited with enough derring-do to become the stuff of legends and the prototype for an endless cavalcade of successors (Fishwick, 1954: 56–70; Rosenberg, 1974:117–18; Somkin, 1967:117–18). Although the name Daniel Boone has virtually become a generic term, no one has yet written a full history of the Boone phenomenon.

In contrast, the much more flamboyant Davy Crockett has inspired a large scholarly, as well as popular, literature (Albanese, 1978, 1979; Beck, 1971; Boorstin, 1965:327–37; Hoffman, 1961; Lofaro, 1985; Shackford, 1956; Stiffler, 1957). This crude, blustering, vulgar individual, the very antithesis of Washington, fascinated his large public almost wholly through his own self-advertisements and outrageous fabrications. However blatant the methods, the fundamental reason for Crockett's lasting presence in the American mind, aided by modern revivals in the film and television media, would seem to be his appeal to some deep craving in the souls of many Americans. As Catherine Albanese puts it, Crockett was the folk hero best able to express the yearnings of those "seeking a middle ground in a civilization that still kept contact with nature. With his dual identity as man of the woods and man of the Congress, he summed up the tensions between the values of nature and history. Even as he embraced the newness of wilderness existence and Adamic myth, he espoused the human political project. Nature and civility in the figure of Crockett, has been made to coexist" (Albanese, 1979:248–49).

Be that as it may, it was the wilderness strain of the man that gained the upper hand among Crockett's numerous progeny in the American Valhalla. Kit Carson, Mike Fink, Cooper's Natty Bumppo, John C. Fremont, Sam Houston, and Buffalo Bill are the most celebrated among many. It seems plausible to trace back to the Boone-Crockett source the entire tribe of cowboy hero and Western outlaw, including Billy the Kid, Wild Bill Hickok, and Jesse James (Steckmesser, 1965), and even many a macho comic book and television character of the present generation. We are dealing here, plainly enough, with folk creations amidst the novel realities of the New World environment, perhaps the spontaneous upwelling of some primordial instinct gushing along original channels.

But the distinctions between Crockett and company and the supernal beings of the Revolutionary era who so thoroughly personify the Providential American mission are deep and wide. The former band of folk heroes do help in defining the American identity and are of least tangential value in promoting nationalistic feeling, but their clientele tends to be limited to certain social strata or to certain sections of the country. On the other hand, the images of Washington, Jefferson, Franklin, Lafayette, and even Patrick Henry and Nathan Hale, all of them of upper-class origin, had managed to capture the fancy and affection of the entire population. For the first time, then, we encounter public eidolons that may be classed as "segmental," that is, entities cherished by no more than fractions of the citizenry as stratified by location, class, party, or special interest. With the passage of time, such segmental figures were to become more numerous and varied, and eventually supreme.

Unquestionably, no post-Revolutionary personage of the early nineteenth century surpassed Andrew Jackson in heroic stature; and, once again, the eidolon functions as a mirror held up to an age, or at least a major fraction of its inhabitants. Although Old Hickory, coming out of the New West, won national acclaim as the victor in the Battle of New Orleans, his symbolic import derives largely from political exploits, populist roots, and sectional self-assertion. As J. F. Wilson suggests, he was a sign of the changing times. "Perhaps a subsequent mythic figure of a scale roughly comparable to Washington could arise only with a new generation celebrating the reorientation of the national community away from the seaboard and embracing with systematic conquest the inner continent" (J. F. Wilson, 1979:38). Since Jackson's career was rancorous, his motivations partisan, his support based, in large degree, on region and class, and his ideology less than crystal-clear ("Jacksonian" is another stock, but ambiguous, political adjective), his image has never quite succeeded in reaching the transcendent heights of a Washington, Lincoln, or Jefferson. And certainly the Jackson cult is much less formidable, and has never attained the international dimensions of the aforementioned (T. A. Bailey, 1966:6–7).

Nevertheless there is little doubt that Andrew Jackson is one of the "residents of a national Pantheon, a collectivity of myths, a supra-historical celestial palace commemorating and dedicated to them and to the values they embody" (Fellman, 1971:67). And, in that hallowed edifice, Jackson fulfills a function, somewhat analagous to Franklin's, since the homespun, uneducated "Jackson, though he is a central figure, remains earthbound and absorbs the negative characteristics that the members of the heavenly Pantheon [Washington, Jefferson, Lincoln] might otherwise be forced to contain themselves. . . . Jackson can represent whatever ambivalent qualities the members of the Pantheon might have without him" (Fellman, 1971:68). Or, put more directly, "If there were no Jackson, then Washington, Jefferson and Lincoln would be less clear and less useful as symbols" (Fellman, 1971:74–75). Thus we can position Jackson as a major tenant in the pantheon, but not at the topmost level, and, arguably, segmental in appeal. However, his greatest significance in the long term may well be the way in which he inherited the institution of a rather diffident presidency from the Virginia-cum-Massachusetts dynasty and began to remold and redirect it along the path it has followed to this day, ultimately greatly enhancing its symbolic as well as political potency. "The power of Congress dwarfed the presidency until Andrew Jackson marched on

Washington. . . . The people . . . found in Jackson reason to begin to love the presidency as an image of themselves. Ironically, but predictably, the more egalitarian the base of participation, the more deeply felt was the tug of royalty" (Novak, 1974:22).

THE LINCOLN PHENOMENON

With the arrival of Abraham Lincoln, we witness the full peopling of the loftiest chamber of the American pantheon. So much has been written about him and the legends that abound after the martyred president (Basler, 1935; Karsten, 1978:98–100; L. Lewis, 1929; E. Wilson, 1954) that further comment may be superfluous. All three of our most highly regarded chief executives, Washington, Lincoln, and Franklin Delano Roosevelt, did indeed preserve the nation and state in periods of profound crisis and, in so doing, determined the direction of our society for generations to come. But rivaling the tangible results of their incumbencies are the symbolic clouds of glory they left streaming in their wake.

The remarkable complexities of Lincoln's personality, including the common touch, his eloquence, and the capacity to appeal to all segments of the nation (ultimately even the South), along with his dramatic accomplishments, all this made him a prime candidate for elevation to the pantheon. But perhaps the circumstances of his death best explain his truly extraordinary emotional hold on Americans and immediate transfiguration to sainthood. Assassinated on a Good Friday in the very last hours of a struggle in which the Union was redeemed through a great blood sacrifice, the multitudes instantly perceived the fallen leader as a Christlike figure (L. Lewis, 1929:92–105)—and John Wilkes Booth as the American Cain or Judas (L. Lewis, 1929:353–56). Indeed, try as one might, the theological implications of Lincoln's career and especially his demise cannot be avoided. The millions who gazed upon his casket or wept as they watched the passing funeral train (Searcher, 1965) underwent what can only be described as a religious catharsis. If that were not enough, we have also the Legend of the Empty Tomb (L. Lewis, 1929:259–62) reinforcing the Myth of the Dying God (L. Lewis, 1929:347–56). The Lincoln phenomenon not only carries us into the universalities of religious feeling but also sharply illustrates, perhaps as much as the Washington phenomenon, the role of the hero in forming and maintaining the nation-idea within a young synthetic nation.

Just as had happened with Washington, but possibly even more spontaneously, rapidly, and intensely, the memory of Lincoln has been honored in every conceivable way. February 12 became a national holiday; his name was bestowed on innumerable places, people, and things; the Lincoln iconography proliferated on every likely surface; the buildings and places associated with the man became shrines; poets, novelists, and dramatists discovered in him a rich and fruitful theme; and his visage became a favorite motif in folk art (Horwitz, 1976:133–44).

Perhaps more than any other historic personage available to Americans, Lincoln was all things to all men. What Carl Van Doren had to say about poets applies equally well to most segments of the population: "The latest Lincoln cult . . . has the distinction of bringing the most revolutionary and most reactionary of poets together to pay equal honor to the sole American whom they all agree to honor" (Van Doren, 1919:777). And, even today, in these unheroic or antiheroic times, the Lincoln cult persists, less enfeebled than that of other national heroes, possibly in part because "the secret of Lincoln's continuing vogue is his essential ambiguity" (Donald, 1959:18). Politicians of every stripe have been eager to exploit the Lincoln image from 1865 to the present moment, for, like all full-blown national heroes, he has been cleansed of partisanship (Donald, 1959). If FDR hitched his image to those of Jefferson, Jackson, and Woodrow Wilson, eventually he identified himself even more closely with Lincoln's. With the best selling efforts of such authors as Carl Sandburg, Stephen Vincent Benét, and Robert Sherwood, among others, it was during the New Deal era that the Lincoln image soaked itself most deeply into mass culture (A. H. Jones, 1974).[7]

Less obvious, but a matter of the utmost importance, has been Lincoln's role in the further transformation of the presidency. As already noted, the process of its sanctification may have taken off with Andrew Jackson, but his immediate successors, with the possible exception of James Polk, did little to magnify the prestige of the office. But, then, through the sheer force of the Lincoln mystique, after 1865 the presidency was ennobled to such a degree that not even the most mediocre or mendacious of the later occupants of the White House have been able to tarnish seriously its sacredness. As Clinton Rossiter has perceptively observed,

> Lincoln is the supreme myth, the richest symbol in the American experience. He is, as someone has remarked neither irreverently nor sacrilegiously, the martyred Christ of democracy's

passion play. And who, then, can measure the strength that is given to the President because he holds Lincoln's office, lives in Lincoln's house, and walks in Lincoln's way? The final greatness of the presidency lies in the truth that it is not just an office of incredible power but a breeding ground of indestructible myth. [Rossiter, 1960:108]

ON A DOWNWARD SPIRAL

We have had at least four presidents since Lincoln whom some would consider national heroes. For the time being, however, our jury of 240 million members has not reached that solid consensus that could elevate any to the stature of Washington, Jefferson, Jackson, or Lincoln. Theodore Roosevelt certainly captured the nation's imagination during his heyday, but, although he glares at us eternally from Mount Rushmore, few Americans today would grant him semidivine status. He may have been "the last great American on horseback, but his cult has not shown the vigor that the Rough Rider displayed during his overvigorous lifetime" (T. A. Bailey, 1966: 7), in part because he has been overshadowed by his more illustrious younger cousin.[8] Nonetheless he and John F. Kennedy seem to be the only twentieth-century presidents whose faces have won the serious affection of American folk artists (Horwitz, 1976:107, 144–54).

Woodrow Wilson has earned a place in the hearts of his countrymen only slightly below that of Theodore Roosevelt as another individual who embodies the spirit of the nation and represents all that is presumably most admirable in Americanism (T. A. Bailey, 1966:5–6; Van Alstyne, 1958). But the appeal of this austere scholar-statesman, hallowed as it may have been by his possible martyrdom on behalf of the comity of nations, has shown more vitality among the intelligentsia than the common herd. Wilson's posthumous reputation may have reached its peak during World War II when many citizens had occasion to regret that a previous generation of Americans had not heeded his counsel. His career provided the material for Darryl Zanuck's high-budget 1944 film *Wilson*, one of the most successful efforts (in critical and technical, if not commercial, terms) at the cinematic manipulation of nationalistic symbols at a time when FDR and his administration were firing off all the available symbolic ammunition on behalf of both internationalism and the war aims of the country (Knock, 1978).

It is still too soon to assess the ultimate locus of Franklin Delano

Roosevelt within the American pantheon. For one thing, the acrimony that attended his four terms and the venom directed at both FDR and his redoubtable spouse linger on, much diluted by his passing, of course, but far less quickly or thoroughly dissipated than was the case with Washington or Lincoln. Concerning his enormous historical importance and effectiveness as an executive there is little dispute among either the general public or professional historians, who, in terms of greatness, rank Roosevelt only slightly below Lincoln, our all-time champion (Murray and Blessing, 1983).

But the question here is rather different: his symbolic prowess, the mythopoeic potential, how bright and enduring an emotional imprint the image will manage to have on our long-term collective consciousness. The elements for such enshrinement are certainly at hand (Orlansky, 1947:240–43; Soule, 1937). During World War II, FDR's photogenic face dominated many a propaganda poster in quasi-religious fashion (Zeman, 1978:74). And a generation ago it was certainly true enough that "those millions who hate him lavishly may as well face the hard fact that *Sunrise at Campobello* will be in the repertory of every amateur company" (Rossiter, 1960:150). Both friend and foe were keenly appreciative of the power of his personality and oratory.[9] And certainly the timing of Roosevelt's demise, in the final weeks of a victorious war, eerily parallels the Lincoln precedent. As I can vividly recall, the shock and grief over his death and the subsequent funeral journey and ceremonies in Washington and Hyde Park convulsed the country in a fashion perhaps equalled only by the Lincoln and Kennedy tragedies or Lafayette's return visit (Orlansky, 1947).

Yet we must hesitate before assigning Roosevelt a permanent niche in our symbolic cosmos. The number of places and objects named after him is almost certainly exceeded by those honoring John F. Kennedy. After four decades, the only item commemorating FDR in the nation's capital is a small, inconspicuous stone block, in contrast to the imposing structures consecrated to Washington, Jefferson, Lincoln, Kennedy, or even the bold equestrian monument to Andrew Jackson; and there are precious few monuments to him anywhere else in the United States. To be sure, the seemingly interminable squabble over the design and placement of a suitably majestic Roosevelt memorial in Washington (Creighton, 1962) reflects the deep uncertainty besetting the art community today over the proper idiom for monuments in general as well as the still smouldering anti-Roosevelt bitterness within certain quarters of the Establishment. But perhaps it is also testimony to the altered mood of

our postheroic epoch, our inability to gush without reserve over
potential national heroes. The most recent presidential candidate
for beatification as a national hero has been John Fitzgerald Kennedy; but since the cult surrounding his memory tells us more
about the presidency as a public eidolon and certain eternal verities
than about the particular qualities of the person, it is best to defer
discussion to a more appropriate section of this essay.

During the post-Lincoln era, the hero-worship of statesmen and
military figures that began in 1775 did continue, but with a zeal
perceptibly less heated. In addition to the presidents already mentioned, we must acknowledge a galaxy of Civil War officers whose
glory outlasted the conflict: preeminently, of course, U. S. Grant,
but also William T. Sherman, Philip Sheridan, and David G. Farra-
gut, among many others, and, gradually but surely, Robert E. Lee,
Jeb Stuart, and Stonewall Jackson. The Indian Wars and various international conflicts up through World War II generated their share
of martial feats and candidates for hero-worship, among them,
George Armstrong Custer, George Dewey, John J. Pershing, Alvin C.
York, Douglas MacArthur, George S. Patton, Chester Nimitz, and
Dwight D. Eisenhower. (The failure of the Korean and Vietnamese
wars to produce any serious claimants for nationwide admiration
may reflect the temper of the times or the depressing character of
those events, or both.) Yet none of these individuals has managed to
inspire more than the most ephemeral or shallow of cults. We may
remember them and respect, or pity, them, but we cannot cherish
any unreservedly with all our heart and soul.

A SPLINTERED CONGREGATION

Since the late nineteenth century, three striking trends have
emerged among those public eidolons with any relevance to nationalistic sentiment. First, we can observe a fractionalization of the
hero-worshipping public, insofar as such a public still persists, and
with such splintering of devotees a considerable diversification in
the kinds of persons being looked up to. A second trend has been
the development of a deep, lasting ambivalence toward many of
these eidolons. They may be admired and loathed at the same time,
even by the same persons, a phenomenon that has culminated recently in the vogue of the antihero. Finally, there has been a decided tendency for the general type, or nameless collections of persons, to replace the individual hero, for the anonymous to push
aside the particular person.

Each of these points merits exploration. Aside from the more eminent of recent presidents, we have been witnessing new varieties of heroes or near-heroes reflecting the changing composition, moods, and aspirations of American society. As already noted, the earliest of the latter-day types was the Western pioneer-frontiersman, then, from the same region, the cowboy and outlaw, stock characters in the American epic, types whose appeal may have been great, but far from all-embracing. Later we greet the self-made entrepreneur, as exemplified by Horatio Alger's protagonists (Hartz, 1964:104–10). With the rise and triumph of big business during and after the Civil War, the name of many a financier, railroad magnate, and manufacturer became a household word. To whatever extent such individuals as Jay Gould, Cornelius Vanderbilt, James J. Hill, Philip D. Armour, Andrew Carnegie, John D. Rockefeller, J. P. Morgan, Andrew W. Mellon, Henry Ford, Henry Kaiser, or Howard Hughes may have been objects of envy and adulation, they are nevertheless segmental in their magnetism. That is to say they embody only a portion of the total cargo of traits and implications borne by the genuine hero, and, of course, they failed to captivate the entire populace.

In fact—and this takes us to the second major trend—such public eidolons were as much divisive in effect as they were agents for unifying the national spirit. Whatever warmth they may have kindled was countered, and sometimes far outweighed, by virulent loathing long after, as well as during, their lifetimes. The same observation applies to many of the more celebrated of our latter-day political luminaries, including Huey Long, the Reverend Charles Coughlin, J. Edgar Hoover, Eleanor Roosevelt, and Martin Luther King, Jr. Perhaps the ultimate in ambivalence of attitude is found in yet another segmental class of fascinating hero-villains with whom Americans have dallied in a love-hate relationship: the master crook. Within an urban twentieth-century setting, the perfect exemplars are Al Capone and John Dillinger.

Two new categories of idols with a plausible claim for heroic status have come into their own only within the past hundred years: the superathlete and the technological wizard. But, once again, their domains fall short of the universal. The former type could not even have been imagined in earlier times since it is only with the advent of mass spectator sports toward the end of the last century that the sport celebrity enters the scene. John L. Sullivan may have been the first indubitable specimen of the genre, but others followed in rapid succession, until by the 1920s and 1930s a dynasty of

such superachievers was literally worshiped, and almost never de-
tested, by a vast, if rather less than total, public. The uppermost
echelon included such stars as Jack Dempsey, Babe Ruth, Bobby
Jones, Bill Tilden, Knute Rockne, Red Grange, Jesse Owens, and Joe
Louis. To a degree probably not rivaled by their post–World War II
successors, many fans thought of them not merely as prodigious
athletes but also as super-Americans whose feats somehow vali-
dated our sense of nationhood. What red-blooded American was not
thrilled to the core when Louis demolished Max Schmeling, darling
of the Nazis, or when Jesse Owens showed Der Führer a thing or
two at the 1936 Olympics?

Although we may dutifully pay our respects to those early American inventors who helped revolutionize our world, among them Eli
Whitney, Samuel F. B. Morse, Robert Fulton, Elias Howe, and Cyrus
McCormick (Jefferson's and Franklin's fame would endure even if
they had never tinkered with mechanical contraptions), they have
never greatly stirred the American masses. It was only when technology achieved unchallenged dominance of everyday life that its
more glamorous practitioners began to knock at the gates of the
American pantheon. It is only slightly excessive to claim that "to
the degree that Americans have achieved a group identity, it has
rested largely on technological superiority" (Wachhorst, 1981:120).
Thus Alexander Graham Bell, Luther Burbank, Charles Steinmetz,
and the Wright brothers—not to mention such fictional champions
as Tom Swift—enjoyed a better press than their forerunners. But no
one within the general category has so enraptured the generality of
Americans as its three most celebrated representatives: Thomas
Alva Edison, Henry Ford, and Charles A. Lindbergh.

Of the three, Edison is probably the most significant. As is amply
demonstrated in Wyn Wachhorst's superlative traversal of the Edi-
sonian mythology, the celebrated inventor and business entrepreneur more closely approximated the complete and total American
culture hero than any other individual in our history, with the possible exception of Franklin (Wachhorst, 1981). In good part, of
course, this is attributable to the impressive number of important
devices he discovered or perfected in the course of a long career, but
also, in no small measure, to Edison's own sedulous cultivation of
his public image. In any event, "the complexity of the Edison image
. . . leaves almost no facet of the American mythology untouched"
(Wachhorst, 1981:4).

The Edison symbol has been a vehicle for every major American theme: the gospel of technological progress, the rural Protestant virtues (hard work, initiative, perseverance, prudence, honesty, frugality, etc.), the success mythology of the self-made man, individualism, optimism, practicality, anti-intellectualism, the American Adam and the New World Eden (America as a new beginning for mankind), the sense of world mission, democracy, egalitarianism, the idealization of youth, and others. [Wachhorst, 1981:3]

By the early twentieth century, the nation's regard for Edison reached extraordinary heights, even though his more substantial accomplishments were things of the past. But residence among the loftiest pinnacles was not to last. Wyn Wachhorst has uncovered the evidence: "My own speculation, based on opinion polls and bibliographic samples from the past half-century, is that Edison has dropped from an indisputable third in the 1920s to sharing sixth place with two or three others in the 1970s. . . . Among the top ten only Lincoln, Washington, Franklin, and Jefferson have stood the test of time, although by that criterion Edison would rank at least fifth" (Wachhorst, 1981:5–6). Following his death in 1931, Edison's fame suffered temporary erosion, but recovered somewhat in the 1960s and 1970s. Permanent installation in the American pantheon seems assured, even though we remain unsure of his ultimate ranking.

If "the function of the culture hero [is] to resolve rationally contradictory cultural values into a single paradoxical reality—to mediate polar tensions" (Wachhorst, 1981:5), then in many ways Charles Augustus Lindbergh filled the role even more admirably than did Edison. It is difficult for those who did not live through the Lindbergh apotheosis to appreciate the unbridled hysteria that burst forth (in France too, but most extremely in America) after the solo flight across the Atlantic in 1927 and especially with the tumultuous welcoming ceremonies upon his return. The "Lone Eagle" seemed predestined to portray the Great American Idol and latter-day folk hero: handsome, brave, resourceful, diffident, individualistic—and a son of the Middle West. The peculiar magic of his achievement was that it so beautifully combined the complexities of advanced technology with a nostalgic reaffirmation of frontier virtues. As J. W. Ward has so perceptively noted, "Lindbergh's flight was the occasion of a public act of regeneration in which the nation momentarily rededicated itself to something, the loss of which was keenly felt" (Ward, 1958:7); "the public projected its sense that the source of America's strength lay somewhere in the past and that Lindbergh somehow meant that America was to look backward in time to rediscover some lost virtue" (Ward, 1958:12). The dramatic flight was thus a great communal ritual in which a receding, romanticized past was harmonized with the problematic technological wonderland of the present in a single intoxicating moment.

In the several years that followed, Lindbergh's fame scarcely slackened, despite his reclusive ways, as he carried on his storybook courtship of the brilliant Anne Morrow and suffered a painful martyrdom when his infant son was kidnapped and murdered. Subsequently, Lindbergh's stock declined precipitously as he became embroiled on the unpopular side of controversial political issues in the early phases of World War II. Thereafter he lived out his final decades enjoying a much coveted obscurity, and his death in 1974 roused only mild excitement among the general public. Thus, despite a brief burst of superbrilliance, the Lindbergh image has settled down to a subdued glow, one far less dazzling than Edison's or Ford's.

Like Edison and Lindbergh, Henry Ford sprang from the loins of the small-town Middle West and reached dizzying heights of folk heroism. Once again, we behold the self-made mechanical genius, the anti-intellectual, homespun ruralist (who acted out his daydreams in Greenfield Village), the wizard who showers us with material abundance, the fabulously wealthy industrialist who retained the common touch. His was a reputation that was partially spontaneous, and indeed unavoidable, given the huge success of the Model T and the abundant folklore inspired thereby; but the Ford image was craftily promoted by the man himself and by his skilful publicist W. J. Cameron. We are fortunate in having two detailed, indeed definitive, treatments of the creation and perpetuation of the myth (D. L. Lewis, 1976; Sward, 1948). Although Ford was also the target of much adverse comment and abuse, no manufacturer before or since has enjoyed such vast acclaim. For many years, the press and general public hung upon every syllable that dropped from the lips of the oracle; and at one point in the 1920s there was serious talk about electing Ford to the presidency. But, finally, as the Ford company matured and became less distinguishable from other firms and the founder dwindled into his dotage, the myth lost much of its luster. The name and the legend endure as significant elements in the American cultural heritage, but no longer rouse much emotion.

The transition from highly individualized heroes to increasingly impersonal eidolons did not occur by chance; instead it reflects the profound restructuring of American society that was well under way by the close of the past century (T. P. Greene, 1970:335–38; Karsten, 1978:104–9). In his study of the more or less laudatory biographies of various celebrities that appeared in selected American periodicals from about 1800 to 1918, Theodore Greene (1970) was able to date the process with some precision. After "that first long-term transition from the early republic's dutiful, socially minded neo-classic gentlemen to the forceful, ambitious individualists of the later nineteenth century, [it was] in the years from 1914 through 1918 [that] independent individualism in turn had become irrelevant" (T. P. Greene, 1970:335). In his penetrating analysis of patterns of commemoration among the objects displayed in the U.S. Capitol, Barry Schwartz discovered premonitory signs of the same transformation. "The post Civil War Capitol exhibited . . . the tendency to substitute for 'personal charisma' the 'charisma of office.' . . . The criterion of commemoration thus shifts from individual to structure, from personal exploits to impersonal functions" (B. Schwartz, 1982:392).

In pinpointing the switch in public attention from the napoleonic tycoon to the organization man as occurring during World War I, Greene argues that this change simply parallels and confirms the advent of our present-day corporate-bureaucratic world. "In the trade associations of the 1920's, in the New Deal agencies, in all the organized activities of World War II and of the Cold War, Americans would settle for the new style of life. More and more of them would find their hopes for affluence, for prestige, even for survival, dependent on the great bureaucracies of business, of government, of the military, and of education. New sanctions and new rationales would grow up to surround the organization life with meaning and value" (T. P. Greene, 1970:337). Unfortunately, "the virtues of efficiency, loyalty, conciliation and cooperation were essentially undramatic ones" (T. P. Greene, 1970:377), so that we can hardly expect to find ourselves celebrating dramatic, durable contemporary heroes in the America of today. Although business firms are much larger and wealthier than ever before, exceedingly few of their executives have attracted much of a claque outside their own headquarters, for this is an age of interlocking directorates, faceless, interchangeable technicians and functionaries, and large stockholders with a passion for anonymity.

Similarly, the character of the contemporary university seems to

be inimical to the public emergence of such luminaries as Charles
Eliot, William Rainey Harper, Nicholas Murray Butler, Benjamin
Ide Wheeler, or Robert Maynard Hutchins or the capability of any
current college president to speak forth on major public issues
with the kind of magisterial authority commanded by his or her
more distinguished predecessors (Nisbet, 1975:108). Recent developments in astrophysics, genetics, biophysics, nuclear physics, computer science, and chemistry have been as profound and important
as anything that materialized in generations past, but no scientific
stars have burst upon the public scene of late (excepting a few media personalities who are not necessarily the discoverers of great
scientific truths), certainly no one with the olympian attributes of a
Newton, Galileo, Pasteur, Humboldt, Darwin, Huxley, or Einstein.
The same depressing statement also applies to the social sciences.
Such a dearth of heroes in basic scientific and scholarly pursuits or
in applied technology is quite simply the result of the fact that
most major results nowadays usually come about through teamwork, often elaborately, expensively organized, seldom from the
lone investigator.

Increasingly, then, those public eidolons having anything to do
with nationalistic sentiment have come to be generalized, collective, or anonymous rather than the projected images of single, identifiable, flesh-and-blood creatures. As already noted, such entities
were being celebrated toward the close of the nineteenth century in
the form of Uncle Sam, the Minute Man, the Pilgrim Fathers, the
Pioneer, Pioneer Mother, and, via many hundreds of monuments,
the idealized Union or Confederate soldier. More recently, we have
the World War I doughboy and the World War II GI, the FBI's G-
Men, and the astronauts. Few ordinary citizens can recall the name
of more than one astronaut; and I doubt whether any reader can
recite the name of even one of the fifty-two American hostages
held for 444 days in the U.S. Embassy in Tehran whose homecom-
ing in January 1981 touched off such a monumental orgy of nationalistic rejoicing. But of all such depersonalized eidolons by all odds
the most important, the one with the most far-reaching implications for the life of the nation and the state, has been the modern
presidency.

A SACERDOTAL PRESIDENCY?

In speaking of the presidency, it is essential to distinguish between
the office and its occupants. It is the former that has acquired such

enormous symbolic vigor in recent years. Individual incumbents, notably the second Roosevelt and John F. Kennedy, may have added cubits to the mythic stature of the presidency, so that, in general, accession to the Oval Office now means instant ennoblement and mounting a pedestal reserved for few mortal beings, however ordinary the person in question might be.

As already suggested, this situation did not prevail in bygone days. The White House of FDR, Kennedy, Nixon, or Reagan is an utterly different institution from that of Thomas Jefferson (Morris, 1977:1). There may have been much muttering in the 1790s about the ceremonial pomp of the Washington presidency, but, subsequently, Jefferson, Madison, and Monroe zealously abjured any displays that hinted at monarchism (Wolfe, 1975:75–76). It was only with the Jackson administration that we glimpse the first clues that the presidency was to become an "elective kingship" (Binkley, 1952; 86–88). The power and prestige of the office took another quantum leap upward during the Lincoln regime. During the century that followed the trend continued, but irregularly so. It was during the Roosevelt years that the presidency became the sacred entity it has remained ever since and we can properly begin to apply the term "imperial."

There may be more than mere coincidence at work in the rather similar trajectory of public regard for the British monarchy. From a nadir in esteem during the eighteenth and early nineteenth centuries, the institution staged a remarkable recuperation during the later years of Victoria's long reign, reaching hallowed heights it has clung to ever since (P. Black, 1953; Cannadine, 1983; K. Martin, 1962). In contrast to the American case, however, the British ruler has lost political power even as he/she was storing up symbolic mana.

With the passage of time, the office of American president has acquired immensely greater power in terms of political clout and prerogatives, work force, and budget, more so than did the legislative and judicial arms of the Federal establishment, which also expanded greatly.[10] But great as the president's power of decision and control may be, ultimately it rests, in large part, on a most primordial resource: the symbolism and image of his office. This fact has become so obvious it has engendered a fair amount of scholarly attention (Binkley, 1952, 1958; Nisbet, 1975:26–30; M. Novak, 1974; Pious, 1979:1–9; Reiff, 1940:101–2; Rossiter, 1960:16–18; Verba, 1965:353–57; Wolfe, 1975:71–107). Put as succinctly as possible, "his [the American president's] office is, in quite modern and sophisticated form, a religion in a secular state. It evokes responses familiar in all the ancient religions of the world. It fills a perennial vacuum at the heart of human expectations" (M. Novak, 1974:4).

It has become essential to the effective operation of the contemporary American nation-state, as well as for the political fortunes of the incumbent, that the presidential image must shine brightly and constantly, that everyone must live in perpetual curiosity about the exalted one, forever eager to hear about his latest words, thoughts, and deeds. One reason for this is the rather unusual job description of the American president as compared with his counterparts within other nation-states. He combines in a single person the responsibilities of head of state (which include an endless round of ceremonial functions), chief executive officer, and head of a major political party. In any case, as Robert Nisbet has rather tartly observed,

> there is the ever-growing centrality of the *image* of the President and, with this, the constantly augmenting attention to the President by press and public alike. Not only what the president thinks on a given public issue, but what he wears, whom he dines with, what major ball or banquet he may choose to give, and what his views are on the most trivial or cosmic of questions—all of this has grown exponentially in the regard lavished by press and lesser political figures upon the presidency during the past four decades. [Nisbet, 1975:29]

And, of course, the president and his aides spend an inordinate amount of time fretting about, and polishing, the image. American political life has reached the point where television plays an absolutely decisive role not only in brightening and guarding the image of the incumbent (local as well as national) but also in determining whether a particular person should even consider running and what the election outcome will be (Meyrowitz, 1985:268–302). Abraham Lincoln would probably never have been nominated had he been available in 1960 instead of 1860; and the corpulent William Howard Taft would have been laughed off the television screen.

Scarcely any of the presidential aura reaches the vice-president, who politically and symbolically finds himself in an anomalous position. More fortunate are members of the president's immediate family, because ever since the first Roosevelt they have been much in the public eye. In particular, the First Lady shares a bit of her spouse's luster (L. C. Jones, 1975:7; Pious, 1979:4). The case of Jacqueline Kennedy may be especially instructive, given her personal glamour and casting in the role of Queen of Camelot and an effective performance as Queen-Widow in the days and weeks following the assassination in a manner reminiscent of ancient monarchies (Wolfe, 1975:415–23). Subsequently, of course, she has remained important copy for journalists, but as celebrity rather than goddess.

In my opinion, the facts lead to the conclusion that, as the state has become the most dominant and central of American institutions, there has been a parallel growth in the potency of the two sturdiest symbolic pillars upon which the state supports itself: the presidency and the flag. The only other governmental institution even remotely comparable to the presidency in terms of symbolic grandeur is the U.S. Supreme Court (Bellah and Hammond, 1980: 76–77; Gabriel, 1956:444–45; Lerner, 1937; Michaelsen, 1970:203–6; Reiff, 1940:101). (The Directorship of the Federal Bureau of Investigation does not qualify; J. Edgar Hoover's rise to heroic glory during his lifetime came about through adroit image-mongering, while his successors have not automatically inherited his halo.) As the ultimate interpreters of the Constitution, a document hedged about with divinity, the Court serves as a "National School Board" (Michaelsen, 1970:203–6) or as a kind of talmudic College of Cardinals. As Alexis de Tocqueville (1947) pointed out at some length a century and a half ago, Americans have stood in awe of courts from the very outset of nationhood; and the judicial system, as articulator of ultimate purpose and justice, provides "a religion independent of churches" (Bellah and Hammond, 1980:76).

Just as happens with the presidency, appointment to the Supreme Court ennobles the appointee rather than the reverse. Although several individual justices have earned enviable personal reputations and are deeply respected by historians and connoisseurs of jurisprudence, none of them, with the marginal exception of John Marshall, have been granted admission to the American pantheon. The U.S. Congress, despite its political might, is not perceived in anything resembling a heroic light by the generality of Americans; and this statement applies even more forcefully to the multiplicity of Federal bureaucracies operating in and out of Washington. The American attitude toward the military establishment has always been ambivalent at best. Whatever symbolic puissance the Army, Navy, and Air Force may have stored up has been by virtue of their fleshing out and enforcing the majesty of the state and flag rather than because of any inherent sorcery of their own.

At no time has the sacredness of the office of president been more explicit than on those six occasions from 1865 onward when a sitting president has expired. The deaths of William Henry Harrison in 1841 (within weeks of his inauguration) and of Zachary Taylor in 1850 do not seem to have caused undue consternation, but they occurred well before Abraham Lincoln had lifted the office of president to soaring symbolic heights. Indeed, "nothing in the American experience comes closer to the apocalypse than the death of a president in office" (Pious, 1979:7). The fact that such a collective paroxysm of shock and grief reflects devotion to a sacerdotal/ monarchical office rather than sadness over the passing of an individual becomes inescapable when one reflects that on only four occasions has the American public been greatly upset by the demise of an ex-president. But there are extenuating circumstances to explain the exceptions. All four ex-presidents—Washington (1799), Adams (1826), Jefferson (1826), and Jackson (1845)—were revered as national idols, men whose gigantic reputations rested only in part upon their residence in the White House. Especially awe-inspiring was the mind-boggling fact that Adams and Jefferson died within hours of each other on the very same day, and that day none other than the fiftieth anniversary of the Declaration of Independence.[11] How many readers can recall where they were or what they were doing when they heard the news of Herbert Hoover's or Lyndon Johnson's death? Yet few of us fail to respond accurately when the same question is posed about Kennedy's assassination.

The deaths in office of two such beloved and masterful statesmen as Abraham Lincoln and Franklin Delano Roosevelt would, understandably, set off emotional tidal waves. But it is much less simple to explain away the stunned reactions of the American public to tidings of the deaths of McKinley, Garfield, and Harding, the latter two arguably the least consequential of our thirty-odd chief executives (Orlansky, 1947:263–65). In essence, it is a symbol that is being mourned as much as, or more than, the man himself. The loss of a president through assassination on four occasions (and near-loss at least two other times) has been especially traumatic (Orlansky, 1947; Verba, 1965; Wolfe, 1975; Wolfenstein and Kliman, 1965). Sidney Verba states the case succinctly: "The assassination crisis is important . . . because it is probably the nearest equivalent in a large modern nation-state to the kind of intense mutual rededication ceremony that is possible in a smaller and simpler society" (Verba, 1965:334).

James S. Wolfe has discerned in John F. Kennedy's career the most complete embodiment to date of the mythic dimensions of the modern American presidency (Wolfe, 1975).

John Kennedy brought a special personal appeal, well-suited
to the new electronic media of communication, into his presidential campaign, and he played his presidency with a distinctive royal flair, pragmatic finesse, and crisis-managing bravado
which easily took on the colors of the Camelot, Contemporer,
and Cosmocrator myths. But it was chiefly Kennedy's death in
office which surfaced and intensified the age-old presidential
myth and its precursors, leading to a retrospective idealization
of Kennedy's presidency and casting a long shadow on the politics of the latter Sixties. Much more than the Inauguration,
which ceremonially elevated Kennedy to the Presidency, Kennedy's death was experienced as a ritualized sacred time and
as a mythic crisis of succession. The Kennedy assassination
was such an unusually deep experience for most Americans
that they found themselves refusing to face it through protest mechanisms, succumbing to their loss in grievous disorga-
nization, perpetuating and archetypalizing the Kennedy myth
through memorialization, and seeking a successor to Kennedy
who would carry on what he had begun. [Wolfe, 1975:2]

During those four heart-wrenching days in late November 1963 encompassing the two assassinations and a state funeral, time and
history seemed to stand still for most Americans, and the deepest
strata of religious feeling were stripped bare for all to witness.

The assassination . . . involved a "shaking of the foundations"
for many, touched human experience at some primordial level,
spoke to our hopes and fears, revealed a primordial religious
commitment to the political community focused on the President. Through the event, people were exposed to the beyond,
experienced transcendence, encountered non-being and being
in the depths of life, confronted the senselessness of existence
itself and were thrown into silent despair, found the terror of
chaos brought to conscious proximity and were driven to a
most solemn re-affirmation of sheltering symbols. [Wolfe, 1975:
2–3]

Through a detailed examination of Kennedy's campaign, inauguration, conduct in office, the assassination crisis, and its aftermath,
J. S. Wolfe documents his thesis that JFK, knowingly or not, enacted
the role of an archaic god-king, "a messianic sacred king recast
from a mythic mold ages old and continually reused" (Wolfe, 1975:
471). If there is merit to this argument, one that must also apply in

its essentials, though less obviously, to Kennedy's recent predecessors and successors, then we have been witnessing one of history's most piquant ironies: the manner in which Americans have traveled full circle from intense antipathy toward the substance and trappings of monarchy during the first wild flush of republican independence to loyal submission to the reigning president-king, the symbolic incarnation of an omnipotent, sheltering state. Such an individual reminds us not merely of the absolute monarchs of early modern times, who ruled mostly by the sword, but rather more of the priest-kings of ancient times, before whom men and women groveled in their hearts. By "pressing the flesh" electronically, the king's touch and his radiance permeate the entire community as they once did through direct rituals in the smaller societies of yore.

WHERE ARE THE HEROES OF YESTERYEAR?

Where do we stand today? One of the few questions on which all observers agree is that ours is a decidedly unheroic era, not only in the United States but in the world as a whole (Walden, 1986). Now that Churchill, de Gaulle, Tito, Nehru, Ben-Gurion, Mao, Pope John XXIII, Dr. Schweitzer, and Franco have passed on to their reward, the only living persons I can think of who are looked up to as national or planetary heroes by the great majority of their constituents may be Castro, Kim Il-Sung, Walesa, and, just possibly, Hirohito. In fact, the acceptance of the demise of heroism is so widespread it has become a sort of journalistic cliché, and any college instructor who has tried to elicit evidence of active hero-worship from his students (as distinct from adulation of celebrities) can confirm its actuality. Indeed, "there is a good deal of reason to believe we are running out of both heroes and the popular capacity for hero-worship, which Carlyle properly saw as vital to any genuine civilization" (Nisbet, 1975:102). Several scholars have noted the wasting away of hero-worship (Fishwick, 1969; Greenstein, 1965; Klapp, 1962:121–24, 142–56; L. Lowenthal, 1956; Meadows, 1945; Nisbet, 1975:102–110; Walden, 1986). They have agreed that "the All-American hero died on Flander Fields" (Fishwick, 1969:180). Robert Nisbet may have hit the nail on the head in claiming that "the acids of modernity, which include equalitarianism, skepticism and institutionalized ridicule in the popular arts, have eaten away much of the basis on which heroism flourished. Technology's reorganization of the world has brought with it a certain built-in disenchantment" (Nisbet, 1975:109). Moreover, beginning in the 1920s, the debunking of the old, traditional heroes developed as a growth industry within the ranks of scholars and journalists.

Although four of our fifteen twentieth-century presidents are candidates for enshrinement in the American pantheon, if not yet full-fledged residents, no other recent statesmen qualify for serious consideration; and there have been only fitful efforts to elevate any recent general or admiral to pedestals in the national Valhalla. Since the Great Depression, business leaders, inventors, and other technological geniuses have failed to capture the public's fancy, and the gap has not been filled by churchmen, educators, scientists, or creative artists. As lamentable as the exit of the hero has been the decline and near-disappearance of the good old-fashioned villain. Once again, I can do no better than to borrow Robert Nisbet's words:

> Just as we seem to have lost heroes in contemporary Western civilization, so in all probability have we lost villains; that is, persons regarded, not as sick, disturbed, victims of social injustice, or delinquent, but as outrightly and incorrigibly evil, base, devoid of any element whatever of virtue, deserving in their own interest and society's of swift and complete punishment. To read about the great villains in the epics, melodramas, and tragedies of other ages is to be put in touch with the same greatness we get in the great heroes, but of treachery, lust, dishonor, instead of virtue ... as the [hero] is, through unique possession of virtue and strength, an exemplar of good, a spur to achievement, the other becomes for us a model of all that is ultimately destructive of the fabric of morality. By that fact, the villain in his way serves the social bond. [Nisbet, 1975:110]

But if we have lost much of our capacity to create thoroughly nasty personal villains, Americans, like other national groups, have never been at a loss in finding entire populations to fear and loathe. Thus over the years we have reviled, in succession, the British, French, Mexicans, Spanish, Russians, Japanese, Chinese, Cubans, Iranians, and Libyans.

In place of the thoroughly detestable villain, veritably Satan incarnate, what we have now is the antihero who is so often the protagonist in contemporary fiction, film, and drama. He or she is not the antithesis of the hero, that is, the villain, but rather his negation. The antihero is a cynical, value-free inhabitant of the crevices of society and its morality, a passionless nihilist devoid of illusion, who affirms nothing and denies everything; and more and more of us harbor a sneaking admiration for the sheer honesty of the creature. If bona fide heroes and villains are now in short supply, the paradoxical fact is that never before has the world, and America, wallowed in such an overabundance of public eidolons. But these are "idols of consumption" rather than "idols of production" (L. Lowenthal, 1956:70), and few have more than the most tenuous connection with nationalism. Hundreds, perhaps thousands, of celebrities now flit across our organized consciousness in the course of a generation, but rarely linger for more than a few months or years. The imperatives of modern commerce and an insatiable craving for novelty and titillation intrinsic to the mass entertainment industries call for a never-ending parade of glittering personalities and overachievers, and, when nothing else is available, the celebration of the trivial. The present century has witnessed the birth of the public relations profession and its expansion into a major industry. Gossip columns, television programs, and periodicals devoted solely to the comings, goings, and foibles of celebrities—some of whom are famous only for being famous— have been flourishing as never before. The vast majority of this army of celebrities fall into two groups that are by no means mutually exclusive: athletes and professional entertainers (musicians, actors, popular writers, television personalities, along with a few stellar artists). Fan idolatry is almost entirely a twentieth-century phenomenon. In earlier days, such incipient organized sport as may have existed did not involve millions of spectators at the playing fields or, vicariously, via radio, television, and the press. Only a few outstanding nineteenth-century entertainers (e.g., Joe Jefferson, Jenny Lind, P. T. Barnum, James O'Neill, Edwin Booth, Lillian Russell) were able to develop national reputations, and then usually only by dint of endless, grueling road tours.

There is no doubt at all about the excitement, even outright passion and adoration, stirred up in the hearts and minds of the American public by athletes and entertainers, though in all too many instances the emotional attachments are short-lived and fickle. In many ways these latter-day celebrities are replacements for the national heroes earlier generations of Americans venerated when the inventory of public eidolons was much more limited. As evidence thereof, we can document the propensity of parents to name their offspring, especially female, after the glamorous superstar of the moment, just as their grandparents had frequently christened babes with such names as Jefferson, Franklin, Washington, and Lincoln. But today's celebrity is a poor stand-in for yesterday's national hero.

The basic argument is strengthened by one apparent exception, the instant adulation of Oliver North by many as a national hero in 1987 despite his dubious credentials. The lieutenant colonel's acclaim is basically that of the celebrity-performer, derived much more from role playing under the television lights than from whatever contributions he may have made to the security and well-being of the United States. Clearly the market for genuine heroes is still quite great; the supply leaves much to be desired.

One can contend that modern sport has become a surrogate for warfare, that, especially in international competition, the teams and their players are the equivalent of armies. Even more obvious is sport as a form of local patriotism, the fact that various cities and regions strenuously identify themselves with the team wearing the local uniform, even though many amateur college athletes and the majority of professional players hail from distant sections of the country. But if the sport celebrity can sometimes be a sort of national hero, he or she is a diminished, dilute version of the real thing and, all too frequently, quite ephemeral in appeal.

No such limited argument is possible for the entertainer. Very few, if any, are closely identified with the nation. The more successful have conquered international audiences; and many are placeless, maintaining residences in two or more countries and remaining on the move much of the time. Moreover, many of the most popular figures in American show business and the arts are natives or citizens of other lands, for example, Greta Garbo, Marlene Dietrich, Charles Chaplin, Maurice Chevalier, Sophia Loren, Xavier Cugat, Itzhak Perlman, Victor Borge, and Arturo Toscanini. The disheartening conclusion must be, as we scan the current scene, that we do indeed live in an age devoid of genuine, durable heroes of recent vintage, particularly those of the nationalistic variety, and insofar as we still pay homage to earlier figures, we are, in essence, living off emotional capital stored up by our forebears.

SUMMING UP

This examination of America's public eidolons in chronological sequence has suggested some important generalizations.[12] Over the past two hundred years, both the number and variety of such items have increased considerably, as American society and its technology have grown in size and complexity. But this growth has also meant a progressive decline in the effectiveness of the eidolons in furthering the cause of nationalism, or, more specifically, that sacred core of ideals around which the young American nation crystallized in the late eighteenth century. A crucial set of national heroes may well have been indispensable for inventing America and sustaining it through a perilous initial century. But, as time went on, the capacity to generate additional, durable national heroes (and villains) seems to have shrunk almost to the vanishing point.

Furthermore, the identity of latter-day public eidolons differs from that of their predecessors. Thus military and political leaders came to share the stage with captains of industry and finance and with wizards of technology, and, ultimately, they too have given way to stars of the worlds of sport and entertainment. Increasingly, our public eidolons have drawn their devotees from diversified, specialized publics rather than from throughout the total population. From intensely personal heroes (however grossly magnified and mythologized) in the early decades of the Republic, we have moved in the direction of the impersonal, abstract eidolon, to the categorical, a trend most notably exemplified by the glorification of the presidency and, to a lesser degree, the Supreme Court. In parallel fashion, such eidolons with nationalistic implications as we may cherish nowadays tend to celebrate the state rather than the nation, a development concisely symbolized by the way in which Uncle Sam has displaced Miss Liberty as the favored national icon.

Certain aspects of America's relationships with its eidolons have not altered appreciably over the years. Despite the enormous impact of recent social and technological change on our behavior, Americans, like other national groups, now as in the past have developed their local folk heroes, many of whom have failed to attract scholarly notice. We also share with the rest of the world a continuing concern for, and sometimes outright worship of, a set of archetypal figures, transnational eidolons who embody basic panhuman sentiments. As noted earlier, the majority of these have been imported into America from the Old World, but we have reciprocated in part by contributing Washington and Lincoln, as exemplars of fighters for freedom, to the planetary pool of archetypes (Karsten, 1978:167, 209).

Another archetype of special interest is the martyr. When the individual in question combines martyrdom with elements of the national ethos, he or she becomes an especially powerful symbol, as would appear to be the case with Nathan Hale, Abraham Lincoln, John F. Kennedy, and Martin Luther King, Jr. (T. A. Bailey, 1966:7–8).

But there are major American martyrs who cannot be characterized as standard national heroes. The most interesting examples are Robert E. Lee and George Armstrong Custer. Given his personal characteristics and military record, it is not too surprising that Lee became the leading national hero of the aborted Southern nation during and especially after the great civil conflict. What is unexpected but revelatory of our innermost human impulses is the way in which Lee came to be accepted eventually throughout the United States after 1900 as a kind of hero (Connelly, 1977). As the military commander of an antistatist cause, there is no logical place for Lee in the National pantheon alongside Washington, Franklin, and others of their ilk; but he has won a place in our hearts as an archetypal martyr—the steadfast, chivalrous, sorrowful, compassionate leader of a losing cause.

Just why Custer, the consummate loser, should have earned such a conspicuous place among the ranks of American popular and folk heroes is one of those enigmas of mass psychology that has never ceased to baffle and intrigue students of the matter (Dippie, 1976; Rosenberg, 1974). But there is no doubt that the 1876 debacle at Little Big Horn in which Custer and all his troops were slaughtered has captured and held our imagination for more than a century, and Custer has continued to be celebrated despite the fact that the massacre can only be explained by his sheer boneheadedness. What is clear is that a relatively minor historical incident, with little relevance to issues of nationalism, was almost instantaneously transformed into a durable but ambiguous myth. The image of the gallant loser somehow touches something deep in our collective psyche. As Brian Dippie explains it, "Custer's Last Stand has established its credentials as a popular myth by demonstrating the requisite staying power. Without altering the myth, Americans can find in it diverse meanings appropriate to the times. Indeed, because the content never undergoes basic change, the myth is at once infinitely flexible and absolutely constant" (Dippie, 1976:140). But this is one myth (or legend) that may tell us less about what it means to be an American than about being a member of the human species in modern times. However, another event that might be compared to the Custer episode illustrates the fact that martyrdom does have considerable utility in boosting statefulness: Masada (B. Schwartz et al., 1986). Israeli officialdom has been strikingly effective in creating a myth, indeed a veritable cult, around the self-destruction of the besieged defenders of this ancient stronghold. The difference between Little Big Horn and Masada lies in the lapse of nearly two millennia between the deed and its celebration in the case of the latter and also the calculated nature of the promotion.

There has been a certain consistency over time in the types of individuals who could be considered genuine American national heroes. Political and military figures have accounted for a disproportionate share of the glory. But the high standing of certain generals and admirals in the perceptions of early Americans is rather difficult to explain, even paradoxical, in view of the fact that the same population was fiercely antimilitary in its attitudes, harboring a deep hostility toward standing armies and the officer caste. Evidently their deeds on behalf of the sacred cause of liberty cleansed the valorous warriors of any taint of association with the professional military. Although a few businessmen-inventors (preeminently Edison and Ford) made the grade, we find no native-born American scientists or even explorers as tenants within our National pantheon. (Columbus, Humboldt, and Einstein were aliens and, in any case, the property of the world, not just the United States.) Also conspicuous by their absence have been judges and members of the clergy (John Marshall may be the only possible exception).

The United States may resemble most other nations in having a dearth of first-rank national heroines—with the possible exception of the semimythical Betsy Ross (Wecter, 1941:476–77) and no female villains, but in one other respect it does stand apart. Although the United States has had its share of prominent, sometimes beloved artists and authors, for example, Longfellow, Clemens, Audubon, Emerson, Alcott, Eakins, Sandburg, Frost, and Norman Rockwell, none has ever attained the towering eminence, the hero's accolades we observe in Italy's Verdi and Manzoni, Finland's Sibelius, Russia's Pushkin, Poland's Chopin and Paderewski, Germany's Goethe, Ireland's Yeats, or Cuba's Martí.

It is clear enough that we have much to learn about national character and the evolution of nationalism in various countries by analyzing their public eidolons. But before we can ferret out the deeper lessons lurking in these phenomena in America, there are many other aspects of symbolic thought and action to be investigated.

THREE ★ ★ ★ ★ ★ ★ ★ ★

PERFORMANCE ★ ★ ★ ★ ★ ★

Dealing with eidolons means dealing with things of the mind. That awkward fact has compelled us to bank heavily on indirect clues concerning attitudes and perceptions, surely never a simple task. But not all nationalistic data are so elusive or incorporeal. We can survey the things people do, the words they use, and the things they make—their observable performance—and such is the business of this chapter and the next. Later we reach even firmer footing by scanning artifacts in the built landscape. Each universe of observations has its peculiar virtues and difficulties, but, in the passage from the inwardly mental to outward action and, finally, to the durable objects of the American outdoors, the lessons about the changing character of American nationalism become easier to learn and the major conclusions more difficult to avoid.

NATIONAL HOLIDAYS

It is a safe bet that every community, past and present, has created its own special, possibly sacred calendar, a cycle of meaningful occasions that repeats itself following a weekly, monthly, annual, or longer temporal pattern. Although little is known about such holiday observances in Colonial America, one can assume replication of Western European practice: the formal celebration of the major, and some lesser, Christian holy days and the much less official enjoyment of certain traditional folk festivals.[1]

With the stirrings of revolutionary nationhood in the United States, we also have the arrival of novel calendric needs and opportunities, and the American zealots promptly rose to the occasion. The fashioning of the first state to embody modern notions of nationalism took place in a partial symbolic vacuum, so that the republican experimenters were obliged to invent, inter alia, not only the first national heroes but also the very first truly national holidays. The process began promptly after the announcement of political independence and has continued unabated to this day. In addition to regular annual observances, the national and local governments would also occasionally proclaim special days of prayer or thanksgiving (Craven, 1956:61–62). Many of the annual occasions have enjoyed only local popularity or have failed to set off any but the most tepid sort of excitement among the citizenry at large, while others have simply sunk quietly out of sight.[2] There are, however, at least five holidays that have played a prominent role in the chronicle of American nationalism as generators of appropriate sentiments or gauges of their intensity, or both.

During the early stages of American nationhood, no two dates have carried a heavier symbolic load than July 4 (Independence Day) and February 22 (Washington's Birthday). They were the earliest of our national holidays; they have prompted more physical fuss and sheer emotional excess than any possible rivals; they have endured, though in altered form, into the present era; and they are among the handful of special days observed in every state in the Union.[3] Thus, if a case is to be pleaded for any holidays serving as formative influences in creating and fostering nationalism, these are the logical candidates.

The first of the annual celebrations of the adoption of the Declaration of Independence came just one year after the event in Philadelphia, Boston, and Charleston on July 4, 1777 (Hay, 1967:17–18; Hazleton, 1906:282–83). This was indeed a totally original American idea and one that set a convincing precedent for all the many countries that have gained political freedom over the past two centuries.[4] After 1777, we can assume a gradual diffusion of the festivities to other population centers throughout the Republic (Hay, 1967), although the detailed historical geography of the process remains to be investigated. According to R. P. Hay, the observance of July 4 quickly became universal. "From the larger towns where it had its origins, the celebration had spread to most eastern hamlets by no later than the middle 1790s" (Hay, 1967:47). The first public celebration of Washington's Birthday may have occurred in Milton, Mass. in 1779 (Warren, 1932:37), followed by New York City in 1784 (Myers, 1972:64); and, once again, it is likely that the practice quickly spread to many more communities even while the Father of His Country was still very much alive.

If the importance of both these holidays was widely acknowledged, it was not possible to realize their full potential during most of the first half-century of national existence because of intense bickering between the Federalist and anti-Federalist camps (Boorstin, 1965:383–85; Butterfield, 1953:120–21). Neither group would concede to the other proprietorship over either holiday or management of its form and content. Even as late as 1832, there was considerable partisan strife over plans for the Washington centenary (Warren, 1932). Nevertheless, it appears that the July 4 and February 22 celebrations reached their peaks of popularity and intensity during the 1820s and 1830s, especially after the Golden Anniversary of the Declaration. Perhaps as much as anything else the strange, seemingly providential deaths "of both Jefferson and Adams on July 4, 1826 . . . symbolized the end of an era of partisanship and also marks the nationalization of the holiday" (Warren, 1945:272; Butterfield, 1953; Hay, 1967:148–71; Peterson, 1960:5). (The fact that James Monroe passed away on July 4, 1831, doubtlessly further confirmed the sanctity of the date.) The advent of the Jacksonian Era certainly stimulated greater participation by the masses (F. M. Green, 1969:124).

No other annual event in the United States has ever come close to rivaling that communal orgy known as the Glorious Fourth for sheer enthusiasm and intensity of patriotic fervor—at least as it was observed in the antebellum period.[5] It was the occasion for massive gatherings of Americans in central public spaces, for lengthy, impassioned orations by leading citizens, often filled with jingoistic bombast, for special church services and sermons, for much cheering and shouting, the display of patriotic regalia, the decoration of heroes' graves, solemn processions, military drills, the shooting of cannons and fireworks, for much twisting of the British lion's tail, elaborate public dinners with endless toasts (and, eventually, less formal picnics), and prodigious quaffing of strong drink (Gabriel, 1956:99–101). But the obligatory, central ritual element was the recitation of the Declaration of Independence. The "National Sabbath" was frequently selected as a particularly auspicious time for the dedication of new public structures and institutions. And, contrary to present-day practice, great numbers of nineteenth-century brides and grooms chose July 4 for their marriage ceremony (Zelinsky, 1984a:11).[6] Despite the boisterousness of the holiday, it was apparent to all that the Fourth of July was the most sacramental of shared moments, the ideal occasion for the reaffirmation of American nationhood (Melder, 1976:38). "Clear evidence of the sanctification of American nationalism, the Fourth of July became literally the holy day of obligation for American patriots. This concept survived the triumph of a secular American cul-

ture as a central component of America's civil religion, so that
well after the passing of providential thought the Fourth of July
remained for public spokesmen the prescribed time for ritualized
pronouncements on the character and consequences of the American experience" (Berens, 1978:155). Washington's Birthday may have
been a more subdued version of the Fourth, for meteorological reasons if none other, but in most fundamental respects it paralleled
the grander holiday.[7]

The latter-day careers of the two prime patriotic holidays have
much to tell us about the changing character of American society
in general and nationalism in particular. Indeed, no sooner had the
Fourth reached its climactic development in the 1830s than we begin hearing cruel jibes about the triteness and tedium of the oratory
(Craven, 1956:87–88) and complaints over the din and commotion
from some of the more sedate pillars of the community (Love,
1904). It may have been boredom or sheer emotional exhaustion, or,
more probably, the shifting mind-set of the population, but by the
1850s, and arguably even earlier in the 1830s and 1840s, observers
detected an unmistakable slackening in both the number of celebrations and their intensity and elaborateness (Hay, 1967:290–302;
Melder, 1976:37). If, as is likely but not yet proved, popular observances of the Fourth may have flourished earliest in the Northeast,
then spread southward and westward, the same spatial pattern may
have been repeated as the practice weakened. "In the 1830s, northern newspapers reported a decline in interest in the festivities in
that section. They declared that in many towns and cities the day
passed without any observance, and they noted general apathy on
the part of the people." But such was not yet the case in North
Carolina (F. M. Green, 1969:134).

Among other vitiating factors, sectional and political strife had
reappeared, as did "special pleading by high-minded reformers. Anti-
slavery and Negro colonization groups, temperance types, women's
suffrage advocates, Sunday school and peace societies all sought to
use the Fourth of July" for their special purposes, thus deflecting
attention from the central meaning of the day (Kammen, 1978:54–
55). The trauma of the Civil War, the lacerating debates leading
up to it, and its sequelae all tended to weaken popular enthusiasm
over any such holiday celebrations. During the Reconstruction period, Southerners were especially lax in observing the Fourth (F. M.
Green, 1969:144–48)[8] but Northerners were becoming negligent as
well.

With the approach of the gala Centennial celebrations in 1876,

almost every self-respecting community rediscovered the importance of observing the Glorious Fourth;[9] and perhaps the most significant set of ceremonies were those held at the highly successful Philadelphia Exposition (Hay, 1967:272–88). One hundred years
later the Bicentennial sparked another nationwide effort to honor
the birth of the United States, but, as discussed below, the 1976
festivities bore little resemblance to the earlier ones. Widespread
and energetic though they may have been, the 1876 activities represented the climacteric in the life-course of the holiday, for, as R. P.
Hay has noted, "the centennial celebrations, grandiose though they
were, represented for most towns, the last frantic efforts to revive a
patriotic holiday that had outlived its usefulness. Many hamlets
which had planned no public observances in recent years and would
stage none in the future rallied in 1876 to give the Fourth of July
the semblance of its former glory" (Hay, 1967:288). Furthermore,
"the gala centennial observance of 1876 brought only a superficial
one-year revival of prewar enthusiasm. Indeed, there were signs
that interest in the Fourth of July had begun to lessen before 1861.
Certainly by 1877, regular patriotic observances were a thing of the
past in most towns. Only the noise of firecrackers remained. The
'American Sabbath' had become just another holiday" (Hay, 1967:
251).

So it came to pass, and so it still remains. The holiday, insofar as
it is still celebrated, has become secularized and is ever so much
quieter than in the past (even the past of my childhood). Only rarely
does it provide the occasion for nationalistic oratory or the reading
of the Declaration.[10] Like many another holiday in contemporary
America, perhaps the greatest emotion roused by its approach is joy
over the prospect of an extended weekend (except for those luckless
years when July 4 falls on a Wednesday). It is interesting to note a
roughly parallel trajectory in the fortunes of the only other national
holiday for which we have any detailed documentation: France's
Bastille Day (Amalvi, 1984). An even sorrier fate than that of Independence Day has afflicted Washington's Birthday, which is now
coupled with Lincoln's as Presidents' Day and is jiggled about annually so as to fall on a convenient Monday. Rare indeed is the public
celebration of February 22 nowadays whether indoors or outdoors.
In the District of Columbia, the day has become notorious for some
remarkable retail promotions, while in the rest of the country far
more people are annoyed by the closing of banks and government
offices than are gladdened by the recollection of our first president.

Although only two national holidays of consequence material-

ized during the antebellum years, there can be little doubt that they
played a not inconsiderable part in building or reinforcing American nationhood. Whatever vicissitudes the celebration of July 4 and
February 22 may have undergone during that formative period, they
did speak unequivocally of the ideas and ideals that defined the
American credo. The second generation of national holidays, dating
from the 1860s onward, were greater in number and different in
character. Clearly the most important of this group has been Memorial Day, or Decoration Day as it is variously known (Myers,
1972:159–64). Several localities in both the North and South invented the holiday almost simultaneously and quite independently
in 1866 or thereabouts; but it was especially popular in the former,
and by 1891 it had become a legal holiday in every northern state
(Dearing, 1952:472). Veterans' organizations were particularly zealous in promoting it as well as other nationalistic holidays (Dearing,
1952:407–8). As seems to have happened earlier with July 4, Memorial Day may have flourished first in the Northeast, then diffused to
other sections of the country while acquiring deep emotional connotations (Handlin, 1961:134–35).

For some years, Americans observed the day with fitting solem-
nity and care, and, in a manner replicating the earlier Independence
Days, parades, orations, military maneuvers, graveyard decorations,
and the dedication of monuments were all in order. But Memorial
Day, like other postbellum innovations, differed fundamentally in
both nature and purpose from its predecessors. Its celebration honored the fallen dead in all of the nation-state's conflicts, but said
little or nothing about the tenets they were presumably defending.
At a more profound level, as W. Lloyd Warner demonstrated so definitively in a magnificent essay (Warner, 1959:227–325), the rituals
of Memorial Day address the universal mysteries of grief, death,
and remembrance rather than just soldierly valor or the virtues of
the nation-state. Much the same might be said of other holidays
that have flourished within modern America while transcending
international boundaries: a Thanksgiving Day that is only marginally nationalistic,[11] New Year's Day, Mother's Day, and Labor Day.
Evidently, as the supremacy of supernatural religion came into
question by the late nineteenth century, the secular holidays that
gradually replaced the ecclesiastical enabled Americans to continue
dealing with human universals. Nevertheless, as Catherine Albanese (1974) has amply demonstrated, Memorial Day, along with
other latter-day secular holidays, has suffered the same fate that

befell July 4 and February 22: the withering away of most of its special meaning.

Abraham Lincoln was scarcely cold in his tomb before the first public observance of his birthday occurred in 1866 (Myers, 1972: 43). Unsurprisingly, Illinois was the first state to adopt February 12 as an official holiday, doing so in 1892, to be followed by sixteen other, predictably non-Southern, states (Myers, 1972:44). Although it did become an occasion of some consequence, especially for public schools outside the former Confederacy, "for the most part no grandly organized and formal ceremonies mark Lincoln's Birthday" (Myers, 1972:46). Flag Day, first celebrated in 1877, has roused even less public ado, while Armistice Day (now a movable Veterans Day), which was designed to commemorate the casualties of World War I, "has remained a halfhearted holiday" (Stewart, 1954:242), and is now barely noticed by the general citizenry. Despite the efforts of the Grand Army of the Republic (GAR) and Italian-American organizations (Dearing, 1952:407–8), Columbus Day has enjoyed even less success, but perhaps somewhat more than Armed Forces Day or Loyalty Day. Another sort of annual event seems to have retained most of its charm: the reunions of veterans' organizations and the regional and national conventions of patriotic organizations. But these are occasions that concern few beyond the immediate localities and memberships.

The fading away or secularization of both church and profane holidays may tell less about the fortunes of American nationalism than about recent holiday observances in general. We need no elaborate documentation to prove that "all [holidays] seem to be becoming the same thing. . . . A holiday has simply become, for most Americans, a day when one is free of work. . . . To regret that they have lost almost all of their associations of dedication and consecration is merely to regret that such qualities seem largely to have disappeared from modern life" (Stewart, 1954:245). But, insofar as national holidays have survived, they have become characteristically statist or martial in form and substance, and only faintly echo the revolutionary notions of the Founders.

OTHER CYCLICAL RITUALS

If the annual variety of national holiday has lost most of its luster, other events linked to the calendar still demand our attention. Indeed, some have left a deep impression on our collective psyche.

One such set of actions occurs so frequently that its performance has become almost reflexive: the Pledge of Allegiance and the saluting of the national flag. A thorough cross-national study of flag etiquette around the world would be a worthwhile exercise, but, in lieu of such an operation, I would hazard the guess that in no other country do schoolchildren and other civilians pay obeisance to the flag so regularly and so often.

It was in the classroom that the campaign began in 1891 for the mandatory daily flag salute, along with the recitation of the Pledge of Allegiance (Brandt, 1971; Dearing, 1952:474–75; L. Harris, 1971; Shafer, 1972:438). Under the prodding of patriotic and veterans' organizations and various periodicals, the crusade scored a resounding triumph. In 1898 New York adopted a flag statute, and within the next several years most other states followed suit (Manwaring, 1962:3). Beginning the school day with the Pledge and salute remains almost universal in elementary schools despite a Supreme Court decision, after a tortuous series of cases, upholding the constitutional right of pupils to refrain (Manwaring, 1962). It has also become customary for adult civilians to salute the flag and even intone the Pledge on ceremonial occasions and at the outset of meetings by official and other organizations.

Another form of pledge, the loyalty oath, along with the related loyalty test, merits at least passing notice in this context even though more often than not it is a one-time affair (Hymans, 1960). Although, or perhaps because, its efficacy is symbolic rather than practical, the role of the oath in nation building has been minimal, except perhaps in the immediate pre-Revolutionary period, when "loyalty tests played a primary role in structuring the Revolution" (Hymans, 1960:61). Considerable political and judicial controversy raged in the late 1940s and the 1950s over compulsory tests and oaths for government and academic employees.

Every four years—the longest regular beat in the ritual rhythm of American life—citizens are caught up in that elaborate extravaganza called "electing a president and vice-president." The symbolic import of this exercise may sometimes equal or exceed the political consequences. Choosing a tenant for the White House is a process divided into five distinct phases: the primary elections and caucuses; the party convention; campaign; election; and inauguration. Although the symbolism of all this feverish activity cries out for comprehensive anthropological treatment, no such study exists for even a single one of these phases and the available scholarly literature only hints at the potential findings.[12]

During the three decades preceding the Jacksonian Era, the selection of chief executives was a relatively gentlemanly exercise, one conducted largely within federal and state legislative chambers. But there is little question that fundamental changes were afoot with the Jackson campaigns of 1828 and 1832 as truly widespread citizen involvement and sharpened partisan feelings developed, or that these episodes served to deepen and widen national consciousness. Thus, for example, in November 1834, a European observer, Michel Chevalier, reported on the torchlight victory march of Democratic partisans following a state election, and noted its quasi-religious character and abundant exploitation of nationalistic symbols (Somkin, 1967:194–95). Such orgiastic happenings seem to have been the nineteenth-century equivalents of twentieth-century sport extravaganzas (Washburn, 1963:42). But it was in 1840, with the unbelievably hyperactive Harrison campaign, that the Whigs hit upon the standard formula for electioneering that has endured and intensified to this day (Gunderson, 1957; Melder, 1976:46–47). It was then that mass rallies and processions burst into full bloom, along with campaign songs, mottoes, pamphlets, scurrilous journalism, banners, buttons, souvenirs, and political paraphernalia of every description, not to mention the revival of the liberty pole and the discovery that an intimate relationship with log cabins was a virtual requisite for the presidency.[13]

We can infer from fragmentary data that the exploitation of national symbols in presidential campaigns, including the eagle, Miss Liberty, the flag, and various stock heroes, was most lavish in the middle and late nineteenth century. Since then, the trend has been toward simple slogans, portraits of the candidates, and other personality items (Collins, 1979; Washburn, 1963). Rough and divisive though many campaigns may have been, there is little doubt that, as Keith Melder has noted,

> on balance, political parties played a positive role in promoting national feelings during these formative [mid-nineteenth century] years, as they have done through most of the nation's 200-year history. They exploited and helped popularize such national institutions as Washington, the presidency, and the Fourth of July. Their leaders became new national heroes. They invented the popular presidential campaign as a new means of expressing national attachments. They promoted the flow of information and helped nationalize public opinion through partisan newspapers, pamphlets, broadsides, and orations. . . . In

fact, political parties themselves became symbols of national
identity and agencies of national allegiance. [Melder, 1976:48–
49]

It has become standard practice for the candidates to expose
themselves to as many potential voters as possible. Initially this
was done largely via horse-drawn vehicles, then later on special
railroad trains, while today presidential campaigners avail themselves of motorcades and jet aircraft as they hop from one gathering
to another. In a sense, such increasingly hurried and extended safa-
ris (usually accompanied by intensive newspaper, radio, and television coverage) amount to trial by ordeal. They remind one of the
journeys in which mythological heroes proved their mettle while
effecting a mystic physical consummation with the sacred soil of
their future dominions. When a sitting president runs for reelec-
tion, the campaign pilgrimage may serve to enhance the mystique
of an already powerfully symbolic presidency by enabling the incumbent to "press the flesh" and thus "to complete the electric
circuit of his symbolic connection" with the people (M. Novak,
1974:41).

It is in the culminating act of the election spectacle, the inauguration, that the symbolic message of the entire quadrennial phenomenon blazes forth most brightly. Unfortunately, what Shils and
Young (1975:135) have written about British coronations applies
only too well to American inaugurations: "About this most august
institution there is no serious discussion at all"—with one honor-
able exception.[14] Nevertheless the meaning of this sacramental
moment is plain enough.

During the early years of the Republic, most of our national leaders, given their puritan and republican inclinations, deliberately
sought to underplay the ritual element in public life. "Against all
pretensions to kingship, they saw the president as merely an office-
holder and his inauguration as merely the commencement of the
execution of his duties as a faithful public servant" (Wolfe, 1975:
55). And indeed Thomas Jefferson, the arch-democrat, managed to
achieve the ultimate in casual, throwaway performances. Over the
years, however, as the supreme affirmation of the power and glory
of the American state, if not the nation, the presidential inauguration has become an extraordinarily ornate, costly, and imposing affair, truly imperial in grandeur. Symbolically, it now far outshines
the vestigial glow of July 4. J. S. Wolfe, quite correctly, emphasizes
the sacred character of the event.

A presidential inauguration is ... "the sacrament of democracy," a key civil-religious celebration in which the nation's sacred values are re-affirmed and its sacred king crowned. Like a coronation, the inaugural ceremony transfers the charisma of office to the new President, provides religious legitimation for his authority, and invests him with symbolic as well as instrumental roles. Like primitive totemic festivals or imperial new year celebrations or Biblical covenant-renewal liturgies, the inauguration provides an occasion for the whole people to unite themselves in rededication to the nation's ideals as they are articulated by the new President as high priest. [Wolfe, 1975:54]

The contention that the inauguration is a religious happening is imbedded within the larger issue of whether American nationalism is truly the equivalent of a civil religion, one to which we shall devote fuller attention at a later point, but the sheer emotional weight and ceremonial pomp of the occasion lend color to the argument. The central moments are, of course, the administering of the oath by the Chief Justice and, following directly, the delivery of the Inaugural Address, perhaps the most liturgically meaningful, carefully crafted, and listened to pronouncement in American public life (Bellah, 1967). In addition to the families of the president and vice-president and the departing occupants of the White House, the proximate witnesses include members of Congress, the Supreme Court, the cabinet, major officers of the executive branch and military, the diplomatic corps, select members of the clergy, and, as distinguished guests, other ranking figures in the national elite, altogether the most glittering assemblage of the revered and mighty to cluster at a single site, except perhaps for state funerals. Looking on are tens of thousands of local residents and those visitors who have performed special pilgrimages. The inaugural parade is a long, splendid affair, involving musicians, marchers, and other performers from every state in the Union. Before and after, the number of balls, parties, and other entertainments is perhaps beyond tallying. However venomous the preceding campaign may have been, we now discover that it was really only a forgettable family squabble, for the inauguration is a season of healing, of muted partisanship, of reconciling the brethren of a single faith.

If the presidential inauguration has gained greater symbolic heft and ceremonial grandeur over time, while the traditional national holidays have grown lax and dilute, we can see an interesting analogy in the history of British coronations. That series of rituals seems to have recorded an all-time climax of majesty, excitement, and showmanship with the investiture of Elizabeth II in 1953 (Shils and Young, 1975). The earlier instances in the eighteenth and nineteenth centuries seem to have stirred much less public interest (Cannadine, 1983). A large part—but still only part—of the explanation for the expanding significance of these events in both the United States and Great Britain is the ever more intrusive role of modern technology. The American print media devote limitless space and resources to every twist and kink of the primaries, convention, and campaign, as well as the inauguration. Radio and especially television make it possible for tens, even hundreds of millions of listeners and viewers in more than one country to become vicarious guests in the entire convention-election-inauguration-coronation phenomenon. The consequences for the nationalizing process, and, more specifically, the reinforcement of the nation-state system, are too obvious for detailed comment.

SPECIAL COMMEMORATIONS

The impress of some exceptional commemorative acts, or those that recur only after extended intervals, may be stronger and more lasting than that of the routinized daily, annual, or even quadrennial ritual. Such "commemoration lifts from an ordinary historical sequence those extraordinary events which embody our deepest and most fundamental values" (B. Schwartz, 1982:377). Such elaborate affairs, which involve the masses liturgically, have been deemed particularly strategic by manipulators of public opinion in new revolutionary nations and those departing sharply in political direction from earlier regimes, such as Soviet Russia, Nazi Germany, Israel, and the United States (Mosse, 1976:54). But they also figure prominently in the life of all self-respecting modern nation-states (Merriam, 1931:151–53).

In the American case, the incidence of special commemorations increased markedly during the late nineteeth century when, as Barbara Powell has noted, "patriotism, renewed and confirmed publicly in commemorative celebrations, was considered by many concerned Americans to be a crucial element in the resolution of the social, economic, and political problems afflicting the nation" (Powell, 1983:68). But the origins of such behavior are to be found much earlier. The practice of proclaiming special fast days and days of thanksgiving and prayer was one inherited from the mother country (Hudson, 1971). It was evidently widespread in Colonial America, but, initially, such observances seem to have been localized and conventionally religious in form. Bernard Bailyn suggests it was only late during the British regime and after independence that they turned secular. "From the mid-1760's on, celebrations of more secular [but still local] anniversaries were added: the anniversary of the repeal of the Stamp Act, of the Boston Massacre, of the landing of the Pilgrims, and of an increasing number of fast and thanksgiving days marking political rather than religious events" (Bailyn, 1967:6).

Some of the initial nonreligious anniversaries revolved about the theme of origins. Thus we find that the historically minded citizens of New England not only launched the first observance of the Pilgrim landing in 1769 but also began the first of an annual series of Forefathers' Days in the following year (Briggs, 1968:14–15), after having observed the centenary of Rhode Island in 1739 (A. Mathews, 1926:410). Virginians did not get around to hailing the founding of Jamestown until the 1807 bicentennial ceremonies (A. Mathews, 1926:415). The early presidents spasmodically, but frequently, proclaimed special thanksgivings, fasts, and days of prayer (Craven, 1956:51–52); but the practice gradually lost its appeal, so that the last national days of fasting were those announced by Buchanan, Lincoln, and Andrew Johnson (Hudson, 1971:16). A twentieth-century effort to revive the tradition came to naught. Frederic Fox provides us with a rollicking account of the sad history of a terminally tepid public reaction to "the national day of prayer" from the early 1950s through 1971 (Fox, 1972). More popular and lasting has been the annual proclamation of a national Thanksgiving Day by the president, a custom initiated by Grant in 1869 and emulated by all his successors, and an occasion, somewhat like the inauguration, for the utterance of sacerdotal messages about the goodness of Providence and references to national symbols and ideals (J. F. Wilson, 1979:56–63).

Over the past few generations, Americans have been unable to suppress the urge to celebrate the grander cycles of time: the centennials, sesquicentennials, and longer intervals that have passed since the occurrence of noteworthy events. Indeed, Albert Mathews finds evidence here for American exceptionalism. "It is quite possible that such festivities have been more common in the United States than elsewhere, for . . . it is in this country, no doubt, that centennial celebrations have been prosecuted with the greatest enthusiasm; indeed the United States may be regarded as their peculiar home" (A. Mathews, 1926:405). The cause, or excuse, for such jubilees may be nothing more earthshaking than the founding of a local community (e.g., Antrim History Committee, 1977), but there is certainly nationalistic significance in the staging of such occasions as the centennials of the Battles of Lexington and Concord (Little, 1961), the establishment of the District of Columbia (Cox, 1901), Lincoln's Second Inauguration (Coblenz, 1967), the bicentennial of Jefferson's birth (Peterson, 1960:432–42) and Washington's (Warren, 1932), or the hundredth anniversary of the Statue of Liberty in 1986.

As often as not, a reenactment of the original event is one of the more spectacular features of the observance (Jackson, 1980:102; D. Lowenthal, 1985:295–301). Thus, when New York City celebrated the hundredth anniversary of the Constitution, President Benjamin Harrison retraced the route of Washington's triumphal inauguration journey and impersonated his predecessor in a restaging of the first presidential oath-taking (Kammen, 1986a:148; Wecter, 1941:139; Whittemore, 1933:160–62). Especially blood-tingling, but presumably harmless, has been the reenactment one hundred years after the fact and even much later, in the most realistic terms possible, of all the major, and many of the minor, military engagements of the Civil War (Hartje, 1973:87–90). But, in general, the Civil War Centennial was far from a howling success, experiencing as it did a troubled, ambiguous career. Americans were uncertain as to just what was being celebrated or how to go about doing it (Hartje, 1973:60–93). And, of course, from 1975 through 1981, there was a similar sequence of costumed recreations of the notable political and military events of the American Revolution (D. Lowenthal, 1977:259–61). In like vein, the annual historical pageant, that is, the fictionalized dramatization of some stirring early history, has become institutionalized in a number of older American communities. Wesley Craven hardly exaggerates in claiming that "the number of historical pageants that invite the tourist's attention, including Paul Green's show at Roanoke Island, is almost unbelievable" (Craven, 1956:180).

Such historical make-believe may not be unique to the United States. It appears to be a fairly popular outdoor sport in Great Britain and perhaps elsewhere,[15] but, echoing Mathews's claim for American eminence in commemorative observances, Thomas Adam asserts that "historical pageants and dramas reflecting the life of the locality are more frequently organized in the United States than in older countries where the historical background of the community can be taken for granted" (Adam, 1937:81).[16] Perhaps the principal lesson to be drawn from all this playacting and frolic is that such mummery is less essential for communities constantly encountering and meditating their history (Ireland, north or south, is an ideal example) than for those, like the United States, or France (Nora, 1984b), for whom the past has become remote, quaint, and rather atrophied, something to be recreated rather than lived.

Of all the time-driven celebrations ever staged in the United States none has ever covered more territory, involved more participants, and, most probably, consumed more cash than the 1976 Bicentennial.[17] Before, during, and after the climactic day, many hundreds of communities in every corner of the country indulged in a staggering number of projects dedicated, officially or otherwise, with only loose coordination by a special Federal commission, to the two hundredth birthday of the United States. They included: dramas, pageants, special publications, ethnic festivals, conservation and preservation projects, regattas, patriotic decorations on all manner of things, traveling exhibits, new community facilities, and literally scores of other kinds of activities. The spatial pattern of official Bicentennial Communities and their activities, as suggested by a map in a report by the American Revolution Bicentennial Administration (1977:1–76), is oddly reminiscent of the probable distribution of such doings a hundred years earlier, as well as the geography of nationalistic place-names: a strong concentration in the Northeast and Middle West, but much lower intensity in the South and West.

The differences from the 1876 festivities are much more striking than any similarities (D. Lowenthal, 1977:264–66; Post, 1976:23; Schlereth, 1980:130–42). The most obvious are the spatial diffuseness and do-it-yourself character of the Bicentennial. Despite much anguished debate in Philadelphia and elsewhere, no metropolitan area was able and willing to undertake another great exposition. It is credible that such indecisiveness may have been symptomatic of even deeper uncertainties.[18] In a total turnabout from the mood of 1876, the Bicentennial celebrants, in an orgy of nostalgia, found themselves attending a coast-to-coast picnic, in essence a vast historical costume party, looking backward fondly toward a sanitized, make-believe past, while studiously snubbing the future. Thus in a sociological analysis of a random sample of 200 Bicentennial events, Brody (1977:104) found that 128 were "oriented exclusively or predominantly to the past," 71 to the present, but only 1 to the future. "What they spontaneously and almost universally preferred and doted upon were not the symbols of age and maturity, but rather the symbols of youth and innocence" (Woodward, 1977:583).

Yet it is supremely ironic that, despite this retrospective posture, all but a minority of disaffected radicals succeeded in totally ignoring the revolutionary significance of the American Revolution (Morris, 1977; Zuckerman, 1978), a much greater cause for concern among the thoughtful than the tasteless overcommercialization of the Bicentennial (Lemisch, 1976). As Michael Zuckerman dolefully remarks, "in such symptoms and symbols, then, we declared our incapacity to connect rewardingly, or even coherently, with our Revolutionary origins. In such irrelevancies and ironies, we acknowledged that the ideas and ideologies of the Revolutionary generation are essentially inert for us" (Zuckerman, 1978:226). Nevertheless there were some minor expressions of antiestablishment distress, again in stark contrast to the harmonious spirit of 1876, and almost all of which were ignored or downplayed by the mass media. The activities of the People's Bicentennial amounted to a Counter-Bicentennial. The indifferent crowd reaction to President Ford and the loud, sustained booing of Mayor Frank Rizzo at the July 4 ceremonies on Philadelphia's Independence Mall reveal attitudes that would have been unthinkable a century earlier (N. Smith, 1977). In the view of a marxist commentator, "more than anything else, Philadelphia's Bicentennial demonstrated the growing impotence of traditional capitalist ideologies—philosophic, religious, political and nationalistic. And it demonstrated the state's response—a heightened barrage of worn-out symbols" (N. Smith, 1977:81).

It is much more difficult to extract any usable generalizations from another series of calendrical occasions: those celebrating the Constitution. Although much revered, at least in theory, this document lacks the powerful symbolic resonance of the Declaration or the War for Independence. In any case, efforts to celebrate its fiftieth anniversary in 1827 roused little interest, while the story of the centennial is one of almost unrelieved organizational ineptitude, near-fiascos, and public apathy (Kammen, 1986a:127–51). However, the record of the sesquicentennial observances under the energetic stewardship of Sol Bloom is much brighter (Kammen, 1986a:282–312); and present indications are that the quality of the Bicentennial activities, which are proceeding even as I write, and the public reaction thereto, are at a level far exceeding that of their predecessors.

WORLD'S FAIRS

During its heyday, there was one other species of events that rivalled or surpassed inaugurations, coronations, or anniversaries of
national independence in terms of mobilizing national sentiment:
the international exposition (Ageron, 1984; Allwood, 1977). Although the immediate antecedents for the series of modern world's
fairs that began with London's Crystal Palace exhibition in 1851
may have been the industrial fairs held in late eighteenth-century
France and Great Britain (Allwood, 1977:9–12), their ultimate origin must be sought in the medieval church fair. And, according to
Robert Post, the latter-day events retained a definite, albeit transformed, sacramental character.

> [A] fair was originally a holy day. . . . The international exhibi-
> tions of the 19th Century no longer had such overt religious
> associations but the world's fair itself assumed some character-
> istics of a quasi-religious celebration. Millions flocked to the
> exhibitions, as pilgrims once did to a holy place. The new pil-
> grims came to renew their faith in their own nations, to experi-
> ence the miracles of Science, to worship at the shrines of Prog-
> ress. Even the great exhibition halls, with their "naves" and
> "transepts," were patterned after medieval cathedrals. These
> halls resounded with organ music, and they were sometimes
> called "Temples of Industry." The Victorian Age had a grand
> vision: for the first time, the Earthly Paradise was drawing
> near. [Post, 1976:23]

John Maass (1973:98–99) deals further with the theological implications of the great exhibitions, noting, inter alia, that "at the St.
Louis Exposition of 1904, [Henry] Adams 'professed the religion of
World's Fairs, without which he held education to be a blind impos-
sibility.' "

The major exposition, operating as it did at more than one level,
may have served to celebrate the Pan-Western doctrine of progress
and salvation through technology. More immedately, however, it
represents all that is good or wished for in the national community;
it is the most elaborate, sophisticated expression of the national
ideology.[19]

In another related sense, as Burton Benedict points out, it is also
a colossal potlatch. "A World's fair is an almost perfect example of
what Marcel Mauss called a total prestation. It is a collective representation that symbolized an entire community in a massive dis-

play of prestige vis-à-vis other communities" (Benedict, 1983:7).
Such expositions were especially urgent devices for the exercise of
moral authority in nineteenth-century America since, in the words
of W. R. Rydell, "the fairs provided visitors with a galaxy of symbols
which cohered into 'symbolic universes.' These constellations, in
turn, ritualistically affirmed fairgoers' faith in American institutions and social organization, evoked a community of shared experience, and formulated responses to questions arising about the ultimate destiny of mankind in general and of Americans in particular" (Rydell, 1980:4–5).

The major expositions were also playing fields on which the leading states of the Western world tussled for symbolic power and prestige, a notion forcefully expressed by Burton Benedict. "A world's
fair can be seen as one of a series of mammoth rituals in which all
sorts of power relations, both existing and wished for, are being
expressed. It is a contest in which the contestants are jockeying for
advantage in the worlds of both commerce and politics. In this contest all sorts of symbols are employed, and there are blatant efforts
to manufacture tradition, to impose legitimacy" (Benedict, 1983:6–
7). The contest could take place on the opponent's turf as well as at
home. As a matter of national pride, the United States, along with a
number of other countries, mounted exhibits of its own native
items at the London exhibitions of 1851 and 1852, at Paris in 1855
and 1867, and Vienna in 1873, but rather ineffectually for lack of
proper financing and organization (Badger, 1979:16; Curti, 1950).

Both the success of the better European fairs and the increasing
popularity of county and state fairs set the stage for a series of ambitious homegrown international extravaganzas. The first of a long
sequence, and arguably the most successful and crucial in terms of
solidifying national pride and self-confidence, was the Centennial
Exhibition of 1876 held in Philadelphia.[20] Excluding a number of
expositions of mainly regional character, the most important of its
successors have been those in New Orleans (1884–85), Chicago
(1893), Omaha (1898), Buffalo (1901), St. Louis (1904), Hampton
Roads (1907), Seattle (1909), San Francisco (1915), San Diego (1915–
16), Philadelphia (1926), Chicago (1933–34), New York (1939–40),
San Francisco (1939–40), Seattle (1962), New York (1964–65), San
Antonio (1968), Spokane (1974), Knoxville (1983), and New Orleans
(1984).

In every respect except the financial (it incurred an operating loss
of over $51 million), the Philadelphia exposition was a smashing
triumph. The attendance was enormous (9,910,966 admissions in a

nation having a total population of some 46 million); the architecture, landscaping, and exhibits aroused general admiration; and the world was stunned by the miracles of American technology. It was at Philadelphia in the summer of 1876 that everyone, citizen and foreign visitor alike, finally realized that, beyond question, the United States had become one of the important nations. As John Maass has put it,

> Before 1876, many Europeans regarded the United States as a second-rate country at the outer fringe of civilization. The Centennial changed this view. . . . The influence of this American Exhibition upon the rest of the world was powerful and permanent. In 1876, the United States first emerged as a major power, which would eventually become an economic, political, and even cultural, super-power. This American dominance was, of course, not caused by the Centennial, but it first became manifest at Philadelphia in 1876. [Maass, 1973:111–12]

The 1876 Exhibition was an exuberant statement of American optimism and materialism. It was also future-oriented, remarkably so for a fair ostensibly commemorating the events of 1776 (Cheney, 1974:90; Post, 1976:23, Schlereth, 1980:139–40). Indeed, the Philadelphia Exhibition may have been the last of the truly uninhibited hurrahs for those glorious "American Things to Come," for by the next decade we detect unmistakable hints of retrospection and incipient disillusion in any number of contexts. I believe David Lowenthal is correct in arguing that "up to the centennial, most Americans were avowed modernists: they felt fortunate to have left the outmoded past behind. The 1880s and 1890s hear a new note: the past has been *better* than the present. The party of Memory for the first time began to outvote the party of Hope" (D. Lowenthal, 1985:123).

But American boosterism continued to be a robust theme at all the later fairs, at least through the New York City show of 1939–40. By all odds, the most brilliant achievement (it even managed to turn a small profit!) was that of the World's Columbian Exposition held on Chicago's South Side in 1893 (Allwood, 1977:81–94; Badger, 1979; Burg, 1976). The time was opportune, for indeed "the exposition was a celebration of America's coming of age—a grand rite of passage" (Burg, 1976:xiii) during the decade when the United States indisputably arrived as a world power, militarily as well as technologically and commercially.[21] Aside from the splendid profusion of exhibits and its impact, for better or worse, on American architecture and city planning for decades to come, this fair was the site for an exceptional number of meetings of national and international learned societies. It seems fair to say that, for these and other reasons, "the World's Columbian Exposition evoked far more commentary than any other exposition in history" (Burg, 1976:xi).

The subsequent American fairs continued, though perhaps less unequivocally or grandly, the basic thrusts of the 1876 and 1893 events, emitting a sort of late afterglow of the Victorian era of total self-assurance.[22] The last of this line was the relatively successful New York World's Fair of 1939–40, but it began to sound a somewhat different tune: the necessity for collective planning, the imposition of social controls for a bright, humane technological future, the blending of freedom with interdependence (Harrison, 1980, 1983). The world had moved into a new, less certain era, so that "the New York World's Fair of 1939 represents a watershed in international expositions. Though there have been many world's fairs since, their character has altered, and they became less important events after 1939" (Benedict, 1983:59).[23]

There were several factors working to transform the world's fair into little more than a glorified trade show and ephemeral amusement park rather than the electrifying cultural/nationalistic occasion it had been. As Burton Benedict has explained, even though some residual chauvinistic drumbeating may have lingered on, "the national competition element in world's fairs was siphoned off by the Olympic Games. The second, third and fourth Olympic Games were all held in conjunction with international expositions—Paris 1900, St. Louis 1904, and London 1908. The Olympics grew and began to take on the characteristics of world's fairs. . . . World's fairs ceased to be the venue of important meetings and congresses" (Benedict, 1983:60). Also contributing to their decline were: the proliferation of national and international trade shows, pure and simple; elaborate, permanent theme parks; the allurements of television and other diversions, as well as relatively inexpensive international tourism. The competition became overwhelming.

It appears that Chicago will be unable or unwilling to produce a sequel to its earlier efforts by staging a fair in 1992 to celebrate the five hundredth anniversary of the Columbus discovery. The disappointing turnouts for the Knoxville and New Orleans fairs of 1983 and 1984 have cast a pall over the prospects for such large-scale efforts in the future. The general outlook for world's fairs has also been darkened considerably by France's decision not to stage an exposition in 1989 to celebrate the bicentennial of the French Revolution. The moral is not that the nation-state has revised its objectives but rather that new means must be used to attain its consistent goals now that the world's fair has become an obsolescent device in the face of social and technological change.

OF ODYSSEYS AND STATELY PROCESSIONS

Two other sets of extraordinary events have also played more than a minor part in dramatizing and heightening national self-awareness: the ritual journey and the state funeral (Merriam, 1931:151–53). There is something quite primordial in the former, with an appeal far older than, but compatible with, that of nationalism: the theme of the hero's quest for rich spiritual or worldly treasure across vast tracts of land or sea that we find so often in ancient epics and folklore. It is an exercise performed in miniature in local parades, but on a much grander platform by the national hero and frequently with telling effect.

Quite early in American history, presidents learned how to collect rich political and nationalistic dividends from ceremonial journeys. In terms of splendor and soaring emotion, no subsequent chief executive has ever quite matched George Washington's achievement in 1789 in the procession from Mount Vernon to New York City for his first inaugural as he was borne by carriage and barge along highways and waterways lined with cheering citizens and through blossom-bedecked triumphal arches to the sounds of odes, choruses, congratulatory addresses, and bands. Every symbolic stop was pulled out in this rousing send-off for the newborn republic.

Washington's successors have often sought excuses to travel extensively throughout the land, in nonelection years, with appropriate pomp and acclamation. Whether the stated intent was partisan or presidential, the probable result was a knitting together of the citizenry as the national leader pressed the flesh and exuded mana. For example, excursions by Monroe (1818) and Jackson (1833) through New England undoubtedly helped relieve intersectional tensions (Binkley, 1958:294; Melder, 1976:20). Many others, notably Theodore Roosevelt, also adopted the device, but perhaps no latter-day president more adroitly exploited the strategy of the journey (as well as radio) than did Franklin D. Roosevelt, and his successors have tried to follow his example.

The things being displayed in such traveling exhibitions need not be flesh-and-blood statesmen. Among the most successful and rousing of nationalistic tours have been those of that holiest of American icons, the Liberty Bell. Reposing in a special railroad car and making frequent stops along the way, the Bell left its Philadelphia home on several ritual occasions, including visits to world and regional expositions: New Orleans, 1885; Chicago, 1893; Allentown, Pennsylvania in the 1890s; Atlanta, 1895–96; Charleston, 1902; Boston, 1903; St. Louis, 1904; and San Francisco, 1915 (Rosewater, 1926:152–93). The cross-country journey to San Francisco seems to have generated especially giddy extremes of hysteria (Rydell, 1980: 409–11). The practice came to a halt only after it was realized that further travel might be fatal to the brittle object. Since then, there have been similar processional displays of revered items, especially in connection with the Bicentennial, for example, the Freedom Train and the Bicentennial Wagon Train (American Revolution Bicentennial Administration, 1977: vol. 1, 61, 95). Particularly interesting has been the elaborate relay of runners bearing the Olympic torch during the summer of 1984 from its landfall in New York City to Los Angeles along a purposefully circuitous route. One suspects that such stagecraft accomplished more for the national esprit de corps than for the cause of international amity.

The homeward odyssey of national heroes and celebrities has often meant general exhilaration and an uplifting of national or stateful sentiments. The pattern has become rather routinized: the voyage or flight across the ocean; an uproarious reception in New York City or Washington; ticker tape parades; an address to a joint session of Congress and/or a ceremony at the White House; a progression from one major metropolis to another; and, finally, the return to the hometown and an ecstatic crowd of friends, family, and well-wishers. Needless to say, the addition of radio and television to the traditional newspaper coverage has vastly amplified the national impact of the event. The persons so honored may be political or military figures, for example, Admiral George Dewey, Douglas MacArthur, or the Iranian hostages (Lang and Engel, 1968); but other types of notables may also qualify, for example, Charles A. Lindbergh, astronauts, Jesse Owens, or Van Cliburn.

The object of such mass adulation or curiosity need not be an American, of course. The cities and highways of America have witnessed many a cavalcade honoring foreign dignitaries, for example, de Gaulle, Pope John Paul II, and numerous monarchs. But far beyond all comparison for its galvanizing effect on the populace and contribution toward a blazing nationalism was Lafayette's grand tour of every state in the Union during his second visit to America in 1824–25 (Brandon, 1950–57; Loveland, 1971:37–38; MacIntire, 1967; Somkin, 1967:131–74). In the course of an incredibly strenuous round of processions, mass meetings, receptions, banquets, and other stately occasions, a considerable fraction of the total population saw, heard, or touched the elderly hero. Fred Somkin hardly overstates the case in reporting that "it was to become over a period of thirteen months something in the nature of a communal pageant, enacted over and over on numerous stages, in which *all that appealed most powerfully* to the American people of the mid-1820's in their still self-conscious role of free men in a free society was to be brought forward and paraded" (Somkin, 1967:132; emphasis in original).

It is no great exaggeration to claim that only a few other events in the Republic's history have so dramatically defined and reinforced the essence of its nationalism as did the Marquis's triumphant return to the country he helped create. Among them are three great state funerals, which combined the ultimate pathos of the extended trip to the tomb with the shattering experience of the passing of a god-king. Although no detailed scholarly accounts are available, the deaths of Garfield, McKinley, and Harding evidently did deeply shock the country (Sheatsley and Feldman, 1965). However, the funerals of all pre-Lincoln presidents were essentially private. The fact that the deaths of William Henry Harrison (1841) and Zachary Taylor (1850), two sitting presidents who were also military heroes in their own right, resulted in little emotional turmoil may tell us something about the status of the presidency during the antebellum period, namely, that it had not yet attained the olympian level that was to characterize it from the Lincoln administration onward.

But, given the charisma of the man, his centrality to the shaping of the nation-state, and the quasi-religious implications of the assassination (on a Good Friday on the eve of an epochal victory) (L. Lewis, 1929:92–105), perhaps no death has ever so profoundly wrenched the nation's psyche as did Abraham Lincoln's. The funeral train moved slowly from Washington to Springfield along a right-of-way lined almost solidly with mourners and with several stopovers at major cities where the casket lay in state (L. Lewis, 1929:105–30; Searcher, 1965). Dignitaries and common folk by the millions marched tearfully past the bier or traveled scores or hundreds of miles to witness the train at every road crossing. It is probable that no other single event in American history, elections excepted, has personally involved a larger share of the total population. Most certainly it was the greatest outpouring of public grief we have ever known, and implied a more intense dedication to the mystique not just of Lincoln but also the nationalistic axioms he embodied. The death eighty years later of Franklin Delano Roosevelt, also on the verge of a mighty military triumph, almost as deeply convulsed the hearts of the American people. Once again, countless onlookers paid their respects to the funeral train as it chugged northward from Warm Springs to the elaborate ceremonies in Washington and, then, to the final resting place in Hyde Park.

The quintessential American state funeral was that of John F. Kennedy in November 1963 at the end of four traumatic days during which the life of the country came to a virtual standstill (Graebner, 1967; Wolfe, 1975:375–83 passim). One of the more remarkable aspects of this emotional crisis was the multitude of spontaneous memorial services, many of them on college campuses (Graebner, 1967). Although the classic funeral journey was lacking (the flight from Dallas to Washington took only hours, and the route from the Capitol to Arlington National Cemetery is only a few miles), there was an intense surrogate experience, for the ubiquity of the television camera lens may have more than compensated. "The shared experience of the assassination weekend, largely mediated by television, gave the nation an unusual sense of unity. Put bluntly, television unified the nation" (Wolfe, 1975:226–67). The funeral ceremony, carefully patterned after Lincoln's (Wolfe, 1975:444), was elaborate, emotionally draining, and yet a catharsis for nearly 200 million sorely troubled Americans. It was also, above all, an affirmation of national unity and common faith.

DROPPING IN ON THE PAST

Important though various recurrent or unique events may have been, it was with the founding of historical museums, parks, and shrines that Americans began to give more persistently concrete expression to their nationalistic impulses (Adam, 1937:79–87; Wittlin, 1970:122–24). The great majority of American museums have been founded in recent decades, and indeed their rate of formation seems to have accelerated recently, with a growing emphasis on the historical variety (American Association of Museums, 1979; Cary, 1975).[24]

The oldest examples were usually quite nondescript in character, a hodgepodge of works of art, stuffed birds and beasts, minerals, fossils, historic relics, and other curiosities.[25] But, with the passing of time, we find a professionalization of museum activity and a differentiation into three broad specialities: the fine arts; science and technology; and history—leaving aside those dedicated to sport, hobbies, and other diversions. Although nationalistic motifs may not be totally absent in the former two, the agenda of historical museums quite definitely includes the bolstering of national and regional pride (Wittlin, 1970). They have functioned under a wide variety of sponsors, among them, federal, state, county, and municipal agencies, historical societies, public and private libraries, colleges, patriotic-hereditary and veterans' organizations, and commercial entrepreneurs. A considerable number are military in character (Cary, 1975), including those located at national battlefields and sites of army and navy installations. The birthplaces, homes, and other buildings associated with political, military, literary, and other American notables have frequently been converted into museums.

One of the most interesting developments of recent years has been the mushrooming of museum villages. As of 1971, no fewer than 120 could be catalogued in 42 states (Zook, 1971), and undoubtedly many more have opened for business since then. These outdoor complexes may be totally synthetic assemblages, such as Old Sturbridge or Greenfield Village, or the carefully reconstructed or rehabilitated older sections of venerable towns, of which genre Colonial Williamsburg and the historic cores of Boston, Charleston, and Philadelphia are prime examples. Some of these places are veritable "living museums" in which costumed actors portray the everyday activities of earlier Americans as authentically as present-day knowledge permits (Carson, 1981). All such activity, along with the broader historic preservation movement, is part of the "museumization" of the American past, to adopt David Lowenthal's apt neologism (D. Lowenthal, 1966), and is not only the most tangible manifestation of general attitudes toward American history but perhaps also the most revealing.

Unlike the situation in many older nation-states of Europe, Asia, and Latin America, where past and present blend seamlessly, Americans have never been on truly familiar, companionable terms with their history. This fact is a product of the basic design of the nation, one that has always taken boundless pride in its newness. During the first century of its existence, the United States was a republic whose inhabitants studiously ignored their past when they were not busy destroying it, all the while keeping their gaze fixed on an elusive future. Later, in a more mature, partially disillusioned phase, when Americans began worrying about their roots, the vital connection was shriveled or gone. In effect, the past had become the property of the highest bidder. Moreover, the latter-day celebration of the American past has been drenched in nostalgia, scarcely the optimum mood for a workable accommodation with one's origins (Dudden, 1961; Jackson, 1980:89–102; Kammen, 1980; D. Lowenthal, 1966, 1976; Nicolaisen, 1979).

Taking Henry Ford's Greenfield Village and the Rockefellers' Williamsburg as the most elaborate, ideologically pregnant examples of what might also be called the "Williamsburgerization" of the nation (Wallace, 1981:84), there is little doubt that Michael Wallace has correctly diagnosed the situation in observing that "the disconnection of past from present and the separation of culture from politics was itself a political act. History was to be confined to providing entertainment, nostalgia, or interesting insights into vanished ways of life. It was not to be freed to become a powerful agent for understanding—and changing—the present" (Wallace, 1981:88). "Most history museums were constructed by members of dominant classes, and embody interpretations that supported their sponsors' privileged positions" (Wallace, 1981:63). Thus, "Colonial Williamsburg . . . doesn't simply borrow and display a historical aura, it embodies a vision of a total social order. . . . CW's order flows from the top down. It is a corporate world: planned, orderly, tidy, with no dirt, no smell, no visible signs of exploitation" (Wallace, 1981:78). It is significant that Williamsburg has become the site for important rituals and political ceremonies, such as receptions for visiting heads of state, and thus a sort of surrogate national capital. Life in Colonial Williamsburg is more predictable, has fewer awkward surprises than our polyglot, occasionally boisterous District of Columbia. It reminds one of the situation of Kyoto vis-à-vis Tokyo.

If Colonial Williamsburg is the ultimate embodiment of the latter-day vision of the American past, the same attitudes are implicit throughout the entire archipelago of museums, museumized places, and signposted sites. In a further exploration of the uses of memory and ritual in American nationalism, we can learn much by considering the pilgrimages American citizens have made to these sanctified places.

From time immemorial, great numbers of pious Hindus and Moslems, as well as Christians, residing in older lands have visited and worshipped at those special localities sacred to their religion. Indeed, such traffic has had major economic and cultural consequences for the places in question. A comparable circulation pattern has also been a standard feature of modern nationalism (Boehm, 1933:234); but, for obvious reasons, such spiritual magnets simply did not exist in Colonial or early Republican America. It was not until the mid-nineteenth century and later, with the rise of historic preservation, monument building on a grand scale, the institutionalized celebration of the national past, improved transportation, and greater affluence, that such lay pilgrimages became a conspicuous feature of American life. Unlike most other forms of symbolic behavior, this is one phenomenon on which we can hang relatively firm numbers.

Predictably, it was Mount Vernon that attracted the first significant contingent of pilgrims, and did so at the urging of its curators (Forgie, 1979:172). After a sluggish start in the 1850s, visitations to this great national shrine have increased steadily and remarkably, at least until the 1970s. Among other things, these figures suggest that a quite appreciable fraction of the American population, along with an undetermined number of foreign guests, have visited the Washington homestead at least once during their lifetimes.

Mount Vernon is not an isolated example. As the railroad and, most especially, the motorbus and personal auto made such places readily accessible to the traveler, patronage became substantial. Thus 134,080 persons were admitted to Lincoln's Tomb in 1927 (L. Lewis, 1929:25); the stream of visitors to Valley Forge swelled from 40,000 in 1906 to 600,000 in 1926 (Burnham, 1982:92); and during the early 1950s approximately 100,000 persons viewed the painting of "Washington Crossing the Delaware" at Washington Crossing Park (Hutton, 1959:171). Greenfield Village set its all-time attendance record in 1976 when it received 1,751,126 visitors (D. L. Lewis, 1976:280). Indeed, among Detroit area tourist attractions only the admission-free Ford Rotunda (destroyed by fire in 1962) drew more visitors than Greenfield Village during the post–World War II years (D. L. Lewis, 1976:280). There were 1,289,302 paid admissions to Colonial Williamsburg in the Bicentennial year, while Valley Forge State Park drew 2,581,443 persons and Monticello 671,487. The number of individuals paying their respects at John F. Kennedy's grave in Arlington National Cemetery is nothing short of astonishing: 700,000 in the first month alone, a value exceeding the 616,406 pilgrims to Lincoln's Tomb during all twelve months of 1963. By June 1971, still arriving at the rate of 10,000 a day, no fewer than 28 million persons had made their way to the graveside (Wolfe, 1975:395).

Table 3.1. *Visits to Mount Vernon, 1858–1980*

Period	Total Attendance
1858–1870 (estimated)	50,000
1871–1880 (estimated)	120,000
1881–1889	163,468
1890–1899	529,871
1900–1909	871,522
1910–1919	1,341,728
1920–1929	3,531,953
1930–1939	5,305,156
1940–1949	6,160,558
1950–1959	10,742,788
1960–1969	12,126,358
1970–1980	11,701,870
Total	52,645,272

Source: Mount Vernon Ladies Association, 1983.

We now have hundreds of historical parks, museums, birthplaces, famous residences, tombs, battlefields, and other buildings and plots of ground that can be called nationalistic shrines, including many administered by state and local agencies and private organizations as well as by the U.S. National Park Service. If both the number of such places and the volume of visits to them have increased markedly in recent decades, as indeed they have, one might contend that their popularity is simply another manifestation of the boom in domestic tourism. A good many of these hallowed sites are also "fun places," for there is undoubtedly plenty of entertainment value at such spots as the Statue of Liberty, Monticello, Mount Vernon (where relatively few visitors bother to see the tomb), Williamsburg, Sturbridge Village, the Washington Monument, or the breathtaking arch at St. Louis' Jefferson National Memorial.

An examination of National Park Service (NPS) statistics for a recent half-century period imparts some color to the proposition that the massive surge in the number of persons frequenting historic and nationalistic sites is part of an even larger, more inclusive phenomenon: touristic or pleasure travel to all manner of recreational opportunities. The number and acreage of national parks, battlefields, historic sites and parks, memorials, monuments, seashores, recreation areas, and other types of real estate managed by the NPS have increased enormously since the establishment of Yellowstone National Park in 1872. It seems reasonable to assume that NPS areas and their traffic not only account for a large share of aggregate recreational experiences in the United States but are also a reasonably representative sample of public preferences for travel-related leisure activities.

In table 3.2 I have displayed visits to three classes of NPS areas by five-year periods during an era when both the numbers of such places and their visitors expanded enormously. Two species of places are of special interest: those that can be considered fully nationalistic, the total of which has climbed from 1 in 1930 (George Washington Birthplace National Monument) to 58 in 1981;[26] and the Civil War sites that one might classify as marginally nationalistic. Ignoring the 1940–44 period, when every variety of civilian travel was curtailed, the general trend for all types of NPS areas has been sharply upward. The grand 52-year totals of 854,925,000 visits to nationalistic areas, 252,910,000 to Civil War sites, and 3,101,178,000 to other NPS areas is impressive, to say the least. On closer inspection, however, the dynamics for the two main categories—nationalistic, broadly defined; and other areas (mostly scenic and recreational)—diverge in suggestive fashion. The nonnationalistic areas have enjoyed truly spectacular growth, and evidently have not yet reached their maximum levels of traffic. On the other hand, the relative increments for both varieties of nationalistic areas have been more irregular. Indeed, in two quinquennia (1970–74 for nationalistic areas; 1975–79 for the Civil War locations) there were actual decreases. The NPS data may suggest that the phase of genuine expansion in pilgrimages to national shrines reached its climax in the 1960s, and that, since then, the volume of such movements has been virtually at a standstill. Indeed, the total number of visits to such places taken as a fraction of the national population has oscillated around the same level since 1967, while the comparable value for recreational/scenic NPS areas has moved ever higher to stratospheric levels. The temporary surge in the Bicentennial quinquennium was just that: temporary, and artificial, and less than expected. Although 1976 was indeed a banner year for most nationalistic shrines, attendance generally failed to live up to expectations, and was only moderately greater than in proximate years. For example, Valley Forge anticipated 30,000 visitors each day during the Bicentennial, but only 15,000 showed up (Powell, 1983:213). "In Philadelphia, officials anticipated anywhere from 14 to 15 million visitors at the shrines of the chief city of the Revolution. Some-

Table 3.2. Visits to National Park Service Areas, by Type of Area, 1930–1981 (in thousands)

Period	(1) Nationalistic Areas	(2) Civil War Areas	(1) + (2)	(3) All Other NPS Areas	(4) Total
1930–34	(N = 7) 1,429	(N = 8) 1,083	(N = 15) 2,513	(N = 45) 17,852	(N = 60) 20,365
1935–39	(17) 18,659 +1205.7%	(9) 8,233 +660.2%	(26) 26,892 +970.1%	(68) 39,770 +122.8%	(94) 66,662 +227.3%
1940–44	(24) 20,589 +10.3%	(12) 4,405 −46.5%	(36) 24,994 −7.1%	(87) 31,337 −21.2%	(123) 56,331 −15.5%
1945–49	(28) 31,601 +53.5%	(13) 6,051 +37.4%	(41) 37,652 +50.6%	(102) 82,944 +164.7%	(143) 120,596 +114.1%
1950–54	(31) 51,152 +61.9%	(12) 10,634 +75.7%	(43) 61,786 +64.1%	(109) 144,931 +74.7%	(152) 206,717 +71.4%

	(1)	(2)	(3)	(4)	(5)
1955–59	(34) 65,334 +27.7%	(12) 14,229 +33.8%	(46) 79,563 +28.8%	(122) 206,142 +42.2%	(168) 285,705 +38.2%
1960–64	(38) 113,566 +73.8%	(13) 32,955 +131.6%	(51) 146,521 +84.2%	(133) 289,778 +40.6%	(184) 436,299 +52.7%
1965–69	(43) 153,016 +34.7%	(15) 51,513 +56.3%	(58) 204,529 +39.6%	(177) 462,989 +59.8%	(235) 667,518 +53.0%
1970–74	(52) 146,853 −4.0%	(16) 68,347 +32.7%	(68) 215,200 +5.2%	(199) 647,665 +39.9%	(267) 862,865 +29.3%
1975–79	(57) 183,633 +25.0%	(15) 40,876 −40.2%	(72) 224,509 +4.3%	(195) 806,475 +24.5%	(267) 1,030,984 +19.5%
1980–81	(58) 69,093	(15) 14,584	(73) 83,677	(198) 454,971	(275) 371,294
Total	854,925	252,910	1,107,835	3,101,178	4,209,013

Source: U.S. National Park Service, annual reports.

where between 7 and 10 million came. In Boston, planners projected more modest numbers and got but a fraction of those. . . .
Surveys showed that travelers were celebrating the bicentennial in
California, the Southwest, and Hawaii instead" (Zuckerman, 1978:
225). Visitor levels in 1980–81 at nationalistic sites returned to the
pre-1976 situation.

In order to provide additional insights into temporary trends in
American nationalistic pilgrimages, I have compiled table 3.3 covering the years 1936–80 for some of the more notable shrines, and
have indicated number of visits as percent of the national population. Unfortunately, figures are not available for the entire group of
nineteen for the entire time span. Consequently, I have segmented
the nineteen and the table into three subgroups in order to ensure
stable universes within each of the designated time periods. In each
of these subgroups there is consistent growth in absolute values
(the war years excepted) and in percentile values in two cases, but
with some suggestion of stasis by the late 1960s, until the attainment of maximum amounts in 1976. During the subsequent four
years, we find a significant decline in both absolute and relative
values; and this diminution, it should be recalled, took place during
a period when general tourism was still expanding quite healthily.
There are grounds for suspecting that such popularity as nationalistic shrines may have enjoyed in recent years is as much a matter of
nostalgia and a sort of voyeuristic titillation as an exercise in true
devotion.

A fuller appraisal of the meaning of the long-term rise, then stabi-
lization, in nationalistic tourism is best deferred until we have considered other collateral evidence. But the post-1976 slump is intriguing. Are we seeing post-Bicentennial fatigue? Or is it the onset
of a long-lived trend that will persist well into and beyond the
1980s. Obviously, it is too early to do more than speculate.[27] Still,
the recent trends do appear to be general and consistent among the
major attractions. Thus, for example, attendance at Old Sturbridge
Village has declined from 667,961 in the peak year of 1972 to
518,968 in 1978, while Greenfield Village has suffered a drop from
1,751,126 in 1976 to 953,670 in 1982, a loss of 45.5 percent.

Most revealing perhaps are recent developments at Lincoln's
Tomb in Springfield, Illinois. The person who travels to that structure, one that is lacking in architectural distinction, is engaged in
the closest approach to absolute nationalistic piety that may be
conceivable under American conditions. The tomb stands near the
corner of an unremarkable cemetery in an unremarkable residential

neighborhood. No one wages an advertising campaign on its behalf; there are no other attractions or distractions in the vicinity; no satellite enterprises, no souvenir or refreshment stands, no amusements for the bored traveler. After many years of steady increments in visitations, 1968 recorded the maximum number to date: 756,432. Since then, the volume of visits has decreased steadily until it amounted to only 296,056 in 1982. I suspect that these numbers may be telling us something important, but just what is not yet clear.[28]

No discussion of nationalistic pilgrimages in the United States can pretend to be complete without contemplating the extraordinary drawing power of the Washington, D.C. area. Within the District of Columbia and neighboring communities we find the greatest aggregation of nationalistic objects, sites, and activities in the entire country, if not the entire world. The throngs of pilgrims who come to gaze or join in ritual, and thus, in a sense, engage in nationalistic communion, are too vast for confident enumeration. The Capitol and the White House are only the oldest of hundreds of government buildings that can suffuse the onlooker with wonder and awe. Sightseers enjoying New York City, San Francisco, or New Orleans can, with a little luck, entirely avoid any reminders of American nationhood or statehood, but such cultural amnesia is literally impossible in Washington.

Beyond all the federal structures, there are the countless monuments and memorials, awesome tombs, the burial grounds of the historically illustrious, military installations, foreign embassies, the museums and libraries, unreasonable numbers of flags, headquarters of numerous national (and international) organizations, and those insistently nationalistic names of streets and traffic circles. The capital city is the setting for rituals and demonstrations large and small and for national conventions of every imaginable sort of group. Washington is as much a theater for the flaunting of symbols as a place for the conduct of government, perhaps more so. And to its streets and corridors come the swarming businessmen, lobbyists, petitioners, diplomats, scholars, scientists, college students from near and distant states and countries, and, above all, the worshipful tourists. Throughout the year, they stream in endless procession, much as they do in Paris, Moscow, Beijing, or Mexico City, but, unquestionably, in greater hordes. Or perhaps the analogy should be with Jerusalem, Rome, or Mecca.

Tourism in Washington, which, inescapably, is tourism with a thick coating of nationalism, is more than a major industry; it is a

Table 3.3. *Aggregate Number of Visitors to Selected, Nationalistically Significant Historical Parks and Sites: United States, 1936–1980*

Group I (1936–1980)[a]

Year	Number of Visitors (in thousands)	Percentage of U.S. Population	Year	Number of Visitors (in thousands)	Percentage of U.S. Population	Year	Number of Visitors (in thousands)	Percentage of U.S. Population
1936	2,413.0	1.88	1951	3,845.7	2.48	1966	12,237.3	6.22
1937	2,884.3	2.44	1952	4,372.7	2.77	1967	13,089.4	6.59
1938	2,665.5	2.05	1953	4,832.8	3.02	1968	12,809.0	6.38
1939	2,637.8	2.02	1954	4,723.3	2.90	1969	13,583.2	6.70
1940	2,930.3	2.21	1955	4,690.1	2.83	1970	13,532.7	6.60
1941	3,252.9	2.43	1956	5,018.4	2.97	1971	13,270.5	6.41
1942	1,973.5	1.46	1957	6,001.5	3.49	1972	10,881.6	5.21
1943	1,232.2	0.90	1958	5,007.1	2.90	1973	11,483.6	5.46
1944	1,441.7	1.04	1959	5,396.3	3.04	1974	10,734.3	5.07
1945	1,859.6	1.32	1960	7,333.1	4.06	1975	11,494.5	5.38
1946	2,669.4	1.88	1961	9,885.2	5.38	1976	13,114.5	6.10
1947	2,940.3	2.03	1962	10,310.0	5.53	1977	12,126.9	5.59
1948	3,216.2	2.18	1963	10,668.2	5.64	1978	12,491.6	5.73
1949	3,447.3	2.30	1964	11,607.8	6.05	1979	11,927.5	5.42
1950	3,525.2	2.31	1965	11,825.5	6.09	1980	11,266.6	4.97

Group II (1954–1980)[b]

Year			Year			Year		
1954	8,290.2	5.09	1960	11,629.6	6.44	1971	20,682.9	9.99
1955	8,259.9	4.98	1961	14,853.0	8.09	1972	17,113.6	8.20
1956	8,795.0	5.21	1962	16,164.9	8.66	1973	17,074.1	8.12
1957	10,040.5	5.84	1963	16,775.6	8.87	1974	17,065.0	8.05
1958	9,139.2	5.23	1964	18,591.1	9.69	1975	17,894.2	8.38
1959	9,738.4	5.48	1965	18,920.5	9.74	1976	21,199.7	9.86
			1966	19,384.5	9.86	1977	17,610.3	8.12
			1967	20,360.0	10.25	1978	18,245.8	8.37
			1968	19,304.3	9.62	1979	17,248.9	7.84
			1969	20,557.9	10.14	1980	16,735.7	7.39
			1970	20,589.3	10.05			

Group III (1972–1980)[c]

Year			Year			Year		
1972	21,812.8	10.45	1975	24,177.5	11.32	1978	23,818.1	10.92
1973	21,847.5	10.38	1976	29,322.7	13.63	1979	22,573.1	10.26
1974	21,943.9	10.36	1977	23,170.6	10.69	1980	22,117.5	9.76

[a] Group I consists of: Lincoln's Birthplace (Ky.); Colonial National Historical Park (Va.); Washington's Birthplace (Va.); Statue of Liberty (N.Y.); Washington Monument (D.C.); Monticello (Va.);* Mount Vernon (Va.).*

[b] Group II consists of Group I plus: Independence National Historical Park (Pa.); Mount Rushmore (S.D.); White House (D.C.); Lincoln's Tomb (Ill.);* Old Sturbridge Village (Mass.).*

[c] Group III consists of Group II plus: Lincoln's Boyhood Home (Ind.); Minute Man National Historical Park (Mass.); The Hermitage (Tenn.);* Greenfield Village (Mich.);* Colonial Williamsburg (Va.);* Valley Forge (Pa.); Ford's Theater (D.C.).

Sources: U.S. National Park Service, annual reports; unpublished tabulations furnished by organizations indicated by asterisk.

rite of passage for old and young, but especially the young. During
and between sessions of the school year, entire classes of students
and troops of Girl Scouts and Boy Scouts jam the well-trodden circuit of sacred stations. In spring and early summer, hundreds of
buses disgorge the graduating seniors from high schools in every
corner of the land. These are students who have scrimped and saved
for months or even years, scraping up travel funds via all manner of
ingenious projects, for what might be the first extended trip away
from home and parents and an experience that will remain deeply
imprinted in their memories.

Just how many tourists, with whatever intentions, have been
flocking to Washington is quite difficult to ascertain or guess (National Capital Planning Commission, 1984b:18). We do have several
estimates for what is surely an enormous quantity; but "the statistical bases for such estimates are somewhat unreliable as a statistically significant survey of visitor traffic in the Washington Area has
never been conducted (National Capital Planning Commission,
1978:12). A plausible figure for total number of visitors in 1974 was
fourteen million (*Washington Post*, Aug. 24, 1975, A12); and the
National Capital Planning Commission (1984a:2) has assumed a
continuing average annual increment of 3 to 5 percent in number of
visitors to the "Monumental Core."[29] The values cited include not
only tourists but also business, convention, and social visitors as
well as demonstrators, many of whom may also have taken in
some incidental sightseeing while in the area. An estimate of
4,650,000 tourists in 1980 (Greater Washington Board of Trade,
n.d.:20; Washington Convention and Visitors Association, 1981:1)
seems unduly conservative when one considers that the recorded
admission for just one popular attraction, the Air and Space Museum, was 10,014,892 in 1983 (National Capital Planning Commission, 1984a:9).[30] The only safe inference is that the traffic has been
immense and has probably been increasing, at least until quite
recently.

ORGANIZING FOR GOD AND COUNTRY

It was not only at historic sites that Americans celebrated their past
and enacted nationalistic ritual. As happened in other Western nation-states, a goodly number of latter-day voluntary organizations
devoted much time, energy, and ingenuity to such celebrations and
rituals amidst their other patriotic deeds. But, as Boyd Shafer cau-
tions, "just how effective they were in making nationalists cannot

be known. Individuals everywhere in the West were subject to so many pressures that would make them nationalists, from their governments and from their parents and their schools as well as from organized patriotic groups, that it is impossible to disentangle and weight the effectiveness of any one" (Shafer, 1972:220). Nevertheless the cumulative impact of veterans and various fraternal organizations has been far from trivial. It was with the formation of the Grand Army of the Republic (GAR) in 1866 by Union veterans that we have the first successful mass organization devoted to nationalist causes (Davies, 1955:30–31). Curiously, despite the enormous political and symbolic importance of the Revolution, its veterans— or at least the enlisted personnel—made no effort to organize themselves (Davies, 1955:3). The one group that did, the Order of Cincinnatus, and one that still survives, limited its membership to commissioned officers and their descendants. Significantly, the Cincinnati generated a great deal of popular hostility in a young republic where antimilitary feelings ran strong (Cunliffe, 1968; Davies, 1955:2–3).

The first serious drive to organize *all* veterans of an American war took place in 1853 and involved the survivors of the War of 1812 (no such effort was made for participants in the Mexican War), but it proved to be a failure (Davies, 1955:22–23). The timing is noteworthy, for this was the same decade that saw the initiation of the first important historic preservation campaign (the Mount Vernon Ladies Association) as well as the earliest erection of meaningful numbers of nationalistic monuments.

The GAR was only the largest and most successful of many veterans' organizations that sprang up in the North in the wake of America's most shattering war; and somewhat later (1889) the aging boys in gray formed the United Confederate Veterans. The GAR quickly grew into a powerful force in the political and symbolic life of the nation, remaining so until the early years of the present century, and more than any other single group was responsible for the propagation of nationalistic ritual on a mass scale (Dearing, 1952; Minott, 1966:25). Following the Spanish-American War, the Veterans of Foreign Wars (VFW) appeared on the scene (Pierce, 1933:52–55), as did the American Legion immediately after World War I. With some justification, the latter describes itself as the "foremost agency for the preservation of American ideals and traditions" (Pierce, 1933:33–51). Both of these huge organizations and their auxiliaries, along with smaller veterans' groups and various associations of military officers (Pierce, 1933:59–70), have continued to play an influential part in American politics and public ritual. And, given the fact that in many hundreds of smaller communities the VFW or Legion hall is the principal social center, the impact of these organizations on American life is too pervasive to be readily assessed.

It was in the 1890s, in so many respects a watershed decade in the evolution of modern America, that great numbers of patriotic-hereditary organizations materialized or came to the fore (Craven, 1956; Davies, 1955:44–45; Manson, 1900).[31] The Daughters of the American Revolution (DAR) and the Sons of the American Revolution are only the most celebrated of these groups (Pierce, 1933:15–32; Strayer, 1958). It was not much later that youth organizations, notably the Boy Scouts, Girl Scouts, and Camp Fire Girls, amassed large memberships, and, despite nominal obeisance to international ideals, developed programs with more than a faint nationalistic tinge (Boehm, 1933:238; Merriam, 1931:118–20; Pierce, 1933:183–202; Rosenthal, 1986). Not to be ignored was the concurrent proliferation of hundreds of fraternal organizations throughout the country, but with special vigor in the Northeast (Schein, 1983).[32] Although a good many were chiefly social in form and purpose, a great number were ethnic and/or religious in nature. A common characteristic, even for those with international affiliations, was the promotion of national loyalty through rituals, publications, and civic activities.

In discussing this varied lot of voluntary associations, it may be possible to draw a distinction between those organizations, mostly older, that sought to instill nationalism "by cultivating an informed interest in the country's 'storied past'—preserving its historic sites, commemorating its great historic events, spreading knowledge of its great warriors, statesmen, and literary figures"—and those others devoted to advocating "particular economic and political dogmas and to the suppression of critical discussions of these dogmas" (Coker, 1934:28).

Be that as it may, these groups pushed the cause of what they considered to be Americanism in a great variety of ways. The activities of the DAR, as detailed by Boyd Shafer, are reasonably representative.

The Daughters held patriotic assemblies to inspire themselves and their communities. They presented copies of national songs and documents to schools, convinced boards of education and legislatures that the American flag should be flown on every school, defied any "misuse" of the flag, and asked that men (not women) doff their hats when it passed. They reviewed the national history, especially its glorious moments, made pilgrimages to historic places, gave entertainments in historical costumes, and erected national monuments. They gave prizes to children for patriotic essays and made certain that the "right" books were in the libraries. [Shafer, 1972:219]

In addition, such associations campaigned to preserve battlefields and other historic buildings and sites, lobbied for various national holidays, created Americanization programs, and did what they could to censor school texts (Davies, 1955:228, 234–44). They often aided in the founding of historical museums as well as monuments (Hosmer, 1965), and the national or regional headquarters of the organization might itself serve as a repository for nationalistic icons, as is the case with the DAR's elaborate, symbol-laden Constitution Hall in Washington (Strayer, 1958:206–27).

Whatever particular form they might take, the operations of the large, impressive array of nationalistic voluntary associations that have been so active for the past hundred years differ quite fundamentally from the patriotic exercises of earlier Americans. The festivities, writings, orations, and art of the latter were, for all their fervor, localized, spontaneous, and lacking any centralized regimentation. Nowadays, in contrast, much of what passes for patriotism is the doing of corporate structures, hierarchical organizations that operate from coast to coast by formula and careful rules. This seems most fitting in a country whose existence is dominated by a complex, integrated national network of political, business, and other organizations.

SPORT

Thus far all the phenomena considered in this chapter are overtly nationalistic except perhaps for the world's fair, which wears its cosmopolitan disguise with only indifferent success. Athletic performance may seem at first an odd choice to round out a treatment of public activities that sustain the statist cause, but, in actuality, no topic is more appropriate. As it happens, none of the modes of public performance so far treated comes close to matching the sheer force of organized sport in both the daily and ritual life of twentieth-century Americans, and thus in supporting and intensifying that statefulness without which the United States could not smoothly function.[33] But first it is essential to distinguish between generalized or unorganized *play*, an attribute of most higher animals, and organized *games*, a uniquely human activity, but one fully developed only in the modern world. In early America, sport and related diversions were localized, relatively spontaneous, and quite unprofessional. Among adults, athletic activity was confined to such things as wrestling, boxing, riding, footraces, bearbaiting, cockfighting, hunting, and fishing, while children amused themselves, as they have for millenia and still do to some extent, with traditional games and frolics arranged on the spur of the moment.

Recreation in general and sport in particular have undergone the most profound kind of metamorphosis since the coming of a full-blown urban-industrial society in the late nineteenth century in the United States and other advanced countries (Guttmann, 1978). Sport became thoroughly regimented at a national, then international scale. Operating under formal rules, central organizations govern the conduct of games, and sport has become a major profit-making industry, its star employees highly paid professionals. Most importantly, the public no longer participates, it spectates. There is, of course, the most intimate web of interrelationships between modern technology (most immediately, transportation and communication), finance, the social, economic, and residential structure, and especially the psychic appetites of a massified population on the one hand, and the excitements of organized athletics on the other. As J. O. Robertson suggests, modern sport helps fill what might otherwise be a paralyzing void in our social existence. "The games and their teams are not only sources of activity and entertainment, their rituals provide opportunities for communication among townspeople who would not otherwise have had any relationship at all" (Robertson, 1980:252).

Vicarious engagement in local sport may indeed be the only social activity that binds together nearly the entire populace not only in small towns but in large metropolises as well. And, by means of radio, television, and the print media, the major sports create coast-to-coast congregations of communicants whose memberships transcend the usual barriers of class, age, religious denomination, ideology, and, recently at least, sex, ethnic, and racial group—and ultimately even region. Sport fanaticism, which in varying degree involves the vast majority of Americans, engenders an intensity of feeling on a daily basis far greater than any roused by conventional religious or political issues. Moreover, the culminating events of the season produce outbursts of mass hysteria that only the rarest of political or military happenings can rival. The street scenes in Pittsburgh or Philadelphia after the home team won the World Series or in Washington when the Redskins triumphed in the Superbowl can only be topped, in my personal recollection, by the delirious mobs in Manhattan on V-E and V-J Days in 1945.

What I am suggesting is a conclusion reached by other observers of the modern world: that we find in contemporary sport a genuine, if this-worldly, form of religion, a mode of worship that, for the majority of the inhabitants of the modernized world, is more meaningful and satisfying than the traditional theologies. This may disconcert the conventionally pious, but the evidence, as forcefully presented by Michael Novak (1976) and, even more extremely, Charles Prebish (1982, n.d.), as well as others (Brohm, 1978; Hobsbawm, 1983b:298–302; Lever, 1969; Mathisen, 1986; Milton, 1972), is incontrovertible. Without repeating Novak's elaborate, eloquent argument or noting in detail the rituals of contests, the raiment, incantations, anthems, conduct of umpires/priests with their rulebooks/bibles, or the uncanny parallelism between stadia and cathedrals, one need only ask oneself what the proverbial Visitor from Mars would believe upon coming across twenty-two actors performing prescribed movements before 100,000 mesmerized spectators in a great oval amphitheater. The answer should be quite similar to the conclusions drawn by archaeologists who examine the ruins of Mayan ball courts.

Like other great world religions, sport is compartmentalized along national lines. A few mass-spectator sports like soccer, basketball, boxing, and tennis have become truly transnational, but, in the United States, as in a number of other countries, certain sports have come to be identified with the nation and its special character, and are treasured as priceless national resources. Even when the sport is not exclusive to the country, its exportability may be limited. Thus we identify Russians with chess, the British with cricket and rugby (and among the elite, foxhunting), and recognize Canada's love affair with hockey, Spain's with bullfighting, Japan's with sumo wrestling, and, possibly, Italy's with bocce. There are also folk diversions and regional specialties that have never attained much nationalistic significance. In the United States, horseshoe pitching, stock car racing, soapbox derbies, square dancing, miniature golf, various card games, and the American version of bowling are examples of the former, and lacrosse, stickball, and rodeos of the latter.

The current sport scene offers little comfort for any advocate of

American exceptionalism. In general terms, American sport enthu-
siasts behave very much like their counterparts in other lands; but
the national peculiarities, like those elsewhere, do help us understand the workings of nationalism. Of the three leading spectator
sports in the United States, baseball, football, and basketball, the
former two, which evolved from British antecedents in the past
century, seem peculiarly compatible with Americanness. At any
rate, outside the United States, only Japan, Canada, and a few Latin
American countries have adopted baseball with any fervor, while
only Canada seems smitten with the American brand of football.

No one seriously challenges the designation of baseball as *the*
National Game, for most Americans have played or passionately
identified with it for at least one hundred years (Crepeau, 1980;
Halberstam, 1970; Voigt, 1976). Morris Cohen (1946:34) goes so far
as to claim "that by all the canons of our modern books on comparative religion, baseball is a religion, and the only one that is not
sectarian but national." In any case, we should have no difficulty in
accepting David Halberstam's contention that "baseball is . . . the
most mythological of sports; it has had the longest history, it is by
its own proclamation our national pastime, and it harbors, I think,
our greatest mythological figures" (Halberstam, 1970:22). And it is
clearly most intimately linked with the American ethos, like the
flag and apple pie, and thus nationalism (Voigt, 1976:79–91). The
American Legion seems to have harbored the conviction that training immigrant youngsters in the intricacies of the game would lubricate the process of assimilation, for Junior Baseball has been part
of their Americanization program (Pierce, 1933:46).

Why this enduring American passion for the game of baseball?
The conventional wisdom, which may be correct in this instance,
is that its popularity arises from a mythic association with the
pastoral theme, the fabled Middle Landscape so central to the
American Dream, and thus with the mystique of the small town
and agrarianism (Guttmann, 1978:91–116). Writing before the professional ranks were as thronged with Afro-Americans and Latin
Americans as they are today, Novak contributes an additional consideration. "Baseball is as close a liturgical enactment of the white
Anglo-Saxon Protestant myth as the nation has. It is a cerebral
game, designed as geometrically as the city of Washington itself,
born out of the Enlightenment and the philosophies so beloved of
Jefferson, Madison, and Hamilton. It is to games what the FEDERAL-
IST PAPERS are to books" (M. Novak, 1976:58).

In some fashion, football seems to have touched an even deeper, more vital core within the national soul, perhaps because of its combination of aggressiveness, territoriality, and fluid interplay between community and individualism, and other attributes best left for anthropologists and psychologists to explore.[34] In any case, its mystique is as baffling to foreigners as cricket's is to Americans.

The spatial and organizational structure of the major sports of baseball, football, and basketball within a nested hierarchy mirrors the design of the American economy and society. Thus fierce competition exists within the junior leagues, high school, college, industrial, minor, and major leagues; but somehow such combat serves to strengthen, rather than erode, loyalty to the overarching nation-state.

It is within the international arena that the nationalistic strain inherent in modern organized sport surfaces most conspicuously. In the America's Cup races, Davis Cup competition, the Pan American games, various international track and gymnastic meets (but not World Cup soccer, for the United States is not yet a serious contender), and, supremely, in both the winter and summer Olympic Games, Americans have behaved as though the national honor were in jeopardy, precisely as their opponents have done. The history of the modern Olympics illustrates the point all too well (Lucas, 1973; Noverr and Ziewacz, 1983:227–33). Revived in 1896 (could there be a more appropriate decade?), their professed ideals, that is, to celebrate the virtues of superior athletes and advance the cause of international friendship, have been belied by the increasing jingoism surrounding the events, a thinly veiled form of surrogate warfare, and, since the 1936 games in Berlin and those of 1952 in Melbourne, their outright politicization.[35]

One need only scan the daily newspapers or view television to corroborate these statements. The results have more than once fanned the flames of American nationalism, for example, the gloating over American achievements at Berlin (followed two years later by Joe Louis's demolition of Max Schmeling, an international morality play if there ever has been any), the unrestrained orgy set off by the American hockey team's surprise victory over the Soviets at Lake Placid in 1980, or the delirium occasioned by the results of the 1984 Summer Olympics in Los Angeles. It is important to remember that in international sport competition we encounter the ultimate distillation of statefulness, of us vs. them, without a trace of meaningful political or ideological content. Yet, through some symbolic legerdemain, we are invited to believe that the victory of a given country's athletic champion or team over another's somehow

ratifies that country's superiority, and hence its citizens', in terms
of all human and social virtues. It is difficult to conceive of a more
vacuous argument.

The volume of journalistic verbiage having to do with sports is
beyond calculation, and recently there has been an upsurge of social
science interest in the topic. Still sadly neglected, however, except
by a handful of folklorists, is the serious study of children's games
and playthings. And we know even less about the nationalistic implications of these items. That little does suggest that there is
much more worth knowing. If the American childhood game of
cowboys-and-Indians is indeed a ritual reenactment of the winning
of the West (Robertson, 1980:162), might it not be rewarding to look
into other such pastimes? Old catalogs show how popular nationalistic games and costumes have been among the young since early in
the nineteenth century (McClintock and McClintock, 1961; M.
Schwartz, 1975);[36] and, then, there are all those toy soldiers and
miniature weapons. We would do well to investigate the impact
such objects may have had on impressionable minds.

At this point in our trek across the symbolic realm of American
nationalism, we have already encountered a highly varied batch of
features, so diversified indeed that readers may have begun to worry
about losing their bearings. This may be a good time, then, to
unfold and consult our road map of motifs, to pick out the broader
lineaments of the terrain before plunging headlong into remoter
domains that are perhaps even more incognito than the tracts we
have left behind.

The exigencies of the printed word are such that our path must
be linear, but linearity does not guarantee straightness. In topologi-
cal actuality, the phenomena we are scanning inhabit a multidimensional space; and, as we saunter twistingly from point to point,
we recognize landmarks already passed and others yet to come.
Thus, for example, we bump into the national hero again in looking
at holidays and museums, and will do so repeatedly when we arrive
at place-names, monuments, and several other themes. Nevertheless, in the particular American case, the scenario I have devised for
the journey, with a certain measure of arbitrariness admittedly—
the progression from the airiest of collective imaginings through
observable actions into the most concrete kinds of objects—does
offer its special rewards, and on more than one level.

As it happens, in scrutinizing nationalistic eidolons, we have begun with symbolic items that are universal throughout the company of latter-day nation-states. Furthermore, these devices are so crucial to the viability of the nation-state that, despite great (and suggestively paradoxical) changes in character, purpose, and strength, they still loom large on the symbolic landscape in the United States and elsewhere. Moreover, they have engaged the hearts and minds of virtually everyone past and present, however altered the mode of engagement. The same statement applies, but with appreciably less force, to the forms of nationalistic performance examined in the chapter just concluded. However potent holidays and most other ritual occasions, world's fairs, and patriotic organizations may once have been, they have begun to matter to fewer and fewer persons as time has passed (once again, we are speaking of the entire assemblage of advanced nation-states), while only a fraction of the total populace gets to patronize historical museums and shrines and the almost universal mania for organized sport is a rather spurious surrogate for genuine nationalism.

If chapters 2 and 3 deal with universals that happen to have an American setting—in which land, incidentally, their expression is especially eloquent—the situation changes in the materials that follow. Chapter 4 has to do with matters verbal and aesthetic. In such sectors of nationalistic activity, personal involvement tends to be more limited, and, for the most part, confined to the talented minority. Further, at this juncture, the American story deviates markedly from that of most other countries. For the first time, we encounter an almost exclusively American practice: the use of nationalistic terms in naming places and certain other objects. And while Americans may have fully emulated other countries by exploiting historiography for nationalistic ends, in other verbal and aesthetic respects the United States has fallen far short of the intensities registered elsewhere. Thus language loyalty, so central an element in defining national identity in most instances, is here basically a nonissue. Although nationalism once flourished in the visual and plastic arts, both high and low, in America, the days of such effulgence are long since gone. As we shall see, achievements in the realms of literature, drama, music, dance, film, radio, and television have been at best unremarkable in advancing the nationalistic or statist cause—in contrast to many another land.

Looking even further ahead, the trajectory of American inventiveness swerves sharply upward, and we depart even more radically from non-American examples, as we enter the zone of the built landscape. With the possible, partial exception of the national-istic monument, the American scene is *sui generis*, truly original in several nationalistic respects.

Even more basic to the ultimate argument of this study than extent of local peculiarity, scale of popular participation, or degree of inwardness, significant though such dimensions may be, is an-other set of trends: alterations in the shape and power of these mul-tiple manifestations of national/statist sentiments over time (and space). But we still have much more ground to cover before uttering the moral of this narrative in unequivocal tones.

FOUR ★ ★ ★ ★ ★ ★ ★ ★

LANGUAGE AND THE ARTS ★ ★

WORDS

The use of language has been important in the shaping of American nationalism and in its public performance, but language per se has not. In this respect, the United States, and all other Neo-European nation-states for that matter, differ sharply from many of those older, traditional nations that emerged *in situ*, discovering their nationhood on the basis of soil, blood, ancient mythology, mother tongue, or some combination thereof (Isaacs, 1975).[1] Whenever and however transplanted Europeans, whether British, French, Spanish, Boer, or Portuguese, sought political divorce from the homeland, the question of language was not a bone of contention (Anderson, 1983:50). Thus, "Americans do not have a language ideology which identifies nation and language; they do not fight for their language as the symbol of their nationhood as many other nations do. They are content to be one of a number of nations speaking the same language" (Ferguson and Heath, 1981:3).[2]

Indeed, the country has never had an official language although, of course, (American) English has taken on that function, de facto, from the very outset. With or without formal Americanization programs, but emphatically through the normal workings of cultural processes and a pervasive public school system, Anglophones have managed to absorb tens of millions of immigrants and their offspring into the language received from Great Britain. It is only quite recently, with the arrival of millions of Spanish-speaking newcomers who resist rapid linguistic assimilation and an ethnic revival that has stressed the retention or rescue of Native American and non-English immigrant tongues, that the exclusive use of English in schools and public life has become an item for widespread political dialogue.

For a brief period soon after independence, one of the dominant creators of American identity did campaign ardently for linguistic autonomy, for the recognition and celebration of a distinctly New World version of English (Bradsher, 1940:272–76; Friedman, 1975: 30–41; Warfel, 1936:129). As lexicographer, polemicist, nationalist, and much else, Noah Webster pressed vigorously at one stage of his long career, by means of the *Speller* and other publications, for a standardized national vocabulary, pronunciation, and orthography distinct enough from British forms to affirm American dignity and self-respect (K. Malone, 1925; Rollins, 1980:36). The only permanent results of his efforts seem to be a few simplified American spellings.

Webster's *Dictionary*, first published in 1828 and frequently revised thereafter, has been immensely influential throughout the English-speaking world as the most complete and scholarly lexicon available until James Murray began issuing the *New English Dictionary* late in the nineteenth century. But, despite the conventional wisdom to the contrary (H. M. Jones, 1964:331–34; Rollins, 1976: 415–16), Webster's great *Dictionary* did not materialize as a chauvinistic document, whatever his initial agenda may have been (Bynack, 1984; Rollins, 1976:416; 1978). Instead the author, as an increasingly conservative, born-again Christian and rather eccentric philologist, molded the most memorable of his many efforts into an argument for social control, quiet piety, and old-fashioned authority. Richard Rollins ably summarizes the essential meaning of his momentous lexicon.

> The *American Dictionary* was the product of an entire lifetime. . . . As such it reflected the events and inheritances of that human life, and contained all the biases, concerns, and ideals of an individual. Indeed, it was an extension of his whole personality. It reflects much about the man and his times, although one must read it carefully to understand the tale it tells. Webster's main concern while writing and publishing it was not to celebrate American life or to expand independence. . . . Instead, he sought to counteract social disruption and reestablish the deferential world-order that he believed was disintegrating. [Rollins, 1976:416]

In the course of events, the problem of the attitudes of Webster and others toward linguistic sovereignty has become moot. The use of American English as a prop for nationalistic zeal is now a nonquestion. By the mid-nineteenth century, the English language, in a multiplicity of dialects, has become the native or official tongue of many countries and, in fact, if not by statute, the dominant language of the world.

If the great mass of early Americans were indifferent to arguments about language being the lifeblood of the body politic, they were highly receptive auditors for the orators of the day. And oratory was as efficacious a medium for promulgating nationalism as any (Curti, 1946:128–29). Until the advent of cheap popular entertainment and printed matter, the spoken word, in the form of sermons, debates, orations, and reading aloud, was the most prevalent genre of group amusement. From earliest Colonial times onward, it was the oftentimes lengthy Protestant sermon that set the pattern. Indeed, the fact that the texts of tens of thousands of such sermons were printed, distributed, and read tells us something about the hold they had over the listening and reading public. In a brilliant, persuasive essay, Bercovitch (1978) has argued that a special variety of sermon, the Puritan jeremiad, one that began as an exhortation to guide the elect toward "the American city of God," gradually became a key part of the more general body of literature and thought expressing that sense of special mission that still suffuses American life. In rather debased form, the tradition survives today in the harangues of some jingoistic fundamentalist preachers. More specific is the claim that the Fourth of July oration is the successor to the earlier jeremiad (Bercovitch, 1978:144–45).

Be that as it may, during the first century of independence, and to some extent for some years following, the July 4th speech was the oratorical centerpiece of national life. The 2,500 examples printed between 1777 and 1876 may represent only a small fraction of the number actually delivered (H. H. Martin, 1958:397). These addresses were clearly one of the major devices to promote national unity and devotion (Huff, 1974). They were saturated with hyperbole and ultranationalistic bombast (C. Larson, 1940; Nugent, 1979: 66–67); and, before long, both form and substance settled into rigid formulae (F. M. Green, 1969:133).

There were other occasions for nationalistic utterances: funeral sermons for Washington, Adams, and Jefferson; receptions for Lafayette; Washington's Birthday; the dedication of monuments or institutions; musterings of the militia; election campaigns; inaugurations; declamations in the halls of Congress (of which Daniel Webster's may be the most memorable); and the lecture circuit (for example, Edward Everett's fund-raising oration on behalf of Mount Vernon). A few individual pieces have ascended to virtually sacramental status: notably Washington's Farewell Address, Lincoln's profoundly eloquent Gettysburg Address and Second Inaugural. Oral delivery of such soul-stirring messages was not confined to overtly political events. Well before the Civil War, the lyceums that were so popular in cities large and small became "the new locus of cultic activity in mid-Victorian America" (Lynn, 1973:19–23) and offered many a silver-tongued orator the chance to extol the glories of America, among other surefire topics; and, subsequently, chautauquas served the same function.

After 1865, "the Memorial Day oration competed in emotional importance with the antebellum Fourth of July address" (Zangrando, 1974:3), but, in general, speech making had begun to lose much of its former drawing power and sorcery. Indeed throughout the world today, oratory seems to be in a general state of decline. The few American exceptions of recent times, for example, John L. Lewis, Douglas MacArthur, Everett Dirksen, Martin Luther King, Jr., or Jesse Jackson, are survivors of a bygone era or alumni of a vibrant Afro-American church culture. Presidential speech making has become relatively informal, as exemplified by Franklin Roosevelt's "fireside chats" and the performances by any incumbent at press conferences. A few formal occasions do remain. The constitutionally mandated State of the Union Message provides the excuse for an impressive ceremony when the president deigns to deliver it in person (J. F. Wilson, 1979:53–56), but such is not always the case (Fersh, 1961). However valuable the contents of these documents may be as evidence of the changing character and mood of the country, there have been few, if any, whose prose has left indelible traces on the collective consciousness of the citizenry. Much the same must be said about keynote and acceptance addresses at major political conventions and campaign oratory. And, of the twenty-two inaugurals by twentieth-century presidents, only two—Roosevelt's in 1933 and Kennedy's in 1961—still reverberate in our memory.

Like every other self-respecting nation-state, the United States has acquired its own special mottoes, a form of speech that can be regarded as the ultimate distillation of the patriotic oration.[3] Only two such phrases have attained official status or something close to it. Although "E pluribus unum," an expression whose origin is rather obscure (M. Deutsch, 1923; 1955), appears on the Great Seal of the United States (Patterson and Dougall, 1976:510–16), Congress has never designated it as the official national motto. That honor belongs to "In God We Trust" by virtue of formal legislation in 1956 (Patterson and Dougall, 1976:514–20). It is a phrase first proposed to Salmon Chase in 1861 by the Rev. M. R. Wilkinson of Ridleyville, Pa. (Ketchum, 1959:22). Just how emotionally uplifting these mottoes may be is open to dispute, but, over the years, Americans have collected quite a treasure chest of stirring catch-phrases that perform yeoman service in the nationalist cause. "Of the people, by the people, for the people"; "I regret that I have but one life"; "Ask not what your country can do for you"; "I have a dream"; "Millions for defense, but not one cent for tribute"; "All men are created equal"; and "We have nothing to fear but fear itself" are characteristic examples.

NATIONALISTIC NAMES ON THE LAND

Few practices within the realm of nationalistic performance raise more intriguing geographic and historical questions than the ways in which nationalistic names were bestowed upon all manner of objects, including people,[4] business firms,[5] commercial products, social organizations, firehouses (Zurier, 1982:40), highways, bridges, taverns (Schlereth, 1985:69), schools (Nelson, 1975:40), military and naval weaponry, and, most especially, places. In fact, it seems safe to claim that in no other nation, past or present, can we find anything like the great number and frequency of nationalistic place-names to be seen in the United States.[6] Let us consider where and when this phenomenon developed and what it may signify.

The place-names in question fall into two general categories. The first, and more obvious, group provides the main substance for the present discussion: places whose names celebrate various patriot-heroes and other national notables and the special ideological aspirations of the American republic. But we dare not ignore another important toponymic practice that is almost uniquely American: the naming of places after the personages and localities of the ancient worlds of Greece and Rome. As many scholars have noted, the widespread belief that the fledgling United States was the latter-day realization of the ideals of republican Athens and Rome (as well as being the New Israel) has had profound implications for our political, intellectual, and artistic endeavors.[7] To recognize classical names in the United States as thinly veiled nationalistic names is to come to terms with psychological reality.

In a previous study (Zelinsky, 1967) I have traced the historical geography of classical terms in the names of American political jurisdictions and post offices, and have demonstrated how a vogue that first materialized in west-central New York in the immediate post-Revolutionary period diffused vigorously over the next several decades until it was strongly imbedded throughout the Middle West, but most particularly in a region we can label "New England Extended." Not so incidentally, within this same territory—roughly the northern third of the nation east of the Mississippi—neoclassical forms of architecture were adopted enthusiastically for the homes of all social classes, not just the mansions of the well-to-do. And probably nowhere else do we find such a profusion of classical motifs in the design of public buildings, banks, shops, colleges, churches, and other edifices. (It would be interesting to find out whether any such regionalization has also existed in terms of personal names and names of business firms.) In any event, it is important to realize that eventually, though quite belatedly, the classical place-naming impulse did penetrate all sections of the country, including the South and West, and the tally of occurrences among the names of political jurisdictions for the entire United States exceeds 2,700, so that this category of names accounts for a respectable share of the totality for our political units.

In an effort to explore the implications of overtly nationalistic toponymy, I have methodically examined three readily accessible sets of data: various Census reports, from which one can derive the names of all counties and minor civil divisions as well as a number of unincorporated places; a Post Office directory published in 1908 that lists every street in the 1,280 leading municipalities of that period (U.S. Post Office Department, 1908); and a recent edition of the annually updated Rand McNally *Commercial Atlas & Marketing Guide* (1982), the single most comprehensive listing of American towns and miscellaneous settlement features. To my regret, I have not yet had the opportunity to study the names of current and discontinued post offices not identified with municipalities, or residential subdivisions and various unincorporated places not included in Census reports, or such physical features as rivers, lakes, hills, mountains, parks, and forests. But even a casual glance at a good gazetteer or a detailed map of the United States will disclose many examples of physical features bearing nationalistic names.

As indicated in the accompanying tables, I have recorded every example to be found in the first two sets of source materials, and selected examples in the third, of places named after each of the duly canonized members of the American pantheon, a roster led by Washington, Jackson, Lincoln, Jefferson, and Franklin, but also including scores of other individuals, many of whom were idolized in the past but are now seldom remembered outside the fraternity of professional historians.[8] I have also admitted a number of eminent persons whose fame and veneration were much more regional than national, for example, Jefferson Davis, Lewis Cass, or De Witt Clinton, but strictly local celebrities have been omitted. The great majority of the persons in question were native or immigrant Americans, but some alien sojourners, such as Columbus, De Kalb, Humboldt, Kościuszko, Lafayette, Penn, and Von Steuben, became in a very real sense honorary citizens and bona fide patriot-heroes. I also believe it legitimate to accept some heroic foreigners who were regarded by nineteenth-century Americans as worthy comrades-in-arms in the sacred cause of liberty: Robert Emmet, Simón Bolívar, Giuseppe Garibaldi, and Louis Kossuth. In addition, the names of such hallowed places and events as Mount Vernon, Monticello, Lexington, Concord, Bunker Hill, Tippecanoe, Buena Vista, Gettysburg, or Ashland[9] radiate such irresistibly nationalistic messages that they must not be excluded. Unquestionably, the genre of overtly nationalistic terms must also embrace a number of powerful abstractions, such as Union, Liberty, Independence, Constitution, Eagle, Providence, or Federal.

Admittedly, there are some ambiguities in, and worthy persons missing from, these tabulations. Thus there is no simple way to ascertain whether the adoption of certain exceedingly common surnames memorializes such individuals as John Paul Jones, Andrew or Lyndon Baines Johnson, Woodrow Wilson, or Captain John Smith, Joseph Smith, or other remarkable Smiths.[10] What scattered evidence I have suggests that very few eponymous places honor these illustrious individuals. Consequently, these popular surnames do not appear in my lists. Moreover, one cannot be sure, without much more local archival research and many more sound, scholarly local place-name studies than are now available, whether a given place-name refers to Abraham or General Benjamin Lincoln or to the English county, or to Andrew or Stonewall Jackson, or to which member of the Lee clan, and so on down a long trail of question marks. Certain terms are also polysemous. Thus Union may refer not only to the political concept but to the junction point for streams, highways, or railroads, or to a social organization. Another source of uncertainty is the fact that certain admissible terms, such as Eden, Excel, Hope, or Joy may pertain to either the concept or a family name.

The identity of the persons whose names are reverently embalmed in the American place-name cover is of more than passing interest. The overwhelming majority of these men (Pocahontas being the solitary token female)[11] won glory and acclaim through exploits in either the political or military realm, and frequently in both. Until the early 20th century, the attainment of the presidency—a powerfully symbolic office, of course—and, in some instances, merely the vice-presidency, was enough to guarantee toponymic immortality, however dubious the personal qualifications of the individual. Few explorers or inventors have made the grade, while scientists, scholars, and creative writers and artists are conspicuous by their near absence, unless we so classify the protean Franklin and Jefferson.

The sheer volume of nationalistic American place-names is impressive. Although only two of our fifty-one state and district names, Washington and the District of Columbia, fall into that category, unless we grant the Penn family patriot-hero status, more than 25 percent of our 3,066 county names are derived from national notables and patriotic terms. It is instructive to compare the Canadian situation with that in this country, since the two nations are so similar in so many other respects, at least superficially.[12] A mere 17, or 6.5, percent of our northern neighbor's 260 counties appear to have been named after Canadian and British notables; and indeed it is difficult to cite even one individual whom the majority of Canadians would accept as a national hero. The international disparity is even sharper when we examine the aggregate number of counties and minor civil divisions bearing patriotic and inspirational terms in their names.

The chronology of American county names, which we can specify with some assurance (Kane, 1960), is noteworthy (table 4.1). The patriot-hero syndrome appeared abruptly, in a great surge, during the first years of national independence (Stewart, 1958:198–99), then gathered even more strength, reaching a maximum during the years 1810–30, accounting for nearly half the name adoptions of that period. More than coincidentally, this is the same period many historians regard as climactic in terms of spontaneous national sentiment.[13] Then gradually, if irregularly, this mode of naming administrative entities, as documented in tables 4.2 and 4.3, lost favor, and effectively vanished after 1920. The namers of city streets seemed to have enjoyed greater freedom of choice and scope for their imaginations than did those who labeled counties and other localities; but, even so, the incidence of streets associated with inspirational terms or the names of patriot-heroes and other national notables is remarkable. The grand total of 18,089 occurrences listed in table 4.4 represents some 8.9 percent of the approximately 203,000 street names in question.

One might argue that the near disappearance of nationalistic place-naming in recent decades could be attributed to a dearth of opportunities. But such is not the case; the explanation is weak motivation. Each year provides us with any number of name decisions for urban and suburban streets, residential developments, apartment and office buildings, schools, hospitals, bridges, airports, shopping centers, and military bases. The current choices are no longer concerned predominantly with description, possession, commemoration, or other forms of celebration, but largely, insofar as one can apply a single epithet to a diversified lot, with image-mongering, with projecting comforting, commercially potent messages. There is little doubt that, in social-psychological terms, we are now living in a toponymic era quite alien to that of the first century of national existence.[14]

Another question, one for which there is no immediate answer, is the extent to which the names being considered here were the initial choices for their localities or, on the contrary, were second or later generation decisions, supplanting earlier names. In particular, given the republican fervor of earlier years, one might expect to find wholesale displacement of names derived from British royalty and nobility by more appropriate selections. It will take a great amount of laborious research to achieve quantifiable results, or to investigate the related question of how many nationalistic place-names have been supplanted by those of another genre. In the meantime, my impression is that the great majority of names alluding to British sovereignty during the Colonial era have been left intact. In any event, an examination of the counties memorializing the more prominent of our patriot-heroes reveals the fact that few have carried any earlier designation. Thus, out of 31 counties currently named after George Washington, only 5 have undergone renaming (one, interestingly enough, was previously called Jefferson). Only 2 of our 26 present-day (Thomas) Jefferson counties have experienced name changes; and the count for the 24 (Abraham and Benjamin) Lincolns, 23 (Benjamin) Franklins, and 21 (Andrew) Jacksons is 1, zero, and 1, respectively (Kane, 1960).

When the locations of six of the most popular nationalistic names are plotted on maps, we are confronted by a set of surprises and provocative, possibly profound, questions concerning the regionalization of the American psyche. The simplest map to describe

Table 4.1. Sources of County Names in the United States, by Category, 1634–1949

Dates	British Notables	British Places	National Notables	Abstract Virtues	Foreign Notables[a]	Other N.A. Places	Exotic Places[a]	Aboriginal Terms	Local Landmarks & Attributes	Local Personages	Religious Terms	Misc.	Total
1634–1699	37 45.7%	31 38.3%	—	1 1.2%	—	—	2 2.5%	7 8.6%	2 2.5%		1 1.2%	—	81 100.0%
1700–1749	39 81.2%	5 10.4%	—	—	—	—	1 2.1%	—	1 2.1%	1 2.1%	1 2.1%	—	48 100.0%
1750–1774	30 63.8%	10 21.3%	1 2.1%	—	—	—	—	2 4.3%	—	3 6.4%	—	1 2.1%	47 100.0%
1775–1789	22 18.0%	6 4.9%	36 29.5%	2 1.6%	3 2.5%	1 0.8%	3 2.5%	7 5.7%	7 5.7%	34 27.9%	—	1 0.8%	122 100.0%
1790–1799	2 1.8%	5 4.5%	42 37.5%	1 0.9%	—	—	1 0.9%	10 8.9%	3 2.7%	48 42.9%	—	—	112 100.0%
1800–1809	—	3 1.9%	45 28.7%	2 1.3%	1 0.7%	—	4 2.5%	24 15.3%	17 10.8%	51 32.5%	8 5.1%	2 1.3%	157 100.0%
1810–1819	—	1 0.5%	83 45.6%	2 1.1%	1 0.5%	1 0.5%	4 2.2%	12 6.6%	5 2.7%	66 36.3%	6 3.3%	1 0.5%	182 100.0%
1820–1829	—	—	116 45.5%	5 2.0%	1 0.4%	—	4 1.6%	23 9.0%	9 3.5%	89 34.9%	3 1.2%	5 2.0%	255 100.0%
1830–1839	1 0.3%	—	116 36.7%	3 0.9%	10 3.2%	6 1.9%	1 0.3%	45 14.2%	21 6.6%	107 33.9%	4 1.3%	2 0.6%	316 100.0%

Period													Total
1840–1849	—	5 1.7%	71 24.4%	1 0.3%	8 2.7%	3 1.0%	—	45 15.5%	25 8.6%	118 40.5%	2 0.7%	13 4.5%	291 100.0%
1850–1859	—	1 0.2%	84 17.9%	3 0.6%	18 3.8%	—	3 0.6%	67 14.3%	55 11.7%	205 43.7%	16 3.4%	17 3.6%	469 100.0%
1860–1869	—	—	47 21.6%	2 0.9%	2 0.9%	4 1.8%	2 0.9%	31 14.2%	29 13.3%	91 41.7%	2 0.9%	8 3.7%	218 100.0%
1870–1879	1 0.4%	—	52 18.6%	1 0.4%	—	5 1.8%	1 0.4%	12 4.3%	23 8.2%	178 63.6%	4 1.4%	3 1.1%	280 100.0%
1880–1889	—	—	28 17.4%	—	2 1.2%	—	—	13 8.1%	24 14.9%	90 55.9%	2 1.2%	2 1.2%	161 100.0%
1890–1899	1 1.9%	—	5 9.6%	1 1.9%	1 1.9%	2 3.8%	—	9 17.3%	17 32.7%	14 26.9%	1 1.9%	1 1.9%	52 100.0%
1900–1909	—	—	27 20.6%	—	2 1.5%	2 1.5%	1 0.8%	23 17.6%	11 8.4%	63 48.1%	1 0.8%	1 0.8%	131 100.0%
1910–1919	—	—	18 15.9%	—	1 0.9%	3 2.7%	1 0.9%	11 9.7%	26 23.0%	51 45.1%	—	2 1.8%	113 100.0%
1920–1949	—	—	1 3.2%	2 6.5%	—	—	—	4 12.9%	10 32.3%	14 45.2%	—	1 3.2%	31 100.0%
Total	133 4.3%	67 2.2%	772 25.2%	26 0.8%	50 1.6%	27 0.9%	28 0.9%	345 11.3%	285 9.3%	1222 39.9%	51 1.7%	60 2.0%	3066 100.0%

[a]Other than British and North American.

Source: Zelinsky, 1983:20–21.

Table 4.2. *Number of Counties and Minor Civil Divisions Presumably Named after Selected National Heroes and Notables*

WASHINGTON (George)	301	FULTON (Robert)	24
JACKSON (Andrew & Thomas)	250	RANDOLPH (John)	23
LINCOLN (Abraham & Benjamin)	190	JASPER (William)	21
JEFFERSON (Thomas)	179	DECATUR (Stephen)	19
FRANKLIN (Benjamin)	159	KNOX (Henry)	19
GRANT (Ulysses)	150	HAYES (Rutherford B.)	18
MADISON (James)	111	CRAWFORD (William Harris)	17
HARRISON (Wm. H. & Benjamin)	104	DALLAS (George M.)	17
MONROE (James)	99	PULASKI (Casimir)	17
MARION (Francis)	91	SHELBY (Isaac)	17
CLAY (Henry)	80	HENRY (Patrick)	16
WAYNE (Anthony)	79	DAVIS (Jefferson)	15
PERRY (Oliver H.)	73	HANCOCK (John)	15
LAFAYETTE (Marquis de)	68	ROOSEVELT (Theodore)	15
COLUMBUS (Christopher)	67	MERCER (Hugh)	14
SHERMAN (William T.)	63	PIERCE (Franklin)	13
CLINTON (DeWitt)	62	HUMBOLDT (Alexander)	12
GREENE (Nathanael)	62	MCKINLEY (William)	12
BENTON (Thomas Hart)	60	ST. CLAIR (Arthur)	12
SCOTT (Winfield)	59	CALHOUN (John C.)	11
SHERIDAN (Philip H.)	59	CUSTER (George A.)	11
WARREN (Joseph)	59	STANTON (Edward M.)	11
ADAMS (John & John Quincy)	57	SULLIVAN (John)	11
GARFIELD (James)	55	DE SOTO (Hernando)	10
CLEVELAND (Grover)	48	HOUSTON (Sam)	10
HAMILTON (Alexander)	45	BUCHANAN (James)	9
CLARK (George Rogers & Wm.)	44	DE KALB (Johann)	9
TAYLOR (Zachary)	43	DEWEY (George)	9
CARROLL (Charles)	40	FILLMORE (Millard)	9
DOUGLAS (Stephen A.)	40	VON STEUBEN (Friedrich)	9
LEWIS (Meriwether)	35	ARTHUR (Chester)	8
POLK (James K.)	35	CARSON (Kit)	8
NEWTON (John)	34	MACON (Nathaniel)	8
PENN (William)	33	TYLER (John)	8
MONTGOMERY (Richard)	32	GREELEY (Horace)	7
WEBSTER (Daniel)	32	JAY (John)	6
FREMONT (John C.)	31	SEWARD (William H.)	5
VAN BUREN (Martin)	31	TAFT (William Howard)	5
BOONE (Daniel)	30	AUDUBON (John J.)	4
MORGAN (Daniel)	30	COOLIDGE (Calvin)	4
LEE (R. E. & R. H.)	29	CROCKETT (Davy)	4
CASS (Lewis)	28	GALLATIN (Albert)	4
LAWRENCE (James)	28	PUTNAM (Israel)	4
MARSHALL (John)	28	PERSHING (John)	3
PIKE (Zebulon)	25	KOŚCIUSZKO (Tadeusz)	2

Table 4.2 continued

LA SALLE (Robert de)	2	SUMTER (Thomas)	2
POCAHONTAS	2		
SEVIER (John)	2	TOTAL	3,771
		(10.8% of all MCDs)	

Source: Zelinsky, 1983:14–15.

and, possibly, explain is that of the occurrence of Franklin—in nearly every instance, obviously, Benjamin Franklin—in the names of counties and minor civil divisions (Wecter, 1941:78–79) (figure 4.1). As might have been expected, the usage has been particularly fashionable in Pennsylvania and New Jersey, that is, the zone in which our eponym was most active or best known. The map pattern leads one to surmise the diffusion of the name westward into much of the Middle West, either in the form of a free-floating idea or as part of the mental baggage of migrants from the source area. One might also attribute the scarcity of Franklins in the South, West, and Northeast to the friction of distance and time. If such an interpretation is valid, what we have in this case is simply another classic example of an innovation emanating from the Midland culture hearth. At this point I am obliged to insert a technical footnote, namely, that in some Southern states a large percentage of minor civil divisions (MCDs) have received numbers rather than proper names. On the other hand, such lacunae in the verbal place-name cover also occur in some non-Southern states, though not as frequently; but, in any case, this practice is not so extensive as to account for any of the basic patterns displayed on our maps.

The configuration of symbols on the Lincoln map is another one that might have been predicted (Karsten, 1978:98–100) (figure 4.2). The thickest clustering is to be found in those tracts of the North Central states settled and organized from the 1860s through the 1890s when the full force of the Lincoln apotheosis was being felt. Understandably, places named after Abraham Lincoln in the post-bellum period are rare in the South as well as in those parts of the Northeast that were well peopled before 1860.

A large, perhaps disproportionate, share of early American patriot-heroes were Southerners. Their ranks include Washington, Jefferson, Madison, Monroe, Richard Henry Lee, Andrew Jackson, Francis Marion, Henry Clay, Nathanael Greene, Daniel Boone, Patrick Henry, and John Marshall among many others, so that one

Table 4.3. *Number of Names of Counties and Minor Civil Divisions Containing Selected Patriotic and Inspirational Terms*

UNION	324	ALAMO	2
LIBERTY	182	ASHLAND	2
CONCORD	46	BUNKER HILL	2
EDEN	42	EQUALITY	2
INDEPENDENCE	39	FORWARD	2
HOPE	39	IDEAL	2
FREEDOM	29	KOSSUTH (Louis)	2
HARMONY	24	LAGRANGE	2
MOUNT VERNON	23	LIBERAL	2
LEXINGTON	21	WALHALLA	2
PROVIDENCE	18	BENEVOLENCE	1
ENTERPRISE	17	BOUNTIFUL	1
PARADISE	15	CONGRESS	1
MONTICELLO	14	CONSTITUTION	1
ELDORADO	13	DEMOCRAT	1
UNITY	13	DUTY	1
EMMET (Robert)	12	ENDEAVOR	1
AMITY	10	EXCEL	1
REPUBLIC(AN)	9	FELICITY	1
AMERICA(N)	8	FRIENDSHIP	1
BOLIVAR (Simon)	8	HUSTLER	1
FRIENDSHIP	8	LOYAL	1
MONTPELIER	6	OPPORTUNITY	1
EXCELSIOR	5	PATRIOT	1
VICTORY	5	PRESIDENT	1
HAPPY	4	RELIANCE	1
JOY	4	SUBLIMITY	1
TIPPECANOE	4	TEMPERANCE	1
PROGRESS(IVE)	3	TRIUMPH	1
PROSPER(ITY)	3		
GETTYSBURG	3	TOTAL	1,011
INDUSTRY	3		

Source: Zelinsky, 1983:14–16.

would feel justified in anticipating a liberal sprinkling of Southern places honoring their memory. But, strangely enough, the actuality defies any such expectation. The maps depicting the location of places named after Washington,[15] Jefferson,[16] and Jackson (figures 4.3, 4.4, and 4.5) tend to resemble each other in their remarkable concentrations of occurrences in Pennsylvania, Ohio, Indiana, and the western reaches of the Middle West,[17] but with severe dearths in the South and West, with the interesting exception of the state of Arkansas, and a relatively weak showing in New England. It is startling, for example, to find no Jacksons at all in South Carolina, one

Table 4.4. *Incidence of Selected National Notables and Inspirational Terms in Street Names of 1,280 Principal United States Cities, 1908*

WASHINGTON (George)	1,036	VAN BUREN (Martin)	128
LINCOLN (Abraham & Benjamin)	713	PIERCE (Franklin)	127
FRANKLIN (Benjamin)	645	CARROLL (Charles)	119
UNION	603	FREMONT (John C.)	117
JEFFERSON (Thomas)	557	RANDOLPH (John)	117
MADISON (James)	525	WAYNE (Anthony)	117
JACKSON (Andrew & Thomas)	524	PENN (William)	116
HARRISON (Wm. H. & Benjamin)	453	CONCORD (IA)	115
GRANT (Ulysses)	439	ASHLAND	103
ADAMS (John & John Quincy)	415	BLAINE (James)	100
CLINTON (DeWitt)	358	CRAWFORD (William Harris)	95
LAFAYETTE & FAYETTE (Marquis de)	328	BENTON (Thomas Hart)	93
LIBERTY	321	PUTNAM (Israel)	92
CLARK (George Rogers & William)	314	HAYES (Rutherford B.)	90
CLEVELAND (Grover)	291	FEDERAL	85
GARFIELD (James)	286	JAY (John)	85
COLUMBIA	283	POLK (James K.)	85
MONROE (James)	277	EAGLE	83
HAMILTON (Alexander)	265	TYLER (John)	81
SHERMAN (William T.)	262	CALHOUN (John C.)	80
WARREN (Joseph)	257	MOUNT VERNON	80
TAYLOR (Zachary)	254	ROOSEVELT (Theodore)	79
HENRY (Patrick)	244	BUCHANAN (James)	75
FULTON (Robert)	233	PIKE (Zebulon)	70
WEBSTER (Daniel & Noah)	226	HOPE	69
CLAY (Henry)	215	FILLMORE (Millard)	68
LEWIS (Meriwether)	210	STANTON (Edward M.)	68
LEE (R. E. & R. H.)	201	HOUSTON (Sam)	67
SCOTT (Winfield)	195	DECATUR (Stephen)	60
LAWRENCE (James)	192	MERCER (Hugh)	59
MARION (Francis)	183	MORSE (Samuel F. B.)	59
LOGAN (John A.)	173	CASS (Lewis)	57
SHERIDAN (Philip H.)	170	KNOX (Henry)	56
MARSHALL (John)	168	SULLIVAN (John)	53
PERRY (Oliver H.)	162	BUENA VISTA	51
DEWEY (George)	158	HUMBOLDT (Alexander)	49
HANCOCK (John)	154	LA SALLE (Robert de)	48
MONTGOMERY (Richard)	153	HALE (Nathan)	46
MORGAN (Daniel)	150	WHITTIER (John G.)	43
MCKINLEY (William)	140	CUSTER (George A.)	42
ARTHUR (Chester)	138	GREENE (Nathanael)	41
DOUGLAS (Stephen A.)	134	SEWARD (William H.)	41
COLUMBUS (Christopher)	130	INDEPENDENT (CE)	40
CONGRESS	128	BOONE (Daniel)	38
LEXINGTON	128	EDEN	38
		SHELBY (Isaac)	38
		CARSON (Kit)	37

Table 4.4 continued

JASPER (William)	37	BOLÍVAR (Simón)	14
EDISON (Thomas A.)	36	MONTICELLO	14
EUREKA	36	POCAHONTAS	11
VON STEUBEN (Friedrich)	35	CONSTITUTION	9
MEADE (George)	34	FREE	9
AMITY	33	REPUBLIC(AN)	9
FARRAGUT (David G.)	33	BEST	7
PROVIDENCE	33	HAPPY	7
PULASKI (Casimir)	33	LUCKY	7
NATIONAL	32	PROGRESS	7
DALLAS (George M.)	30	VICTORY	7
GREELEY (Horace)	30	ELYSIAN	6
MCCLELLAN (George B.)	30	FORTUNE	6
VICTOR	30	TIPPECANOE	6
HARMONY	29	ALAMO	5
PHOENIX	28	EAGER	5
KOSSUTH (Louis)	26	JUSTICE	5
DE KALB (Johann)	25	ACME	4
LONGFELLOW (Henry W.)	25	ANTIETAM	4
PRESIDENT	23	CHOICE	4
AUDUBON (John J.)	22	JEFF DAVIS	4
REVERE (Paul)	22	PROSPER	4
AMERICA(N)	21	FAITH	3
PARADISE	21	GARIBALDI (Giuseppe)	3
PIONEER	21	GETTYSBURG	3
ENTERPRISE	20	ALERT	2
FRIENDSHIP	20	BETTER	2
JOY	20	BRILLIANT	2
LAGRANGE	20	CERRO GORDO	2
TECUMSEH	20	FORWARD	2
CROCKETT (Davy)	19	IDEAL	2
BENEFIT	18	MODERN	2
GALLATIN (Albert)	18	CONFIDENCE	1
MACON (Nathaniel)	18	EQUALITY	1
POE (Edgar Allan)	18	FELICITY	1
UNITY	18	FLAG	1
KOŚCIUSZKO (Tadeusz)	17	FRATERNAL	1
STONEWALL (Jackson)	17	FREIHEIT	1
DE SOTO (Hernando)	16	MONTPELIER	1
ELDORADO	15		
FREEDOM	15	TOTAL	18,089

Source: Zelinsky, 1983:16–18.

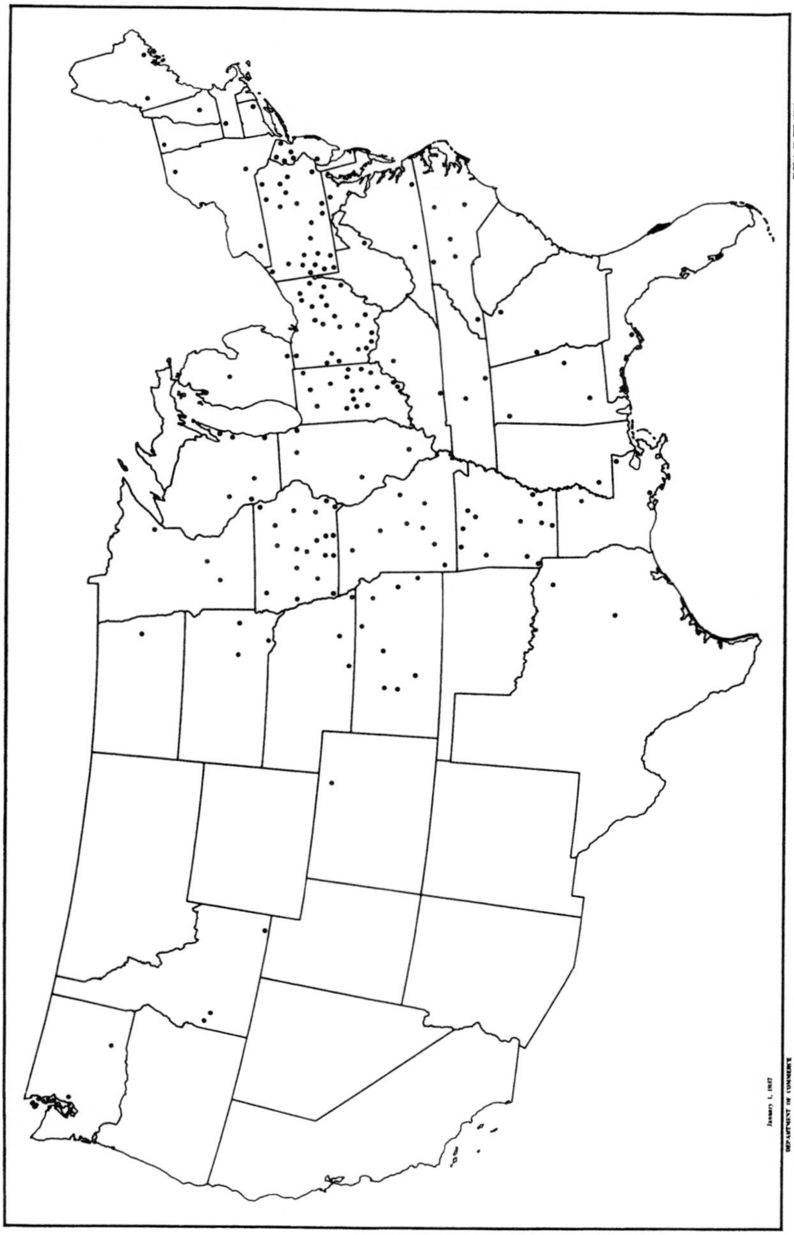

Figure 4.1. *Franklin in Names of Counties and Minor Civil Divisions*

Source: Zelinsky, 1983:24.

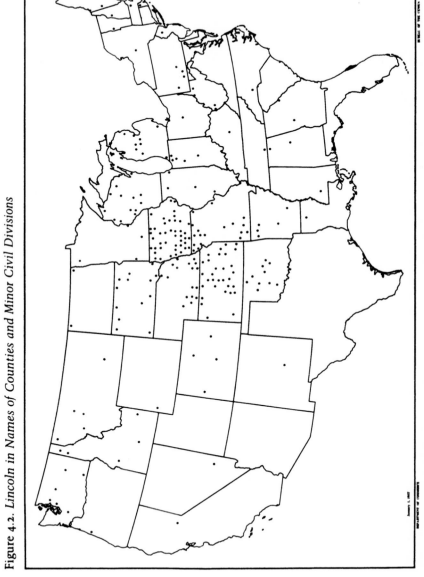

Figure 4.2. *Lincoln in Names of Counties and Minor Civil Divisions*

Source: Zelinsky, 1983:28.

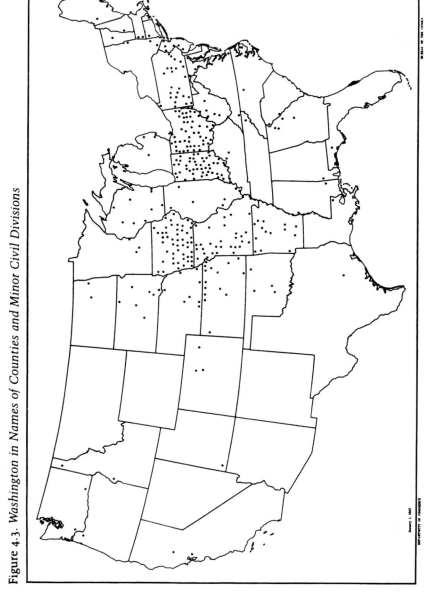

Figure 4.3. *Washington in Names of Counties and Minor Civil Divisions*

Source: Zelinsky, 1983:25.

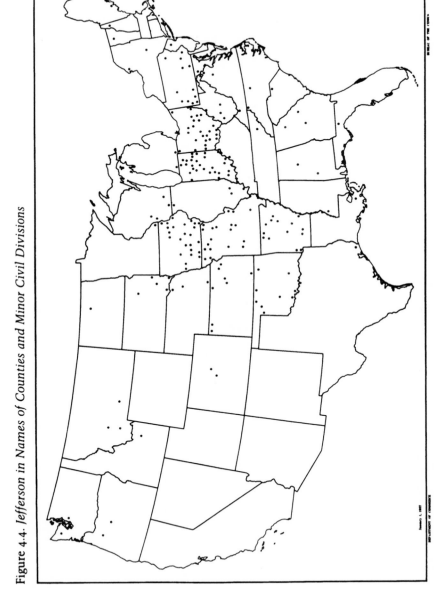

Figure 4.4. *Jefferson in Names of Counties and Minor Civil Divisions*

Source: Zelinsky, 1983:23.

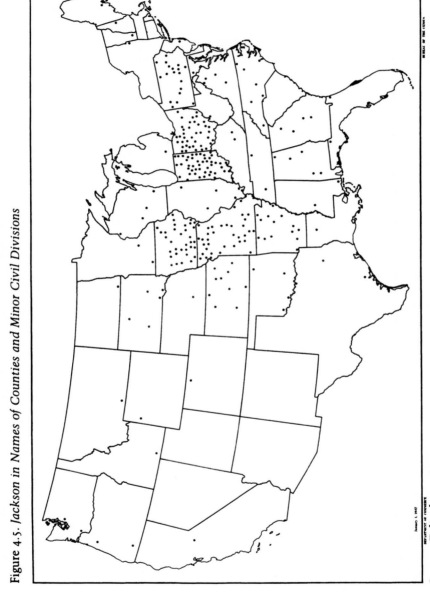

Figure 4.5. *Jackson in Names of Counties and Minor Civil Divisions*

Source: Zelinsky, 1983:27.

of the two states claiming our seventh president as its native son. In a possible bit of historical irony, the South partially redeems itself by having bestowed the term Union on a fair number of places, presumably during the antebellum era (figure 4.6); but even here the general distribution pattern closely resembles that in the preceding maps. An intriguing novelty is the strong showing of the term Union in West Virginia. Can this be the result of the traumatic decision in 1863 to secede from Virginia and adhere to the Federal Union?

A final, summary map (figure 4.7) attempts to display the relative popularity of overtly nationalistic place-names throughout the United States by indicating the total number of all such items within the ten counties closest to each county. The rationale of the procedure, a kind of spatial averaging, is that it eliminates much of the "noise" in the phenomenon, including whatever randomness may occur in local patterns, and reduces the deceptive visual impact of counties that vary so greatly in size and shape.

Whatever its virtues, figure 4.7 fails to tell us anything definite about the relative strength of nationalistic items within the totality of place-names because the aggregate number of place-names varies from one locality to another. Table 4.5 remedies that deficiency to some extent. The percentile values presented therein express the frequency of a dozen leading nationalistic terms within the names of the estimated aggregate number of political entities and agglomerated settlements in each state as of 1982. One may assume similar results were we to tabulate the entire range of nationalistic terms. The two summations of data (figure 4.7; table 4.5) confirm and fortify some of the inferences drawn from the other maps and permit us to make others:

(1) This particular mode of place-naming has been especially important in the east-central portion of the United States, and, with one notable exception, this area coincides nicely with the territory identified in other studies as being culturally and demographically tributary to the early Midland Culture Hearth of Pennsylvania and the Delaware Valley. Although we cannot be certain without creating a series of maps documenting the date at which the MCDs were named, the map strongly hints at a Pennsylvania origin, then westward diffusion over an ever-widening arc. Further support for this notion comes from the modest, but noticeable, cluster of nationalistic items in central North Carolina, an area colonized by significant numbers of migrants from early Pennsylvania and Maryland.

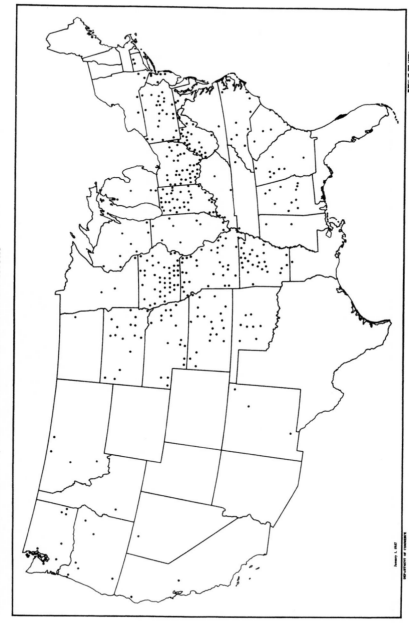

Figure 4.6. *Union in Names of Counties and Minor Civil Divisions*

Source: Zelinsky, 1983:26.

Figure 4.7. *National Notables and Inspirational Terms in Names of Political Jurisdictions*

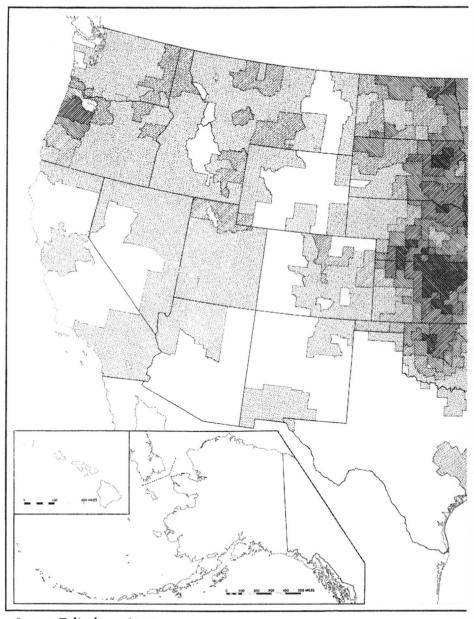

Source: **Zelinsky,** 1983:22.

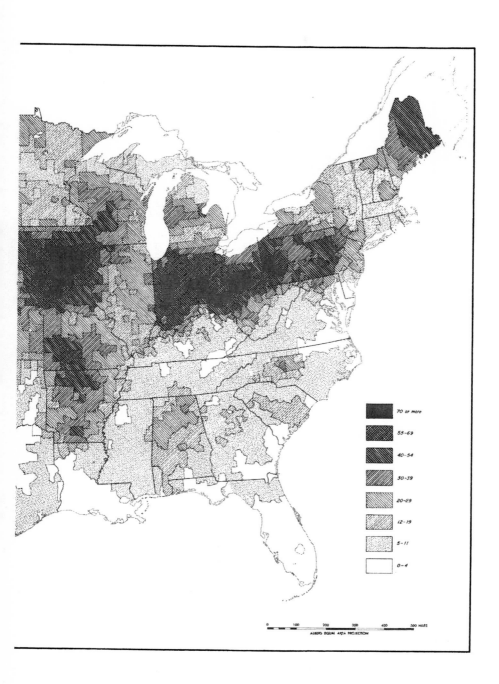

Table 4.5. *Incidence of Selected Nationalistic Terms in Names of United States Cities, Towns, Counties, and Townships, by State*

State	Number	%	State	Number	%
Iowa	326	8.5	New Hampshire	17	1.3
Indiana	335	7.3	South Carolina	29	1.2
Missouri	217	5.8	Utah	13	1.2
Nebraska	92	5.3	Colorado	22	1.1
Ohio	345	4.7	Connecticut	19	1.1
Kansas	158	4.5	Delaware	8	1.1
South Dakota	71	3.2	Nevada	6	1.1
Arkansas	117	3.0	New York	91	1.1
Oklahoma	62	3.0	Florida	36	1.0
Alabama	85	2.2	Kentucky	48	1.0
West Virginia	84	2.2	Minnesota	36	1.0
Idaho	27	2.1	Louisiana	27	0.9
New Jersey	68	2.1	Massachusetts	27	0.9
Wisconsin	92	2.1	North Dakota	12	0.9
Pennsylvania	241	2.0	Washington	23	0.9
Oregon	39	1.9	Texas	57	0.8
Rhode Island	12	1.8	Vermont	12	0.8
Tennessee	71	1.8	Mississippi	29	0.7
Montana	25	1.7	California	33	0.6
North Carolina	76	1.7	Arizona	7	0.5
Georgia	59	1.6	Wyoming	3	0.4
Michigan	72	1.5	New Mexico	4	0.3
Maine	36	1.4	Hawaii	1	0.1
Maryland	44	1.4	Alaska	0	0.0
Virginia	69	1.4			
Illinois	92	1.3	UNITED STATES	3,475	2.1

Note: Selected nationalistic terms are: Adams, Franklin, Grant, Harrison, Jackson, Jefferson, Liberty, Lincoln, Madison, Monroe, Union, and Washington.

Source: Zelinsky, 1983:19.

(2) It is doubtful whether we can explain the scarcity of nationalistic place-names in New England Extended, especially in New York State, and in most of the South, excepting the Ozark Region, in terms of the diffusion process. The disparities in levels of frequency between those in the Pennsylvania-Midwest concentration and those in the Northeast and South are simply too great.

(3) The map patterns reflect the fact that nationalistic place-naming was time-specific, that is, that it was largely concentrated within the first several decades of national independence. Consequently, place-names of this type are rare or nonexistent in areas

that have been recently settled or developed, such as southern Florida and many parts of the West.

(4) We lack immediate explanations for the fading away of nationalistic place-name decisions and the later advent of different types of names for towns, suburbs, and other places. Until more facts are available, we might speculate that changing fashions in names signify important shifts in value systems and the ways in which we perceive our nation and the world.

We are left with three mysteries concerning the relative distribution of nationalistic place-names in the U.S., and clear answers for none. The first is so obvious that I have had difficulty not mentioning it up to this point: that strange hiatus in the State of Illinois (figure 4.7; table 4.3). (But, interestingly, I have found no such Illinoisan deficiency in the incidence of nationalistic terms in cemetery names in the course of some current, as yet unpublished, research.) If there is any validity in the contention that the popularity of nationalistic place-naming worked its way westward from Pennsylvania across the Middle West, then that sharp dropoff between the clusters in Indiana and the equally dense concentrations in Iowa and Missouri makes little sense in historical-geographic terms. Whatever the explanation may be, it is clearly intrinsic to the state itself, since the incidence of nationalistic place-naming continues at a high level in Indiana, Iowa, and Missouri right up to their boundaries with Illinois. The most authoritative compilation of data on Illinois toponymy offers us no clues (Adams, 1969), and it would be foolish indeed to attribute the anomalous situation to any deficiency in national sentiment on the part of the state's residents. The only plausible alternative is some peculiarity in the laws or regulations governing place-naming within the state.[18]

There may be larger implications in the reluctance of New York and much of the territory historically associated with it to participate vigorously in the toponymic developments immediately to the south. What we are witnessing may be two closely related versions of the same cultural phenomenon, that is, the celebration of American national virtues through the medium of place-names, occurring at precisely the same time and being directed in parallel spatial channels, one neoclassical in character, the other overtly nationalistic, but with rather little transference of behavior from one source area, or its nearby hinterland, to the other. Is it conceivable that one variant of nationalistic toponymy simply excludes the other, that only so much "psychic space" is available for either one or the

other? One way of pursuing an answer would be to analyze the
relative frequency in nineteenth-century Pennsylvania and New
York of two types of names conferred on infant lads: such fore-
names as Franklin, Jefferson, Washington, and Andrew Jackson as
compared with the likes of Ulysses, Junius, Marcus, Adrian, Cornelius, or Horatio.

But the most intriguing problem is the poor showing of overtly
nationalistic place-names in the South, excepting, once again, the
marginal Ozarks. Evidence that cultural or psychological factors
may underlie Southern standoffishness may be read from intrastate
patterns within Missouri. Although the state as a whole ranks high
in total number of occurrences, nationalistic place-names are few
and far between in the lower Missouri Valley and the Bootheel, precisely those areas most deeply affected by Southern culture in antebellum times. Similarly, we may read some significance into the
observation that Southerners did adopt classical place-names with
some frequency, though quite belatedly, and that such items are
less transparently nationalistic in character than the names of patriot-heroes.

What are we to make of this form of Southern deviance? It is
essential to note that the naming decisions covered in this study
were predominantly local in character. Some, notably the county
names, originated or were ratified at the state level; most of the
others were arrived at by the officials or ordinary citizens of counties, townships, municipalities, and other small entities, sometimes
quite informally. Thus it is not too farfetched to assume that, during the first eighty years or so of the Republic, the process of place-
naming was an unobtrusive measure of political attitudes, perhaps
even a subtle kind of "loyalty test." Thus, if this supposition has
any merit, the citizens of, say, New York, Pennsylvania, Indiana,
and Iowa were subconsciously voting their confidence in the Union,
its founders and leaders, and the principles they proclaimed through
their selections of place-names, while the good people of such
states as Virginia, South Carolina, and Mississippi were expressing
through the same mechanism certain hidden feelings and reservations.[19] Such an interpretation does not, of course, preclude the
possibility that, after the Reconstruction period, the South began to
be as nationalistic as the non-South, if not more so, in keeping with
what seems to be our general subjective consensus about the South
nowadays. Although it is easy and tempting to equate nationalism
with militarism, as is often done in the case of the American South,
the two phenomena are far from identical. The evidence that the

South has traditionally harbored a strong militaristic strain in its ethos is more convincing than the argument that Southerners are mainstream, American-style nationalists. I am quite prepared to admit that this excursion into the regional geography of the American political mind may have been misdirected, but only after we have gathered and sifted evidence from other unobtrusive measures of attitudes that could confirm or falsify these speculations.

I have left to last what may be the most fundamental question one can pose about the purposeful naming of things: What psychological impact, if any, do message-bearing names have upon their users? The effects may be considerable for certain types of commercial enterprises and products and perhaps a few other categories of objects. However, when we consider the names of places, there are no clear-cut answers. It is quite possible that the current romantic vogue in the naming of streets, subdivisions, and other localities is serving its purpose, especially since the seductive words so exploited remain in more or less daily use. But I suspect that place-names derived from dead or dormant heroes, events, and ideals become lexically opaque in short order and that few of us are any longer aware even subliminally of their import (Nicolaisen, 1976). Among many possible examples, consider Madison Avenue, Madison Square Garden, and Madison, Wisconsin. Each of these names casts its special semantic spell, but would any of us immediately think of James Madison on hearing them?[20] Or—to carry the argument to its bitter end—even if we did make the connection, how many of us would appreciate Madison's ideological significance?

The conclusion I must draw is that our numerous nationalistic place-names are durable, but archaeological, features of the American scene. They remain as sensitive, half-mute testimony to the ways in which a powerful tide of nationalistic euphoria surged over the land in our earlier years rather than as part of the living language. They are also effects rather than causes. One would be hard put to argue that such names were essential building blocks in the construction of our novel nation-state, but they do serve admirably as clues to a remarkable mind-set. Thus, tracing patterns of frequency in nationalistic place-names over time and space raises original questions and poses new answers to older questions concerning some of the most fundamental problems in American geography and history.

THE HISTORIANS AND TEACHERS SPEAK

Toponymy is only one of several verbal channels through which nationalism seeks expression. Perhaps the words of teachers and historians are the most crucial. Among the truisms that are so self-evident they scarcely need noting is the fact that no nation or nation-state can long endure without its historiography—its common pool of memories, a consensus on the nature of its past as it may have been, or should have been. Such a memory bank may take varied shapes, among them: oral legend and folklore; song, fiction, and drama; monuments; and museums. But, in modern times, formal, written histories with some pretense of objectivity for consumption by both literate children and adults are deemed absolute necessities.

The young United States of America found itself in a problematic situation when it came to creating a usable body of historical literature, as did the interested foreign scholar. At the time of the Revolution, the only respectable historical narratives to be found in the few bookshops and college and private libraries dealt with British and West European topics or the world of ancient Greece and Rome. A few provincial chronicles had begun to appear, usually the output of part-time scholars, but they were limited to individual colonies and were far from definitive.[21]

The absence of an institutional base was inhibiting. No federal, state, or local archives had yet materialized, relevant documents were widely scattered in Europe and America, and many were missing or destroyed. Although some local and state historical societies appeared in the early nineteenth century, mainly in the Northeast (Whitehill, 1962), and subsequently initiated publications, American historiography did not become fully institutionalized until the 1880s with the creation of university chairs and departments and a nationwide professional association with erudite journals and annual conventions (Shafer, 1972:203). Indeed, it was only at the remarkably late date of 1934 that the United States finally established its National Archives, long after similar steps by Western European governments (H. G. Jones, 1969; McCoy, 1978; Shafer, 1972:201). Such tardiness and the political bickering preceding and following the inception of this institution may tell us something about underlying American attitudes toward history.

On a more positive note, during the early decades of independence, America was home for a remarkably lively intelligentsia, a set of would-be historians immensely energized by the Revolution.

They, and humanity at large, were keenly aware of how world-shaking an event they had witnessed. They had been participants or observers, or could still converse with the Founders and Framers, so that it was still a breathing reality whose meaning and purpose they were determined to express. Most of all, they were impelled by a burning sense of mission. Theirs were not the mundane chores of journalist or scribe, but rather the lofty office of creators.[22] It was their charge to discover or create, then interpret a usable past (T. A. Bailey, 1968; Boorstin, 1965:362–73; Fisher, 1912; Friedman, 1975: 18–30; Nye, 1960:42–43; Plumb, 1970:89–90; Schlereth, 1980:209; Shaffer, 1975; W. R. Smith, 1966; Stephens, 1916; Van Tassel, 1960: 31–46; Zenderland, 1978:vii–xvi). "American historians worked from the assumption that the United States could only be welded into a nation by the articulation of a cohesive national heritage" (Shaffer, 1975:28). And it was a particular novel species of nation they sought to fashion, fulfilling a charge articulated by Jerald Brauer. "The historian . . . 'is our most important secular theologian,' responsible for describing and defending the covenant that makes us a people, being always ready both to 'explain how this country has achieved its uniqueness' and to warn against the intrusion of alien influences" (Brauer, 1976:46).

But, like historians in other emergent modern nations, the task of the American chroniclers was complicated by the centrifugal tug of localisms. "Bringing to their work a sense of common enterprise, they self-consciously set out to form the entire American past into a pattern that contradicted the reality of American life. Local loyalties and internal dissensions were persistent facts, but national unity became the interpretive credo" (Shaffer, 1975:2). In this endeavor they were greatly abetted by the belief, one that had already begun to sink deep roots into the American psyche, of the providential role of the United States in world history, that, in the rather ironic phraseology of J. H. Plumb, "America was cleaner, purer, less corrupt and more in the way of God and godliness than the evil world which had been left behind in Europe. Indeed, America was to be the tribunal before which all history was to be judged" (Plumb, 1970:89). Thus Clinton Rossiter did not find it surprising that "the invocations of a heroic past and visions of a glorious future [were] indulged in by men as different in style as David Ramsay, Jedidiah Morse, Parson Weems, Jared Sparks, John Quincy Adams, William Holmes McGuffey, Rembrandt Peale, John Trumbull, Daniel Webster, John Marshall, and, pre-eminently among historians who felt the hand of God laid upon America, George Bancroft

kept the apparatus working at full blast" (Rossiter, 1971:124–25).
Interestingly enough, the push for a unified historical vision came
chiefly from the writers and thinkers of New England, along with
the bulk of learned effusions of all sorts and many of the other
more influential notions in the formative period of nation-building
(Plumb, 1970:90–91).[23]

In terms of immediate tactics, two approaches seemed especially
effective: the biographical and the broad continental perspective.
Filio-pietistic accounts of early heroes reached a public panting
with eagerness as Daniel Boorstin and others have noted (T. P.
Greene, 1970:38–39; Van Tassel, 1960:66–76). "Long before there
was any substantial literature specifically recounting the national
history, there were American biographies of every shape, size, and
description. Biographers rushed in to fill the vacuum of national
history" (Boorstin, 1965:366).

The authors generally used eulogy and fictionalized anecdote to
fashion legendary figures. "The existence of living memories and
corroborative documents . . . might have proved embarrassing for
the creators of a national hagiology had it not been for the sense
. . . of the great mission of America" (Van Tassel, 1960:66–67). The
supreme exhibit within the genre was, of course, the imaginative
life of Washington by the ineffable Mason Locke Weems, who also
composed accounts of Benjamin Franklin and Francis Marion. In its
many successive incarnations, the volume was an enormous best
seller, far surpassing in sales the more sober, scholarly efforts of
the likes of John Marshall, Jared Sparks, or Washington Irving; and
it has fixed the image of Washington in our collective consciousness too solidly for it ever to be revised by the plodding efforts of
mere scientific historians (Forgie, 1979:36–49). Quite apart from its
achievement in national myth making, Weems's *Life of Washington*
is also a landmark publication by virtue of being perhaps the earliest successful example of the mass marketing of popular literature,
that avalanche of low- and middle-brow printed matter that was
soon to dominate the reading habits of the Western world.

Although George Washington was the most surefire of subjects
for the biographer, he was only one of many, for it was the rare
statesman or military hero among the first generation of free Americans who escaped literary enshrinement. And, of course, the industry is still very much alive. There are probably more full-length
biographies and studies of Abraham Lincoln than of any other historical figure, with the possible exception of Napoleon, and the
bulging catalog of Lincoln titles now runs to the many thousands.

Since the days of Grant, it is assumed that ex-presidents and other political and military notables will not only arrange for the publication of their papers but, in the line of duty and possible profit, will also authorize biographies or write their own reminiscences. The appetite for biographies of national figures remains insatiable, and, despite the existence since the 1920s of a lively debunking tradition, the bulk of this literature remains celebratory, and its net effect is to advance the interests of the nation or the state.

Following another track, several early nineteenth-century writers sought to chronicle the full span of American history over time and space, but with only middling luck at best. It was the long-lived George Bancroft, equipped as he was with the needed technical skills, literary talent, and sheer stamina, who finally scored a critical and commercial knockout with his ten-volume epic begun in 1834 (Boorstin, 1965;369–73; Kraus, 1953:115–27). Since then, we have had any number of encyclopedic treatments of American history for popular and pedagogical consumption, more often than not the product of multiple authorship. In general, their tenor has been chauvinistic and uncritical, the persistent leitmotif being American exceptionalism, the nation(-state)'s transcendent virtues, and the sacred destiny of the United States. Even after the critical, scientific mode of historiography began to dominate serious inquiry and writing, that is, past the turn of the century, most chronicles of the American past remained staunchly nationalistic in tone and purpose, and often displayed a streak of social darwinism (Kraus, 1953:190–241). Only recently, but well after Henry Adams and Charles Beard began to pose uncomfortable questions, have any notes of self-doubt or awareness of the darker underside of America's history crept into any considerable body of work. There is little doubt that, in sum, the historians of the United States have played a crucial role in framing and perpetuating the myths that are so vital to a vigorous nationalism.

Difficult though it may be to measure such things, can there be much question that the greatest impact of printed histories was registered in the schoolroom? This may be as appropriate a point as any to consider the role of public education in the evolution of American nationalism. Clearly no other institution has been so instrumental in that cause or more deserving of the extended discussion, which, fortunately, it has received (Balch, 1890; Beale, 1936:55–78, 174–207; Carlson, 1975; Elson, 1964; Michaelsen, 1970; Pierce, 1930; Roorbach, 1937:104–28, 165–201; Wiggin, 1962). American schools are hardly unique in this respect since the governments and pedagogues of all nation-states since the French Revolution have been keenly aware of the criticality of the educational strategy and have exploited it to the hilt (P. Black, 1953:40–49; Merriam, 1931; Miliband, 1969:179–264; Scott, 1916; Shafer, 1972:195–99). But what sets the United States apart from virtually every other country is its lack of a fully centralized educational bureaucracy, one responsible for formulating and administering the curriculum throughout the entire public school system, in addition to managing plant and personnel. Instead, in a land that has had free, compulsory, and universal primary instruction, and at least some secondary education of the same description, for the past several decades, it has been the state and local school boards that have supervised curriculum, selected textbooks, and hired and fired teachers. Yet, quite astonishingly, these thousands of localized decision-making units, along with the parallel parochial school systems (mostly Roman Catholic, Lutheran, and Jewish) have arrived at remarkably similar agenda.

Such a phenomenon raises intriguing questions about the workings of social psychology. The salesmanship of the more aggressive textbook firms operating nationwide is only a minor part of the explanation. Much more basic is a preexisting consensus among opinion-makers and leaders, as well as the public at large, as to the core package of ideas and attitudes that constitute the American Credo. Without any formal mechanism for discussion and debate, agreement was reached on these issues by the early nineteenth century, when American public education was still in its infancy. As public schools multiplied rapidly, they required no central office to dictate what knowledge, beyond reading, writing, and arithmetic, should be drummed into the heads of their young charges. "Everywhere one major purpose of education, at all levels, came to be the making of 'good citizens,' and that meant, in popular thinking, the making of national patriots" (Shafer, 1972:195). It may not be too extreme to suggest, as did D. W. Brogan, that "the public school was America's 'formally unestablished national church'" (Michaelsen, 1970:62).

Formal instruction in American history, now mandated by all states, did not begin until 1827, when Massachusetts and Vermont (New England again!) were the first to demand it in their schools (Roorbach, 1937:104; Shafer, 1972:195–96). But the process of nationalistic indoctrination was already well under way by then, largely through the exertions of a single individual, Noah Webster.

Best known, and not unjustly, for his herculean lexicographic labors, actually Webster's greatest impact on his beloved country may well have been as a pioneer of cultural nationalism (Warfel, 1936: 92–94). As early as 1787, his *An American Selection*, intended for school use, was thoroughly saturated with patriotic messages. But it was the Webster *Speller* that best justifies the claim that "he did more than any other man to unify America" (Warfel, 1936:94). From 1783 to 1847, no fewer than 24 million copies of this wildly popular volume were sold to schoolchildren and their parents (it is worth noting that the total population of the United States in 1847 approximated 21 million); and they taught more than spelling, grammar, and correct linguistic usage, for these small books were crammed with a variety of nationalistic homilies and quotations (Bradsher, 1940:275).[24]

From the mid-nineteenth century onward, American schools have had their pick of a long series of basic American history texts. Although they have evolved in both style and content while presenting an ostensibly authoritative vision of the American past and its meaning, they have always served staunchly, at least until quite recently, as "guardians of tradition" (Elson, 1964; FitzGerald, 1979). The early geography texts were also influential in molding the minds of young scholars (Carpenter, 1963:246–70); and in this area no figure was more pivotal than Jedidiah Morse, an historian who, inter alia, could also lay claim to being the first professional geographer in America (Hauptman, 1978:425–26; Van Alstyne, 1970:65–66). Morse's *The American Geography* and the texts of his successors were unabashedly propagandistic, and their advocacy of westward expansion, Manifest Destiny, and the role of the frontier predates their official exposition by the elite (Hauptman, 1978). Like similar publications in other lands, American school atlases from the earliest years up to the present are implicitly nationalistic in content and arrangement. The United States claims a large plurality of plates, and they almost always appear in the forward section of the book.

By the middle of the past century, the works of Webster, Morse, and others were overshadowed by those of the even more celebrated William Holmes McGuffey (Carpenter, 1963:79–86; Lynn, 1973:9–24; Minnich, 1936). In its many editions and millions of copies (it is still not entirely out of print), McGuffey's *Reader* was for many years standard fare for the majority of elementary classrooms. In essence, it was a catechism of nationalism for " 'McGuffey's' was more than a textbook or a literary collection of 'elegant extracts'; it was, in sum, a portable school for the new priests of the republic" (Lynn, 1973:23).

From the 1880s onward, America's public schools have been obliged to assume an even greater burden than ever for ideological indoctrination and preserving national unity. The rapid urbanization and industrialization of the country and, most particularly, the influx of vast swarms of aliens so culturally remote from the older British-Teutonic stock, meant unprecedented challenges to the established belief system. The newly formed patriotic-hereditary and veterans organizations went to some pains to make certain that American history and ideals were being properly taught in the schools (Davies, 1955:234–44; Dearing, 1952:402–3, 471–86 and passim; Strayer, 1958:67–76). In addition to imbibing nationalism from their history, civics, geography, and literary textbooks, the pupils also learned flag etiquette and the Pledge of Allegiance. The approach of national holidays was the cue for special recitations, pageants, musical programs, study projects, and other such activities.

The zeal of the self-appointed guardians of Americanism reached a climax of near-hysteria in the 1910s and 1920s with the inauguration of "Americanization" programs aimed principally at immigrants and their offspring through the public schools (Carlson, 1975; Hartmann, 1948; R. Lewis, 1930; Michaelsen, 1970:149–56; Minott, 1962:72–89). Spurred on by the war effort, scores of patriotic organizations labored strenuously to assimilate the newcomers into their system of values as promptly as possible. What was being force-fed to these clients was a curriculum based on Republicanism, middle-class ideals, and nondenominational Protestantism; and it was flawed by the inherent paradox that "Americanization education in the interest of liberty . . . became . . . an imperious demand for individual conformity to societal norms" (Carlson, 1975:4). It is not at all certain how effective these efforts may have been, but the opinion that "the Americanization campaigns had the greatest impact on those who organized them" (Wallace, 1981:68) seems unduly severe.

In contrast to the past century, when such questions seem never to have occurred to anyone, the twentieth century has witnessed much sporadic anxiety over the ideological purity or reliability of teachers as well as how best to civilize the invading hordes. Coercive programs to ensure loyalty by teachers have not been uncommon; and there has been particular pressure to teach an idealized, sanitized version of the American past in uncritical fashion (Beale, 1936:174–207).

Such defensiveness may well be in reaction to a profoundly significant development in the scholarly world, something that may represent one of the first serious challenges from within to the spiritual hegemony of the nation-state. As we shall see, we can discern parallel happenings in the other social sciences and the worlds of art, music, letters, and journalism. Among professional practitioners, the vogue for "scientific history" that began in Germany in the mid-1800s and reached American shores by the turn of the century eventually spawned a brand of skepticism that is incompatible with the earlier vocation of the historian, that of simply justifying and glorifying one's native land (Kennedy, 1973:86–87). And, of course, the pressure of recent events that violate cherished beliefs, yet cannot be ignored, drives the scholar further into the wilds of agnosticism. Thus revisionism has come to be respectable, if still controversial, within the halls of Academe, and not just within the United States. P. M. Kennedy forcefully states the transformation of the historian's mission.

> In historical circles today the patriotic historian has virtually disappeared from the universities and research institutes of Western Europe and the United States. . . . In contrast, there are a number of historians in the West, particularly Germany and the United States, whose writings could be labelled "anti-nationalistic," by which it is not meant that they are against the nation *per se*, but that they are deeply critical of the past (and usually also the present) policies of the government, and believe that the patriotic ideological values and ambitions of previous generations which they see as often being humbug and concealing much calculated greed and ambition should be discarded from their national life. [Kennedy, 1973:84][25]

By the 1960s, such disaffection at the more rarefied levels of scholarship, combined with a succession of domestic social upheavals, economic malaise, and military disappointments overseas, had its effect on the writers of history and social studies texts for America's public schools. If there had been virtual unanimity in tone and content in such publications over the preceding hundred years, with their uncritical trumpeting of nationalism (Nietz, 1961: 234–69; Noah, Prince, and Riggs, 1962), while changes occurred

rather slowly and pretty much in unison, the situation has been
utterly different for the past twenty years (FitzGerald, 1979). Now
we find considerable diversity of outlook and approach among competing texts, much nervous shifting of direction, and even turn-
abouts, in the race to keep abreast of the times and to minimize
the pressures of conflicting ethnic/religious/political constituencies. Although old-fashioned nationalism is by no means extinct in
elementary and secondary school texts or some popular periodicals,
the former consensus has been shattered. Unlike the author of political orations or the designer of coins, stamps, or monuments, the
chronicler of history is obliged to be quite explicit and factual about
what happened in years gone by and to extract rational interpretations from such material. The current inability to agree on the nature and implications of our past may be symptomatic of inner
uncertainties about national identity and purpose.

ICONOGRAPHY

As Aldous Huxley has noted most perceptively, "Nations are to a
very large extent invented by their poets and novelists" (Huxley,
1932:50).[26] That did not happen in the case of the early United
States, but certainly not for lack of trying by its literati. If Americans were formerly adherents of an oral culture, they also seem to
have been visually oriented, not only to pages of print, but also to
images, first those appearing on canvas and other media cultivated
by artists and craftsmen and, subsequently, on movie and television
screens.[27] And quite often, of course, these images were projections
of the public eidolons that have been so influential in shaping or
reflecting American nationalism. Thus it was through mass immersion in nationalistic iconography that the inhabitants of the young
republic molded their identity and perceived their destiny.

If students of nationalism know less than they should about the
impact of visual items (Neil, 1975:51), it may be because of the
tribal ways of most scholars as detected by Neil Harris. "The energy
concentrated upon written texts as points of departure has accompanied an indifference toward those shifts of style and form that
belong to physical objects. The history of stylistic change has been
left in the care of art historians" (N. Harris, 1979:196).

With the gigantic exceptions of the flag and eagle (both to be dealt
with at a later point), most of the imagery created or commissioned
by the government has not been nearly as effective as the material

issuing from the private sector. Indeed, official efforts along this line have usually been routine in character and very much what one has come to expect of every well-organized nation-state. They need not detain us long.

After the adoption of a national flag, the most pressing business for the fledgling United States, iconographically speaking, was the design of its Great Seal, something that came to pass in 1782 after many a false start (Fleming, 1982; Hunt, 1909; Krythe, 1968:27–32; Patterson and Dougall, 1976; Silverman, 1976:320–23, 366, 416–18). It is fateful in the annals of America's symbolic life for introducing the red-white-and-blue shield into the public realm and, most especially, for launching the eagle on its spectacular nationalistic flight. With an ideal combination of the themes of freedom, fierceness, and dignity, the American bald eagle was the perfect choice for the national totem; and it immediately escaped the narrow confines of the seal to begin roosting on every possible perch. If the obverse face of the Great Seal has, at least indirectly, made its mark, virtually all citizens studiously ignore the reverse side with its mystifying pyramid and eye and inscrutable Latin motto.

Again, in keeping with the deportment of a proper nation-state, the United States began issuing a series of official medals in 1776 (Loubat, 1878). These gold and silver collectibles were intended to honor eminent personages and stirring events, including, since 1893, presidential inaugurations (Dusterberg, 1976). Although the medals normally contain some nationalistic symbols, for example, Miss Liberty, in addition to effigies of the persons being honored, their general impact has been minimal since both production and circulation have been quite limited, at least until quite recently. Only the last few official inaugural committees have begun to exploit the money-making potential of medals by marketing them in larger quantities (Dusterberg, 1976).

The U.S. Treasury and Post Office have never stinted in their use of nationalistic images on coins, paper currency, postage stamps, and various certificates; and the same is obviously true of virtually every other nation-state in the twentieth century, even though the subject has never received much systematic attention. The notion of emblazoning a country's ruler on its coins, tokens of divinity, so to speak, predates Hellenic and Roman practice, and indeed may coincide with the invention of metallic currency. The United States has so honored certain of its chief executives while occasionally including nonpresidential heroes, for example, Franklin. Other familiar items, for example, Miss Liberty, the eagle (Herrick, 1934: 246–57), and Graeco-Roman motifs (H. M. Jones, 1964:229) have also received their numismatic due.[28]

With larger surfaces at their disposal, the designers of paper currency have managed to make the dollar bill and other denominations virtual anthologies of nationalistic images. Although postage stamps may be much smaller than banknotes, the frequency of new issues makes up for their minuteness. The faces of national heroes and statesmen have adorned every standard series of stamps since the first were engraved in the 1840s, and many of the commemoratives celebrate events of nationalistic import (Poulsen, 1986). But, as is true in other graphic media, it is the American Revolution and its dramatis personae that dominate the philatelic scene.[29] No one has ever tried to gauge the psychological impact, subliminal or otherwise, upon the public in the United States of constant, daily exposure to this barrage of symbols on articles we cannot refrain from handling. The occasional charges of partisanship over selection of subjects may indicate nothing more than political paranoia.[30] If it were not for the persistent hoarding of the Kennedy half-dollar, I should be inclined to minimize the value of currency or stamps in the cause of nationalism; but it is not at all clear whether the collectors of that 50-cent piece are acting out of devotion to a sacred memory or speculative greed (Wolfe, 1975:410). In any case, a critical analysis of the changing imagery on American currency and stamps would be well worth the effort.[31]

For the past several decades, the governments of the more advanced nation-states have been using posters for recruiting purposes and to promote various peacetime causes, but with special intensity during World Wars I and II.[32] It was during the 1914–18 conflict that we find the greatest flowering of this genre as the various belligerents recruited the most eminent artists of the time to stiffen the national resolve—and with results that are strikingly similar whatever the venue (Coffey, 1978; Crawford, 1979; Darracott and Loftus, 1972a; Keay, 1975; Richards, 1978). The propaganda posters are doubly derivative, the medium having been expropriated from show business and the images from traditional older sources. Thus we find Miss Columbia, Uncle Sam, the Statue of Liberty, flag, and eagle all starring in American posters (Coffey, 1978; Darracott and Loftus, 1972) and their counterparts in the output of foreign poster artists.[33]

There was somewhat less reliance on posters during World War II, in part because of paper shortages, but even more because of the availability of radio and film (Darracott and Loftus, 1972; Judd, 1972; Stanford University, 1972; Zeman, 1978). National differences in form and content were even less apparent than they had been thirty years earlier.

The one form of iconography initiated or inspired by governments anywhere in the world about whose psychosocial impact we know least is undoubtedly the official uniform. Such costume, whether worn by members of the military, police, or judiciary, or by civilian veterans, Boy Scouts, Girl Scouts, and the like, is often heavily symbolic in and of itself; but the message may be reinforced by means of the national colors, medals, specially designed buttons and ornaments, inscriptions, and miniature flags (Merriam, 1931:148–49). My impression, in lieu of any serious study, is that uniforms have been a less significant factor in the symbolic life of Americans than is true for most other countries, but that they may have gradually gained in importance over the years, especially in the military. Indeed, it seems that a reasonable degree of standardization in the dress of the Northern soldier did not materialize until the later phases of the Civil War (Windrow and Embleton, 1973:90).

More than anything else, after the military and political dust had settled, it was a set of visual images that acted as the catalytic agent transforming the inhabitants of the thirteen former British colonies and their descendants into that remarkable synthetic community we can call the American nation. These magical icons were the work not of government but of a band of artists, trained and untrained, both elite and folk, who plied their trade while interacting with the entire free population in the most intimate fashion imaginable. Because the paintings, engravings, drawings, and other art products bursting with nationalistic energy were sold, displayed, reproduced, imitated, and, above all, placed in one form or another where they would be visible every waking hour in the homes and workplaces of virtually everyone, they may not only have been more potent as formative factors in the nationalization process than the written or spoken word but more sensitive measures of the true feelings of rank-and-file men, women, and children than any sort of written document. Sermons, pamphlets, orations, and other verbal exhortations are created by the talented few for finite audiences; holidays, rallies, festivals, and other rites are fleeting affairs; but certain images endure as our constant companions. They burn themselves indelibly, hauntingly into the deepest recesses of our souls. If we assume, for the sake of argument, that nationalism is a kind of religion, then, as Fred Schroeder has so eloquently phrased it,

> At rallies, on feast days, on sabbath days, religion can presume that a mass audience will operate as the anonymous recipients of a consistent and unvarying ritual, but when the rally is over and the festival is past . . . then the religion needs sustenance. The sustenance must come by means of dispersing the religious experience among the homes and into the lives of the masses. . . . *No state or tribal religious control can continue without a mass-sanctioned aesthetic*; that is, as in all popular arts, the product must sell. It must anticipate needs, it must respond to unstructured criticisms of the constituency, it must flex with social-psychological changes that have been wrought by other forces . . . but at the same time must provide for individual, family and clan worship that is consistent and compatible with the politics and government of the day. . . . When a popular art work really expresses the beliefs of the people and responds to their needs, it will resist all imposed changes, all higher criticism, and will achieve the outlaw immortality that all popular culture strives toward, not to be recognized until much later by upcult critics. [Schroeder, 1977:126–27; emphasis added]

As it happened, the art community of America, such as it was, was ill prepared for the challenge of independence and nation-building, perhaps even more poorly equipped than the literary establishment. Indeed, all aspects of aesthetic endeavor in Colonial America were still just that: colonial. (The isolated brilliant achievers, such as the poet Edward Taylor, won recognition only posthumously.) As of 1776, the producers and products of higher culture were still being shipped from Britain or continental Europe, while the more talented native sons were still going abroad for training, inspiration, and material reward, and often remained far away.

Nevertheless, with the coming of political freedom, nationalistic Americans felt powerful jolts of adrenalin coursing through their arteries, and they began to flex their cultural biceps. Thus in this exuberant dawn of self-discovery, there began the long struggle for cultural and intellectual independence and for full parity with the rest of the world. It is a story told well and in much detail by several scholars (N. Harris, 1966; Ketcham, 1974:244–62; Kohn, 1957: 39–89; Krout and Fox, 1944:332–69; L. B. Miller, 1966, 1967; Neil,

1975; Silverman, 1976).[34] The growing pains lasted an agonizingly long time, and even after the emergence of world-class poets and novelists in the 1840s and 1850s in the persons of Poe, Hawthorne, Melville, Whitman, and Dickinson, European condescension toward American cultural striving persisted. It was not until the twentieth century, in some instances only after World War II, that Americans finally stopped slavishly following European styles and models as their work in drama, musical composition and performance, architecture, and fashion, as well as verse and fiction, merited and received full acceptance by critics abroad.

Americans were much more fortunate, or at least self-satisfied, in the realm of the visual arts. Painters and their ilk were stunningly successful with the American public, however reluctantly worldwide recognition may have arrived. It is important to realize that in the eighteenth and early nineteenth centuries the gaping chasm that now separates the avante garde and other sophisticated professionals in the worlds of art, literature, and music from popular and folk practitioners of such crafts simply did not exist anywhere. Insofar as there were mass publics then, they were catered to by creative persons of all levels of skill and pretension. This was particularly true of the young United States when, as Elinor Horwitz has abundantly documented in her study of folk arts and crafts,

> Americans of all degrees of education, sophistication, and wealth loved their land with a total lack of restraint. They were insatiable in their desire to praise the country and to hear it praised in ringing oratory. They venerated the symbols of their nationhood and wanted to display them—all of them—everywhere, always. For, after all, a symbol can only be fully enjoyed when it's seen close at hand every day, hanging over the door, over the mantel, on a pole; woven into the coverlet, painted on the tea set, inlaid on the cupboard. The new patriotic iconography inspired artists, folk artists, and craftsmen alike. [Horwitz, 1976:11]

Many years later, we encounter the same revolutionary gusto in Mexico, especially in its extraordinary mural art. There may be another analogy in the creative ferment in Soviet Russia during the first dozen years after the overthrow of the Czarist regime.

Artists by the score—the homegrown variety, Americans educated abroad, and immigrants, such as J. A. Houdon or Emanuel Leutze—impelled by idealism or the prospect of monetary gain, capitalized on the opportunity. The choice of subjects was preor-

dained, given the artistic genres then in vogue and the cataclysmic
forces that stirred artists into action: the heroes and events of the
American Revolution. Indeed, from 1776 to the present moment,
modified by time and changing tastes though they may be, this
same cluster of themes has remained absolutely central to American nationalistic iconography and also, in only slightly lesser degree, to other phases of the symbolic life of the country. By seeing
the Revolution through the eyes of its artistic interpreters then
and later, we have defined, then redefined, what it means to be
American.[35]

In the days before photography, it was by painting or drawing
portraits of whatever patrons were willing to sit still long enough
and able to pay for the privilege that a handful of (usually itinerant)
artistically inclined individuals were able to eke out a living of
sorts. By the close of the Colonial period, some (like Benjamin West
and John Singleton Copley) had achieved genuine virtuosity and
launched a tradition that was to serve their successors well. Within
a few years, the portraitists of the new republic had learned their
craft adequately and rose to the demands of a market clamoring for
likenesses of their demigods. And if the results could be passable
aesthetically, their real meaning was political and symbolic.

"The portrait image has been an element of human history,
whether in ancient magical shapes and mysteries or as reflected
truth. It has moved populations to reverence. It has been an imple-
ment of substantiation and a weapon of attack" (Sellers, 1962:1).
Quite apart from the use of outsize photos of the candidates or
incumbents in American and other elections, note the truly mon-
strous blowups of the faces of Marx, Engels, Lenin, and the current
head of state in the Soviet Union or the similar use of gigantic
images of Mao and company in revolutionary China. It is precisely
parallel to what happened in revolutionary America—but here as a
bottom-up phenomenon, not top-down.

Of all the familiar faces, none has ever been more familiar before
or since than that of George Washington. During his lifetime, he
sat for portraits and busts many times, and submitted at least once
to measurements for a lifesize statue.[36] After his demise, representations of the man increased rather than diminished in number (Eisen, 1932). Indeed Washingtonian iconography became something of an industry as able artists, such as Gilbert Stuart, devoted
much of their career to copying and recopying their more successful efforts. But the handiwork of the professionals was only a bare
beginning. By means of engraving and lithography and through the

activities of artisans, the figure of Washington soon appeared in every possible physical medium on every possible object and surface. It is quite impossible to overstate their ubiquity even today, but the rage for visual reminders of Washington reached its climax in the early nineteenth century. The face and entire six-foot-plus figure of this charismatic individual were the proper stuff for myth: the calm, but powerful, features, the inescapable nobility. They will forever haunt the memory and imagination of America.

Other major figures of the Revolutionary era and many a lesser one sat for their portraits or busts, or else the artist drew upon his imagination to satisfy the cravings of a worshipful public. Some of the results are memorable, even moving. There is, for example, Thomas Sully's sensitive rendition of Thomas Jefferson, but, above all, the better portraits of Benjamin Franklin. They were powerful symbolic ammunition in both France and the United States (Seller, 1962:138). Perhaps more than any other single American countenance that has attained notoriety, Franklin's expresses the full range and complexities of the national character, just as did his long, many-sided career. In Franklin's face we see ourselves as in a mirror; in Washington's we see, or saw, what we might aspire to, but never reach.

If depictions of national heroes meant money in the bank for the artist of early America, the most ambitious aspired to the loftiest of genres: history painting. These large, complex, panoramic renderings of battle scenes and great historical events might take years of effort, but the rewards, financial and professional, could be considerable. Although arriving on the scene somewhat later, the symbolic impact of the more popular canvases of Revolutionary themes upon the budding national consciousness may have been even greater than that of the ever-popular portraits. The most successful of the earlier practitioners was John Trumbull, whose four huge Revolutionary scenes were installed in the Capitol rotunda in 1826–27 (Curti, 1946:55–56; Jaffe, 1976; Kammen, 1978:79–80). Undoubtedly the most celebrated of these and the one most lavishly admired by his contemporaries has since become a principal icon of American culture: his *Declaration of Independence*. Other competent artists of the period, such as Thomas Sully, Asher Durand, and Jacob Eichholtz, also performed admirably in the same idiom.

But all other efforts have been at least partially eclipsed by the single noblest example of American history painting: Emanuel Leutze's immensely popular *Washington Crossing the Delaware*, executed in 1849–51 (Hutton, 1959). Indeed, it may be the only work of art that every adult American can identify, and its didactic value has been incalculable. Its only possible competitor, another instantly recognizable picture that, like Leutze's, has been copied, parodied, and exploited countless times in countless ways is Archibald Williard's *The Spirit of '76*, which, appropriately enough, was first exhibited at the 1876 Philadelphia Exposition (Pauly, 1978). Thanks to the crafty promotional efforts of businessman James Ryder and cheap mass reproduction via lithography, it soon achieved universal fame.

Williard's painting is also noteworthy as perhaps the last American nationalistic production on a Revolutionary or any other subject that could be treated at all seriously by the critical establishment. During the past one hundred years, only four nationalistic art objects have secured a firm niche in the hearts of Americans: Bartholdi's Statue of Liberty, Norman Rockwell's *The Four Freedoms*, Joe Rosenthal's carefully posed photograph of the raising of the flag at Iwo Jima, and the Vietnam Veterans Memorial. You will seek in vain for any discussion of the first three in the histories of American art. A possible fifth item, or group of items, and a favorite theme for commercial artists, Custer's debacle at Little Big Horn, is to be found more frequently hanging over bars than in art museums.

If elite, popular, and folk art overlapped in subject and even intent during the first century of nationhood, only to part company after the 1870s, we can detect some significant changes in emphases during the earlier years, variations in choice of symbols or in their handling that reveal the shifting currents and preoccupations of the American mind. Throughout the antebellum period, certain items recur with much regularity: Miss Liberty, the eagle, Revolutionary figures, presidents, heroes of the army and navy, and depictions of momentous events. We find them not only in paintings and engravings but in all manner of household and other artifacts, including those in glass and ceramic (Klamkin, 1973; Knittle, 1927; Lindsey, 1967). But a closer look suggests changing sensibilities. After reviewing the artistic themes of the period, Kammen observes that the ideas of Liberty and Power, but especially Liberty, "obsessed the American mind from the opening of the Revolutionary crisis until about the close of James Madison's presidency" (Kammen, 1978:96). He discerns a transition from an era concerned with Liberty to one absorbed in the issues of Peace and Plenty that was consummated by the 1820s.

Thus, the decade after 1796 comprises the watershed between a Revolutionary culture whose attitudinal axis was the concept of Liberty and a republican culture whose aspirational axis was the expectation of Prosperity—eventually expanded, after about 1825, to "Peace and Plenty." And just as Liberty had its cluster of iconographic symbols—Miss Liberty, the pole and cap, the eagle, and the printing press—so, too, did Prosperity have its cluster of images. They include the cornucopia, bowls of luscious fruit (especially bulging bunches of grapes), ripe grain being harvested, and most of all, the plough. [Kammen, 1978:98–99]

By the middle of the nineteenth century, as the immediacy of the Revolution and its ideals had begun to fade, rather different motifs in nationalistic iconography began to evolve. As we shall learn in the following chapter, the national flag escaped from relative obscurity to become a conspicuous, even dominant element, and pretentious monuments, formerly disdained as "so Old Worldly, so aristocratic, so un-republican" (Kammen, 1978:106), began to populate the American scene indoors and out. However, even with the passing of time, representations of the Founders and Framers and Revolution-related items continued to monopolize the affections of both providers and consumers of nationalistic arts and crafts. Perhaps the only major additions to their repertoire were the person of Abraham Lincoln, whose presence still broods over the land in many forms, and, of course, the Statue of Liberty. Few post-1865 celebrities stirred up more than momentary excitement among the makers of the images.[37]

By the second half of the nineteenth century, a third mode of graphic expression (following portraits and history painting) found favor among America's partisans: the depiction of its natural wonders and beauties. Such artistic expression documents an earlier, but relatively inarticulate, tenet of the American credo: the redemptive value of the landscape, the idea of community through nature (B. Novak, 1980:15–17). "Americans never tired of pointing out the moral lessons derived from their landscape which, they insisted, suggested freedom, exuberance, and optimism" (L. B. Miller, 1967:702). Although "reliance on nature as proof of national greatness began in earnest immediately following American independence from Great Britain" (Runte, 1979:14), this development matured belatedly. In part this was because of the sheer unavailability in the eastern United States of any spectacular scenery that could rival Europe's stellar attractions (pace, Tom Jefferson!), with the sole exception of Niagara Falls. In due course, Niagara did indeed become the subject of American boasting in word and picture and a genuine national symbol of some consequence for the United States, but evidently not for Canada (Horwitz, 1976:28). But the opening salvo in the campaign to bolster national pride by means of landscape painting was the work of the gifted artists of the Hudson River School who demonstrated, quite handsomely, that the glories of Eastern hills, ravines, and wilderness could rival those of Europe's humanized landscapes. With the discovery of the vivid Amerindian nations of the Great Plains and the exploration of the Rockies and the even wilder West beyond, another group of artists, including George Catlin, Albert Bierstadt, Thomas Moran, Charles Russell, and Frederic Remington, earned much acclaim and even fortune with their drawings and paintings of these marvelously exotic settings. In so doing, they certified them as powerful cultural icons, not overtly nationalistic, to be sure, but perhaps all the more effective for that (Runte, 1979:11–32). "Translated into engravings and woodcuts for popular distribution in newspapers and magazines, the works of Albert Bierstadt, C. E. Watkins, and other artists provided the visual component of cultural nationalism" (Runte, 1979:25). In visual as well as literary and folkloristic terms, the West had become the grand metaphor for America (H. N. Smith, 1950).

In this general context, one ought to consider the map of the conterminous United States as a meaningful national icon, though precious little has been written on the topic (Horwitz, 1976:32). Indeed, the outline of the forty-eight states has become a familiar symbol and an emotionally potent one in advertisements, outdoor signs, and various folk media. There is also the consideration that maps of British North America, along with the Colonial newspapers and informal networks of correspondents, preachers, and other travelers, may have been crucially instrumental in sowing the seeds of future nationalism. Writing about the publication of regional and continental maps during the middle third of the eighteenth century, Lynne A. Leopold-Sharp (1980:32) notes "accurate maps of individual colonies and regional areas played an important role in the colonists' recognition of the American land: they reinforced the fact that the colonies were but one part of the larger North American continent."

By the late nineteenth century, if the evidence from a study of patriotic and political china is at all indicative, the treatment of early heroes and their deeds had become less fashionable in American art and artifacts (Klamkin, 1973:57–58). Insofar as we still find the Revolution being portrayed, it has been drained of ideological meaning and has become little more than a series of battles.[38] Michael Kammen intones a requiem for the lost import of an earlier day. "We no longer hear very much about political independence and republican government. . . . The American Revolution viewed as a moral and governmental event gives way to a bloody war, plain and simple. There is a very real sense in which the Revolution came to be reduced to battles, regiments, and colorful uniforms— and thereby got trivialized" (Kammen, 1978:85).

An analysis of commemorative objects displayed in the U.S. Capitol confirms this supposition (Fairman, 1927; B. Schwartz, 1982). The post–Civil War Capitol reveals a tendency to celebrate the structural aspects of American society, rather than the heroic individual or their ideals, incumbency of office rather than remarkable achievement, so that Barry Schwartz can conclude that "the result is an iconography that became more present-oriented, less heroic, and less charismatic, a pattern that attested to the fact that America, at last, had become an unrevolutionary culture" (B. Schwartz, 1982:396). In other public sculpture of the final quarter of the nineteenth century, we find that "particular individuals participating in identifiable historical situations were gradually replaced by non-specific people as archetypes of courage, valor, and quiet determination" (Kammen, 1978:83), a development we have already detected in the general discussion of public eidolons.

From the 1870s through the 1920s, nationalistic iconography in America generally languished, reworking hackneyed motifs in uninspired, generally sentimentalized, romanticized fashion (Kammen, 1978:85–89). Perhaps the most enthusiastic exploiters of the icons of nationalism were cartoonists and advertisers, of both the commercial and political breeds. From the Harrison campaign of 1840 onward, designers of political paraphernalia showed little reticence in dragging out not only pictures of their standard-bearers but also any and all of the standard props, including Uncle Sam, Miss Liberty, eagles and flags galore, the Liberty Bell, Statue of Liberty, plows, national mottoes, sacred buildings and documents, and the occasional log cabin. Such symbolic extravagance may have reached its climax in the colorful campaign of 1896 if the published material on campaign buttons, posters, badges, bandannas, banners, and other artifacts can be relied upon (Bristow, 1971, 1973; Collins,

1979; Fischer, 1980; Thieme, 1980; Tripp, 1976). But they also suggest that such political gear has become less florid in recent times, resorting less often to national symbols and turning instead to personality items (Collins, 1979; Tripp, 1976).

National symbols have been less prominent in the newspaper and magazine advertisements that have flourished since the late nineteenth century than in the political arena, but they are by no means negligible, especially in wartime (Atwan, McQuade, and Wright, 1979; Cobb, 1978). Although Miss Liberty is not a frequent guest, we do come across Washin·, n, Lincoln, Uncle Sam, and the eagle fairly often, along with the occasional invocation of the pioneer, the U.S. Capitol, Panama Canal, Golden Gate Bridge, Roosevelt Dam, Mount Rushmore, and the one-room schoolhouse (Cobb, 1978:50–51, 54–55, 74, 88–91, 94–95).

The Great Depression that began with the stock market crash of October 1929 ushered in an era of greatly altered sensibilities in all departments of American life, or perhaps brought to the fore developments that had been festering below the surface since the turn of the century. Among the most startling of changes was that in nationalistic iconography. The combination of socioeconomic trauma and, for the first time ever, federal patronage on a massive scale for thousands of distressed artists resulted in a remarkable renaissance of nativistic art products: a mixture of regionalism, social realism, and the rediscovery of the peculiar essences of traditional America (C. C. Alexander, 1980; Contreras, 1983; G. O. Larson, 1983; Marling, 1982; McKinzie, 1973).[39]

Previously, American artists had automatically adopted imported European styles in their uncritical celebration of national heroes, ideals, and triumphs. It is supremely ironic that just when, in the 1930s, they finally discovered an authentically American idiom, they were to use it in a reflective, critical, but not necessarily hostile, fashion to deal with the problems of national history and identity, and without the bombast and saccharine of previous generations. The bulk of murals, easel paintings, and other art projects commissioned by the Treasury Department's Section of Fine Arts, the Works Progress Administration, and other New Deal programs were concerned with local history, industry, and resources or were general salutations to the notions of progress, technology, and a brighter, more humane future. However, an important minority reworked the familiar Revolutionary themes, and not a few of these "transcended the naive, undiluted patriotism of 1900, and link[ed] national legend with personal sympathy for political rebellion and social protest" (Kammen, 1978:90).[40]

Yet another artistic era materialized with World War II and its sequelae. Even though, as C. C. Alexander recognizes, it was "obviously a great patriotic event in itself, the Second World War nonetheless signalled the incipient decline of the nationalistic impulse in the American arts" (C. C. Alexander, 1980:242). Although regional and folkloristic motifs linger on in certain unfashionable circles and periodically threaten to erupt on a grand scale, mainstream "art for art's sake" in the United States for the past four decades has been thoroughly cosmopolitan in mood and form and preponderantly nonrepresentational in style. But this new internationalism has generated products in the United States as well as other advanced countries quite at odds with those created by the old-fashioned international consensus of the 1700s and 1800s. If the journeymen of the profession can still earn their bread and butter with militaristic comic books or the occasional jingoistic poster or ad for government or business firm, today's would-be authentic artist would not be caught dead sincerely daubing a nationalistic canvas or casting a straightforward bronze monument to any hero past or present on his or her own initiative. As in so many other realms of late twentieth-century aesthetic endeavor, the serious practitioner has become an alienated creature. When the occasion or commission arises, as it did during the Bicentennial, for handling the old national themes, the result can be tongue-in-cheek or downright satiric (Kammen, 1978:90–91). After a journey of more than two hundred years, nationalistic art in the United States seems to have reached a dead end, its mission accomplished, its energy spent.

OTHER AESTHETIC ENTERPRISES

If American practitioners of the visual arts, high and low, were signally successful in mobilizing nationalistic sentiments, the story is rather different when we consider other departments of aesthetic endeavor. Other countries have cherished certain novels, poems, and musical works and the culture heroes who were their makers to such a degree that these creations and larger-than-life geniuses have been crucial elements in the birthing of a national spirit. Thus Italy has had its Alessandro Manzoni and Giuseppe Verdi, Poland its Henryk Sienkiewicz, Cuba its José Martí; Russia found itself defined by Pushkin and Gogol and an illustrious company of nine-

teenth-century Slavophile composers, as Scotland did through Robert Burns or Ireland through the writers of its Celtic Revival. The
mighty rhetoric of Christopher Marlowe and William Shakespeare
has taught the English what it means to be English. The aspirations
of the coalescent nations of Europe found eloquent voice in the
strains of Bohemia's Smetana, Finland's Sibelius, Hungary's Liszt,
Spain's de Falla and Albeniz, and Norway's Grieg. Or, in some cases,
a more generalized pride in their civilization and the feats of their
more brilliant countrymen would serve nicely. It sufficed to convince the Germans, with that long rollcall of Luther, Goethe, Schiller, Beethoven and company, of the importance of being German or
the French of their obvious superiority over lesser beings.

Just why the United States has never had a genuine counterpart
to the cited examples during its formative years, no verbal or musical epic around which to muster its emotional energies, is not entirely clear. The near absence of legitimate theater or a musical
stage until a later epoch made it quite improbable that the likes of a
Victor Hugo, Mikhail Glinka, or Richard Wagner could spring from
American soil. Yet scribblers have abounded from the earliest moments to the present, and all too often have found publishers. Morbidly sensitive to the jibes and jeers of the cultural mandarins of
the Old World, the literati of the infant republic struggled mightily
to attain respectability, a campaign that has been documented in
detail (Bolwell, 1939; Bradsher, 1940; Ketcham, 1974:244–55; Nye,
1960:235–67; Silverman, 1976; Spencer, 1936, 1957; Werner, 1932).

Their two principal aims were closely related: to establish a worthy national literature; and to promote American nationhood by
means of such writings. Was it the dearth of native talent or an
inhibiting sociocultural environment that thwarted their efforts? If
the poetry and fiction of Philip Freneau, Joel Barlow, or Washington
Irving was quite acceptable, neither it nor the veritable flood of
doggerel and prose from the pens of the less inspired ever truly set
ablaze the hearts and minds of the American masses. Compounding the problem is the brilliance of the political prose that issued
from Paine, Jefferson, Franklin, the Adamses, Madison, Hamilton,
and many others. Widespread illiteracy (obviously no handicap for
the nationalistic artist or artisan) is, of course, part of the explanation, as was the rudimentary development of the publishing business or a national critical apparatus. One can also appeal to the
anti-intellectual bias that is widely suspected to be a chronic feature of American life; but the universal enthusiasm for the best in
early painting and engraving tends to give that argument the lie, as

does the nobility of the political literature and its large, receptive audience.

Whatever the reasons for the nonappearance of any verbal block-buster in the nationalist cause, lesser items abounded, and they were not totally lacking in impact. Such literary worthies as Long-fellow, Lowell, Bryant, Whittier, Holmes, and, later, Emma Lazarus created stirring lines that have been widely anthologized, then re-cited and memorized by generations of schoolchildren, as were the lyrics to the more successful patriotic ditties, extracts from the great orations, and other set pieces (Stevens and Stevens, 1917).

Rather surprisingly, and in contrast to the works of Webster, Morse, McGuffey, and their ilk, nationalistic motifs seem to have been quite secondary in the extensive nonpedagogical children's lit-erature that flourished during the early nineteenth century in the form of giftbooks, storybooks, travel books, histories and geogra-phies, literary annuals, counseling and etiquette manuals, tracts, and periodical miscellanies (MacLeod, 1975; Randall, 1969). Such transcendent beings as Washington, Franklin, Webster, Clay, and Jackson may have been held up as models for emulation, but it was generalized moral preachments that largely preoccupied the au-thors of this new genre.

The arrival of cheap mass-circulation periodicals by the second half of the nineteenth century brough with it an entirely new, less reputable form of juvenile literature: the dime novel (Curti, 1937; Wecter, 1941:341–63). The enormous popularity of such lowbrow reading matter and its initial emphasis on Revolutionary themes leave little doubt "that it was a factor, and probably an important one, in the development of American patriotism and nationalism" (Curti, 1937:769). After the Spanish-American War, the American Revolution began to lose its appeal for addicts of pulp magazines, as the Wild West (an indirectly nationalistic theme) gained primacy (Wecter, 1941:342–43). The present-day inheritors of the tradition are the comic books, and, by transposition, some television series, that extol the valor of Americans fighting in recent wars. We dare not underrate the impress of this cultural undergrowth upon pliable young minds.

On a higher adult plane, nationalistic themes have never van-ished from American fiction and drama, but neither have they ever come close to dominating the literary scene (with the marginal ex-ception of that secular Southern bible, Margaret Mitchell's *Gone with the Wind*). A detailed discussion would carry us well beyond the scope of this essay,[41] but a fair assessment of the significance of nationalist indoctrination in "serious" literature over the past hundred years would have to be: modest and declining. Ever since the days of James Fenimore Cooper, the historical novel has claimed a wide readership in the United States; but foreign locales are as popular as domestic ones, while local color, romance, and exciting adventure generally figure more prominently than any nationalistic messages.

Only rarely have plays or films featuring national heroes or the stirring events of American history earned commercial or critical success.[42] The one historical personage that offered much hope for the theatrical producer was not Washington, Jefferson, or Franklin, but rather Abraham Lincoln, most notably in the form of Robert Sherwood's *Abe Lincoln in Illinois*, a genuine critical and popular hit on both stage and screen. The Lincoln boom, no doubt instigated in part by F. D. Roosevelt and his supporters (A. H. Jones, 1974), was but one more manifestation of a renewed nativistic fascination with the American past and its culture and folklore during the New Deal era. It involved work by some of the more notable history-minded, middlebrow authors of the period, including Maxwell Anderson, Carl Sandburg, Stephen Vincent Benét, and Howard Fast. In the realm of music, Earl Robinson's cantatas *Ballad for Americans* and *Lonesome Train* were the aural equivalents of the populist murals of the 1930s. But, again, as happened in the art world, this creative vein had been worked to exhaustion soon after World War II.[43]

One might expect much more of the motion picture in the annals of American nationalism. Since the dawn of cinema, the United States has taken a leading role in developing the technical, commercial, and, rather incidentally, artistic potential of the great new entertainment medium, with sociocultural results so profound and varied we are still far from understanding them fully.[44] Robert Sklar's statement that "the fact is that the careful analysis of movie dreams and myths has scarcely begun" (Sklar, 1975:197) is still valid despite the flood of literature on most other aspects of cinema.

There can be no dispute over the capability of film for rousing violent emotion, the still festering row over Griffith's *The Birth of a Nation* being a classic case in point, or for mobilizing latent nationalistic sentiments. If non-Russians find it hard to resist the cry for motherland and revolution in *Potemkin*, *Chapayev*, *Lenin in October*, or *Alexander Nevsky*, imagine the emotional havoc visited upon Soviet citizens. Emil Gance's epic *Napoleon*, produced in the early 1920s, is reputed to have had a decisive impact on the mind-set of the young Charles de Gaulle (and in its recent revival with a new musical score, it is powerful enough to make a Bonapartist out of almost anyone). It is also well known that the Nazi regime used both documentary and fictional films to strong effect in whipping up a fine chauvinistic frenzy; and the filmmakers of the People's Republic of China are striving earnestly to do the same. Less frenetically, the fine documentaries made by Canada's National Film Board have certainly contributed toward whatever sense of nationhood may exist in that country (MacCann, 1973:32–42).

We find no parallels within the American film experience. When movies burst upon the scene, the structure of nationalism had already hardened and revolutionary ardor had long since cooled. The role of the movie industry was not to challenge values or promulgate challenging new visions, but one of affirmation, to restate and repackage the enduring political, social, and cultural myths of America. It was an assignment that was especially crucial during the troubled 1930s when so much of American life was in flux and people in unprecedented numbers sought solace in darkened cinema palaces.[45] The most comforting myth was that of the Middle Landscape, that of agrarian, small-town America, so neatly exemplified in the films of Frank Capra and Walt Disney (Sklar, 1975: 195–214). Only rarely have commercial producers taken chances on historical films with nationalistic themes, as happened with *Abe Lincoln in Illinois*. The classic instance may have been Darryl Zanuck's *Wilson* (1944) (Knock, 1978). An elaborate, costly effort, it won critical respect and may have brightened Woodrow Wilson's image while modestly advancing the cause of internationalism (with an American flavor), but it lost money at the box office, and molders in the limbo of half-forgotten movies.

Like almost every other major belligerent, the United States did not hesitate to exploit the film medium during the two world wars, but with uncertain results (Bohn, 1968; Brownlow, 1979; Jowett, 1976:293–332; MacCann, 1973). Newsreels, documentaries, outright propaganda, and fictional entertainment were all commandeered for use in 1917–18, but rather crudely, resorting to overstatement and ethnic stereotypes rather than serious ideas or ideals (Brownlow, 1979). Employing a more restrained approach, the Hollywood recruits fared rather better during World War II, when the seven educational films in Frank Capra's *Why We Fight* series were widely exhibited and admired and seemed to have had a tonic effect on both civilian and military morale (Bohn, 1968).[46] At the same time, the commercial studios, and Warner Brothers in particular, turned out a number of exciting movies with wartime messages. But Capra and the other cinematographers engaged, directly or otherwise, in the war effort initiated nothing new in the way of national symbols but simply recirculated warmed-over images and clichés. Despite much bureaucratic and congressional infighting, various New Deal agencies created quite a library of documentaries to help push their programs; but, with the exception of Pare Lorent's remarkable achievements, these films seldom matched the effectiveness of their British and Canadian counterparts (MacCann, 1973).

If the direct contribution made to American nationalism by the film industry may have been modest in effect, the movies—and television—did support the cause in a most meaningful way, but quite accidentally and indirectly. By presenting a constant stream of images of so many places throughout the huge territorial expanses of the country, these visual media (and, to a lesser but significant extent, popular song and magazines as well) inculcated a sense of proprietorship and identity with the land that would be difficult to achieve via any other strategy. Thus even the most sedentary of twentieth-century Americans enjoy a vicarious familiarity with, and affection for, their varied land that reinforce their national and stateful proclivities.

Like film and the visual arts, radio and television offer quick, effective devices for nationalizing the masses of immature twentieth-century nation-states, especially in those Third World countries where the literate comprise a small minority (Merriam, 1931:164–67).[47] In the case of the United States, however, the electronic media arrived after the fact. At best they broadcast and intensified established images and cultural axioms while they served as conduits for nationalistic performances that would have been enacted in their absence, albeit not necessarily in precisely the same fashion. Thus political stump speeches and slogans, conventions, campaigns, elections, inaugurations, and all manner of public service messages are all grist for the microphone and video camera, and so too the ticker-tape parades, international sport competitions, state funerals, special anniversary celebrations, and other rituals. Television, in particular, may well be the strongest vehicle for sustaining myth and ritual in contemporary America (Goethals, 1981); but it has not been particularly effective as a creator of original symbols or even heroes, except those of the most ephemeral sort. As for radio, even during its heyday in the 1930s and 1940s, it served only marginally in sustaining nationalism. The rare exceptions, such as Norman Corwin's World War II radio dramas (C. C. Alexander, 1980: 227–28), which are almost never mentioned nowadays, only serve to confirm the basic irrelevance of radio to the cause of modern American nationalism.

Of all the modes of human expression, perhaps none has greater immediate emotional power, and thus the potential for quickening nationalist passion, than does music. The effect on individual or mob may be only fleeting, but it can be powerful and decisive. There seems to be a general rule that revolutionary euphoria uncorks a great burst of political music, as happened, for example, in France during its revolution and eighty years later in the Paris Commune. The American experience confirms the rule. Although only the jaunty *Yankee Doodle* has endured, we have evidence that it was just one of hundreds of rousing songs composed during the American Revolution (Moore, 1846). These new melodies or original verses set to older traditional tunes undoubtedly aided the war effort substantially as well as hastening the advent of a culturally unified nation. Subsequently, nationalistic songs continued to resound throughout the land, providing an effective means for bonding a widely dispersed, diverse population. George Washington was, of course, a favored subject during the early years, and was hymned to the point of deification (Lawrence, 1975:96). *Hail Columbia* (1798) attained instant popularity, and "seems to have played a helpful part in keeping people loyal to the Union," as did *The Star-Spangled Banner* (Werner, 1932:28–29). The Civil War prompted another eruption of songwriting on both sides of the conflict, primarily for use among noncombatants, and several numbers have remained popular to this day. In his perceptive study of Civil War music, James Stone (1941) draws a sharp distinction between what was sung by the troops—overwhelmingly the popular music of the prewar period, though sometimes in parody versions, and almost nothing in a nationalistic vein—and the music that buoyed the spirits or bloodlust of the civilians. "Patriotic songs are one of the ways in which commands to civilians are expressed" (Stone, 1941:547).

The significance of music seems to have declined rather steadily in subsequent wars. The Spanish-American conflict has left us with only one durable ditty, the frivolous *There Will Be a Hot Time in the Old Town Tonight*. World War I yielded three or four items of lasting value, but if World War II inspired a few hits, their popularity was fragile, and none are current today. The Korean and Viet-

namese conflicts and lesser unpleasantnesses have left no residue
at all on the musical scene.

We can observe much the same trajectory in the realm of songs
for political campaigns (Lawrence, 1975; Silver, 1971). Like so
many other standard devices in the political armamentarium, the
campaign song flourished for the first time in 1840 among Harrison's partisans (Gunderson, 1957:123–47), then remained reasonably important for most of the following hundred years. But such
music has gone into eclipse within the past several decades according to Irwin Silber. "The decline in campaign singing which first set
in after World War I was further accelerated after the second great
war. Radio and television were rapidly replacing the old-fashioned
campaign rally, and by the sixties, the new 'cool' media completely
dominated the vote-getting process" (Silber, 1971:281).

If there are some places where nationalistic music has remained
important, one of them has certainly been the public school. The
genre figures prominently in school songbooks (Kraske, 1972; Pierce,
1930:217–21). *America, America the Beautiful, Columbia the Gem
of the Ocean,* and the like are practiced in class, and frequently
performed at assemblies and ceremonial occasions. They may not
be forgotten later, but just how often adults sing any of these numbers, aside from our official and unofficial national anthems, is difficult to judge. In another setting, brass bands and their martial
music, and especially the hymns of the various armed forces (which
bear a close resemblance to college fight songs) have, if anything,
gained in popularity in recent years. It may be significant that their
apolitical lyrics embody a militarism that was uncharacteristic of
the spirit of early America.

When the British adopted *God Save the King* as their national
anthem in 1745 (Boyd, 1980:xiii–46), they initiated a precedent
that every sovereign country in the world has eventually felt constrained to imitate (Boyd, 1980; Merriam, 1931:147; Nettl, 1967;
Wakeling, 1954). Such emulation suggests their potency,[48] and indeed "national anthems, like national flags, are among the purest of
political symbols" (Zikmund, 1969:73), though few can rival the
Marseillaise for sheer power and durability (Vovelle, 1984).

The nonexistence of a national anthem was acutely embarrassing
for loyal unionists at the outbreak of the Civil War. Despite a
widely publicized drive supervised by a distinguished committee in
1860–61 and the offer of a $500 prize (a munificent sum in those
days), none of the 1,200 entries were deemed acceptable (White,
1861). The United States was surprisingly slow in making its offi-

cial selection, and most citizens today would privately agree it was not the wisest of choices. We have more than adequate documentation of the history of the composition of the poem entitled "The Star-Spangled Banner" and how it was set to a popular tune ultimately derived from a Germanic source (Boorstin, 1965; Delaplaine, 1947; Kouwenhoven and Patten, 1937; Sonneck, 1914). The verses met with instant public approval, but the musical setting gained ground quite slowly (Nye, 1966:69).[49] Only after much prodding and lobbying by nationalistic organizations did Congress finally designate it as the national anthem in 1931. Despite the adequacy of the lyrics, the tune lacks the raw emotional punch of the *Marseillaise, Deutschland über Alles*, or even *Dixie*, much less *The Battle Hymn of the Republic*; and its singability leaves much to be desired. The anthem has also suffered from overfamiliarity. It is sung, or hummed and mumbled, quite perfunctorily, before countless athletic events and at all sorts of public meetings and ceremonies; and we hear it, to distraction, at the beginning and end of the broadcast day for many a television station. (In contrast, Mexican law strictly prohibits the performance of the national anthem at any but the most solemn of occasions.) For all these reasons, and also the relative lameness of *My Country 'Tis of Thee* and *America the Beautiful*, another far more singable and stirring composition, Irving Berlin's *God Bless America*, has acquired the status of a de facto national anthem, one for which many Americans now rise and bare their heads.

Many countries include their indigenous music and dance within the storehouse of deeply cherished national symbols. The United States has not been so fortunate. Although it has its share of authentic folk music, it would be unrealistic to claim any strong connection with the nationalist cause for the blues, jazz, bluegrass, cowboy laments, or square-dancing, however rich their cultural worth may be. At another level, that of art music, unlike several European cases, not many American composers have seriously striven to identify themselves with the folk and popular idioms of their native land. With the exception of George Gershwin, the works of the few that have succeeded (for example, Aaron Copland and, most particularly, Charles Ives [Kammen, 1978:89]) have been enjoyed only by that limited fraction of the population patronizing symphony and ballet performances. But I cannot close this discussion of the role of music in the making and maintenance of American nationalism without noting that, despite certain lacks and weaknesses, nationalistic and martial numbers, mostly holdovers from the past, remain among the more significant mainstays of the nation-state. Indeed it is impossible to imagine public life without such songs, hymns, and marches in the United States, or any other viable nation-state for that matter. Above all, the rousing marches of John Philip Sousa retain their powerful appeal and remind us of an era of unquestioning national self-assurance (N. Harris, 1983).

The pieces of the puzzle are beginning to lock together.

As we have threaded our way through a large mass of highly varied materials, it has become evident that the outward signs and symbols of American nationalism tend to fall into regular patterns. Despite a number of loose ends and some apparent contradictions, the most effective organizing frameworks for these regularities seem to be time and space. Indeed, the perceptive reader may already have discerned the grand schema toward which this essay is wending, a model that best accommodates all the evidence thus far adduced having to do with symbols as causes and effects of American nationalism. But the most irrefutable testimony is still to come. Encoded in the built landscape of the United States are solid clues: tangible, relatively durable, overlapping strata of national and statist objects generated by several generations of citizens and their agents. Let us decode the clues.

FIVE ★ ★ ★ ★ ★ ★ ★ ★

NATIONALISM ON THE LANDSCAPE

In every sovereign country of the modern world, the workings of the state have set their mark upon the land.[1] Nowhere today is this more evident than in the United States. Such a statement would have made little sense two hundred years ago, for the landscape did not begin to change immediately when the United States became independent on July 2, 1776. Back then the humanized landscape of the young republic was essentially a replica of the Western European models from which it was derived; and tangible signs of central authority were exceedingly few and far between either here or abroad. As the country and its state apparatus matured, however, America gradually acquired the full complement of physical trappings that have become standard for the self-respecting nation-state, and even initiated a few of its own.

THE IMPRESS OF THE STATE

It was in the realm of internal political boundaries and land division that the federal presence first expressed itself in meaningful material form. It was only belatedly, after our international boundaries were finally stabilized, that they became visible by means of monuments, border stations, custom houses, and, in some instances, especially along the Mexican border, physical barriers. The fact that by far the greatest part of American territory was acquired by, and settled under the auspices of, the central government has had profound implications for the shaping of the map and settlement features. The creation of new states and territories, following the original thirteen, meant that federal officials delineated interstate boundaries, often doing so in distinctively geometric fashion, and then proceeded to subdivide and dispose of the land in accord with a simple, highly standardized scheme. Indeed "nowhere else was so much land surveyed in so short a period according to one

standard method" (H. B. Johnson, 1982).² Approximately half the
total American population now resides on land parcelled out since
the mid-1780s under the rules of the federally managed rectangular
survey system. The result is that a very large fraction of our property and fence lines, field boundaries and roads, and many of our
county and minor civil division boundaries are perpetual witnesses
to the brawn and legitimacy of the state; and it is not difficult to
believe that we have absorbed the lesson, even if only subliminally.

During the early decades of the Republic, the federal establishment was relatively tiny in size and had not yet consolidated its
power, a situation reflected in its then puny physical plant. In
1816, the total civilian work force of the U.S. government included
no more than 4,847 persons, and it had increased to only 36,672
in 1861 (Craig et al., 1978:163). (By March 1984, the figure had
climbed to 2,895,587.) Even in Washington, D.C., for many years
the Capitol was the only structure to invite serious attention by
reason of bulk or architectural aspiration. The rest of the newborn
capital city was an embarrassment or ordeal to domestic and foreign visitors. Outside the District of Columbia, the only serious
material evidence of central authority was a string of lighthouses
along the Atlantic Coast acquired by action of the first Congress in
1789—"the first structures over which local communities had no
control" (Stilgoe, 1982:111), probably because of the inadequacies
of local finances.³

Eventually, however, federal edifices rose up in every corner of
the land, often dominating the immediate scene by virtue of sheer
size or stylistic bravado. For the world as a whole, administrative
buildings related to the central government have become prominent features in the urban scene only rather recently (Merriam,
1931:151). But by the mid-nineteenth century in the United States
every up-and-coming metropolis considered itself entitled to a federal courthouse, the larger and more pretentious the better. As Lois
Craig has pointed out, "towns everywhere clamored for federally
funded buildings as an indication of stature. And Congressmen
obligingly served them up. For example, Memphis received a courthouse even though no federal courts were held there. . . . Indeed to
people in towns such as Dubuque, Iowa and Astoria, Oregon, federal buildings represented the latest in architectural style and technology and, symbolically, membership in the Union" (Craig et al.,
1978:163).

The ubiquitous U.S. post office building with its centerward
siting became a conspicuous part of the American scene after the

passage of some years; and, at least until quite recently, standardized architectural styles affirmed the watchful presence of Uncle Sam. On a more intimate scale, we also find within all cities countless mailboxes, formerly painted olive drab, but more recently an eye-catching red, white, and blue. Other federal buildings now abound: National Guard armories, recruiting offices for the armed forces, Social Security offices, and, in county seats, offices of the U.S. Department of Agriculture. Certain localities are also graced by the presence of custom houses, federal penitentiaries, Veterans Administration hospitals (of uniform design), divisional offices of various bureaucracies, and federal lighthouses, canals, and waterways. Furthermore, in terms of both acreage and sheer number of specialized structures we can hardly ignore the facilities of the Army, Navy, Air Force, and Coast Guard.

The national military cemetery is a peculiarly interesting and effective device for promoting the statist mystique (Mosse, 1979). Prior to the Civil War era, no national government had paid much attention to the possibility of the organized burial of battle casualties and veterans; but in 1863 the United States initiated the widely imitated practice with the dedication of the Gettysburg Battlefield (Mosse, 1979:7–8; Patterson, 1982). Since then, the number and acreage of the American examples—largely, but not exclusively, on home territory—have expanded greatly, becoming rather standardized in their landscaping (Mollenhoff, 1983; Steere, 1953–54a, b, c). They have not been ignored by the public; in fact, some, most notably Gettysburg, have become tourist attractions, with results that are visually questionable (Patterson, 1974); but the crucial consideration is that soldiers' cemeteries "were characterized by order and the subordination of the individual to the community" (Mosse, 1979:9).

And there are other constructed objects to remind us of an expansive, intrusive central regime. Over the years, the Corps of Engineers has transformed the appearance of many parts of the country with its dams, dikes, and associated flood control and navigational projects. Within a multistate region, the Tennessee Valley Authority has imprinted itself boldly upon the land since the 1930s; and other landscape legacies of the New Deal, especially the buildings, tree plantings, and other creations of the Civilian Conservation Corps (CCC) and Works Progress Administration (WPA) have indelibly altered the face of the United States (Cutler, 1985). It is also difficult to ignore the federal presence in the public housing projects to be seen in so many of our cities. And, although they do not fall into any convenient category, we dare not overlook the nearly ubiquitous, basically statist American Legion and VFW halls. Along our highways we frequently encounter large billboards exhorting us to invest in federal bonds or to enlist in some program or service directed from Washington. Smallest and least visible of these stigmata of a centralized state, but far from trivial, are the stone and metal markers implanted in the ground by the Geological Survey and Coast and Geodetic Survey.

Widespread and striking though they may be, the rectangular survey system and the aggregation of federal structures are not the only visible evidence of a seemingly omnipotent state. The federal government owns and manages a formidable fraction of America's territory; and such lands may be distinctive in appearance as well as being frequently signposted and fenced. Especially prominent among such landholdings are, of course, the various national parks, forests, and monuments that have become so treasured a part of American life. It is unlikely that any other country has set aside so much real estate or lavished so much money and attention on communal playgrounds and wilderness areas. Americans can claim another first in this instance, for the world's national park movement did indeed originate in the United States in 1872 (Nash, 1970); and we can see "the national park movement in America . . . as an outgrowth of the nineteenth century American search for national pride" (Powell, 1983:72).

Another important way by which the central state has imprinted itself upon the land has been via a national highway system. Although the federal government involved itself quite early in road programs and other internal improvements, it did so in desultory fashion for a long while, and lagged behind most other advanced countries in this respect. Indeed, it was not until 1925 that a federal agency finally mandated a national highway numbering system and began the installation of standardized signs (Stewart, 1953:13–14). But, since the mid-1950s, the U.S. Department of Transportation has financed and supervised what may well be the world's most grandiose public works project: the Interstate Highway System. The implications, direct and indirect, have been immense for many aspects of our economic and social geography, and not least for the American landscape. Most immediately, there are the homogenized highways themselves with their uniform engineering standards and system of signs, never letting us forget the supremacy of the state.[4] But conspicuous by their absence—for reasons probably rooted deep in the national psyche—are two items quite commonly found in other lands: a national railroad system and a national airline.

Although the visible impress of the state is inescapable throughout the length and breadth of America, it is in the nation's capital that we encounter by far the most concentrated and powerful expressions of statist ideas. And indeed, the City of Washington was designed with that purpose in mind. "In the realm of broad (and somewhat trite) generalities the most fundamental fact about Washington is that it was created for a definite purpose and has been developed according to a definite plan. Therein lies its unique distinction among American cities and among all existing capitals in the western world" (Federal Writers' Project, 1937:3–4). Here is still another instance in which Americans can claim priority in invention, for Washington was the first totally synthetic capital city, creating a precedent for Ottawa, Canberra, Brasilia, Islamabad, New Delhi, Ankara, Belmopan (Belize), and other such latter-day efforts (Fifer, 1981; Henrikson, 1983:124). The only possible earlier claimant is St. Petersburg, which was founded in 1701; but that was a multipurpose development, one that did not become the seat of the Russian Empire until 1714.

As is well known, the original physical plan for the District of Columbia embodies the thoughts of Washington, Jefferson, and other luminaries as well as L'Enfant's.[5] The remarkable street layout and placement of official buildings resulting from their deliberations were, at least for the first decades of national existence, curiously at odds with the temper of the times and an egalitarian populace, and provided a paradox that has not escaped John Reps's notice. "All the baroque design motifs of European planning developed over the years in the old world suddenly and splendidly found application in this virgin setting for the capital of the newest of the world's nations. It was a supreme irony that the plan forms originally conceived to magnify the glories of despotic kings and emperors came to be applied as a national symbol of a country whose philosophical basis was so firmly rooted in democratic equality" (Reps, 1967:21).

Yet the city founders may have been shrewdly prescient of what lay in store in this calculated physical expression of the deeper implications of the new constitutional principles. The tableau of twentieth-century Washington superbly expresses the role of the metropolis vis-à-vis the country and the world at large. The theatrical ensemble of majestic vistas and plazas, great phalanxes of em-

bassies, government and national association offices, heavily symbolic architecture (as discussed below), sophisticated landscaping
and nighttime illumination of crucial structures, and the regiments
of statuary (Evans, 1981)—all these and other elements combine to
overpower the viewer. One's first pilgrimage to Washington can be a
blinding religious experience, a rite of communion.[6] An adequate
discussion of Washington, D.C. as a concrete expression of nationalism and statism calls for a lengthy monograph rather than this
cursory note. In any event, it is difficult to think of any other national capital that so consummately pronounces the nation-state
creed in material terms.

The items discussed thus far are unambiguous expressions of the
existence and workings of the American state. As we turn to other
landscape features that transmit nationalistic messages, we learn
that they are, for the most part, products of the "American nation,"
in the particular sense in which we have defined that term, but not
totally so. We also detect some lively statist influences.

NATIONALISTIC MONUMENTS

Monuments and memorials of varied form abound in the United
States as they do in many other parts of the world. But here they are
especially interesting by virtue of sheer numbers and the fact that
so many are nationalistic in intent or effect. Furthermore, an exceptionally large share of these nationalistic items originated through
local or private efforts, not by governmental decree, and thus are
authentic expressions of nationhood.

The simplest way to define a "monument" is to identify it as any
object whose sole function at present is to celebrate or perpetuate
the memory of particular events, ideals, individuals, or groups of
persons—especially those "excellences worthy of permanence"
(Friedlander, 1976:epilogue). (Monuments are also usually, but not
always, visually obtrusive.) So defined, the concept may embrace
tens of millions of gravestones and many other items of purely local meaning. But our concern is limited to those monuments that
honor some element of the nationalistic credo, and, to make matters simpler, those that are freestanding outdoor constructions. The
most characteristic examples are in the form of statuary, obelisks,
columns, towers, arches, cairns, special templelike edifices, and
such relics of military glory as tanks, cannon, naval vessels, an-
chors, aircraft, and rockets. Although they may be much less conspicuous, we may also admit to this category many of the historical

markers that line our higways (L. V. Coleman, 1933:83–84; Leng-genhager, 1967–70; Pisney, 1977).

The concept of the monument is, of course, closely akin to that of the memorial, but there is a critical distinction to be made. The memorial object serves more functions than does the single pur-pose monument, and almost any kind of item can be pressed into service. Thus we have memorial parks, gardens, forests, bridges, auditoria, stadia, highways, benches, government buildings, and in-stitutions of every description, not to mention the memorializing name that can be attached to anything. If a few items do straddle the line between monuments and memorials, such as the tombs and some birthplaces or homes of presidents and other national notables (C. Jones, 1962; Laird, 1971), for the most part, the divi-sion between the two groups is clear and useful.

By their very nature public monuments, of whatever descrip-tion, verge close to sacredness, not unlike the temples, shrines, and historic landmarks with which they are often associated. In-deed, as Marvin Trachtenberg has so tellingly characterized them, monuments "function as social magnets, crystallizations of social energy, one of the means civilization has devised to reinforce its cohesiveness and to give meaning and structure to life. Monuments are a way men transmit communal emotions, a medium of continu-ity and interaction between generations, not only in space but across time, for to be monumental is to be permanent" (Trachten-berg, 1976:15). Given the profound implications of the monument for the geographer, historian, anthropologist, and other students of humankind, it is unsettling to discover the meagerness of its litera-ture.[7] Neil Harris's flat statement that "there is no adequate study of American monuments" (N. Harris, 1966:375) applies to the world in general and all its major divisions, with the splended ex-ceptions of a detailed monograph on Quebec (Hébert, 1980) and another on French monuments to the casualties of World War I (Prost, 1984).[8] The best stopgap yet available for the American scene is Friedlander's (1976) photographic essay with its short, but perceptively eloquent, epilogue by Leslie George Katz, while in a brief essay J. B. Jackson (1980:89–102) tantalizes us with the hidden strata of meaning lurking within the monument. The few general treatments or commentaries that touch on the United States vary greatly in quality and factual heft, but all are essentially sketches (Doezema, 1977; Geist, 1978; N. Harris, 1966:188–98; Krythe, 1968; Laas, 1972; Trachtenberg, 1976).

If nothing approaching a general census of monuments exists for

the United States, we do have a handful of local publications of
good quality cataloguing and discussing monuments and outdoor
art in general. Fittingly enough, the list includes the District of
Columbia and environs, an area undoubtedly boasting the densest
aggregation of nationalistic and other public monuments within
the nation (Evans, 1981; Goode, 1974; Zangrando, 1974); but a few
other major metropolitan areas have received their due: New York
(Fried and Gillon, 1976; Saltus and Tisné, 1923; Sharp, 1974), Chicago (Riedy, 1981), Philadelphia (Fairmount Park Art Association,
1974), Boston (Whitehill, 1970), San Francisco (Snipper, 1975), Detroit (Nawrocki, 1980), and Pittsburgh (Gay and Evert, 1983). And
then we have accounts of monumental statuary for just a few
smaller localities: Newark, N.J. (Thurlow, 1975), Fresno (Fresno
Mall Art Committee, 1973), and Morris County, N.J. (Bostick,
1978). For the great intervening gaps I can offer only some relatively
casual impressions, namely that every urban center of consequence
has at least a few monuments consecrated to the memory of nationalistically significant ideals, events, and personages. But even
at the bottom of the settlement hierarchy it is not uncommon to
find a marble shaft or other monumental object in a crossroads
hamlet honoring the local war dead and veterans or some hero or
cause dear to the nationalist's heart.

The siting of nationalistic monuments presents us with some
interesting questions. Many of them rest, in umbilical fashion, at or
near the events they commemorate, often in rural places. But the
more imposing examples are generally urban in location, and usually lack any territorial bond with whatever is being celebrated. In a
few spectacular instances, the site itself contributes mightily to the
monument's effectiveness. Thus the artful placement and orientation of Bartholdi's Statue of Liberty in New York Harbor dramatically underscore its intent and have helped it become the national
icon it now emphatically is (Handlin, 1971; Higham, 1984; Pauli
and Ashton, 1969; Trachtenberg, 1976). Similarly, one cannot imagine the visually and symbolically overpowering Jefferson Memorial
Arch standing anywhere but on its inevitable site along the St.
Louis waterfront. And, within Washington, it would be difficult to
improve upon the appropriateness of the siting of the Washington
Monument. At the other extreme, however, we have Borglum's
mammoth carvings on Mount Rushmore, a site determined by
physiographic and lithologic circumstance (Fite, 1952). Despite the
remoteness of the monument—it was not accessible to the public
by road until some years after the project began—the object and its

image have gripped the national imagination as have few other rivals for nationalistic affection.

Within our cities, we most often find the nationalistic monument within the ceremonial center(s), plots of ground not necessarily coincident with the central business district's functional center. Such hallowed spaces may adjoin the city hall, county courthouse, federal buildings, or civic centers with their auditoria and museums, points where processions and mass meetings begin or end on solemn occasions. The installation of the monument adds substantially to the symbolic aura of its environs, or, at the very least, "man's created equivalent of a natural landmark" (Friedlander, 1976:epilogue) lends the sort of visual punctuation to the scene that even the infidel cannot ignore.[9] Indeed, many an otherwise emotionally neutral parklet or street intersection gains identity and radiates symbolic meaning solely because it contains a monument of note. Beyond the principal ceremonial centers, there are alternative choices: bridge approaches, parks, cemeteries, and college campuses, which are also, of course, foci of concentrated communal energy. On a humbler level, many a city neighborhood has dedicated a small patch of landscaped, flag-bedecked ground to an Honor Roll that lists and lauds the local residents who have served in the armed forces. It would seem that monuments and/or flagpoles dominate our civic ceremonial centers in much the same manner as temples or cathedrals have done in the premodern cities of the Old World or Latin America. And church buildings are conspicuous by their near-absence from both the ceremonial and business centers of the American city.

Although monuments may proclaim the glories of national events, notables, and abstractions, the great majority have achieved only local notoriety. But they are overshadowed by a potent few that have transcended place and time to become the durable objects of universal American devotion, a company that includes: Mount Vernon, the Washington Monument, Lincoln Memorial, Independence Hall (Maass, 1970; Rhoads, 1976:241), the Liberty Bell, the Statue of Liberty, Old North Church, Plymouth Rock, Old Ironsides, Monticello, the Tomb of the Unknown Soldier, Mount Rushmore, and the Vietnam Veterans Memorial. Who could possibly count all the miniature replicas and photos of such monuments sold by gift and souvenir shops?

What specific phenomena do our nationalistic monuments represent? Most frequently national heroes and epochal events, less frequently such noble abstractions as Independence, Victory, Freedom,

Patriotic Valor, Equality, Progress, often to the accompaniment of
the actual hardware of battle, or through the use of eagle, flag, idealized beings, and other artistic devices. Within the first two categories, the emphasis falls overwhemingly on the military and political, especially if we ignore items of local interest. We commemorate great wars and battles, major treaties, and the Declaration of
Independence, and there are innumerable likenesses of presidents,
generals, and various patriots, but, aside from Columbus,[10] few explorers and even fewer inventors, except perhaps in New York City,
that hotbed of cultural strivers and consumers (Saltus and Tisné,
1923). Leading American figures in the arts and sciences are conspicuous by their rarity. A sculpture honoring Longfellow may be
the only example of this genre within the District of Columbia
(Goode, 1974:26–27); and one must search long and hard across the
land to track down monumental remembrances of such candidates
for culture hero status as Francis Scott Key, Mark Twain, Whitman,
Emerson, Edison, Ford, or Lindbergh.[11]

   If every American president, leading statesman, martyr, notable
general and admiral has received his monumental due, there are
three historic personages whom we encounter with special regularity in stone and metal incarnations. Statues of, and abstract
monuments to, George Washington are so widespread as to be uncountable, as are other forms of his iconography (Eisen, 1932). The
most extended treatment of "Lincoln in Marble and Bronze" discusses eighty-seven examples selected from a much greater population of such effigies (Bullard, 1952), while one authority claims
that "the number of statues, busts, and portraits bearing Franklin's
name is exceeded by no other American except possibly that of
Washington" (Riedy, 1981:272). In addition to actual individuals,
the American landscape contains many idealized representations of
certain mythic types: Miss Liberty in her many guises, the Minute
Man, the Pilgrim Fathers, the Pioneer Mother, Union (and Confederate) soldiers, and the World War I doughboy. Indeed, some of these
items seem to have been mass-produced for an eager market, as was
the "American Doughboy" series manufactured by a plant in Chicago (Bostick, 1978:23). Also worthy of mention in this context are
the many small-scale replicas of the Statue of Liberty set up by the
Boy Scouts of America during the 1920s in small towns throughout
the United States, but mainly in the Middle West, few of which
have survived to the present time (Jackson, 1982; Schlereth, 1982).

   The chronology of our nationalistic monuments offers as many
insights and questions concerning the changing American ethos as

does the spatial distribution of their dramatis personae. Although no examples have survived, Colonial America did have a few monuments honoring British royalty and statesmen, the most famous of which was the equestrian statue of George III toppled and melted down by a New York City mob on July 9, 1776 (Saltus and Tisné, 1923:xvi). The earliest—and, for a long while, only—durable landscape feature denoting nationalism was the Liberty Tree or, in its literally stripped-down version, the Liberty Pole, a device whose ultimate origin as a symbol of life or freedom may stretch back into prehistoric millenia. Specific trees, usually pine, decorated with rebellious inscriptions were gathering places for the insurgents; the tall poles often bore the Liberty (or Phrygian) Cap on their peaks (Albanese, 1976:58–68; A. M. Schlesinger, 1952). Evidently the tree/pole device and its reproduced image were quite effective in stimulating national fervor and in annoying the British and their adherents. In any event, the phenomenon did outlive the Revolution for a few years and was also adopted by the French Jacobins (Ozouf, 1976:303–16). Eventually it faded from the American scene, but hickory poles were erected for the presidential campaigns of the 1830s and 1840s, with a last hurrah in the Frémont effort of 1856 (A. M. Schlesinger, 1952:456–57). Even more ephemeral were the arches and decorations arranged for the grandest of occasions, such as Washington's inaugural journey or Lafayette's 1824–25 tour of a hysterically receptive republic.

Aside from the short-lived Liberty Tree/Pole, the post-Revolutionary American landscape was remarkably bereft of monuments of any sort for several decades; and exceedingly few of the rare pre-1850 nationalistic items have survived. Although "by 1774 Plymouth Rock had become a symbol worth capturing by the Sons of Liberty" (Craven, 1956:32), a formal dedication was delayed until 1820 (Somkin, 1967:107–10), and it was not until well into the nineteenth century that it became an object of widespread veneration (Commager, 1975:191). The first public sculpture in New York, then as now our largest city, was an effigy of Alexander Hamilton, ca. 1810, although it is not clear whether it was displayed indoors or outside (Sharp, 1974:5); but "by the middle of the 19th century, New York City was still relatively devoid of any substantial public sculpture" (Sharp, 1974:6). The first monument dedicated to Washington, fourteen years in the making (1815–29), was completed in Baltimore thirty years after his death (J. M. Hatch, 1978:204).

It is probably correct to claim that "the American monument

tradition starts . . . with the Bunker Hill Monument in Charlestown, Massachusetts . . . the first historical marker of major consequence in the United States" (Laas, 1972:7). Initiated in 1823, with
a cornerstone laid on the fiftieth anniversary of the battle in 1825—
by Lafayette, appropriately enough—amidst a most elaborate ceremony, the monument was finished eighteen years later (Ellis, 1843;
Wright, 1953). The Concord Monument did not take nearly as long
to complete, for it was dedicated six years earlier on July 4, 1837
(Sarles and Shedd, 1964:56). But perhaps no such project is more
imposing or dramatic, or longer in construction, than the Washington Monument in the nation's capital. After many years of discussion, it was finally begun in 1848, but not completed until 1885.
This same period also witnessed the opening chapter of the American historic preservation movement, with the acquisition by New
York State in 1850 of the Hasbrouck House, George Washington's
headquarters at Newburgh—our very first house-museum—and
shortly thereafter with the rescue of Washington's Mount Vernon
estate, as a small band of determined women acquired and restored
the building and grounds, converting the place into the first of
our great monument-shrines (Hosmer, 1965; G. W. Johnson, 1953;
Thane, 1966, 1967).

If there were two or three conspicuous early pioneers, the urge to
build nationalistic monuments did not begin to take hold in a serious way until the 1850s, and it was only after Appomattox that the
movement became genuinely contagious. Thus an 1856 statue of
Benjamin Franklin may have been the first such object in Boston
(Riedy, 1981:272; Whitehill, 1970:8). The earliest significant item
in New York City dates from the same year: Greenough's equestrian statue of Washington in Union Square; and until then "there
was no monument to commemorate our struggle for independence,
nor was there a single statue in recognition of the achievements of
our national and local heroes" (Fried and Gillon, 1976:vii–viii). The
first public monument anywhere in Ohio was the Perry Monument
(1857–60), unveiled in Cleveland, but later moved to Toledo (Hargrove, 1977:23), while, in both Chicago and Morris County, N.J.,
1876 was the year for their initial national monument (Riedy, 1981:
3; Bostick, 1978).

During the half-century or so following the Civil War, there was a
veritable explosion of monumental sculpture in the United States,
most of it imbued with nationalistic motifs (Sharp, 1974:6; Whitehill, 1970:15), and

in large part sponsored by civic groups, patriotic organizations and private citizens eager to commemorate wartime heroes. Small towns with modest funds purchased inexpensive, hastily manufactured bronze or granite soldiers. The larger urban centers either constructed granite ensembles of soaring columns with garlanded maidens personifying such worthy attributes as War, Victory, Valor and Peace, or memorialized valiant officers in minutely detailed statues. But the most lavish projects honored the great war leaders. [Fairmount Park Art Association, 1974:188]

And, of course, other great national heroes. In the victorious North, the profusion of military monuments was truly extraordinary (Baruch and Beckman, 1978). A questionnaire mailed to postmasters of the 354 cities and towns of Massachusetts in the early 1900s disclosed the fact that 233 of these places boasted one or more memorials to the officers and men of the Union Army to a total of 348 items. These were in addition to some 34 GAR halls and the many "memorial" libraries and other public buildings so dedicated (Roe, 1910). In similar fashion, though necessarily in rather smaller numbers, the Southern states honored the "Lost Cause" with many poignant sculptures of the men in gray, especially during the period 1900–10 (Davis, 1982; Emerson, 1911; Widener, 1982; Winberry, 1982, 1983).

It is essential to point out that, with few exceptions, these costly projects were conceived, initiated, and funded mainly by the citizenry in grass-roots fashion rather than by federal or other governmental agencies. Today, as in the past, when Congress or local administrations have been asked to appropriate money, the results have usually been slow, grudging, and partial. Instead, patriotic associations, ad hoc organizations, public-spirited businessmen, and even schoolchildren have provided most of the cash and enthusiasm. Furthermore, the process of funding, creating and dedicating these monuments stirred up a fine frenzy of excitement we would find difficult to imagine nowadays. The public responded to newspaper appeals and the passionate oratory of committee members and followed every detail of project design and choice of sculptor until the festive day when tens of thousands assembled around a site awash with dignitaries (Fairmount Park Art Association, 1974: 136–37). The scene at the Washington ceremonies described by J. M. Goode was characteristic: "Sculpture became a peculiarly 'Vic-

torian event.' This meant that the dedication of a statue often resulted in the closing of all businesses, with crowds of 20,000 or
more attending the band concerts, parades, and marathon speeches
that accompanied nineteenth-century dedications in Washington"
(Goode, 1974:25). And, subsequently, the monument site would often provide the stage for anniversary and other public celebrations.

By the time of World War I, and certainly by the 1920s, there was
a precipitous decline in the number, size, and importance of nationalistic monuments and notable stylistic changes in those that were
constructed (Jackson, 1980:95–97). "War memorials erected from
1920 onward were generally smaller stone tablets with appropriately engraved inscriptions," (Baruch and Beckman, 1978:ix). In his
treatment of Boston statues, Walter Muir Whitehill found very little to discuss within the post-1950 period, and "in the past decade
when there has been space to fill, it has been by an abstraction
rather than a portrait of anybody" (Whitehill, 1970:15), in keeping
perhaps with general trends in the world of art. Similarly, "few figural monuments have been installed in Chicago in recent years"
(Riedy, 1981:177); and a catalogue of Fresno's publicly owned art, all
of it dating from the 1960s, fails to mention anything at all of a
nationalistic bent (Fresno Mall Art Committee, 1973). These trends
may transcend international boundaries. In tabulating the dates of
monuments in London and Washington, David Cannadine (1983:
164) found a strong parallelism in the temporal profiles of the two
capital cities. Quite clearly, in recent years the art community and
the public at large have lost nearly all interest in celebrating national virtues in monumental form. Turning to J. M. Goode again,
we find that "the marble and bronze renditions of idealized heroes
in carefully executed uniforms, or the togas and honorary laurel
wreath of antiquity, are less frequently produced in the 1970s. Today the meanings of the Classical and Biblical themes and symbols which were so familiar to the public until the early twentieth
century are generally obscure, or altogether forgotten" (Goode,
1974:26).

The practice of memorializing the combatants in recent wars
may not have gone entirely out of fashion, but the method of imple-
mentation certainly has. Thus we have the new fashions as reported by Bernard Mergen.

In 1948, the editors [of *The American City*] were happy to report that a survey of 740 Chambers of Commerce revealed that
265 communities had built or were planning memorials, in-

cluding 42 auditoriums, 29 recreation parks, 20 athletic stadiums, 19 hospitals, and a variety of airports, art centers, fountains, and museums. Only 19 of the war memorials were statues or monuments. The non-military nature of the majority of the memorials and the Fine Arts Commission's explicit warning to avoid "cast-iron soldiers or a pile of cannon balls," suggests that the Iwo Jima memorial taking shape in the minds of the sculptor and the committee [for the Marine Corps War Memorial] raising funds to pay him was an anomaly. [Mergen, 1983:3]

Most of the monuments built or planned of late are abstract in design (Hubbard, 1984:25; P. C. Johnson, 1945), for example, Saarinen's immense catenary curve in downtown St. Louis.[12] An essentially nonrepresentational project may also be a hybrid of monument and museum, as exemplified by the Franklin Delano Roosevelt Memorial proposed for Washington's Tidal Basin, which still languishes in a legislative limbo (Creighton, 1962).

The joint dilemma of the art community and a citizenry anxious to assuage its grief and bewilderment by erecting a lasting tribute to the martyrs of statism is nowhere more poignantly illustrated than in the recent furor over the Vietnam Veterans Memorial on the Washington Mall (Clay, 1985b; Hine, 1982; Howlett, 1985; Marling and Silberman, 1985; Mergen, 1983). The art establishment prevailed, for the most part, since the dominating central portion of the monument is nonfigural; but the opposition party—peopled largely by veterans' groups, nationalistic organizations, and citizens of basically conservative political-social coloration—did manage to salvage a victory of sorts by emplacing three life-size bronzes of American fighting men, along with an American flag, off toward the edge of the site. Contrary to all expectations, the central element, the low, black marble wall, containing nothing but the names of the casualties, has been a major success, emotionally as well as aesthetically. Nevertheless the larger question of how to design public art with legible messages in acceptable forms remains unsolved. That may be one of the reasons why the country still lacks any important monument to the troops involved in the Korean conflict (Phelps, 1985). Be that as it may, a great half-century burst of monument building has bestowed upon the American landscape thousands of durable artifacts. A few may have been shifted to different sites and some destroyed, but the great majority linger on to remind us of an era of uninhibited national glorification.

We are left with two interesting historical problems: Why the long delay—some seventy or eighty years after Independence—before the general advent of the nationalistic monument? And why has it become less fashionable in recent decades? The first question is especially intriguing in view of the fact that, as we have seen, nationalism manifested itself so vigorously in several other mediums during or immediately after the Revolution: hero-worship, national holidays, the folk and popular arts, oratory, place-names, and personal names. Among the more obvious explanations, we have the technical and financial. During the early Republican period, there were too few native or imported artists and too little surplus wealth for monumental projects. But Clive Bush may have hit upon a more fundamental reason: "There is a history of long resistance to public statues during the first 30 or so years of the republic's life. The predominantly ex-Puritan populace preferred to internalize in conscience their moral imperatives, rather than have them induced externally by artifacts all too easily connected with idolatry and popery" (Bush, 1977:38). Or at least the Protestant, frequently Calvinist, rulers of the young nation's moral conscience were so inclined (P. C. Johnson, 1945:9).

As for the second problem, one might argue two points: first, that since the 1920s, the art community has been unable or unwilling to find proper designs for nationalistic monuments; second, that the majority of the monuments in question would be war-related and that the nature of our wars may contribute much of the answer. Thus the two most traumatic conflicts, those most integral to our communal hoard of symbols, the Civil War and, however belatedly, the Revolution, have generated more than their share of public art. In part, this may have been because they were fought on American soil. On the other hand, such events as the War of 1812, the Mexican, Spanish-American, Korean, and Vietnamese wars and World War I (all, except the first, foreign affairs) have, to a significant degree, polarized the national community or burdened us with ambiguous afterthoughts and, consequently, have yielded a meager monumental legacy. However, this argument founders on the fact that American participation in World War II was enthusiastic, unequivocal, and generated great pride in our martial exploits, yet produced only a slight ripple on the visible landscape. We must search more deeply for explanations, but can do so only after considering some additional facets of the American scene.

THE NATIONAL PAST MUSEUMIZED

There is a not so subtle difference between the nationalistic object that is solemn and celebratory and one that is didactic or merely amusing. If the former, the genuine monument, has fallen out of fashion of late, the other group has multiplied remarkably in recent decades. It is an entity for which we have no convenient generic term, but embraces such phenomena in the constructed landscape as historic sites and landmarks, preservation projects, museums, and their variegated ilk. True enough no sharp break is visible between the two extremities of what is in reality a continuum—Monticello, for example, belongs to either camp, depending on the attitude of the visitor—but the essential distinction is profoundly meaningful.

The monument is visible testimony of an active faith, one which deeply engages the hearts and minds of its participants: the internal covenant made palpable. On the other hand, museumized objects may speak of matters historical and nationalistic, but, whatever the maker's intent, at a considerable psychological remove, as just another roadside attraction. Significantly, they seldom claim the same locational priority within our towns and cities as do the monuments, but are scattered hither or yon wherever historical happenstance or commercial guile may happen to dictate. We gaze at the famous battlefield, the boyhood home of, say, James Buchanan, or Fort Ticonderoga, or Williamsburg as we would at a television screen or a stage (and these places may indeed mount pageants and reenactments), as passive spectators. Insofar as we absorb the historic data, it is through a gentle romantic haze, and things have become somehow simplified, denatured, and cosmeticized. The fact is that Americans have never learned how to cohabit congenially with their past. As future-oriented creatures during the first century of our national existence, this may not have been a problem; but after the rendezvous with the future proved to be less satisfying than had been anticipated, we have increasingly sought solace and refuge in a factitious dream-time: a young America of heroic deeds and unblemished seraphim.

I would suggest that the historic preservation movement, which has been busy remaking some crucial fractions of the American scene in recent years, and which came into being in the last quarter of the past century, along with most of our patriotic and hereditary organizations, may have been, in part, the first serious exercise at backward-glancing nationalism (Maass, 1976b; Wallace, 1981).

Among its objectives was the instruction, and thus the spiritual salvation, of an increasingly disaffected or simply ignorant public. Thus the all-important Williamsburg reconstruction was deliberately conceived as a device for "constructive *civic* action," a way of strengthening "a citizen's commitment to defend the principles of liberty" (Adam, 1937; Carson, 1981:32; Geist, 1978; Wallace, 1981); and such motivation was not entirely absent from the minds of those who initiated other projects in this genre, for example, those of the Daughters of the American Revolution (Somerville, 1979; Strayer, 1958:32–34). The zeal that Americans have displayed over the past hundred years in packaging significant leftovers in the interest of a rather diffuse nationalistic sentimentality may well exceed anything achieved by other countries, as claimed by Nicholas Zook. "In no other country have such vast sums of money been expended for the rescue and refurbishing of old and significant sites and structures. In no other country have so many dedicated individuals donated so much time and energy to preserve historic landmarks in order that this generation, and future generations, might share through them the trials and glory of our forebears" (Zook, 1971:7). On the other hand, in this country, as elsewhere, the historic preservation movement, and that larger phenomenon within which it is subsumed, the museumization of the past, is complex in origin; plainly more than jingoism is involved (D. Lowenthal, 1966, 1976). Furthermore, the movement serves several purposes, including a rather cold-blooded commercialism (Lee, 1982). Since a full discussion would take us too far afield, I shall have to content myself here with a simple inventory of what we can see in the built landscape in the way of memorabilia bearing nationalistic overtones.

The earliest efforts to museumize our past dealt with the abodes of presidents, and the impulse to convert such places into tourist attractions is far from spent. In fact, it is not only presidential residences that are being preserved, refurbished, or reconstructed but also birthplaces, graves, tombs, and other places associated with our chief executives and even some of their vice-presidents (Haas, 1976; Hampton, 1928; Laird, 1971, 1980; U.S. National Park Service, 1979). The brief moment of glory enjoyed by Plains, Georgia may represent the *reductio ad absurdum* of this trend. The newest wrinkle in such voyeurism may be the presidential library (T. A. Bailey, 1966:57–59; T. Schlesinger, 1981:704–7). Since FDR initiated the practice, an unwritten rule has compelled every successor (and Herbert Hoover to boot), or his admirers, to have an imposing edifice erected to house his papers and other relics. But such institutions serve more as a magnet for tourists than as a summons to scholarship.[13]

Public museums have flourished in the United States for more than a century, but initially they tended to confine their interests almost exclusively to the fine arts and natural history, or to science in general. In the past few decades, however, these institutions have proliferated remarkably in number and variety; and, among the more specialized establishments, the historical and the military figure prominently (E. P. Alexander, 1979; American Association of Museums, 1979; Wittlin, 1970). The historical and military museums operate under a wide diversity of auspices, including federal and local government agencies, special-purpose associations, and commercial proprietors; but, whether their coverage is local or continental, the message—overt or otherwise—is a commitment to the glory of the national past. Americans have been especially zealous in creating that specialized type of museum known as the Hall of Fame (T. C. Jones, 1977; Soderberg and Washington, 1977). Although the great majority are concerned with celebrities in the worlds of sport and entertainment, the earliest—and perhaps most important—was the nationalistically oriented Hall of Fame for Great Americans at New York University (1901) (T. C. Jones, 1977: 339–52); and one may suspect nationalistic motives underlying the general movement.

Although the United States has more than its share of conventional and unconventional museum buildings, Americans seem also to have pioneered in the museumization of the outdoors (Schlereth, 1981). Scores of forts with some claim to historic interest have been preserved, signposted, and otherwise made available to the public (Haas, 1979). And has any other nation preserved and made open-air museums out of as many battlefields as has the United States?[14] Moreover, nearly every structure and site significantly associated with the American Revolution and Civil War seems to have acquired historic landmark status or at the very least a roadside marker (Boatner, 1973; Cromie, 1975). The United States has witnessed an unparalleled proliferation of house-shrines and house-museums honoring national and local notables of every sort (L. V. Coleman, 1933).[15] Although Americans may have borrowed the notion of the museum village from its European inventors, they have developed it with remarkable zest (Alderson and Low, 1976; Haas, 1974; Zook, 1971). These complexes may consist of authentic structures that have been preserved or rehabilitated, or they may be latter-day replicas not necessarily situated at the places they are supposed to represent. In their most sophisticated version they become living museums in which suitably trained and costumed performers similate the everyday existence of the village residents (Carson, 1981; Wallace, 1981). Although they function to entertain the public and to instruct them concerning the presumed realities of the past, the element of nationalistic indoctrination is not entirely absent from the museum village, and it is inescapably present in such institutions as Williamsburg and the Lincoln Heritage Trail (Zook, 1971:34–35, 83–87).

Finally, at an even further remove from the traditional historical museum, we find another American innovation, the theme park (Starbuck, 1976). Even though it may be only a glorified amusement park and, of course, profit-making enterprise, seldom does it lack some historical attractions with an implicit nationalistic message. Unfortunately, the one venture that did make American ideals its controlling theme, "Freedomland in the Bronx, New York, lasted only a few dismal years" (Starbuck, 1976:20).[16]

It is important to realize that the twentieth-century museumization of the American past, like the wave of monument building that preceded it, is mainly the work of the private sector and nongovernmental associations. Federal agencies, such as the National Park Service, may play a role, along with state and municipal governments, but the critical impulse flows from citizens' groups, voluntary organizations, philanthropists, and entrepreneurs, and government intervention is usually after the fact. What we may be experiencing is a vague, lingering echo of an early robust nationalism, the search for reassurance through the tangible artifact. Nowhere is this more evident than in the ways Americans chose to celebrate the Bicentennial of independence.

In every respect, including manifestations in the built landscape, the 1976 festivities differed sharply from the happenings one hundred years earlier. "The centralized nature of the 1876 festival contrasts vividly with the dispersed quality of the Bicentennial" (D. Lowenthal, 1977:264). The latter involved thousands of locally generated activities rather loosely coordinated by a national commission. Conspicuous among the bicentennial projects, which included all manner of displays, pageants, reenactments, and other excitements, were the many additions to the visible scene. In addition to the predictable new museums and other civic buildings, historical landmarks, and works of art, walls and lampposts across the land blossomed forth with patriotic devices and murals. Hitherto innocent surfaces were daubed with red-white-and-blue stripes and five-pointed stars. And, as David Lowenthal has noted, the Bicentennial intensified an already vigorous form of architectural fetishism. "Long before the Bicentenary, ersatz Independence Halls of every size and material had sprung up all over the country, serving as banks, schools, libraries, courthouses, shopping centers, and prisons. In 1976 these replicas became still more numerous" (D. Lowenthal, 1977:263). Whether or not South Bend, Indiana is justified in claiming to be the originator of the idea, cutely anthropomorphic, red-white-and-blue fireplugs often "in the likenesses of Revolutionary War soldiers and other American heroes" materialized in many cities, so that "the fireplug troops now outnumber the combined forces of Washington's several ragtag, eighteenth-century armies" (Schlereth, 1980:216). In contrast to the countless traces of the nation's two hundredth birthday party strewn far and wide across the American landscape, many of which may survive well into the next century, a few buildings in Philadelphia's Fairmount Park are now the only visible reminders of the 1876 celebrations.

But the fundamental point to be made about the Bicentennial applies to the entire range of activities and objects that it inspired: that it was an exercise in retrospection and historical make-believe.[17] As we have already observed, "it was all so different from the centennial celebration of 1876, when the most modern machines and technology were displayed at the Philadelphia Exposition as favored symbols" (Woodward, 1977:584). That exhibition "scarcely referred to history at all—a complete contrast to the 1976 celebration that lovingly recalled and recreated the past and constantly invoked it" (D. Lowenthal, 1977:266). Indeed, the American celebrants of 1976 had very little to say about the contemporary situation and even less about the future. The unspoken implication may have been "that the nation's greatness lay wholly in the past" (D. Lowenthal, 1977:266). Yet, strangely enough, the past with which we so lovingly dallied was somehow lacking in authenticity. It was a remote, selectively filtered past, an idealized vision of youth and innocence; and, what was most remarkable in a celebration of the events of 1776, any allusion to revolutionary ideas was in distinctly bad taste (Zuckerman, 1978). The landscape consequences of this attitude, the failure to contrive any fresh new symbols, was the mass production of some souvenirs, and a spate of references to a sanitized creation myth. If it arrives, will the Tricentennial bring something different?

FLAG AND EAGLE

Who can deny the exceptional importance of the national flag in
the hearts and minds of contemporary Americans—or in their visible landscape? Indeed, "for many Americans the flag is literally a
sacred object" ("Who Owns the Stars and Stripes?," *Time*, 1976:15),
and "the flag . . . is a symbol so charged with emotion that people
cannot look at and judge, even, whether or not the design is aesthetically good or bad" (Pullen, 1971:184). In part, as a prominent
student of flag lore has suggested, this is because "our nation lacks
both a royal family and a single dominant religion. Hence, in
searching for an encompassing symbol, the majority have traditionally rallied around the flag. We invented—the first people to do so—
an annual Flag Day. Our children pledge allegiance to the flag. . . .
Unquestioning loyalty to the flag has been considered a fundamental American principle" (Whitney Smith as quoted in Wolfe, 1975:
61). And among some segments of the population flag fetishism has
gone well beyond the threshold of hysteria (Balch, 1890; L. Harris,
1971; Woelfly, 1914). Although we lack the detailed research to confirm the notion, I am inclined to accept the statement that "the flag
has always occupied a much stronger place in American life and
mythology than have flags in other countries" ("Who Owns the
Stars and Stripes?," *Time*, 1976:15), except perhaps for the word
"always." It may not be too extreme to argue that, as *the* organizing
symbol of our nation-state and of the Americanism that is its civil
religion, the flag has preempted the place, visually and otherwise,
of the crucifix in older Christian lands.

Is the United States unique among the countries of the world in
its obsession with its national flag, and, specifically, in the propensity to display it in public places? In lieu of published data or a
methodical worldwide survey, any answer must be provisional. I
have the impression that the combination of green, white, and
red—the order in which they appear on the Italian flag—has been
used with increasing frequency recently to denote things Italian
in signs and advertisements within the United States. But from
the scattered information and recollections available to me, my
guess is that the only countries that rival America in the frequency
with which the citizenry exhibit the flag of their own free will may
be the Scandinavian (Lassen, 1985) and especially Sweden (Abler,
1983; Hägerstrand, 1984; Leighly, 1985), where the national colors
(blue and yellow) are conspicuously presented on a great variety of
objects. Many Swedish homes and vacation cottages are equipped

with flagpoles from which the national flag is flown frequently, but rather more in the spirit of hospitality than nationalism (Häger-strand, 1984). The Swedish flag code is almost as elaborate as the American, and flag display is prescribed for no fewer than sixteen holidays, religious as well as national.[18] The incidence of national and provincial flags in Canada is significant, but well below the level of its southern neighbor. I recall seeing very few flags of any sort, except in government installations, in Mexico, Central America, Great Britain, and Ireland during my travels there; and I am told that the private display of the national flag in both Brazil (Schiller, 1982) and Australia (Albinski, 1985) is exceedingly uncommon. In the course of several thousand kilometers of highway and ship travel through Germany, France, Belgium, Switzerland, and Turkey during the summer of 1983, I took special pains to note flags along the way. In the case of West Germany, I did not observe a single national flag aside from those on naval and merchant ships and government buildings; and very few were visible in the other countries, with the single interesting exception of Switzerland. In that land a fair number of private residences fly the red-and-white national banner, but the frequency of such displays is well below the modest level to be seen in Canada and, presumably, Sweden.

Thanks to the efforts of various vexillologists, we know all that anyone could reasonably wish to know about the legal, heraldic, and most other aspects of the history of the American flag (Hope, 1973:292–96; Krythe, 1968:1–26; Quaife, 1942; Quaife et al., 1961; W. Smith, 1975). But we know much less, indeed very little, about the actual history and geography of public or private flag display in the United States. A few scholars have amply documented the enduring vitality of the flag in our folk arts, especially on items destined for domestic use, including furniture, fabrics, china, crockery, wall decorations, quilts, and virtually every imaginable, and some unimaginable, objects (Horwitz, 1976:54–75; Mastai and D'Otrange, 1973). Anyone who has browsed through American newspapers and magazines of the twentieth and the late nineteenth centuries can hardly avoid noticing the extensive exploitation of the flag in mast-heads, advertisements, cartoons, and corporate logos, as well as on commercial products and company stationery. The American flag may well have attained peak intensity in the popular arts during the period extending from the 1960s through the Bicentennial when "Middle Americans" and adherents of the Counterculture waged a kind of guerrilla campaign against each other using the flag, following quite different modes of reverence and taste, so that

it appeared in various guises on things and surfaces that might not
have been thinkable earlier.

But despite the extraordinary significance of the national flag in
American life, scholars have shown no interest in its place within
that tableau of outdoor objects we designate as the landscape, except for its display on school buildings and grounds (Balch, 1890;
Davies, 1955:219; Dearing, 1952:472), and a solitary academic sor-
tie that examines flag display in a working class neighborhood of
Philadelphia on Flag Day (Cybriwsky, 1972:200–202). Nevertheless
even the most casual sort of fieldwork quickly reveals how conspicuous and pervasive a role our national flag plays in the present-day American scene. It inevitably adorns every federal, state,
county, and municipal facility, and we find flags on or next to, as
well as inside, museums, public and private schools, and many or
most office buildings, hospitals, cemeteries, apartment buildings,
and churches (Hayes, 1926:120). Surprisingly few factory or ware-
house structures lack flags, and often the pole and associated landscaping are large, elaborate, obviously costly affairs. A high percentage of service stations and other highway-related establishments
display the flag on poles, exterior walls, or windows. We also encounter it on streetside holiday decorations, trucks and autos, advertising signs and billboards, clothing, and many a manly tatoo. In
brief, it is ubiquitous. Perhaps most revealing of underlying attitudes is the large number of private residences having flagpoles or
other flag hardware that fly the national banner constantly or on
selected occasions. As is the case with all the other places noted
above, with the possible exception of federal and school buildings,
such manifestations of patriotism are quite voluntary, as well as
rather expensive; they are not the product of any ukase from on
high. Indeed, federal laws and regulations governing flag display,
designed, in part, to prevent commercial use and desecration, were
not promulgated until well into this century (Collins, 1979:24).

It is important to note that no other types of flags—the nearest competitors being the corporate banners of some franchise operations—approach such ubiquity. Unlike the Canadian situation,
where the provincial flag may rival the national device in popularity, one rarely observes the flags of states or our larger cities
except on official structures. Indeed, most citizens would not recognize any if they did happen to see them.

Much less widespread, but still quite numerous, is another symbol related to the flag, but more directly kin to the national seal:
the red-white-and-blue shield.[19] This familiar design abounds, of

course, in markers along the national highway system; but it crops up repeatedly in corporate and association logos and many kinds of commercial and noncommercial signs. It is but one facet of a more general recent phenomenon that has escaped serious attention, except in connection with the Bicentennial celebrations: the red-white-and-blue motif (D. Lowenthal, 1977:263; "Who Owns the Stars and Stripes?," *Time*, 1976:13).

The frequency with which this color combination shows up—almost always in the indicated sequence—in the logos of major and lesser business firms and on every conceivable sort of sign and public decoration—is actually quite astounding.[20] In some instances, obviously, the choice of hues is calculatedly allusive, but much more often, I suspect, the subconscious mind has been at work. The designer divines, in instinctive fashion, that these are the colors most likely to strike a responsive chord in the general psyche. One might argue that the juxtaposition of red, white, and blue is visually jarring and thus ideal for advertising and related purposes, but other tricolor formulae can be even more effective as attention-getters. Perhaps the most convincing evidence of the nationalistic import of these colors is their relative rarity in public spaces in Canada and, I believe, other foreign lands as well.

These three interrelated items—the flag, shield, and red-white-and-blue motif—are so omnipresent in such numbers that perceptual saturation may have set in. They recede comfortably into the familiar visual background against which we tend to notice mostly only the out of the ordinary; but if they were absent, we might well be vaguely disturbed. As I can attest from field experience, much concentration is needed to perceive the full extent of their physical presence; but, when one does go through the exercise, the degree to which the American visual scene is punctuated by these symbols is truly mind-boggling.

Less flamboyant than the national flag and its derivatives but almost as ubiquitous and as richly suggestive of popular attitudes regarding the American republic is our national totem, the eagle. This magnificent creature, wings outstretched, appears, usually in metal, wood, or plastic painted black or gold, on countless homes and outbuildings as well as on nonresidential structures and signs. In residential settings we find the fowl perched over house doorways and garage entrances, atop flagpoles, on gable ends, walls, mailboxes, snow guards, and door knockers, and delineated on all manner of decorative items on porches and lawns (Lynch, 1979: 150–54, 355, 359, 386). And the term *eagle* occurs with more than random frequency in the names of natural features, business firms, and other man-made phenomena.

As we shall learn shortly, the history of the eagle's place in American life has been quite different from that of the flag. Although, as a heraldic device, the eagle in one form or another has been prominent in the military and political insignia of many empires and states, for example, Rome, Germany, Austria, Poland, and Russia, from ancient times to the present (Herrick, 1934:179, 230), the eagle was not a common motif in the British North American colonies (Isaacson, 1975:v). But it did burst upon the American consciousness suddenly and triumphantly with its incorporation into the national seal in 1782 (Hunt, 1909; Krythe, 1968:27–32; Patterson and Dougall, 1976; Silverman, 1976:320–23, 366, 416–18). In the posture in which we know it so well, the spread-eagle version of the American bald eagle, it was, as Philip Isaacson argues, a canny choice. "The bird was an exclusively American form, inherently majestic and visually simple. Its strength and independence corresponded exactly with America's self-image, and the simplicity of its shape made it the perfect vehicle to express that image. The eagle could be so readily understood and so easily used that by 1810 it had become the country's most popular emblem and the universal badge of an American" (Isaacson, 1975:6). Marshall Smelser has articulated the eagle's truly profound symbolic value: "Probably no modern civilized nation has venerated its national emblem as much as Americans. To them it has assumed a moral value transcending the mundane purposes of national identification. As a tribal totem it satisfies the real and almost universal hunger for a public symbol of spiritual kinship above any invulnerable to the contentions and changes of politics—and for which no other totem is available to the United States" (Marshall Smelser as quoted in Albanese, 1976:261–62).

In the two centuries since its adoption, the eagle has remained a conspicuous, often exciting element in American iconography (Bush, 1977:304–5; Herrick, 1934:231–47; Hornung, 1941; Krythe, 1968:40–46). Much of the symbol's instant popularity in the early republican years may be attributed to its consorting with Miss Liberty in some widely influential engravings (L. C. Jones, 1975:5; Kammen, 1978:95–96). In 1791, it appeared atop what was perhaps the earliest formal patriotic monument in the land, the Beacon Hill Monument (Hitchcock and Seale, 1976:39). Very quickly the eagle began to decorate every possible object produced by folk and commercial artisans for use within and outside the home (Horwitz, 1976:

35–39). Thus, for example, it was to be found on andirons, wall-paper, stirrups, circus wagons, butter molds, trivets, snare drums, weathervanes, coverlets, and cast-iron banks (Cahill, 1942); paper decorations, furniture, political buttons (Isaacson, 1975:164–93); "mastheads of journals, broadsides, recruiting posters, young ladies' watercolors, sheet music, playing cards, Pennsylvania frakturs, copybooks, labels for canned goods, currency, governmental documents, and any other material where a patriotic suggestion had even the most remote relevance" (Isaacson, 1975:167); military insignia (Campbell and Howell, 1963); tavern signs (Melder, 1976:51); on the prows, sterns, and pilot houses of ships (Pinckney, 1940); on firefighting companies and their equipment (Isaacson, 1975:186–90); presidential campaign posters (Tripp, 1976); and other political paraphernalia (Isaacson, 1975:193); political cartoons (Weitenkampf, 1952:374); glassware (Knittle, 1927:224–25 passim); circus carousels (F. Fried, 1964:165–70); newspaper and magazine advertisements (Cahill, 1942:94–95; J. C. Taylor, 1976:24–27); wartime posters (Darracott and Loftus, 1972:58; Yanker, 1972:53–56); and, of course, on coins (Herrick, 1934:246–57).

In terms of sheer numbers, the American eagle may be as prevalent today as it was during the halcyon decades of its youth. Indeed, there is reason to suppose it has yet to reach its peak as a decorative accent on the exterior and grounds of the American house. Nevertheless some of the symbolic stuffing may have leaked out of the bird. The smaller number of latter-day craftspeople who still exploit the eagle motif may not be displaying quite the verve and inventiveness—or uncritical national pride—of their predecessors (Horwitz, 1976:51). And Isaacson observes, perhaps with some justice, that the eagle "no longer embodies our national aspirations. . . . When the Country was young, it needed a symbol that would tangibly express its intention to maintain its political individuality. The eagle was a perfect vehicle to express that determination, but that goal was achieved long ago, and the sense of mission has since gone out of the bird. *It is still a staunch image but without the animate force it once had*" (Isaacson, 1975:84; emphasis added).

If the eagle has largely compensated whatever loss in symbolic cargo it has suffered through sheer numerical proliferation, the historical career of the American flag has been radically, surprisingly different both quantitatively and qualitatively. During its early career, the national flag was remarkably unimportant to the citizenry at large (and it was many decades before its design and dimensions attained strict standardization) (Quaife, 1942). The negative evidence is impressive. In an exhaustive treatment, *The American Revolution in Drawings and Prints*, that covers the period up through 1789, Cresswell (1975) does not include a single representation of the flag. Similarly, the largest collection of songs and ballads of the Revolutionary period fails to include any reference to the flag even in its earliest versions (Moore, 1846). In what may well be the most nearly definitive catalog of American political iconography on textiles we shall ever see—1,501 illustrations in all—the earliest American flag depicted is to be found on an 1815–16 bandanna celebrating the Battle of New Orleans, while the first to appear in a symbolic mode shows up on an 1819 kerchief (Collins, 1979:68–71). An analysis of some 2,500 Fourth of July orations delivered between 1777 and 1876 notes that the flag was seldom mentioned before 1845 and the Mexican War (H. H. Martin, 1958:401). As of 1794, as M. M. Quaife has remarked,

> the Stars and Stripes had never been carried by our army, nor would it be for another generation to come. We had no navy to display it abroad, and while it floated over some merchant ships and over land fortifications, the vast majority of Americans never came in contact with a fort or with a ship at sea. Since they seldom, if ever, saw the Stars and Stripes, and never, until the Mexican War of 1846–48, fought under it, they did not possess the sentiment of love for the Flag which today is shared by all Americans. [Quaife, 1942:99–100]

If the ascendancy of the flag began in earnest with the Mexican conflict and perhaps also with the growing popularity of Francis Scott Key's "Star-Spangled Banner," "the start of the Civil War encouraged for the first time on a wide scale the display of the national flag" (Mastai and D'Otrange, 1973:130–33; W. Smith, 1975: 91). Mastai and D'Otrange are quite specific in dating the emotional coming of age of the flag.

> The cult of the national flag, as it has endured to this day, was a direct outcome of the Great Rebellion. . . . Edward Everett, in Boston two weeks after the attack on Fort Sumter, spoke of "the flag, always honored, always beloved [but now] worshipped." The word was by no means too strong. And what had been a stern and solemn enthusiasm in wartime became a joyous delirium at war's conclusion. As one writer asserted: "After the fall of Sumter [to federal troops] Cincinnati was fairly iridescent with the red, white and blue." Cincinnati was but typi-

cal of all cities, towns, and villages over the length and breadth of the land. [Mastai and D'Otrange, 1973:130]

But the climactic era of flag worship was still to come. Indeed, it was only in 1943 that the Flag Code, originated by voluntary associations, was legalized by Congress (Horwitz, 1976:73). Flag Day was first celebrated in 1877, but the movement to popularize the holiday did not really take off until 1890 (Myers, 1972:173–83; Davies, 1955:218). From the late 1880s onward, and especially during the 1890s, organized zeal on behalf of the flag attained fever pitch. Not too coincidentally, as we have seen, this was also the period when many of our patriotic-hereditary organizations were founded or began to flourish, when fresh varieties of xenophobia began to sprout, and when old-fashioned imperialism attained its maximum virulence. In 1888, the influential, mass-circulation *Youth's Companion* launched a sustained campaign to install a flag over every schoolhouse in the nation, as well as for the universal adoption of the Pledge of Allegiance (L. Harris, 1971). Simultaneously, in 1889, the GAR proposed that flags be flown by all public schools in New York, then later in other states, and labored mightily against flag desecration and to induce civilians to salute the flag, something they had seldom done previously (Davies, 1955:219–22; Minott, 1962:25). Indeed, we can attribute much of the modern ritual surrounding the flag to the exertions of this first large veterans' organization and its successors. And their efforts bore fruit in the 1890s as Mary Dearing discovered. "When a G.A.R. committee first mounted a school platform to present its flag to an attentive young audience, the flying of the Stars and Stripes over educational institutions was virtually unknown. By 1895 the commander in chief was able to boast that they floated over 17,988 of the 26,568 public schools within the twenty-one Grand Army departments" (Dearing, 1952: 472).

Unfortunately, the available verbal documents say nothing about the flying of flags by private dwellings, business establishments, or public buildings other than schools, or the changes in this practice over time. But we can extract useful information from two sources: the illustrated county atlases of the late nineteenth century and especially the 1870s (Thrower, 1972) and present-day field observations. A sizeable minority of the hundreds of county atlases included not only maps and general accounts of the history and geography of the locality but also—for a consideration to be sure—marvelously detailed engravings of many of the principal farm-

steads, town dwellings, and commercial structures and, occasionally, the countenances of their proud proprietors.[21] We can be certain that the artists idealized their subjects to some extent, but we
can be equally certain that, in this era of exuberant materialism,
they overlooked no detail, however trifling, that might brighten the
image of their patrons. Thus the drawings of house, shop, or courthouse are photographically precise; and, among the multitudinous
gear depicted, we can espy lightning rods, dinner bells, birdhouses,
weathervanes, croquet hoops, the very slats of the shutters, and on
the passing vehicles and pedestrians, the carriage hardware and
every flounce on the ladies' skirts. If flags or flagpoles had been
visible, the artist would not have dared to omit them.

I have examined some forty-nine illustrated atlases, with a median publication date of 1875–76, for counties in Ohio, New York,
Pennsylvania, and Michigan, states in which I also carried out field
observations. (Illustrated county atlases are rare or nonexistent in
Wisconsin and states outside the Midwest and Middle Atlantic region). Only 16 of the 3,417 single-family dwellings appearing in
these publications were shown flying flags, and another 6 had poles
but no flags, for a grand total of 0.6 percent of the buildings enumerated (Table 5.1). Since we are dealing here primarily with upper-
class citizens, that is, those most financially capable of expressing
their patriotic urges in tangible form, this value may overstate the
general prevalence of American flags on the residential scene of the
1870s. Flags were much more numerous in the vicinity of nonresidential structures. Of the 246 public edifices (schools, churches,
government buildings, etc.) tabulated, 8.9 percent sported flags or
flagpoles, while the score is 11.0 percent for the 767 commercial
and manufacturing establishments. Architectural eagles were so little in evidence in these early atlases there was no point in noting
them.

During the summers of 1981 and 1982, I systematically observed
flags, flag hardware, and eagles on the exteriors and grounds of occupied single-family dwellings in rural tracts and smaller towns
on days other than national holidays along automobile traverses
through the following areas: central Pennsylvania, southwest New
York, northern Ohio, southeast Michigan, south-central Wisconsin,
southern Ontario, western Connecticut and Massachusetts, western Maryland, eastern West Virginia, western Virginia, and north-
central North Carolina. Deliberately omitted were observations of
nonresidential buildings and grounds, that is, places in which the
incidence of flags is so great as to be uninteresting. Virtually all

government facilities fly at least one flag; a conservative estimate for shops and office buildings would be 25 to 30 percent and for factories and warehouses well over 50 percent. I was able to record both flags and eagles only on those trips for which an assistant was available.

Flag display by American homeowners occurs in a variety of ways. The most elaborate is on a large metal flagpole set in a carefully landscaped plot that may contain decorative objects as well as flowers and low shrubs. But in many places the pole may be much shorter and simply inserted into the grass; and, in the extreme case, the flag may be only the tiny object schoolchildren brandish while watching parades. Although these poles, or just the flags, usually stand in front of the house, they often appear on lawns off to the side and, occasionally even in the backyard (thus making a full count from the highway rather difficult). Nearly half the poles observed would seem to be flying the flag night and day throughout most or all of the year; on the others the flag may appear only on holidays and other special occasions. On a significant minority of houses, we find flagpoles attached at an oblique angle to the porch or wall or flags draped on a window or wall or from the porch railing, some of them small pocket-size affairs.[22]

The incidence of all these forms of flag display among the 11,763 residences observed in 1981–82 was 4.7 percent, several times greater than the value derived for portions of the same areas a century earlier. At 4.2 percent, the popularity of the eagle is almost as great. Although it would be useful to have a denser network of field observations in the states and province already mentioned and in others as well, the data in table 5.1 seem to support one major conclusion: a remarkably sharp disparity in the propensity to display flags and—to a lesser but still significant degree—eagles, as between the Northeast and the South at the present time (and inferentially earlier as well). Although the flag-and-eagle syndrome may be strongest in portions of Ohio, New York, New England, and Wisconsin, it is far from trivial in all the observed portions of the Northeast, except for some parts of Pennsylvania dominated by pietistic German-Americans. But southward from the latitude of Winchester, Virginia there is an abrupt falling-off in the phenomenon; and in the Deep South one can travel many miles before finding even a single private home displaying the national banner, or the Confederate flag, for that matter. Its incidence there is relatively low even on nonresidential properties. This North/South differential would hold even if one were to make allowances for the

Table 5.1. *Premises of Occupied Single-Family Dwellings Observed for National Flags, Flagpoles, and Eagles*

Area	Premises Observed for Flag Items	Flags on Freestanding Poles (No.)	(%)	Flags on Buildings (No.)	(%)	Poles without Flags (No.)	(%)	Total Flag Items (No.)	(%)	Premises Observed for Eagles	Eagles on Houses or Outbuildings (No.)	(%)
Ohio												
1875	1,440	4	0.3	0	0.0	2	0.1	6	0.4	—	—	—
1981	567	24	4.2	8	1.4	38	6.7	70	12.3	—	—	—
New York												
1875	337	3	0.9	0	0.0	0	0.0	3	0.9	—	—	—
1981	731	33	4.5	16	2.2	28	3.8	77	10.5	—	—	—
Connecticut/Massachusetts												
1982	440	22	5.0	13	3.0	8	1.8	43	9.8	440	27	6.1
Wisconsin												
1981	701	33	4.7	0	0.0	33	4.7	66	9.4	701	8	1.1
Pennsylvania												
1875	1,017	5	0.5	0	0.0	4	0.4	9	0.9	—	—	—
1981–82	1,621	44	2.7	18	1.1	33	2.0	95	5.9	834	47	5.6
Maryland/West Virginia												
1982	642	10	1.6	5	0.8	21	3.3	36	5.6	642	49	7.6

Michigan												
1875	623	4	0.6	0	0.0	0	0.0	4	0.6	—	—	—
1981	486	5	0.8	1	0.2	20	4.1	26	5.3	—	—	—
Subtotal (North)												
1875	3,417	16	0.5	16	0.0	6	0.2	22	0.6	—	—	—
1981–82	5,188	171	3.3	61	1.2	181	3.5	413	8.0	2,617	131	5.0
Virginia												
1982	2,942	15	0.5	16	0.5	24	0.8	55	1.9	2,942	114	3.9
North Carolina												
1982	714	0	0.0	2	0.3	1	0.1	3	0.4	714	17	2.4
Subtotal (South)												
1982	3,656	15	0.4	18	0.5	25	0.7	58	1.6	3,656	131	3.6
Ontario												
1981	2,919	48	1.6	2	0.1	34	1.2	84	2.9	0	0	0.0
Total												
1875	3,417	16	0.5	0	0.0	6	0.2	22	0.6	—	—	—
1981–82	11,763	234	2.0	81	0.7	240	2.0	555	4.7	6,273	262	4.2

Note: 1875 is a median date for information gleaned from atlases. The data for 1981 and 1982 are from field observations.

Source: Zelinsky, 1984b:82.

greater percentage of poorer homes in the South. It is interesting to note that the incidence of the new maple leaf flag and the older imperial ensign in Ontario, which suffers competition from the provincial flag, is well below the comparable value in the U.S. Northeast, but also far above the Southern value. And, of course, eagles are nowhere to be seen on Canadian buildings.

This observation of a steep latitudinal gradient parallels closely the discovery of that equally sharp disparity between North and South in the incidence of nationalistic place-names already noted. What we may be witnessing in the cases of both place-names and tangible nationalistic symbols are but two visible manifestations of a deep, stubbornly durable disconformity between the cultural and social mind-sets in these two major regions.

In any case, the evidence adduced above leads inescapably to the conclusion that the public display of the American national flag—and derivative items—has increased mightily over the past two centuries and may still be increasing today, and that this fact suggests some important changes in the collective emotional life of our citizenry.[23]

THE BUILDINGS SPEAK

"The buildings which a society constructs convey information at a symbolic level. Collectively, they are a formal expression of its needs, values, and aspirations" (Lambert, 1978:10). And, in keeping with this axiom, the buildings of the United States do indeed speak to us eloquently of our political and other ideologies. Unfortunately, however, students of the American landscape have not yet acquired total fluency in the language and dialects of structures. If architectural historians have learned how to decode the messages of the more elaborate, sophisticated items and if cultural geographers have acquired much understanding of rural dwellings, fences, and barns within the folk genre, we are just beginning to look seriously at the popular, or vernacular, buildings that constitute by far the largest part of this great family of artifacts. But even with the limited knowledge at our command, it is clear that nationalism has been one of the more influential factors in shaping building styles from the earliest years of independence until the present moment. It is also apparent that nowhere else in the built landscape is the transition between nation and state as hazy as it is in the realm of architecture.

American nationalism has expressed itself visually most unequivocally and persistently through the medium of the Classical Revival. Although the imitation or updating of Hellenic and Roman models has occurred everywhere throughout the Western World in modern times, no other land has espoused the movement with equal enthusiasm or has so wholeheartedly absorbed neoclassical motifs into the national idiom. Nowhere else has classicism so deeply pervaded so many strata of life and society, or done so with so pointed a political moral. As we have already seen, the theme of America as Athens or Rome reincarnated and perfected appears in our place-names, personal names, oratory, fine arts, and iconography in general. But, most of all, it was by means of their temple-like buildings that Americans flaunted their spiritual manifesto and self-image before the world (Gowans, 1964:243–84; H. M. Jones, 1964:269–72; Nye, 1960:270–73). Perhaps no one has explored this notion more effectively than Alan Gowans.

> They thought of classical architecture, first of all, as symbolic of liberty, of freedom from tyranny. . . . In the United States that symbolism . . . stood for the patriotic Protestantism of one-hundred-per-cent Americans, a religion with none of the "subversive" taint of "Tory" Episcopalians or "foreign" Roman Catholics. Temples were an "officially proper" form for churches just as they were for homes, courthouses, or state capitols. Questions of convenience or appropriateness hardly entered into the matter; it was the patriotic symbolism that counted. [Gowans, 1966:70]

> Most of all, classical revival architecture seemed a witness to the success of the great American experiment "of the people, by the people, for the people." Capitals and pediments and gleaming white walls, embodying in their identical classical forms and proportions common ideals and standards everywhere from Maine to Alabama, seemed visible refutations of old sour predictions that the new republic would fall apart into anarchy like the city-states of antiquity. [Gowans, 1964:276][24]

Thus during the first six or seven decades of the republic, Greek Revival and closely related forms of architecture were the preferred styles for a broad range of public and private buildings. Although Thomas Jefferson may have been the single most influential advocate for the style, this was a development whose time and place had arrived, and undoubtedly would have materialized fully even without the efforts of the Sage of Monticello. The neoclassical craze may have reached worldwide proportions, eventually penetrating localities as farflung as South Africa, India, and Japan, but it reached its climactic intensity in the United States in sheer quantity and functional diversity; and special architectural nuances evolved that rendered the American forms nonexportable to other lands for ideological or other reasons. Even in nearby Ontario, perhaps the most Americanized of Canadian provinces, British Colonial Classicism distinctly deviates from the brand that flourished just south of the border (Gowans, 1966:71).

One obvious expression of American distinctiveness was the adoption of white paint for neoclassical frame structures and, subsequently, for the great majority of vernacular buildings of whatever style. Such a passion for whiteness may be unparalleled elsewhere, and, as John Stilgoe maintains, was more than a random mutation in popular taste. "White [for houses] was more than a fashionable color. It was new, completely new, as new as a democratic government free from Parliament, and men and women embarking on the experiment in nationhood embraced it passionately. Along with a new flag, new currency, and new ordering of land, white lead paint announced a new country and a political philosophy grounded in liberalism" (Stilgoe, 1982:169).

It is difficult to say whether Classical Revival architecture first took hold in domestic design or in the public realm, or whether the two developments occurred simultaneously. In any event, the fact is that by the early nineteenth century this politically resonant style had become deeply entrenched within New England and the territory westward thereof colonized by New England ideas and natives, so that humble cottages as well as the most opulent residences took the form of temple-homes. Both stylistic detail and political implications varied with region. "In Northern eyes, classical forms were associated, however vaguely and often contradictorily, with individual freedom. They were the expression of that all-pervading confidence in equality of opportunity" (Gowans, 1964: 279). But in the South, where the Classical Revival arrived rather belatedly, apparently through the migration of persons and ideas from the Northeast (Zelinsky, 1954), and where its adoption was confined very largely to aristocratic plantation houses and upper-class city mansions, it became the embodiment of Southern conservatism, "the symbol and assurance that sound society could perfectly well combine ideas of liberty with the institution of slavery" (Gowans, 1964:281).

The passion for neoclassical styles that began in early America extended well beyond the private dwelling, and it still lingers on in attenuated form. Both early and late, we have had church structures that simulate Greek temples, and not just those built for Christian Scientists. In addition, college and exposition buildings, lodge halls, railroad terminals, monuments, prisons, libraries, commercial emporiums, and even factory buildings have clung to the same stylistic persuasion, though less so with the passing of time. Even in the 1980s we can find classical elements in American office buildings, service stations, restaurants, or tombs. Among the more suggestive of the many manifestations of the Classical Revival is its nearly universal adoption to adorn that most sacred of American enterprises, the bank, from Strickland's 1818 building in Philadelphia up through the mid-twentieth century (Gowans, 1981). But perhaps the most persuasive form of evidence that neoclassicism struck a chord deep within the general American psyche is the way in which, over the years, classical elements have been appended to simpler folk housing. Thus when the proprietor of a humble clapboarded I-house or a rudimentary brick farmhouse crossed a certain threshold of affluence, he would often tack a classical portico onto the front or have windows and other exterior details redone in the classical mode.

In terms of outright symbolic puissance, it is among government buildings that the Classical Revival has triumphed most completely. Clearly the single most influential model has been the National Capitol (Fairman, 1927; Feeley, 1957; Gowans, 1981:123–24; Hitchcock and Seale, 1976:121–46; Krythe, 1968:140–67; L. B. Miller, 1966:40–78; M. A. Scully, 1984).[25] Although other federal buildings quite independently adopted a neoclassical form during the early nineteenth century, it was the Capitol (the name itself is significant) that most other official structures sought to emulate, especially after it finally assumed its present dimensions during the Lincoln presidency. Indeed, the building has become far more than an architectural prototype, having risen to the level of transcendent national icon, along with the Statue of Liberty, the Washington Monument, and a favored few others, so that we find it in advertisements (Cobb, 1978:88, 91), posters, business logos, folk crafts, souvenirs, and all manner of places.

The style of the national Capitol has been copied most slavishly in many of our state capitol buildings, but the process was gradual. "At the close of the eighteenth century there was no universally acceptable image of what an American state capitol should be" (Hitchcock and Seale, 1976:48). It was during the 1820s and 1830s that "statehouse design passed through a transition that led suddenly to the adoption of a new architectural style, Greek Revival" (Hitchcock and Seale, 1976:69). Then, after the national Capitol had become the symbolic anchor of the American Union in the 1850s, we find widespread mimicry of it in state capitols and other structures (Craig et al., 1978:141), sometimes, as in the case of the buildings in Providence or Austin, to the point of near duplication (Hitchcock and Seale, 1976:187). During the late nineteenth century and early twentieth, the architecture of official buildings, including state capitols, evolved through a series of interesting variations, but all still well within the general bounds of neoclassicism. It was finally in 1922 that "the requiem for American Renaissance capitols was sung at Charleston, West Virginia . . . when that state commissioned a Cass Gilbert Capitol from the master himself" (Hitchcock and Seale, 1976:271).

The progression of architectural styles for the much more numerous county courthouses has closely paralleled the history of state capitols (Harper, 1971; Ohman, 1985:67–70; Pare, 1978). Greek Revival buildings dominated county seats during the second quarter of the nineteenth century, then persisted intermittently thereafter (Hitchcock and Seale, 1976:172–84). The designs of the post–Civil War era tended to lag behind the fashions in commercial and residential building. "Almost unbelievably, the present decade [the 1970s] still saw Neo-Classical court houses erected. Such is the one for Butler County at Morgantown, Kentucky, dedicated in the fall of 1975" (Hitchcock and Seale, 1976:248). Scholars have just begun to survey the city halls of the United States (Goodsell, 1984; Lebovich, 1984), but I strongly suspect that, when that task is completed, it will document a similar procession of styles: the ascendancy of Greek Revival styles by mid-nineteenth century, then a series of classically derivative designs up until the very recent past. One hardly need mention the fact that echoes of classicism reverberated in hundreds of U.S. post office buildings throughout the land until just a few years ago.

Although psychoanalyzing a civilization through its architecture is fraught with peril, it is hard to avoid certain suspicions stemming from stylistic shifts within the American neoclassical genre. Thus there may be some merit in Alan Gowans's contention that "there succeeded to Greek simplicity and Roman dignity the bombastic eclecticism of mid- and later-19th-century America" because "Jeffersonian classicism seemed to have lost its basis in historical fact," that the actuality or ideal of a utopian republic of freely associating yeomen that had inspired Americans during the first half century of national existence was no longer within reach (Gowans, 1964:282–83). But we still face the obstinate persistence of classicism in American buildings—in dilute, modified form, to be sure—into the present generation. Aside from simple inertia, the explanation may be seen in the changing connotations of this particular style. What had been a spontaneous expression of deeply felt convictions—the possibly unique early American ideology—harbored by both officeholders of the fledgling state and the populace at large may have gradually come to proclaim nothing more than the authority of the governmental apparatus. And, as a statist symbol, the latter-day neoclassical style would have much in common with what we see in government buildings in many other countries, including the Stalinoid examples in the Soviet Union and Eastern Europe. Thus it is possible that an architectural entity that was once blatantly nationalistic eventually became less distinctively American and, following the same convergent trend observable in other departments of culture, subsided into just another transnational phenomenon.

Turning to other architectural developments, there are at least two—the log cabin and the one-room country schoolhouse—that are laden with folkloristic and sentimental value but are only peripherally linked with nationalism (Cohn, 1979:175–92; Gulliford, 1981). On the other hand, another building style with strong nationalistic implications has recently achieved unusual popularity in the residential and commercial sectors: the Colonial Revival (Ames, 1985). Although we can note some overlap in physical details between it and the neoclassical, they differ decisively in two respects. First, there is continuity, and, of course, change in the latter over a span of nearly two centuries, while the Colonial Revival is separated by at least two generations from its supposed antecedents. Second, the Colonial Revival, a product of both elite and popular culture, is an expression of nationhood rather than statehood, but a nationhood much altered from that of the pristine republic (Gowans, 1986:9–11; Rhoads, 1976, 1977; V. J. Scully, 1971:19–33). We have here an ideal case of what Eric Hobsbawm calls an "invented tradition." "Their peculiarity is that the continuity with [a historic past] is largely factitious. . . . they are responses to novel situations which take the form of reference to old situations, or which establish their own past by quasi-obligatory repetition" (Hobsbawm, 1983a:2).

Serious research into the genesis, evolution, and significance of the Colonial Revival has only recently begun, but a few things are clear. It materialized rather abruptly in the 1880s, a movement "inspired from the beginning by nationalistic sentiment—the desire to have in America an *American* style distinct from European modes" (Rhoads, 1970:242).[26] The style developed as a conflation of the Georgian, Federal, Greek Revival, various Colonial folk housing models, and perhaps a liberal dash of the architects' imagination. The timing is most intriguing. One might have anticipated at least a nominal architectural salute to the Revolutionary period at the 1876 Exhibition, but, as John Allwood points out, "it is particularly interesting to note the absence at Philadelphia of Colonial revival buildings among the State's pavilions—the first and last time that any State was to produce a building designed along modern lines at an American international exhibition" (Allwood, 1977:53). In its architectural form, the Colonial Revival seems to be another symptom of a larger syndrome: the organized statefulness and historic nostalgia that crystallized shortly after 1880 and have been with us for the past hundred years (Stump, 1981:52; Wallace, 1981).

If any single structure has played a role in this movement comparable to that of the national Capitol in neoclassicism, it has been Philadelphia's Independence Hall. After being "fitted up in impressive style in 1854" (Rosewater, 1926:135) following years of relative neglect, it gradually captured the popular imagination and spawned countless progeny in the cause of nationalistic piety (Maass, 1970). Its impact has increased over time. And it appears that the Colonial Revival in general has not yet reached its culmination by the late twentieth century (Gowans, 1968:212–13; Rhoads, 1976:254). Rivaling Independence Hall in its general impact has been Colonial Williamsburg, the early Virginia capital resurrected in an ideal manner during the 1920s under Rockefeller auspices. The claim that much of late twentieth-century America has undergone Williamsburgerization is not too extreme (Wallace, 1981). Among the middlebrow homes of suburbia, "Colonial" models of one sort or another, but often distinctly reminiscent of Williamsburg, rank among the most popular and respectable; and we find service stations, office buildings, furniture stores, shopping malls, and supermarkets as well as other structures zealously, if anachronistically, cultivating much the same appearance of what we think colonial structures should have looked like. As is also the case with our recent museums, we may be conspiring to fabricate in these buildings a mythical past to foster some sense of national community, but a nationhood with no explicit spiritual commitment.

One need only travel north to Canada and inspect its public and private architecture in order to appreciate how deeply a particular nationalism has permeated the minds of American builders. Despite the many overt similarities between the two national communities, whose ultimate origins are, of course, rooted in the same soil, their political philosophies have taken separate paths and so too some fundamental elements of social outlook. Thus we do not find in Canadian domestic design anything closely resembling the Colonial Revival of the United States. And while neoclassical elements may appear in some public and commercial buildings, and a few residential ones, they are far from dominant and are relatively muted in expression. Ideologically, such Canadian edifices speak not of republicanism or the redemptive zeal of their American kin, but of other ideals, those associated with a constitutional monarchy (Lipset, 1965).

PUTTING THE PIECES TOGETHER

We have examined a large, motley array of objects, practices, perceptions, and other phenomena that are meaningfully connected with American nationalism. It is obvious that there is much variability along several dimensions within this universe of items. Thus they differ considerably in date of origin, durability, strength of development, direction of change, relevance to nationalism, and degree to which they are causal or symptomatic. After reviewing some seventy-odd entities, I have concluded that we can extract the maximum amount of meaning by setting them within a temporal framework. I suggest four categories of phenomena:

1. Those that appeared during the era of revolutionary ferment or immediately thereafter. Some have been short-lived, others have survived to the present, but, without exception, the survivors are weaker now than during their earlier careers. The group includes

Brother Jonathan
eagle I (i.e., the eagle in its
    earlier incarnation)
historiography
holidays
individual heroes
Liberty Tree
literature

Miss Liberty
names of business enter-
    prises and products
neoclassical architecture
oratory
paintings of heroes and
    events
pedagogic texts

personal names
place-names

sacred documents
song

2. Another group of items materialized on a significant scale during the middle third of the past century or shortly thereafter, but have subsequently vanished or lost most of their popularity. They are as follows:

Americanization programs
campaign paraphernalia
campaign songs
dime novels
landscape painting

monuments
posters
technological heroes
world's fairs

3. The most populous category includes phenomena that, with but two exceptions (the rectangular survey system and political boundaries) appeared in a major symbolic way from the mid-nineteenth century onward and have either continued gaining in strength or have maintained whatever maximum level they ever attained.

archives
battlefield parks
celebrities
Colonial Revival
eagle II (i.e., as a statist
    symbol)
federal structures and works
flag
generic eidolons
historic preservation
historical museums
inaugurations
loyalty oaths
national cemeteries
national parks
nationalistic voluntary
    organizations

Olympic Games
pilgrimages
Pledge of Allegiance
political boundaries
presidency
presidential libraries
rectangular survey system
red-white-and-blue motif
reenactments of major
    events
sport
state funerals
theme parks
Uncle Sam
Washington, D.C.

4. Finally, there is a miscellaneous collection of phenomena that are historically unique (the Bicentennial) or for which data are inadequate or whose temporal careers are too uncertain to permit

assignment to any of the first three groups. (I do have my private hunches about the proper loci for several, but shall restrain myself.)

Bicentennial	map of the U.S.A.
children's games and toys	medals
coins and stamps	mottoes
Constitution	national anthem
country schoolhouse	parades
drama	political parties
film	presidential campaigns
folk crafts	radio and television
folk music	ritual journeys
language	Supreme Court
log cabin	uniforms

At first glance, the messages transmitted by these four classes of phenomena seem contradictory and likely to confound any effort at generalization. But a second careful look suggests a coherent, consistent pattern: nationalistic symbols and related forms of behavior as evidence of a transition of the American community from nationhood to full-blown statehood, from nationalism, sensu stricto, to statefulness. Thus we find all the items in group 1, with the sole exception of Brother Jonathan, intimately associated with a spontaneous form of national feeling. As already noted, each flourished during the early decades of independence, then dwindled, either to disappear completely or linger on feebly and dilutely. The third group are all symptoms or props of statism and are still on the ascendant or have stabilized on a high plateau of power. Most or all of them also fit into the category of "invented traditions." Thus, as one cast of characters has drifted off the stage, they have been gradually supplanted by another company performing from a very different script. The nine entities listed in the second category are also, without exception, directly or indirectly statist in function. In each instance, the decline or disappearance of the item is explainable in terms of altered technological and social circumstances, but not by any weakening in the vitality of the statist creed. Given our current state of knowledge, the residual batch of phenomena assembled in group 4 can neither confirm nor negate the scenario about to be presented; but I strongly suspect that additional data will bolster the case.

We have finally reached the point where some confident asser-

tions about the evolution of American nationalism are feasible.[27]
The history of the phenomenon falls into three general phases or
periods as described below. Each period has its distinctive central
character, but no precise date at which it begins or ends. Transitions are too gradual and the overlap of certain attributes great
enough to frustrate efforts at strict periodization. Need I add that,
as is true for any such social or historical schema, not every last bit
of data can be tucked tidily into the proper slot? The human world
is not the world of physics and chemistry, but it does contain some
approximation of orderliness.

Phase 1 extended from the 1760s or 1770s through the 1840s,
those early decades of imminent and actual independence when a
pure, pristine nationalism was exceedingly powerful and as yet un-
besmirched by statism. It surpassed in vigor all competing interests
except the enthusiastic Christianity with which it was entangled in
a complex, mutually nourishing symbiosis. The emergent state was
honored and respected mainly to the degree that it embodied the
lofty national principles. A faith in the unique virtues and transcendent mission of the Republic that was deeply, genuinely inter-
nalized inspired the hearts and minds of most men and women. In
landscape terms these feelings may have been externalized (perhaps
spontaneously, without deliberation) in the style of the one artifact
indispensable to every family—the dwelling—but after Yorktown
no other physical cues were required in public spaces to keep national fervor close to fever pitch. Americans expressed their nationhood through hero-worship, singing appropriate songs, adopting nationalistic names, observing the great holidays, and enjoying paintings, oratory, and printed matter celebrating their remarkable new
republic. If a date must be set for the climax of this emotional
surge, let it be 1824–26. We had then the near-coincidence of Lafayette's return visit (1824–25), which occasioned an orgy of celebration unsurpassed before or since for sheer scale and excitement, and
the awe-inspiring simultaneity of the demise of John Adams and
Thomas Jefferson on July 4, 1826, the fiftieth anniversary of the
Declaration.

With the passing of the Revolutionary generation and the living
memory of the early heroic struggles and providential blessings,
not to mention the advent of sectional strife, massive immigration,
industrialization, and profound economic and social innovations,
American nationalism had entered its second phase by the eve of
the Civil War. Nationalism, now intermingled with a nascent stat-

ism, retained much, but not all, of its pristine élan. And it had begun to metamorphose. The heroes, events, and ideals upon which was grounded the nationalist creed of the first generation of Americans had moved beyond immediate reach, receding into a remoter emotional space. At such a juncture the nationalistic monument entered the scene as a device both necessary and effective for jogging the collective memory. The eagle, once a totem bursting with libertarian messages, was converted into a content-free emblem, one, which like the flag, simply declares identification with the state, and nothing more. Similarly, the neoclassical style, once so laden with ideological baggage, dwindled into one of several popular architectural clichés, but the one style most serviceable, like flag and eagle, for connecting a building with the overarching federal regime, with centralized authority rather than any special principle. Such innovations as the world's fair, historic preservation, Uncle Sam, state funerals, national parks, and a vast array of federal structures entered the scene, along with a presidency that was undergoing sanctification. The 1890s may have been the decade in which this second phase blossomed most luxuriantly.

The third and current period of American nationalism, its emphatically statist phase, began to germinate as early as the 1880s, but was not to attain its apogee until the late twentieth century. Insofar as it harkens back to the past, it has been a synthetic, nostalgic nationalism no longer rooted in the historic circumstances that bred its predecessors, and one with little or no awareness of the contentious ideas that made early America such a special, often suspect place in the eyes of the world. And it is deeply, decisively different from the initial phase because, as Robert Nisbet mordantly writes, "nostalgia is the rust of memory. Having, as it were, lost the past from our present, we look back on it fondly, and so often vapidly. It is a poor substitute for the sacred" (Nisbet, 1975: 90).

To the degree that any traces of the primordial nationalism are still detectable, it is a nationalism no longer at odds with American statism, a conflict, it might be argued, that could well have been simmering below the surface in earlier times. Instead the two strains of thought now cohabit snugly. The United States has thus become a full-fledged nation-state. The symbols, rites, and other nationalistic practices in vogue today are essentially nonideological and nonethnic in character, and simply proclaim the power and glory of Uncle Sam. Quite clearly the emotional temperature of nationalism is much lower than in its heyday (and such is also the case for statefulness except in moments of crisis), if for no other reason, because of the many new competing demands upon the time and psychic energies of a fully modernized, complex society. Like the active practice of religion, the observances of nationalism have become a sometime and rather tepid thing. For Americans coping with a bewildering world of shifting values, the essence and uniqueness of America are now items to be investigated casually at museums and costumed spectacles; spiritual refuge is to be found in the arms of the state. Showing the flag, especially during periods of international tension, or at Olympic games, will have to do as the proper antidote to doubts about purpose or identity. On a daily basis we pay homage to the presidency and quadrennially experience the orgy of an inauguration. In the contemporary world, with its odd mixture of sophistication, cynicism, and wishful thinking about the past, the traditional nationalistic monument is obsolete. In the infrequent instances when something absolutely must be built, the approved design is fashionably ambiguous. What is more generally appropriate, however, is the artfully framed, illusionist historical museum in all its many forms and, for the vernacular structure, a Colonial Revival treatment, the mythopoeic reenactment of the past as it should have been.

With considerable hesitation, I would like to venture the speculation (one barely concealed in the preceding paragraph) that we may have been entering, ever so gradually, a fourth period, the "poststatist" episode of our national life course. Thus far the most convincing body of evidence to bolster any such suggestion comes from the marked dropoff in the number of visitors to our nationalistic shrines since 1976; but hard numbers must be mustered from other modes of symbolic performance before we can hail the oncoming era with much assurance. If there is any merit to this notion, it is a phase rooted in the disillusionments of World War I and its aftermath. Just as has been the case with earlier transitions, there is no sharp break with the past, if indeed we are moving into such a distinctly different collective mood, but rather an overlapping of attitudes and values. Thus we retain the same cast of symbolic characters that peopled the stage in the third period, but we may be viewing them in a new light. Obviously, we shall have to wait until the next century to learn how much substance there is to this conjecture.

Against such a backdrop of the rise of the state and its attendant statism and of a once vibrant nationalism that has traveled through at least three distinct episodes in its devolution, I believe we can begin to make some interesting sense out of the diversified welter of national and statist objects in the American landscape, and also in the shifting nature of our public eidolons and overtly nation- and state-related activites. Conversely, such a schema, if pursued methodically in further landscape studies and other realms of scholarship, may suggest new insights into the changing structure of American thought and behavior.

Because the evidence remains so fragmentary, we must be more reserved in speculating about the historical geography of nationalism in the United States than about its history. Nevertheless, such data as we do possess all point toward a single hypothesis: that nationalism seems to have developed earliest and most vigorously in the New England and Middle Atlantic states, then subsequently grew lustily in those sections of the Middle West settled from this northern segment of the Atlantic Seaboard, while it lagged far behind in the South. As already noted, the present-day (and presumably earlier) incidence of flag and eagle display and holiday observances by region supports this notion; and a complete survey of nationalistic monuments is likely to provide further corroboration. The historical geography of nationalistic place-names and classical town names (Zelinsky, 1967), allows no other interpretations; and studies of three phenomena with definite psychological linkages to the specifically American brand of nationalism—political cultures, utopian communities, and old-line fraternal orders—all document sharp North/South disparities in keeping with the spatiotemporal scenario described above (Elazar, 1972; Porter and Luckermann, 1975; Schein, 1983).

The sequence of phases postulated for United States nationalism is specific to one country. It need not apply to many, or even any, other lands. I am not pleading American exceptionalism, an issue that does not directly concern us here (Bell, 1975; Veysey, 1979), but rather the notion that historical circumstances have differed so greatly among the 150-odd actual and would-be nation-states of the late twentieth century that the chronicle of state and national development may not be closely duplicated in any pair of them. Like the United States, some have begun their corporate life as nations, then metamorphosed into states; others were initially states that fostered nationhood en route to becoming nation-states; in still other cases, nation and state appeared at roughly the same time.

My suspicion is that, whatever the path followed, however various may have been the period, formative sociopolitical setting, pace of development, and incidental difficulties, all of the world's countries today seem to be trudging toward a common destination: the perfected nation-state.

*We are like flies crawling across the ceiling of the Sistine Chapel:
we cannot see what angels and gods lie underneath the threshold
of our perceptions. We do not live reality; we live in our para-
digms, our habituated perceptions, our illusions; the illusions we
share through culture we call reality, but the true historical reality of our condition is invisible to us. How can you fix up history if you cannot see it?*
—William Irwin Thompson

All the many lines of evidence we have reviewed in the previous
chapters render quite explicit what has been generally merely implied by most other students of the American scene: a gradual, but
profound, transformation in the essential character of the community that calls itself the United States of America. (A glance across
the border at the far different Canadian experience would serve to
reinforce such an interpretation of the American materials.)

Unlike the conventional nations of the Old World, this "first new
nation" began life without strong historical or territorial traditions
or the usual preconditions of a common religion, language, or other
such cultural bonds, but rather on the basis of a novel ideology. As
a voluntary association of defiantly individualistic citizens with a
special sense of their differentness and transcendent mission, young
America barely tolerated the yoke of statehood. But, whatever the
wishes and ideals of the first generations of Americans, the pressures of the modernization process asserted themselves with a force
that grew with each passing year. The logic of the new economics
and technologies began to be expressed politically through the medium of a burgeoning state apparatus, parapolitical organizations,
new social and psychological arrangements, and a varied repertory
of revised symbols and modes of behavior. The inevitable outcome,
arrived at with relatively little social disruption in most other

countries, was ratified in the United States only after prolonged
bloody slaughter. But the conclusion of the Civil War left no doubt
as to the supremacy of the state, physically and spiritually.

Thereafter what had been a nation that was only incidentally a
state has graduated into a nation-state. Increasingly, over the past
century and a quarter, it has been one in which the vestigial elements of nationhood became weak and subservient within the polity and also much altered from their pristine condition. Thus today
the United States qualifies as a full-fledged member of that kindred
guild of nation-states that includes all the advanced countries of
the world and some of the aspiring less-developed entities as well.[1]
As I have noted previously, the route may differ from case to case—
sometimes the state precedes, then helps fabricate the nation; occasionally state and nation sprout in tandem; or, as in the American
example, nation spawns state—but the end results are much the
same. Our forefathers may have found selfhood and identity in
their locality, or *pays*, and church, or, at the furthest remove, in
their culturally kindred "folk" spread well beyond the horizon.
Now we live in a world where statefulness is the only acceptable
condition for human beings and where to be a stateless person is as
hideous a form of social leprosy as the imagination can contrive.

One may debate the function of symbols and symbol-related behavior in the progression from nation (or state) to nation-state,
whether they operate as cause or effect, or both. Were these phenomena integral to the psychological transformation, which, I must
insist, is as much a part of the modernization process as the political, economic, or technological, or are they incidental accessories?
Obviously there is opportunity for further research and discussion.
In the meantime, what is abundantly clear is the value of the symbolic life as a record of what is happening in other realms of social
change.

There is no doubt in my mind that the large, otherwise confusing
mass of American data we have examined makes sense when set
within the nation-into-state scenario. I have developed the argument in some detail, using a spatial as well as chronological framework when possible, in tracing the careers of such items as monuments, the flag and eagle, nationalistic museums and parks, and the
varied physical apparatus of the state. But the same sequential logic
applies to the shifting cast of characters in the pantheon of heroes,
villains, celebrities, and impersonal eidolons who have engaged
the emotions of Americans over the years—and to the presidency.
The historical geography of nationalistic place-names finds mean-

ing only within such a nation-into-state scheme, and the same must be said about the history of holidays, all manner of commemorative acts, nationalistic pilgrimages, world's fairs, a variety of political rituals, hereditary and patriotic organizations, historiography, the popular and high arts, international sport competitions, and all the other topics touched upon previously. There are further conclusions to be extracted from such data, but first we must dispose of some unfinished business.

THE GENESIS OF AMERICAN NATIONALISM

The skeptical reader may detect one potentially fatal flaw in my thesis. How can one argue the precedence of nation when the social entity known as America first comes to the notice of the world no sooner than 1775 or 1776 with the work of the Continental Congress, to be followed, of course, by more durable political structures? Isn't it conceivable that it may have been the fledgling state, however shaky at the outset, that somehow forged a nation and a sense of nationalism among its disparate populations? At least one historian has written in this vein, maintaining that the loyalty of the rebels in 1776 was directed primarily to their locality, not to the larger cause, and that "the grander sentiment" was effected through the heroic exertions of Washington and a few other leaders.[2]

If the military success of the Revolution was, admittedly, a near thing, and even making the further concession that it was only with the greatest of good luck that the framers of the Articles of Confederation and the Constitution breathed political life into their creations, there is nonetheless a varied and persuasive body of evidence that an American nation had begun to emerge before the military conflict with the motherland (Arieli, 1964:62–70).

During most of its early existence, the term *American* connoted nothing more than a territorial expanse; but by the middle decades of the eighteenth century it began to take on a warmer, more particular meaning (Nye, 1966:52–54). The first definitive signs that the colonists had begun to perceive themselves as collectively distinct from their British kin arrived with the War of Jenkins' Ear, as noted by Albert Harkness. "This enterprise is of considerable interest as an illustration, if not actually one cause, of emergent Americanism. . . . Indeed, both sides employed these words ['American' and 'European'] to designate one another as early as 1741" (Harkness, 1950:88).[3] And Paul Varg cites even firmer evidence dating from a few years later. "In the fall of 1759, during the celebrations of the conquest of Quebec, the name 'American' became something more than a geographical expression. The use of the term suggests nascent nationalism" (Varg, 1964:181).

By means of careful content analysis of news accounts in American periodicals during the period 1735–75, Richard Merritt (1966b) has demonstrated a decisive shift some years before the Revolution in the array of terms used to refer to the territories inhabited by the colonists, as *American* and other words suggesting a sense of incipient national solidarity rose sharply in frequency. The same author has also suggested some of the means whereby such a change in mind-set might have occurred (Merritt, 1966a). An effective intercolonial postal system was in operation from 1753 onward, distributing books, pamphlets, magazines, newspapers, and other products of an actively growing press as well as correspondence. Intercolonial exchanges of other types were also on the upswing, including numerous migrants, preachers, and artisans, in addition to merchants and their wares.

Further proof of the spread and standardization of ideas, and presumably attitudes, comes from a rather unexpected source: folk housing. In his meticulous analysis of the surviving early common dwellings of a central Virginia locality, Henry Glassie has documented a remarkable change that took place spontaneously around the middle of the eighteenth century: the adoption rather abruptly by ordinary farmers of certain cosmopolitan building designs that had come into vogue throughout Anglophone America and that replaced the localistic folk building traditions that had been so universally practiced in earlier years (Glassie, 1975:176–93). From such testimony he infers major social change. I believe that more than coincidence was at work when archaeologist James Deetz reached much the same conclusion in his enchanting *In Small Things Forgotten* (1977) after scrutinizing all manner of humble artifacts from eighteenth-century America. "In ways great and small, gravestones, grave pits, houses, refuse, cuts of meat, recipes, ceramics, furniture, and cutlery inform us that a great change was worked between 1760 and 1800 on the world view of most of Anglo-America" (Deetz, 1977:127). Such relatively sudden shifts in weltanschauung are not proof positive that a parallel transition was in progress from localism to nationalism in the specifically political/ideational realm, but such a suspicion is hard to avoid.

What may be the most convincing kind of evidence supporting the case for a pre-1776 germination of American nationhood comes from the churchly sphere. It must be remembered that the theologically (and, inferentially, politically) disaffected comprised a considerable fraction of the early emigrants from the British Isles and the Continent. There is more than a little plausibility in the contention that adherents of evangelical Protestantism may have been especially predisposed to revolutionary impulses (Middlekauff, 1970). In any event, church groups nominally under the governance of European authorities may have grown restive under such long-distance constraints, living as they were under the novel conditions of the New World, so that it is possible that "zeal for ecclesiastical nationalism helped to develop a zeal for political nationalism on the part of the leaders of the churches of America" (Humphrey, 1924:440). It is also arguable that colonial church synods, especially the Presbyterian variety, may have served as models for subsequent federal entities (Humphrey, 1924:66).

What is incontestable is that the earliest social phenomenon of any magnitude to vault across provincial boundaries in British North America was the first Great Awakening (1725–50), a revivalistic frenzy led by Jonathan Edwards and other eminent divines that convulsed a goodly portion of the colonial population from New England to Georgia. Some political fallout was inevitable. Jerald Brauer summarizes the evidence persuasively.

> The Great Awakening has been interpreted as the first colony-wide movement that bound together many diverse interests among the thirteen colonies and provided a thread of unity that ran throughout the group. Some historians have gone so far as to argue that it was the first movement that gave the colonies any sense of common identity. . . . The converted believer basked in his own uniqueness, which inevitably led to intense dissatisfaction with the traditional, with things as they were. [Brauer, 1976:21]

Robert Bellah goes even further. "It is the national community [resulting from the Great Awakening] with its religious inspiration that made the American Revolution and created the new nation" (Bellah and Hammond, 1980:13).[4]

Religious ferment may have been important and perhaps even crucial in the eventual birthing of nation and republic, and will bear looking into at a later point. But other forces were certainly at work, factors not classifiable as sociocultural. The economic discontents of the colonists, which historians have so often reviewed, had considerable effect, as did the home government's obvious diffi-

culties and miscalculations in devising viable political mechanisms
for administering a varied, distant set of obstreperous colonies. But
the factors of distance and administrative ineptitude were not necessarily decisive. Despite much bumbling, the British managed to
retain a hold on their East Indian empire until 1947 (not to mention
other remote colonies), even though it was much more distant and
immensely more populous and politically complex than the North
American colonies.

Not the least of the factors contributing to, and later sustaining,
nationhood and statism was the fighting of wars or the prospect
thereof. As already suggested, the participation of militia from several colonies, side by side with British regulars, in that long series
of wars fought by the mother country against France, Spain, and
others overseas as well as in Europe, had the unintended effect of
breeding common intercolonial sentiments. This was especially
true in the case of the Seven Years' War, which also had as its political aftermath much resentment amongst the nascent American
nationals toward the Crown and its solicitous handling of the van-
quished popish denizens of Quebec.

One of the relative weaknesses in the stockpile of items conduc-
ing to nationalism during the prehistory and history of the republic
has been the absence of a consistently hateful national enemy (Nye,
1966:48). If virtually every Old World nation has been blessed and
solidified by some eternally dreaded foe (A. D. Smith, 1981:74–78),
Americans have not enjoyed that emotional luxury, at least not for
more than a few years at a time. While it lasts, war has, of course, a
marvelously unifying effect (Robertson, 1980:324–35);[5] but, before
1945 and the discovery that the Soviets would do admirably as the
satanic Other for as long as we pleased, it has been difficult to keep
such therapeutic loathing at a proper pitch between wars.

For a time, the American Indians captured the general imagination as *the* foe (Commager, 1975:186–88), but they failed to measure up as a military threat; and, since their subjugation, attitudes
toward them have been ambivalent and even tinged with romantic
admiration (Cawelti, 1976). The Spanish and Mexicans (Americans
have scarcely deigned to notice the Canadians) have been cast in
the role of villains only intermittently. In contrast, there has been
the enduring, but remarkably many-sided, relationship with Great
Britain. Powerful though both may have been, neither Anglopho-
bia nor Anglophilia gained the upper hand during the nineteenth
century (Brock, 1971; Burns, 1957:41–48; Crapol, 1973:3–18), and
eventually the attitudes of both parties have mellowed into a sta-

ble, amiable "special relationship."[6] If the model of a superior English civilization was a persistent cause of psychic tension and uncertainty as to identity throughout the Colonial period and for long
afterward (J. P. Greene, 1969:205–18), one of the more potent forces
unifying early Americans, and one not entirely extinct even today,
was a generalized antipathy toward the decadence and corruption of
the Old World and the counterimage of a fresh, innocent, redemptive America (Commager, 1975:186–88). "British and European society has served as a model of what the United States should *not*
be" (Nye, 1966:48).

One must take care neither to overstate nor understate the case
for a pre-1776 American nation. But even after we have filled in
more of the gaps in our knowledge of the social psychology of the
colonists during the first three-quarters of the eighteenth century, it
is unlikely that the following verdict will be greatly revised. What
seems credible is that a dawning sense of American peoplehood had
indeed developed during the period 1750–75, in large part subconscious, it is true, but also overt enough to furnish the psychic
wherewithal for the political and military struggles to follow. If the
Americans of 1775 were not yet inflamed with a raging sense of
nationhood comparable with that, say, in Ireland in 1916 or among
the Hindus of 1947, there was nonetheless enough of a perception
of a common destiny and set of ideals among most strata of society,
along with a shared set of differences with the European home-
lands, to give the colonists the spiritual energy to make their unlikely bid for independence. And such a budding awareness of nationhood was all the more remarkable in view of the sharp economic, environmental, social, and demographic discontinuities among
the colonies and the considerable differences in their political
structures. There was little doubt in the minds of the more articulate leaders of the Revolution that, as John Adams declared, "the
Revolution . . . was complete in the minds of the people, and the
union of the colonies, before the war commenced in the skirmishes
of Concord and Lexington" (Curti, 1946:8) or, as Patrick Henry
noted in 1775, "the distinctions between Virginians, Pennsylva-
nians, New Yorkers and New Englanders are no more! I am not a
Virginian, but an American" (Curti, 1946:15). Bernard Bailyn has
aptly summarized the psychological and political situation of the
decisive years just before the Revolution:

> By 1776 . . . Americans had come to think of themselves as in a
> special category, uniquely placed by history to capitalize on, to

complete and fulfill, the promise of man's existence. . . . In the
period before independence . . . explorations were made in new
territories of thought, the first comprehensive maps sketched,
and routes marked out. Thereafter the psychological as well as
intellectual barriers were down. It was the most creative period
of American political thought. Everything that followed assumed and built upon its results. [Bailyn, 1967:20–21]

One observation is absolute: No truly national symbols existed
before 1775. When we speak of the conception and gestation of
nations, we are in the presence of the profoundest of social mysteries, even when dealing with the relatively transparent history of
America. It is doubtful whether we can ever get to the innermost
heart of the matter. But, if the presence or manipulation of symbols
is not always among the first causes for the creation of nations, and
if they may be missing during earliest infancy, one may still argue
forcefully for their indispensability during the formative adolescent
years, and for their utility during the nation-state phase. All the
factual material leads to that emphatic conclusion for the United
States.

Before we get down to the principal business of this final chapter,
there are a few other aspects of the nationalization process to consider or reconsider. If both the nature and intensity of American
nationalism have varied substantially in the course of 230 years or
more, the same must be said concerning its spatial aspects (Meinig,
1986:396–97). This is true not only in America but in other countries that have managed the transition to a vigorous nation-state.[7]
A particular section of the country assumes the lead in terms of
both economic and political development, then, by whatever means
are available, extends its power and nationalistic notions into the
lagging regions of the national territory. As already noted, the
spatiotemporal patterning of nationalistic place-names and of flag
and eagle display strongly suggests that it was in the core region of
early America, that is, southern New England and the middle Atlantic states, that nationalistic fervor flourished most energetically,
and possibly still may. I also strongly suspect that similar findings
would emerge from the plotting of the locations of nationalistic
monuments and holiday celebrations over time. Distinctions along
residential and class lines are also plausible. Fifer (1976) claims
that, during the great debate over the ratification of the Constitution during the 1780s, the pro-Constitution forces were relatively

strong within the towns and among elite groups, but weaker in the more remote, agrarian areas.

By general consent among chroniclers of American thought, it is to New England we must turn for the genesis of the nation-idea, as is true for so many other early advances in technology and in a wide range of social and intellectual activities. Even such early travelers as Isaac Weld (1807) remarked that "in New England the national spirit was stronger than elsewhere" (Van Alstyne, 1970:129). Casting itself in the role of the New Israel and espousing the providential mission that lies so close to the core of early American nationalism, New England first articulated the shape of the nation to be. Its leadership became clear when the region served as the hearth for the Great Awakening, which, as we have seen, was the first loud interprovincial signal of the approaching Revolution (Berens, 1978: 29). Then by dispersing themselves, their ideas, and culture throughout most of the rest of inhabited America, New Englanders and, in appreciable measure, the peoples of the Middle Colonies as well, laid the groundwork for an independent nation of unique character (Melder, 1976:9–10; Shaffer, 1975:57).

The antithesis to the vanguard role of New England is obviously to be found in the Deep South, where, according to the evidence adduced in this study, nationalism appeared tardily, or weakly, or both. A possible paradox, the fact that Southerners are relatively militaristic, as attested by their notably great, valorous participation in the Revolutionary War, the Mexican War, and other conflicts, is more apparent than real. Nationalism and militarism are by no means synonymous, a fact that can be confirmed by a glance through the anthropological literature. An explanation for the paradox may lie in the possibility that the South generated an alternative nationality, one that was valid enough in its own terms but distinct from that of the Northeastern Core Region. Consequently, the measures applied to gauge standard American nationalism may not be wholly relevant in the states that eventually formed the Confederacy. Recent writers have developed a convincing case to the effect that the South has not been just a backward or deviant region but rather the home of a quite specific, self-aware ethnic group that, like every legitimate nation, felt strong internal promptings toward political autonomy (Kohn, 1957:108–9; McCardell, 1979). Despite the failure of its military bid for independence, this ethnic group has managed to retain its distinctiveness even in the face of massive modernization (Killian, 1970; Reed, 1972).

As is the case with mainstream American nationalism or any other variety elsewhere, the origins of the Southern nation are obscure, possibly unfathomable. The peculiarities of the habitat and economy may have been key factors, along with the infusion of great numbers of Africans; and there may be some merit in the argument that an exceptionally large percentage of Celtic (Scots, Scotch-Irish, Irish, Welsh) settlers among the pioneer generations may have imparted much of their ethnic heritage to the embryonic South, in contrast to the predominantly English transfusion of culture further north (McDonald and McWhiney, 1980; McDonald and McDonald, 1980).

No discussion of the spatial components of American nationalism could be complete without some mention of the interrelated themes of the West and the frontier. Beyond question, these phenomena have contributed in a major way, whether as metaphor or physical fact, to defining the American's sense of self and thus his nationalism, probably to a greater degree than in any other neo-European land with extensive pioneer settlement, with the possible exception of Australia.[8] The topic merits, and has received, extended treatment (Cawelti, 1976; Kohn, 1957:22–23; H. N. Smith, 1950; Steckmesser, 1965; Wilbur, 1973), as have the related themes of the pastoral ideal in America (Marx, 1964) and Europe's perception of America as a possible earthly paradise (Sanford, 1961). There is no need here to review the long-lived, still smoldering controversy over the validity of the Turner Thesis as it applies to the shaping of political and social institutions. Suffice it to say that the composite image of frontier and West has entered deeply into the American identity, and that it is linked in the most profoundly meaningful way with the civil religion of the United States.

AMERICANISM AS A CIVIL RELIGION

Up to this point, I have evaded any direct statement of the full agenda of this study, preferring to let the facts speak for themselves. Now it is time to be blunt. The theological and ecclesiastical terms used at various points in earlier passages have not been mere figures of speech. One of my central theses is simply that civil religion has become the dominant faith of the contemporary world, and further, that we cannot dissociate this notion from the latter-day ascendancy of nationalism and statism. The worldwide triumph of civil religion is valid enough even though, as has happened with other universalizing churches, the various national chapters are divided among themselves.

Succinctly defined, "by civil religion we can mean any set of beliefs and rituals, related to the past, present, and/or future of a people ('nation') which are understood in some transcendental fashion" (Hammond, 1976:171). It is obviously a concept closely related to, though not quite synonymous with, statism. The rise of civil religion is another manifestation of modernization, and it has flourished in precise inverse relationship to the decay of conventional Christian dogma and practice or the erosion of other ancient faiths in an effort to fill the void left by their abdication from the hearts of humankind. Carried to its extreme, the glorification of nation or state, or both, results in a kind of substitute theology.[9] Carlton Hayes (1926, 1960) has described the phenomenon more fully and lucidly than anyone else (even though his publications failed to excite the attention and controversy they merited). The essence of his "Reflection on the Religion of Nationalism" is worth quoting at length, since I can hardly improve upon the statement.

Since its advent in western Europe, modern nationalism has partaken of the nature of a religion. . . . It is now evidenced throughout the world. Everywhere it has a god, who is either the patron or the personification of one's *patrie*, one's fatherland, one's national state. This deity may be referred to, in familiar, even jocular style as Uncle Sam, John Bull, Marianne, Hans, or Ivan. Yet it is the god of a chosen people, a jealous god, preeminently a god of battles.

Nationalism, like any religion, calls into play not simply the will, but the intellect, the imagination, and the emotions. The intellect constructs a speculative theology or mythology of nationalism. The imagination builds an unseen world around the eternal past and the everlasting future of one's nationality. The emotions arouse a joy and ecstasy in the contemplation of the national god who is all-good and all-protecting, a longing for his favors, a thankfulness for his benefits, a fear of offending him, and feelings of awe and reverence at the immensity of his power and wisdom; they express themselves naturally in worship, both private and public. For nationalism, again like any other religion, is social and its chief rites are public rites performed in the name and for the salvation of a whole community.

Interior devotion to nationalism is expected of everybody,

though in this respect a little allowance may appropriately be made for human frailty. So long as public rites and ceremonies are decently observed, the hearts of individual worshippers need not be too closely searched. . . . There can be no question of the popular and compelling character of external nationalist worship. Blasphemy and sacrilege have customarily been regarded as heinous crimes, and the present-day person who allows a flitting mental doubt to find expression in sneer or jest at the expense of the national cult is eligible for madhouse or for jail. [Hayes, 1960:164–66]

It is much easier to admit the veracity of such observations when they are directed at societies other than one's own (J. A. Coleman, 1970). Thus American readers can absorb with some equanimity accounts of "the religious nature of Russian Marxism" (McDowell, 1974; Zeldin, 1969) or the pagan rituals of National Socialist Germany (Mosse, 1976), or can calmly consider the possibility that Japan or Mexico may have a civil religion of sorts (Bellah and Hammond, 1980:27–85). But turning the spotlight on the United States can jangle sensibilities, as Robert Bellah (1967) and Sidney Mead (1967) discovered when they published their widely noted essays, which, in my opinion, are restatements of the obvious. The ensuing tumult has not entirely subsided (Richey and Jones, 1974; Thomas and Flippen, 1972; J. F. Wilson, 1971, 1979). In part, the dispute reflects the queasiness of theologians, and perhaps the intelligentsia as a whole, about relaxing conventional definitions of religion, which exclude whatever fails to classify itself as ecclesiastical or does not profess belief in the supernatural and/or the hereafter. To do so, we seem to fear subconsciously, may mean blasphemy and the risk of being struck dead by lightning. In actuality, any system of beliefs constitutes an authentic religion if it embodies the supreme values of a society and its members and has the capacity to mobilize the deepest of emotions. Using such criteria, nationalism qualifies handily. My claim is that we cannot begin to comprehend fully the symbolic life of the United States without setting it within the context of a civil theology.

Like any other widespread phenomenon, civil religion varies substantially in kind and intensity among national communities, and has assumed different forms with the passing of time. Many permutations are possible in the relationships among the (conventional) church, state, and civil religion. Perhaps the simplest is that of the present-day theocracy, so neatly exemplified by Shiite Iran but also approximated in modern Israel. In such places, all three forces so deeply interpenetrate one another that for all practical purposes distinctions become moot. But in contrast to the premodern theocracy, the mystique of the state has acquired a psychological potency not experienced hitherto. A symbiotic embrace between state and orthodox church also characterizes such countries as Falangist Spain, Japan (especially before 1945), Czarist Russia, and the United Kingdom in which a single dynast reigns over, or controls, both entities, but where the state assumes the task of propagating and executing the civil religion. In still other cases, such as Revolutionary France, Nazi Germany, Maoist China, Mexico, the Soviet Union, and North Korea, the state has fabricated its own secular faith and has gone to great lengths to proselytize the masses. What makes the American case quite possibly unique—and here one can certainly plead exceptionalism—is the fact that, for nearly all of its existence, the civil religion has enjoyed a life of its own quite independently of both church and state, even though it has had important dealings with both (J. A. Coleman, 1970). In all other modern nation-states, the state has acquired title to its civil religion and has borne the burden of cultivating and guarding the faith.

In one other crucial particular the United States has stood out amongst even that small band of countries that perceive themselves as divinely commissioned to save the world through their example and whose general characteristics have been identified by Clinton Rossiter.

All self-conscious nations develop a sense of peculiar worth and importance, and thus like to think that success in pursuing their own purposes will bring benefits, just as failure will do harm, to men of other nations, even to men in every part of the world for generations to come. A select few, however, have been especially persuaded by such factors as time, geography, size, success, ideology, and necessity to think and act seriously as nations that have been granted special blessings and are therefore bound by special obligations. England, France, Germany, the old Spain, the new China, the old and new Israel, the Soviet Union, and . . . the young United States are perhaps the most instructive examples of nations in which a belief in high destiny has been, whether persistently or only discontinuously, a forceful presence in the lives of men great and small. [Rossiter, 1971:44][10]

But if Catholic Spain, Holy Russia, Protestant Britain, or the Islamic Caliphate have read some special import into their destiny, it has been as the randomly chosen vicar of the eternal, unchanging True Faith and a light unto the world at large. God might very well have pointed His finger elsewhere. The American self-perception is quite special. For one thing, American nationalism has been international in character from the very outset, especially at the outset but to a certain extent even today. Lafayette and other true believers from abroad were among the progenitors; the doors of the civil chapel remain swung open for right-minded, born-again aliens; the gospel has been carried around the world through a variety of mechanisms; and revolutionary upstarts elsewhere have been, and perhaps still are, inspired by the American example. (The closest historic parallel may be early Bolshevik Russia which, among other things, attracted many a zealot from other lands.)

But even more special is the belief that this miraculous culmination of man's earthly mission could only have come to pass in a particular epoch in a particular chosen land. "If not *uniquely* American, the idea of a protecting Providence was *characteristic* of American patriotism. Indeed, so primary was this theme that no study of American nationalism can possibly ignore it and remain faithful to the historical past" (Hay, 1969b:80; emphasis in original). And criteria for admission to this charmed company of believers and the means for promulgating the faith have been qualitatively different and new.[11] These facts, along with the sheer intensity and persistence of the thoroughly religious conviction of being a chosen people charged with a redemptive mission for humankind to be executed from a specific territorial base during a specific era have indeed made this country qualitatively distinct from other lands (Hay, 1969b:80).[12] Russel Nye provides a forthright definition of this distinctiveness.

> The search by Americans for a precise definition of their national purpose, and their absolute conviction that they have such a purpose, provide one of the most powerful threads in the development of an American ideology. All nations, of course, have long agreed that they are chosen peoples; the idea of special destiny is as old as nationalism itself. However, no nation in modern history has been quite so consistently dominated as the United States by the belief that it has a particular mission in the world, and a unique contribution to make to it. [Nye, 1966:164]

And no other country has ever been so officially articulate in trying to express its national mission.[13]

If the American civil religion eventually acquired all the complexities and trappings of a traditional church after consummating its rendezvous with the state, the first clear signs of its existence appeared even before there was a state to which it might be joined. It was not an accidental occurrence, nor was it a makeshift contrived by the architects of a nation lacking the standard raw materials available in the Old World. Instead it was the logical efflorescence of both theological and political trends that had been simmering in Europe for some generations, and which found unusually fertile soil in the Promised Land of America, as E. L. Tuveson has noted. "The American apocalyptic prophets inherited rather than created much of their ideology, and . . . millennialism was no American invention. It was a logical development of premises, begun before in Britain, about God's plans for universal salvation through history, the revealed will being interpreted in the light of successive world events. . . . In one sense, indeed Manifest Destiny was thrust upon the United States" (Tuveson, 1968:92). Thus during the course of the eighteenth century, the political idealism of the Enlightenment merged with the providential and millennial enthusiasms of evangelical Protestants to brew a heady new mixture indeed in a land where no single denomination held universal dominion (Ahlstrom, 1975; Brauer, 1976:29–54). Despite its theological paternity, the resulting credo eventually became nationalistic and this-worldly.

And, once again, it was New England that led the rest of the nation in this quest for the New Jerusalem—and toward a twentieth-century materialization the seventeenth-century divines could scarcely have foreseen. Sacvan Bercovitch makes the case forcefully.

> Despite their allegiance to theocracy, the emigrant Puritans were part of the movement toward the future. Their rhetoric and vision facilitated the process of colonial growth. And in sustaining that rhetoric and vision, the latter-day Jeremiahs effectually forged a powerful vehicle of middle-class ideology: a ritual of progress through consensus, a system of sacred-secular symbols for a laissez-faire creed, a "civil religion" for a people chosen to spring fully formed into the modern world—America, the first-begotten daughter of a democratic capitalism, the only country that developed, from the seventeenth through the

nineteenth centuries, into a wholly middle-class culture. [Ber-
covitch, 1978:27–28]

Although a given denomination might try to effect ecclesiastical
monopoly within a single province (and with only partial success
even in New England), the political realities of national independence compelled mutual tolerance. "Each [church] wanted freedom
for itself. . . . it had become clear that the only way to get it for
themselves was to grant it to all others" (Mead, 1963:35). Moreover,
church organization was generally quite imperfect; there was much
fluidity within and among the various sects with many individuals
floating freely from one group to another; and, despite the occasional spurts of revivalism, formal membership and church attendance were at low ebb during the eighteenth and early nineteenth
centuries.

Thus, even if there had been a strong central state at the outset, which, of course, was lacking, it would have been in no position to establish a state church. Yet, paradoxically, divided among
and within themselves though they might have been, the various
churches were peculiarly important in effecting the Revolution
(Hatch, 1977; Heimert, 1966; G. Miller, 1976; Plongeron, 1982) and,
then, in lending substance and meaning to the infant republic, in
inculcating republican ideals and a sense of national community
(Bellah, 1978:21). And, in the process, the structure of formal religion itself began to undergo major transformation. The second
Great Awakening (1780–1830), which encompassed far greater numbers of worshippers over a much broader territory than the first and
may have been even more uninhibited in form, obviously, but not
accidentally, coincides in time with a most critical period of nation
formation and the most fervent realization of nationalism (Bellah
and Hammond, 1980:14; D. G. Mathews, 1969). Donald Mathews
pointedly connects the two outbursts: the religious and nationalistic. "The constant visitation of evangelical preachers and their
preaching the same values, norms and vision of society throughout
the United States helped create a distinct moral community. Thus
the Revival helped make religion one of the major determinants of
public discourse everywhere in the country. . . . Because the Revival
enveloped the entire country, it was a nationalizing force that created a 'common world of experience'" (D. G. Mathews, 1969:39–
40).

This remarkable spasm of public piety was one of the end results
of a process initiated by the Reformation three centuries earlier.

The flight from formal practices and ecclesiastical rigidities, the emphasis on individual initiative and salvation, and the internalization of religion all meant the loss of any central, institutionalized locus of churchly authority. I do not wish to imply that the early American churches were the sole, or even principal, custodians of the civil religion, but simply that they were conspicuous actors in the drama of its creation. Indeed, some theologians have taken some pains to denounce the "heresy" of the supremacy of the state and the very notion of a civil religion (Wood, 1977). But, of course, an influential wing of American Protestantism has continued to be wildly chauvinistic up to the present moment. The gist of the matter is set forth succinctly by John Wilson. "What had been proved in the American experiment was certainly not that the Christian religion was unimportant to the civil government, but that its contribution could, without benefit of establishment, as well be indirect and informal as explicit and legal" (J. F. Wilson, 1979:14).

The genesis of the American civil religion was overwhelmingly a mass phenomenon, one that involved the hearts and minds of the great unchurched majority of the population rather than something emanating solely from the pulpit. For, in the words of Catherine Albanese, "the 'real religion' of the American people lies to a greater degree outside the confines of traditional definitions. To state the matter baldly, the American penchant for teeth-brushing or flag-waving may have as much or more to do with religious orientation than church or synagogue attendance" (Albanese, 1976:7).

For the great mass of Americans today, traditional religion, generally acknowledged to be a good thing, has been relegated to a rather remote emotional corner far from the vital center of life. It is un-American not to have some religion, but it matters little which one (as long as it is not too far out), what its creed, or how zealously you practice it (Dohen, 1967:8). And the extent to which the mainstream churches, Catholic and Jewish as well as Protestant, have been homogenized and Americanized by the greater society may equal their contribution to the shaping of its civil religion (Dohen, 1967; Herberg, 1960).

Thus a lively civil religion materialized in the United States in its earlier years, the creature of the spiritual thirst of the population that ministrations of the older faiths could no longer fully slake, and without the active intervention of the nascent state. We can equate this civil religion with the first stages of nationalism and a passionate belief in America's providential destiny, whose outward symbolic forms we have already encountered. As Robert Hay reminds us, such symbols may well have been urgent necessities, for, by any objective measure, the new country was a third-rate power in economic and military terms. "America's psychological necessities doubtless account, in large measure, for the pervasiveness of the Providential legend. . . . The material abundance which the Industrial Revolution brought in its wake together with America's development into a great world power provided new justification for the American experiment. But, during the Republic's first century, it had been the conviction of Americans that they were heaven's favorites which had done most to sustain a nation of patriots" (Hay, 1969b:100–101). It was, of course, the American Revolution itself that provided the vital center of the new faith, the stockpile of raw materials for the symbols and mythologies that were to follow and, however modified, are still with us (Albanese, 1976; Kammen, 1978; Lipset, 1963:74–75).[14] The Revolution was, in the purest meaning of the concept, a religious experience for the participants, and not just in the narrow sense that preachers and theologians may have paved the way for the political event. Verily, "the American Revolution was *in itself* a religious experience, a hierophany collectively manifested and received which provided the fundamental basis for American civil religion as we know it" (Albanese, 1976:6). It is difficult for us, more than two centuries after the fact, to sense more than dimly the incandescence of emotions kindled during this Revolution/Civil War, or the degree to which it mobilized the human capacity for awe in the face of suprahuman events. It was emphatically a mass phenomenon involving everyone (if we exclude slaves, aborigines, loyalists, and bondsmen) from the meanest to the loftiest strata of society (Morris, 1977).[15]

No artifact of the human mind is static, not even the religions whose adherents strain so mightily to freeze into immobility. Would a resurrected Gautama Buddha know what to make of the Buddhism practiced in his name in Tibet, Burma, or southern California? How closely do the rituals and pronouncements of the Vatican City resemble those of First Century Christians? Would the firebrands of the First International recognize the doctrines emanating from the Kremlin or Beijing? In precisely the same fashion, American civil religion has undergone profound revision since its initial formulation, but without loss of continuity.

The spores of the statism that eventually became the main substance of American civil religion were sown in the early days of the nation with the drafting of the Constitution and the design of the

District of Columbia. The subtle shift in ideological/religious orientation in the four score years preceding the Civil War can be traced in the rising fortunes of the sanctified idea of Union. The concept had been celebrated in verse and other forms even during the Revolution (Werner, 1932), but it was only during the stressful decades leading to Sumter that it attained complete canonization (Nagel, 1964; Nye, 1966:75–79), ultimately to reach a climax in the truly religious mysticism of Abraham Lincoln (E. Wilson, 1954). During its heyday, Union permeates the psychological scene in many ways, including song, oratory, and visual symbols, as described by Paul Nagel. "Union's symbols invariably conveyed a sense of comfort and reassurance. The figures used were familiar, often in fact inherently unexciting and usually mechanical. But each suggested a quality of synthesis indispensable to the idea itself. The images chiefly encountered are chains, ships, constellations, and other markedly tangible representations such as vases and architectural patterns" (Nagel, 1964:211). But what had started out as a "spiritual Union . . . rising from a concept of sublime human fraternity" (Nagel, 1964:71), and however lofty Lincoln's vision thereof may have been, eventually hardened into a faceless central authority imposing its will upon a submissive citizenry.

What the Revolution had meant to the cause of pristine nationalism in theological and political terms was roughly equivalent to the impact of the Civil War on the statist phase of American civil religion. But the differences in their symbolic legacies are more valuable than the parallels in illustrating the metamorphosis of the nationalist faith. Whereas the Revolution was the source of a brilliant constellation of symbols whose luster still brightens the collective memory, the lessons, symbolic or other, of the Civil War are obscure, except perhaps for their testimony as to human folly and the inevitability of monolithic government. If the Civil War was a symbol of anything, then, more than "a full century after the event, it is still difficult to make out the character of that symbol" (Kammen, 1978:258–59; Handlin, 1961:133).[16] Outside the South, few Americans are now aware of the events of 1861–65 or care to reflect on their significance.

The only durable additions to the national pantheon to emerge from the conflict were Abraham Lincoln and Robert E. Lee; but the legends that grew around these two figures feed upon primordial emotions and are only in part specific to the particular war. In any case, it was "awkwardly apparent that Lincoln and Lee were exceptional Americans rather than representative Americans" (Kammen,

1978:258). The only significant holiday inspired by the Civil War, Memorial Day, has not only declined in popularity, like all other national holidays, but has evolved into a generalized salute to military glory that is combined with a timeless meditation on death and renewal.[17]

I believe that the failure to manufacture new national symbols since the middle of the past century testifies to a certain spiritual vacuity in the latter-day statist creed.[18] As a substitute for originality, older items were recycled or given different emphases, for example, the eagle and flag, even as others, for example, Miss Liberty and the monument, lost most of their mana. Arguably, since 1865, and certainly since 1876, significant accessions to nationalist myth, iconography, music, architecture, and literature have been few and far between.

One of the unmistakable symptoms of the degeneration of Revolutionary idealism was the prevalence for a protracted period, in places high and low, of the doctrine of Manifest Destiny, especially from the Mexican War through the McKinley administration (Merk, 1963; Weinberg, 1935). But its crassly expansionist tone and not so covert racism (Burns, 1957:206–10), as well as its geopolitical impracticality, all of which ran counter to the high-mindedness of the original national creed, have rendered such territorial jingoism obsolete. There is no doubt, however, that the doctrine lingers on clandestinely and in newer guises.

When any of the great supernatural religions progresses from its lowly beginnings to official status and nominal spiritual suzerainty over large communities, it collects a large stock of ritual and physical gear along the way. One might even argue that the price of such political and material prosperity is the loss of the inner spark, that outward conventions and physical show become more dearly esteemed than genuine salvation. Be that as it may, we can easily demonstrate a truly uncanny similarity between the workings of the fully mature statist civil religion of countries such as the United States and the operations of orthodox Christianity during its heyday.[19] The individual is born into the state and remains a compulsory member of the national congregation until his death unless he elects the difficult apostasy of emigration. The compulsory registration of birth, marriage, divorce, and death by the state usurps the very same functions once performed by the parish priest. Schooling in public, that is, government-controlled, schools is mandatory for all those children not enrolled in parochial institutions. A strong case can be made to the effect that, locally managed though they may be, the public schools of America, in the words of D. W. Brogan, serve as the country's "formally unestablished national church" (Michaelsen, 1970:62), and are the single most important instrument for the inculcation of public piety (Carlson, 1975; Michaelsen, 1970; J. F. Wilson, 1971:7–9). The tax-supported schoolroom of today serves precisely the same purposes as did the cathedral and parish classes of an earlier day, for in both instances the transmission of knowledge and skills is really secondary to immersion in religious and societal norms.

The modern nation-state has made its flag into a literally holy object, the equivalent of the cross or communion wafer; and nowhere is the observation more apt than in the United States. Furthermore, national anthems and related compositions have displaced church hymns. Carlton Hayes relentlessly pursues the multiple parallelisms between the two forms of faith.

> There are universal liturgical forms for "saluting" the flag, for "dipping" the flag, for "lowering" the flag, and for "hoisting" the flag. Men bare their heads when the flag passes by; and in praise of the flag poets write odes, and to it children sing hymns and pledge allegiance. In all solemn feasts and fasts of nationalism, the flag is in evidence, and with it that other sacred thing, the national anthem. An acute literary critic in his purely secular capacity might be tempted to cavil at phrases in "Rule Britannia," in "Deutschland uber Alles," or even in the "Marseillaise;" he might object, on literary grounds, to such a lame beginning as "Oh say, can you see?" But a national anthem is not a profane thing and does not admit of textual criticism. It is the *Te Deum* of the new dispensation; worshippers stand when it is intoned, the military at "attention," and the male civilians with uncovered heads, all with external show of respect and veneration. [Hayes, 1960:167]

We have already seen how national heroes, martyrs, and villains have preempted the emotional space once occupied by the Holy Trinity, the saints, and Satan and his imps. The birthdays of Washington, Lincoln, Jackson, and other revered leaders have displaced the saints' days, while Independence Day, Memorial Day, and other nationalistic commemorations have rivaled church holidays on any scale of public excitement. The deaths and funerals of the greatest of the national greats have touched off convulsions of religious fervor, the like of which no traditional religious event has ever matched in America. We have an ample galaxy of places hallowed

by their association with national heroes or their deeds, a far
greater number than of American sites cherished by devout Christians. And to such places as Valley Forge, Mount Vernon, Plymouth
Rock, Independence Hall, Lincoln's Tomb, Monticello, Arlington
Cemetery, Faneuil Hall, the Statue of Liberty, the Liberty Bell,
the many sanctified cemeteries and battlefields, and especially all
the many temples and tombs of Washington, D.C. stream endless
throngs of pilgrims performing their holy obligations. Throughout
the land, graven images of the national demigods, related eidolons,
and miraculous events and their portrayal on paper, wood, canvas,
glass, ceramics, and every other conceivable medium have upstaged
a more venerable iconography featuring Jesus Christ, the Virgin
Mary, the saints, and biblical episodes.

Like any proper faith, the American civil religion venerates its
sacred documents. Chief among them, of course, has been the Declaration of Independence, which underwent apotheosis soon after
its signing (Albanese, 1976:182–88; Hazleton, 1906; Maass, 1976a;
D. Malone, 1954:248–68; Wills, 1978:323–62). It matters little that
only a small minority of the population have ever read all of its
noble language or are familiar with more than a couple of its incantations. Sacredness is enhanced rather than lessened by inaccessi-
bility or by being vested in archaic, even incomprehensible tongues.
Also numbered among the most divine of national scriptures are
Washington's (or Hamilton's) Farewell Address (Forgie, 1979:25),
two or three of Lincoln's major addresses, and, preeminently, the
Constitution (Kammen, 1986a). (Is it necessary to note again that
personal acquaintance with the documents is hardly necessary to
fetishize them and to strike awe into the hearts of the faithful
flock?) (Albanese, 1976:202–19; Lerner, 1937:1294–1305; Marienstras, 1976:145–50; Reiff, 1940:101; Schechter, 1915). Its symbolic
radiance far outshines the literal import of the words. Today as

> in the nineteenth century the American Constitution [has] op-
> erated as the central myth of an entire political structure. . . .
> There reigned everywhere the tacit understanding that it was
> the one unifying abstraction, the one symbol that might com-
> mand all loyalties and survive all strife. The Constitution thus
> served multiple functions for a society that lacked tradition,
> folk-memory, a sovereign, and a body of legend. . . . America's
> veneration for the Constitution became steadily more intense
> in the years that followed the Civil War. [Elkins and McKitrick,
> 1961:184]

Holy writ must have its properly ordained priesthood to interpret inner meanings. If the President embodies the godhead of the civil religion, if historians act as the lay clergy (Mead, 1977:74), it is the federal courts that furnish the regular clergy, most of all the robed justices of the Supreme Court who preside as the high priests to proclaim dogma and explicate talmudically the hidden sense of divine writ (Lerner, 1937:1312).[20]

Thus there is literally no aspect of a fully constituted supernatural church that lacks its direct counterpart in the American civil religion. This is true even in the realm of missionary effort. In terms of cash, personnel, and number of establishments, no nation-state has been more active, or hyperactive, in sending church missions beyond its borders than has the United States.[21] Whether they intend to do so or not, the missionaries, be they Catholic or Protestant, preach not only the Christian gospel but also, implicitly, that of the American civil religion smuggled within the technological, cultural, and other precepts dispensed to their flocks. Or, as happened so blatantly in Hawaii, they prepare the way for economic, political, and demographic incursions by their countrymen.

Americans have also exported their creed via a variety of nonecclesiastical channels. Their philanthropic outreach abroad, both private and governmental, in the form of disaster relief, schools, orphanages, medical facilities, training programs, libraries, and other cultural projects (Curti, 1963), has long operated on a scale far outdistancing that of any competitors. Intentionally or not, such generosity has enhanced the image of the donor country, and has softened whatever resistance the beneficiaries might have had toward the message of Americanism. Clearly this has been one of the principal results of the Peace Corps over the past quarter-century (Hapgood and Bennett, 1968; Textor, 1966; Windmiller, 1970). Its program is the exact lay equivalent of the overseas Christian missionary effort.

Two additional aspects of American foreign relations are related to the civil religion and should not be overlooked: the philhellenism of the nineteenth century that so greatly influenced policy toward the Greek struggle for independence (Borza, 1973); and the special relationship with modern Israel in recent years, something that runs far more deeply than the influence of the Jewish lobby. In both instances, theological factors (broadly defined) have produced results that may not have been necessarily in the material interests of the United States.

WHAT LIES IN STORE?

The fact that both supernatural and civil religions, along with political and social systems, are in a constant state of flux, that they
are evolving into new and unexpected forms, is so fundamental an
axiom of history, yet so easily overlooked, that it will bear many
repetitions. The temptation to read portents of things to come in
the symbolic entrails of contemporary nation-states is very great
indeed. But perhaps the richest lesson of the past is how foolish it is
to foretell the future. Furthermore, the task of the prognosticator is
peculiarly difficult in the 1980s because of the remarkable, truly
fundamental changes in modes of social interaction and individual
mind-set, of public and private discourse, taking place in response
to the growing tyranny of telecommunications. Although it is
manifestly impossible to grasp fully what is going on so rapidly at
this very moment, it is not at all implausible that the advent of
television as the dominant (mostly mindless) purveyor of information and amusement is at least as revolutionary a development for
humankind as the arrival not too many generations ago of printing
and universal literacy. As Meyrowitz (1985) and Postman (1985)
have so chillingly argued, we have already entered a McLuhanesque
"Age of Show Business" and inhabit Aldous Huxley's *Brave New
World*. What all this implies for the evolution of political consciousness is far from clear. All I dare do in concluding this biography of the American civil religion as revealed through its symbolic
patterns is to summarize the situation today, and let the reader
indulge in his or her own speculations.

Two facts are undeniable. First, as I have taken some pains to
demonstrate, there have been enormous changes over the past two
hundred years in the nature of the American nation and nation-
state and, more particularly, in the nationalism and statism without which the polity could not function effectively.[22] It would be
shortsighted not to expect equally profound changes over the next
century. Secondly, like others elsewhere, the American nation-state
and the statism which is its mainstay are beset with difficulties and
dangers that threaten their viability. It is still much too soon to
decide whether Robert Nisbet is on solid ground in claiming in his
Twilight of Authority (1975) that the present situation is analogous
to that of Western Europe on the eve of the Reformation and the
breakup of feudal society, when the old order gave way to modernization, but some of the parallels are intriguing.

Clearly, we are at the beginning of a new Reformation, this time, however, one that has the political state rather than the church as the central object of its force; a force that ranges from the slow drip of apathy to the more hurricane-like intensities of violence and terror. The first great Reformation, that of the sixteenth century, was also a period of twilight of authority in the West. It was terminated by the rise of the national state and the gradual retreat of church, kinship, guild, and hereditary class.

Today we are present, I believe, at the commencement of the retreat of the state as we have known this institution for some five centuries, though what the consequences will be no one can be certain. [Nisbet, 1975:6]

The first clear signals of distress began, I suspect, with the defection of a few intellectuals and creative artists during the past century. The darker blasphemies of Hawthorne, Melville, Henry and Brooks Adams, Ambrose Bierce, and the elderly Mark Twain, along with those of their counterparts in Europe, were harbingers of a widespread disillusionment among the intelligentsia in the past seventy years. Nowadays it takes much flexing of the imagination to reconstruct the situation as it existed during the early nineteenth century when not just statesmen, bureaucrats, and professional warriors but virtually all poets, dramatists, musicians, artists, and novelists threw themselves, heart and soul, into the nationalist cause, eventually to be joined by the rank and file of the population. At a certain point, which I would place in the 1820s or 1830s in the United States, nationalism saturated the community, becoming as much a part of the normal routine of existence and the inner mental life of the populace as Roman Catholicism seems to have been within its realm during the medieval Age of Faith. Later, whatever the misgivings of a prematurely disenchanted vanguard, the statist faith, the riper latter-day offspring of nationalism, attained uncontested dominion over all strata of society in the advanced countries. Merle Curti has summarized the situation quite effectively.

It was not until well toward the end of the century that Brooks and Henry Adams ventured a pessimistic conception of American destiny. This failed to win any general support. Indeed, not until the verge of the Second World War did any considerable number of people question the quasi-axiom that America was

to bring to the common man plenty, comfort, opportunity, adventure, and peace. Then the old near-Calvinistic conception
of the fundamental evil in the universe, the basic weakness of
man, the tragedy of his fate, brought forth foreboding words
among a small circle of intellectuals. A considerable number of
the plain people still believed in America's destiny, though less
exuberantly, to be sure, than in former times. [Curti, 1946:64]

It was the gruesome, senseless brutalities of World War I that shattered this consensus among the intelligentsia and, soon after,
among many ordinary citizens.

In the world of letters and the arts, a seemingly endless crisis in
styles, standards, and objectives had set in by the 1920s, and alien-
ation from public and self became the byword. No longer could the
critical observer look at the world and honestly convince himself
that the nation-state was the vehicle for perpetual progress, physical security, social harmony, personal felicity, and the answers to
the riddles of the universe. World War II did little to restore loyalty
to the statist credo. George Orwell hardly overstated the case when,
in the late 1940s, he declared: "In societies such as ours, it is unusual for anyone describable as an intellectual to feel a very deep
attachment to his own country" (Orwell, 1953:192).

By the 1960s and 1970s, the statist faith seemed to be approaching its nadir in the United States, especially among the youthful
(Bellah and Hammond, 1980:196), as Paul Goodman reported. "Our
case is astounding. For the first time in recorded history, the mention of country, community, place has lost its power to animate.
Nobody but a scoundrel even tries it. Our rejection of false patriotism is, of course, itself a badge of honor. But the positive loss is
tragic and I cannot resign myself to it. . . . This loss is especially
damaging in growing up" (Goodman, 1969:97). As our examination
of public celebrations and the boom in nostalgia has suggested, the
future no longer appeals to the masses as a blissful haven (Bell,
1975:197; Zuckerman, 1978:242). It is, of course, too early to draw
firm conclusions from the post-1976 slump in pilgrimages to nationalistic shrines, but perhaps even the past, however glamorized,
may be beginning to lose its allure. The loss of an ideological
faith[23] called into question by urban rioting and the agony of Vietnam was widely perceived as only one item in a general debacle
that involved the disintegration of social norms, the debasement of
language, and the malfunctioning of the economy. The litany of
tribulations, as recited by Robert Bellah, is depressing.

The erosion of language . . . is a symptom of the erosion of common meanings, of which there is a great deal of evidence in our society. This takes the form, which is by now statistically well documented, of a decline of belief in all forms of obligation: to one's occupation, one's family, and one's country. A tendency to rank personal gratification above obligation to others correlates with a deepening cynicism about the established social, economic, and political institutions of society. [Bellah, 1975:x]

As a logical accompaniment to the more general erosion, the old tried and true nationalistic symbols seemed to be losing much of their vitality. The trivialization of national holidays, the near extinction of monument building, outright desecration of the flag, and, possibly, a dismaying decline in voter turnout during presidential elections (Asher, 1980), were only some of the unwelcome clues. "Western society in general has experienced a decline in nationalist sentiments and a concomitant decrease in the force of civil religions" (Liebman and Don-Yehiya, 1983:136). Americans might take some dubious pride in being in the vanguard of this worldwide malaise, just as they had been in earlier political and ideological innovations. "This very fact, however, has pitched them into a spiritual predicament for which they are ill prepared" (Ahlstrom, 1975:504).

However diseased its spiritual marrow may have become, there is no doubt that the nation-state system in general has been afflicted, internally and externally, by a number of serious challenges of a political, economic, and military nature. One of these, the so-called ethnic revival (Hechter, 1973; A. D. Smith, 1981; Williams, 1982, 1984) has had only a modest impact on the solidarity of the American nation-state. It has been a much more serious issue in recent years in countries such as Great Britain or France, which had long been assumed to have extirpated separatist movements, but where the Scots, Welsh, Bretons, Corsicans, Alsatians, Occitanians, and others have unexpectedly begun agitating for greater autonomy. Such ethnic restiveness has also been a matter of growing concern in countries such as Belgium, Spain, Yugoslavia, the Soviet Union, India, Guyana, Iran, Canada, and many African republics, to take some conspicuous examples, where subordinate groups have never been fully reconciled to membership within multiethnic states (Barnet, 1980:307–8).

In the United States, a resurgence of ethnic feeling among Native

Americans and descendants of European immigrants and African slaves has produced some interesting social and cultural results, along with some minor political reverberations, but without posing any meaningful threat to the territorial integrity of the nation-state. There may be a regional component in the belated stirring of self-awareness among the Cajuns of southern Louisiana and the Hispanic peoples of the Southwest, but, again, no hint of a secessionary movement. Undoubtedly related to such rediscoveries, or contrivances, of ethnicity has been a renewed interest in regionalism among Americans as evidenced by a notable surge in the number of regional and local organizations, periodicals, and other literature, cookbooks, festivals, and the like.

Although it may be difficult to measure the phenomenon quantitatively, it is clear that the traditional American antipathy toward government in general has become more vocal and intensely felt in recent times, reflecting, one might suppose, "a loss of purpose, identity and, ultimately, dignity in the face of increasing bureaucratization" (A. D. Smith, 1977:30).[24] Although I must insist upon a significant distinction between the machinery of government and the state-idea, any disenchantment with the latter is likely to be reflected in even greater hostility to the more tangible and onerous manifestations of the once sacrosanct state.

The foregoing "postnationalist" trends—the new regionalism and ethnicity and also the resurgence of religious fundamentalism, all of which are closely associated with symbolic behavior and the emotional temper of the citizenry—can be construed as revulsion against "the God that failed," a nation-state that has not adequately delivered the promised spiritual (and material) goods (Nisbet, 1974: 28). Other equally corrosive forces are at work that are not so directly cultural. Even at its apogee, the nation-state never succeeded in fully abolishing all the older loyalties: to family, locality, gemeinschaft, and a great range of voluntary associations. But it is a newer set of technological, economic, and intellectual developments that has a much greater potential for dethroning the nation-state.

At a rather rarefied level, one might advance the argument that the worship of science, which sometimes assumes the form of scientism, is the new universalizing religion that is the proper heir of the traditional faiths and of statism; but, except among committed professionals, this is a remote, bloodless theology incapable of quickening Everyman's pulse (Zelinsky, 1975).

Since the 1950s, with the advent of advanced nuclear arms and delivery systems, it has become plain to the man on the street that not even the superpowers command the capability to perform that most elemental of all state functions: protecting their citizens against hostile attack and possible mass annihilation (Barnet, 1980: 305). Melville Watkins states the obvious in commenting that "the military technology of the electronic age—the most advanced of any part of the new technology—has rendered obsolete nineteenth-century notions of national sovereignty and national independence. The bomb shelter is not a very satisfactory place in which to wave a flag, and fallout shows a fatal lack of respect for national boundaries. Not surprisingly, there has been increasing recognition of the need for disarmament, world law, and a global police force" (Watkins, 1966:292).

Another less malign technology, electronic telecommunications, has been even more effective than the printing press in violating the sanctity of international boundaries.[25] Leonard Doob's observations are truer today than when they were written more than twenty years ago. "In the twentieth century, dictators and patriots, we think or hope we know, are pursuing a will-o'-the-wisp at a time when international communication is developing so rapidly and efficiently. True, most people behind whatever curtain is designated, including ones created by the West, are not straining to become cosmopolitan and are in fact hearing very few of the international communications. But there are cracks produced by radio and television, science, and the exchange of peoples" (Doob, 1964:52–53). With the nearly universal marketing of transistor radios and tape players and the capability of transmitting news events, soccer matches, sermons, movies, or whatever to a global viewership via satellites, it becomes more and more difficult to advance the aspirations of statism. Even such relatively hermetic nation-states as the Soviet Union, South Africa, and Albania cannot totally quarantine unsavory alien messages. In similar fashion, dramatic declines in travel time and costs for international trips have meant enormous increments in the volume of exotic tourism and in the circulation of students, young hitchhikers, and other travelers among all manner of countries. Whatever the results, they are certainly not likely to make the world more jingoistic.

Recent advances in communication and transportation are among the factors that have led to the ascendancy of that most serious rival of the nation-state: the multinational firm (Barnet and Müller, 1974). It has become painfully clear that "the basic unit of economic policy—the nation-state is not appropriate to the problems of late-twentieth-century capitalism" (Heilbroner, 1983:77). With net worths and technical resources far richer than those of many nominally sovereign states and operated by sophisticated staffs with only vestigial allegiance to their native lands who allocate investments and transfer goods and jobs with little regard for international boundaries, the largest of the multinationals have become leading movers and shakers of the world economy and thus, indirectly, of the political decisions of nation-states.[26]

It is not solely in the economic realm that the nation-state is undergoing emasculation. National governments find themselves particularly helpless when confronted by a host of increasingly worrisome environmental problems, especially those involving the atmosphere and oceans. Of necessity, these governments are compelled to surrender some of their authority (and thus symbolic legitimacy) to international bodies of one kind or another and to hope that such collaboration will safeguard the local along with the global habitat.

Less immediate a menace, but one with interesting long-range potentialities for usurping the hegemony of the nation-state, is a thriving network of nongovernmental transnational organizations. Although transnationalism has existed since the dawn of nationalism as its unobtrusive puny sibling, especially in the realms of the sciences and humanities, the phenomenon has begun to flourish vigorously only in the twentieth century. Today there are several thousands of these groups, some regional in scope, others global, whose members seek to advance and coordinate their interests in such endeavors as humanitarian and ecological activities, sport, the arts and sciences, and many forms of self-realization with scant regard for the niceties of national affiliation (Field, 1971; Galtung, 1980; Inkeles, 1980; Skjelsbaek, 1971; Toffler, 1980:339–41). The persons and local cells who participate in such far-flung camaraderie might be seen as the frontier homesteaders of an embryonic world society. Even though the individuals in question account for only a minute fraction of the world's population, their knowledge, skills, and generally elite status endow them with a measure of influence far greater than their numbers might suggest. At the very least their presence serves as a standing rebuke to the grandiose pretensions of the nation-state.

All the trends sketched in the preceding paragraphs were visible enough by the 1960s, and it would have been perfectly forgivable then to predict the imminent withering away of the nation-state. But, for better or worse, social history seldom progresses along straight, predictable grooves. What seemed so obvious and inevitable a few years ago has not come to pass. In fact, there has been a certain resurgence of statefulness in the United States and elsewhere during the 1980s. For all its infirmities and mindlessness, the nation-state still lumbers along. Indeed, in the Third World, which may be lagging behind the highly advanced countries in this as well as other respects, old-fashioned statism seems to be still on the rise (Anderson, 1983; A. D. Smith, 1979).

In the United States and other postindustrial lands, statism may well be enjoying a (pen)ultimate (?) flush of glory, and for the same reasons that ethnicity, regionalism, fundamentalist piety, greed, and nostalgia in all their variations have staged comebacks. First, there is the distressing realization that the future that once beckoned so alluringly has become a dark, forbidding place that obviously frightens us; the womblike certitudes of the past have considerably greater appeal. Secondly, none of the available substitutes for the nation-state are as yet practically or emotionally acceptable. A truly welcome alternative is not yet on the horizon.[27]

Thus, in moments of special stress, we find even normally alienated intellectuals nestling in the arms of the motherland. I suspect that, in this curious ideological lull of the 1980s, we can observe some instructive parallels between traditional churches and the civil religion. Although the intellectual and theological foundations of Christianity were shattered several generations ago, its adherents cling to it like drowning persons reaching for a life raft. In just the same way, we inmates of the nation-state hang on to its crumbling prison walls for dear life. Neither the old-time religion nor statism is a candidate for instant death. But the difference between now and then, between the nervous present and the days when supernatural or statist faith was whole and unassailable, is a profound one (as Matthew Arnold mournfully declaimed while he stood on Dover Beach). No longer are all the days and hours of our lives completely immersed in the faith; no longer do all thoughts and actions fall spontaneously into the hallowed patterns. Instead we can detect elements of hysteria in a reversion to an unattainable past. Beset by other concerns, even the most ardently pious and nationalistic among us must pump ourselves up at certain moments before we can simulate the proper emotions. But we dare not look within, into the dark empty center. What more can I say?

NOTES ★ ★ ★ ★ ★ ★ ★ ★

CHAPTER ONE

1. Or to claim, as Louis Snyder has, that "there is nothing 'natural' about it: its building was as artificial as the construction of the Panama Canal. There is little 'rational' about it: it is not necessarily a predestined way of life for the human animal" (Snyder, 1976:3). However, one cannot help wondering about the plausibility of Manuel Castells's suggestion that the European city-state, or leagues thereof, may have been just as viable a route to a modern world. "Those cities, marching along this alternative historical road, had much more direct access to modernity, and their success is still expressed in their superior level of cultural pluralism, political democracy, and economic efficiency" (Castells, 1983:14). Murray Bookchin (1987) has explored this general notion at considerably greater length.

2. In another passage, Steiner expresses his views even more vehemently (Steiner, 1967:59). "Nationalism is the venom of our age. It has brought Europe to the edge of ruin. It drives the new states of Asia and Africa like crazed lemmings. By proclaiming himself a Ghanaean, a Nicaraguan, a Maltese, a man spares himself vexation. He becomes one of an armed, coherent pack. Every mob impulse in modern politics, every totalitarian design, feeds on nationalism, on the drug of hatred which makes human beings bare their teeth across a wall, across ten yards of waste ground. . . . If the potential of civilization is not to be destroyed, we shall have to develop more complex, more provisional loyalties" (Steiner, 1967:152).

3. It is impossible to overstate the power and sacramental qualities of the modern nation-state. "Statism affirms the centrality of state interests and the centralization of power at the expense of nongovernmental groups and institutions. In terms of symbols and style, statism reflects the effort to transform the state and its institutions into the central foci of loyalty and identification. Statism gives rise to values and symbols that point to the state, legitimate it, and mobilize the population to serve its goals. In its more extreme formation statism cultivates an attitude of sanctity toward

the state, affirming it as an ultimate value" (Liebman and Don-Yehiya, 1983:84–85). "The state is the ultimate value which gives everything its meaning. It is a providence of which everything is expected, a supreme power which pronounces truth and justice and has the power of life and death over its members. It is an arbiter which is neither arbitrary nor arbitrated, which declares the law, the supreme objective code on which the whole game of society depends. . . . It is no longer incarnated in one man. It is abstract. . . . In its universality, in its combination of transcendence and proximity, we once again encounter the classic sacred. . . . What makes it sacred is not that it sets itself up as God, but the fact that the people accept it, live it, and look upon it as the great ordainer, the supreme and inevitable providence. They expect everything of it, accept its every intention, and inevitably and inexorably think of their lives and of their society in relation to it. Such is indeed the sacred. Without it our state is *nothing*. No purely rational loyalty suffices for the modern state . . . it is love and devotion which are required. The state is the sacred toward which our utmost in adoration is directed. . . . The state is constantly increasing its demands, together with its areas of competence, so that it can no longer be tolerated except as a mystique—and it is indeed through a mystique that the citizen responds. The more the state asks of the citizen and endangers him, the more he is ground down, the more his response is one of adoration. That is all he can do under the circumstances. This, again, is an obvious sign of the sacred—that which terrifies the most arouses the greatest intensity of awe" (Ellul, 1975:80–82).

4. I have been particularly impressed by, and benefited substantially from, the scholarly publications of Anderson (1983), Gellner (1983), Hayes (1931, 1960), Isaacs (1975), E. L. Jones (1981), Kohn (1944), Merriam (1931), Shafer (1972), and A. D. Smith (1977, 1979, 1981). Also of considerable value have been Deutsch (1966), Doob (1964), Huizinga (1959), Kamenka (1976), Kedourie (1961), King (1935), Kohn (1962), Leclerq (1979), Lemberg (1964), Miliband (1969), Nevitte (1979), Rocker (1978), Seton-Watson (1977), Snyder (1959, 1976), and Williams (1981). Most of these publications include extensive references, but for major bibliographic compendia, see Deutsch and Merritt (1970)—no fewer than 6,208 entries—and Rokkan, Soden, and Warmbrunn (1973).

5. It matters little whether we credit England or France as being the cradle of nationalism, since nationalizing trends could well have been simultaneous in the two countries. Hayes claims that "by the seventeenth and early eighteenth centuries, national patriotism was developed more generally and more acutely in England than in any other country—more so than in France or Spain or Sweden, and much more so than in Italy or Germany or eastern Europe. Indeed, we may affirm that modern nationalism, as we

know it today, had its original seat in England" (Hayes, 1960:38–39). From another point of view, "modern nationalism, which demands such overriding loyalty and commitment . . . must be interpreted in terms of the great revolutionary crisis in the history of humanity, which began with the French Revolution and which has continued ever since" (Symmons-Symonolewics, 1980:386). Palmer, on the other hand, envisions a somewhat earlier origin: "The Seven Years War aroused considerable national feeling" (Palmer, 1940:99), presumably in both Britain and France, and, arguably, in British North America as well. The only safe assumption is that something so gradual in its gestation could have emerged in any of the more socioeconomically advanced countries of the era and that ever since, the dating and location of the onset of nationalism has been closely correlated with the historical geography of modernization.

6. Miliband (1969:179–264) does discuss the ideological dimension of the state in capitalist society, but mainly in terms of education and information media, and devotes only a single page to the manipulation of symbols. Writing from a neo-Marxist perspective, Nairn is especially scathing in his comments on the ineffectuality of Marx, Engels, and their followers in analyzing the state and for their inclination to downplay nationalism (Nairn, 1977:18–19n). His own efforts are only partially successful. The statement that "nationalism is always the joint product of external pressures and an internal balance of class forces. Most typically it has arisen in societies confronting a dilemma of uneven development—'backwardness or colonization'—where conscious middle-class elites have sought massive popular mobilization to right the balance" (Nairn, 1977:41–42) is not very helpful in understanding, for example, the genesis of nationalism in England and France.

7. One of George Eliot's more sympathetic characters states the case eloquently: "A creative artist is no more a mere musician than a great statesman is a mere politician. We are not ingenious puppets, sir, who live in a box and look out on the world only when it is gaping for amusement. We help to rule the nations and make the age as much as any other public men. We count ourselves on level benches with legislators. And a man who speaks effectively through music is compelled to do something more difficult than parliamentary eloquence" (Eliot, 1979:217). Robert Nisbet approaches the question at a different level, but reaches the same general conclusion. "To make Frenchmen out of Burgundians, Germans out of Bavarians, and Americans out of Virginians or Californians, was no easy matter in the nineteenth century, and it is inconceivable that ordinary, unspoken unwritten economic or political forces could have accomplished this" (Nisbet, 1975:67).

8. Firth (1973) offers as well-rounded and sensible an exploration of the

history and definition of the concept of symbols as one can hope to find, but he fails to reach any firm conclusions. For the ways in which our "symbolic universes" or "symbol spheres" legitimate social and political organizations, see the oft-quoted, worthwhile discussions in Berger and Luckmann (1966:85–118) and Gerth and Mills (1954:274–305).

9. Or, viewing the matter in a less congenial light, "because of the youth and rapid growth of America, nationalist ideology is more artificially confected there than in any other nation. It did not grow from experiential and cultural roots, fertilized and watered by a watchful imperial ruling class, as in Britain. It was, like other artifacts of the New World, a conscious ideological construction, in the work of which ruling powers in the state, the media and the educational system all combined. The ideology consists not in the assertion of the superior virtues of the (German/British/Japanese) race but in the pretense that America is not a race or nation at all but the universal Future. It lays arrogant claim to the universalism of virtues—an incantation of freedoms and rights—and asserts in that name a prerogative to blast in at every door and to base itself in any part of the globe" (E. P. Thompson, 1983:240).

10. The United States is an ideal laboratory for testing hypotheses about the origins of ethnic groups of the hyphenated variety, as well as for observing the formation of nationality on a broader scale. Many immigrants who had not been aware of the fact in their native villages abruptly learned they were, or were considered to be, Italians, Germans, Ukrainians, or Yugoslavs, or whatever, perhaps even before their compatriots back home received the revelation (Kosiński, 1980:47, 52–53). The best general study of ethnic phenomena in America may well be Greeley (1974).

11. Implausible as it may seem, geographers, political scientists, and other scholars have yet to delve into the interrelationships between territory and political life in anything approaching definitive fashion—aside from their work on the delineation of international boundaries. Three of the more substantial treatments of the territorial dimensions of national entities (Duchacek, 1970; Gottmann, 1973; Knight, 1982) have little to say about the symbolic or psychological aspects of the topic. Yi-Fu Tuan (1978) touches on the question, but all too briefly. But, whatever the symbolic import of America's territory per se, there is no question as to the emotional resonance of the map of the country, even in bare outline (Horwitz, 1976:32).

12. Because of their absence or minor importance during the formative stages of American nationhood, such items as territory, dress, cuisine, and language will receive minimal notice in the following chapters. Following the same reasoning, there is to be almost no mention of the absence of national railroad, airline, and telecommunication systems or the failure to

develop a national university or a centralized educational system, standard items in most advanced countries (Zelinsky, 1973:50–52).

CHAPTER TWO

1. In the only definitive study to date of the visual personification of a nation, Agulhon (1979a) has traced the varied, complex, and contradictory career of the French Marianne as she has appeared in sculpture, paintings, cartoons, coins, stamps, and literature, and the ideological implications thereof. At the international scale, the almost universal phenomenon of adopting a totemic mascot—usually in facsimile, sometimes in the flesh— for colleges, secondary schools, and professional athletic teams is ripe for anthropological plucking.

2. It is noteworthy that Uncle Sam (and Brother Jonathan) seem to have found less favor in the South than in the rest of the country (Ketchum, 1959:32, 84). Can this be an instance of Southern lack of enthusiasm for American nationalism, or rather statism, as it evolved in the Northeast?

3. For useful, but more specialized, approaches to the phenomena of heroes and hero-worship in America see Beck (1971), Brophy (1975), Browne and Fishwick (1983), Fishwick (1954, 1969), T. P. Greene (1970), Jewett and Lawrence (1977), Karsten (1978), Klapp (1949), and Soule (1931).

4. "The emergence of this single figure of outstanding personal qualities, whether he is the actual leader and director of the armed struggle for independence, or whether he is one who distinguished himself during that period and so inherits the claim to power, is of crucial significance in the formation of nationhood. . . . How can we imagine the United States without the figure of George Washington, Venezuela without Bolívar, Ireland without De Valera, or India without Nehru? Conversely, the absence of such a prominent national figure in the early years of independence is clearly a substantial bar to the creation of national identity. Without such a figure, nationalism becomes, as it will become in the mature state, a much less definite thing, a sentiment attached to an abstraction, to a flag or to a phrase" (A. D. Smith, 1977:138).

5. "By 1779 . . . Franklin could well reflect that his portrait had accomplished its full share as promotion for the American cause. Franklin portraiture had played a substantial part in the build-up of the Franco-American alliance. Its political importance remained, but in a new way, and one less immediate to his diplomatic purposes. Both his presence in France and the spread of his portraits were serving in some measure to sustain those undercurrents of liberal thought which were carrying France toward revolution. For all that the Phrygian cap symbolized, this man's face was even

more specifically a symbol. In it lay rejection of the traditions of the past and confident, sagacious discernment of the future—things no conventional symbols could represent as well as that broad mouth and those amused, attentive eyes. It was the first time in history that a half smile had meant so much or that the form of a corpulent old man signified the overthrow of empires" (Sellers, 1962:138).

6. Another hero-come-lately, Paul Revere, ranked second in all but one of the tests. Interestingly, the names of Benedict Arnold and John Wilkes Booth also occurred with some frequency. In responding to a companion questionnaire that solicited any names that came to mind in connection with American history up to 1865, the students consistently placed Washington at the top of the list. Lincoln, Jefferson, and Franklin followed closely in that order (Frisch, 1983). In a replication of Frisch's experiment, I administered the same questions to two large undergraduate classes at the Pennsylvania State University in March 1984 ("American History before 1865" and "World Climates"). The results were remarkably similar. For example, asked to list those ten names, excluding public officers and military leaders, 74 of the 115 respondents in the geography class cited Betsy Ross. Following far behind, in order, were: Lewis and Clark; Benjamin Franklin [sic]; Christopher Columbus; Paul Revere; Eli Whitney; Daniel Boone; and Pocahontas. There were a number of curious surprises in the results, including the fact that a dozen of the respondents seemed to believe that Florence Nightingale was an American.

7. "Above all other historical personages, . . . Lincoln came to dominate the era of Franklin D. Roosevelt. In a time of partisan strife and international conflict, the development had profound implications. The Great Emancipator symbolized neither party nor nationality, but freedom and democracy, unity and charity, moreover, his image revived the memory that, even in a bloody Civil War, the United States had somehow survived" (A. H. Jones, 1974:24).

8. " 'Our Teddy' was shot in the chest by a fanatic during the presidential campaign of 1912, while 'battling for the Lord' (and a 'third term') as a Bull Moose. If he had only died, the cult could have boasted a glorious martyr— one fighting the good fight for Progressivism. But the tough old Bull Moose survived, and his anguished bellowings at President Wilson from 1913 to 1919 were often more embarrassing to his friends than bothersome to his foes" (T. A. Bailey, 1966:7).

9. Personal charisma—that stunning, mysterious aura that emanates from certain individuals even when they are silent and immobile—is a quite real, if unexplainable, phenomenon. It is perhaps most common among actors and creative persons, but some fortunate statesmen have been born with it. That Roosevelt and three or four other persons I have

encountered in the flesh were endowed with it is something to which I can testify personally. I laid eyes upon FDR twice, once at a considerable distance from the back of a large crowd, the second time at close range and by pure chance. While strolling near the southeast corner of the White House grounds one day early in 1942, I saw the gates suddenly swing open as the presidential limousine hurtled past en route to a ceremonial reception for Queen Wilhelmina at Union Station. For the briefest instant, FDR's eyes locked with mine, and it was as though a bolt of electricity passed through my body. That is not my usual reaction to politicians.

10. The political prowess of the White House has never been quite as great in practice as it may seem in theory or appearance because of the constraints imposed by the constitutional system of checks and balances, the inertia of a deeply entrenched bureaucracy, and the sheer force of public opinion (Roelofs, 1976:164–75). Nevertheless, no other governmental institution in the Western World commands anything like the administrative and symbolic leverage manipulated by the American chief executive.

11. It is unsettling to realize that three of the first five presidents (Adams, Jefferson, and Monroe) all expired on the same sacred date, July 4. Surely the odds for that type of coincidence fall into the astronomical category.

12. Thus far we have paid little attention to the geography of national heroes except to note the emergence of certain figures identified with the West and the frontier. But one of the most puzzling features of the initial generation of heroes associated with the Revolution and America's political genesis, and indeed of subsequent nineteenth-century heroes, is that so few of them were connected with New England and New York. Although these Northeastern states exercised so much leadership in matters cultural, technological, and political, the dominant heroes—Washington, Lafayette, Jefferson, Franklin (a juvenile migrant from Boston), Jackson, Lincoln—do not bring that part of the country to mind. New England must comfort itself with luminaries of the second and lower rank: for example, John Adams, John Hancock, or Paul Revere.

CHAPTER THREE

1. For a brief, but illuminating, introduction to the general phenomenon of American holidays, see Stewart (1954:222–48). Myers (1972) and J. M. Hatch (1978) offer a profusion of useful historical and other details in encyclopedic format for some hundreds of notable dates in the American calendar.

2. Two volumes aimed at the juvenile and elementary school markets of

the United States (Dupuy, 1965; Hoff, 1967) discuss major national and patriotic holidays and a number of the minor ones as well. Among the latter are some with only regional appeal, for example, Lee's Birthday, Alamo Day, and Patriot's Day, and those that come and go without attracting much public attention, for example, National Freedom Day, Loyalty Day, Independence Day, Labor Day, Veterans (Armistice) Day, Thanksgiving, and Christmas—which exhaust the list of federal legal public holi-(1946:136–41) is well worth reading, as is Bernard Lewis (1975) on the more fundamental theme of the deliberate fabrication of holidays to serve the interests of the nation-state. In the same vein, Jennifer McDowell (1974) has written on the relative success of Soviet public ceremonies, while Mona Ozouf (1976) has dealt definitively with the extraordinary profusion of civic festivals and the like and their significance during the frantic first decade of the French Revolution. "La fête est alors l'indispensable complément du système de législation. . . . On pourrait ajouter l'individu rebaptisé citoyen dans la fête" (Ozouf, 1976:16).

3. "Technically speaking, the United States still has no national holidays. There are a small number of federal 'legal public holidays' designated by the President and Congress, but these apply only to the District of Columbia and to federal employees wherever they may be. Each state designates its own holidays. If New Year's Day, Washington's Birthday, Memorial Day, Independence Day, Labor Day, Veterans (Armistice) Day, Thanksgiving, and Christmas—which exhaust the list of federal legal public holidays—happen to be observed in each of the states, it is because each of them separately has taken the appropriate legal action" (Boorstin, 1965: 375).

4. "The most remarkable feature of the Fourth is that it has no roots in the farther past and no religious connotations. It is wholly patriotic, that is, secular. Although such holidays have since that time become common throughout the world, they were not customary before 1776, and undoubtedly the American celebration had much to do with the establishment of similar days in other countries" (Stewart, 1954:236).

5. For general accounts of July 4 celebrations and their significance, see: Bercovitch, 1978:144–45; Berens, 1978:114–15; Boorstin, 1976:375–90; Calkin, 1976; F. M. Green, 1969; J. M. Hatch, 1978:197–200; Hay, 1967; Kammen, 1978:54–55; Melder, 1976; Myers, 1972; Stewart, 1954:236–37.

6. In the nineteenth century, both church and secular holidays, including Easter, Thanksgiving Day, December 24, 25, 26, and 31, and January 1 were much favored as wedding dates, but nowadays they are shunned.

7. General accounts of the holiday are available in: Boorstin, 1965:351–53; J. M. Hatch, 1978:197–200; Myers, 1972:63–70; Stewart, 1954:237. George Washington was the only member of the Revolutionary pantheon

whose birth date achieved universal recognition. Only belatedly, beginning in 1931, were steps taken to observe Jefferson's birthday (Peterson, 1960: 273–74), and, as of 1966, the occasion was officially noted in only four states, all south of the Mason-Dixon Line (T. A. Bailey, 1966:10). The anniversaries of Lafayette's birth and death have enjoyed only ephemeral popularity, reaching some sort of peak around World War I (Loveland, 1971: 146n). Strangely enough, there seems never to have been any organized effort to celebrate Franklin's birthday.

8. Historical happenstance may have contributed to the postbellum apathy of Southerners. "Perhaps because of General John C. Pemberton's surrender of Vicksburg on July Fourth, the whites in much of the South did not celebrate Independence Day" (J. G. Taylor, 1982:133).

9. There is evidence of widespread popular participation in the July 4, 1876 festivities, for example: "Something like twenty-five thousand out-of-town visitors converged on Indianapolis, then a city of sixty thousand, and similar migrations occurred all over the country. Everybody took part, or so it seemed. . . . frequently one finds a note that the Centennial Fourth was an opportunity for national rededication" (Nugent, 1979:65).

10. "In a Hamiltonian world . . . the Fourth of July ritual, with its optimistic references to Providence, the Founding Fathers, and the Present Generation, was little more than a Jeffersonian time lag. Its themes were too simple to explain the complex domestic ills related to industrialism" (Hay, 1967:298). The character of the vestigial July 4 oratory is remarkably different from that of the halcyon years. "Mention is made of 'the unity of English-speaking peoples,' 'the brotherhood of Anglo-Saxon democracies,' and 'our British cousins.' . . . The one enduring theme which permeates these orations as a whole from Revolutionary times down to the present is the idea of Franco-American friendship" (C. Larson, 1940:25).

11. If the holiday has an American flavor and some whiff of nationalism, the explanation may be its connection with the Pilgrim legend and the nativistic cuisine that tradition has ordained for the feast on the fourth Thursday of November.

12. The most comprehensive account to date (Boller, 1984) is totally anecdotal in form with no attempt at generalization or critical analysis. Much more intellectually informative, though limited to the period 1788–1860, is Washburn (1963). There is a particular dearth of analytic treatment of the political convention.

13. Excepting the definitive account of the 1840 campaign (Gunderson, 1957), we have only one other attempt to explore the symbolic implications of any of these events, Michael Novak's (1974) treatment of the 1972 campaign.

14. Namely Wolfe's (1975:54–70, 482–84) examination of the signifi-

cance of the 1960 Kennedy inauguration written, fittingly enough, from a theological perspective. Less probing, but also useful, in understanding the ritual of inauguration is J. F. Wilson (1979:47–53, 74–79) and Michael Novak (1974:20). The literature on inaugurations is bulky. Freitag's (1969) selected bibliography lists no fewer than 1,517 titles; but even the most comprehensive accounts, such as Durbin (1971) are superficially descriptive. Indeed, most of the literature is pure journalistic fluff.

15. In addition to a considerable complement of historical observances occurring annually in Great Britain and Northern Ireland, there are two well-organized societies (one Royalist, the other Roundhead) that have been restaging the battles of the English Civil War in full gear and uniform. And, if I can believe my correspondent, other groups of history buffs have been reliving the Wars of the Roses and the early Viking raids (Prince, 1981).

16. It is worth noting that the parade is a constant feature of all the celebrations discussed thus far, including major holidays, anniversary rituals, inaugurations, and, though usually indoors, the party convention. Sad to say, no folklorist, cultural historian, or art critic has yet undertaken the serious study of this colorful, important phenomenon. Indeed, "one of the most ignored cultural events of American life is the public parade. A contemporary visitor is likely to find himself unprepared for their frequency, their length and devotion to symbolizing, in a kind of official public theatre, what are often bigoted, nationalistic, military, and sectarian goals" (Bush, 1977:44). Although it may be true that "parades of the eighteenth century were far more significant in the life of the American people than they were later or are today, for they were needed in crystalizing national opinion and promoting home interests" (Pinckney, 1940:56–57) and "the parade as an art form or as a political symbol is all but dead" (Jackson, 1980:102), they are still numerous and quite alive, especially in the holiday and commemorative exercises of smaller communities. There may be some significance in the fact, as reported by Roger Stump (1986), that such events are relatively infrequent in the South.

17. The official documentation is enormous, being barely summarized in the five-volume report of the American Revolution Bicentennial Administration (1977). For briefer descriptive accounts, see: Brody (1977); Cramer (1981); Hartje (1973); J. M. Hatch (1978:624–28); Longstreet and Lamprecht (1975). We still await the much needed, detailed critical interpretations of the event, but useful short commentaries are available in: Lemisch (1976); D. Lowenthal (1977); Morris (1977); Schlereth (1980:130–42); N. Smith (1977); Woodward (1977); and Zuckerman (1978).

18. "I do not happen to regard present feverish bumbling in connection with celebration of the Bicentennial as the worst of our national afflictions,

but the whole spectacle of futility in this instance is a perfect image, it seems to me, of the condition in which we find ourselves. What one celebrates—whether in family, religion, or nation—is tradition, or a set of traditions. The sight of literally thousands of bureaucratic bodies struggling to find something to celebrate, some way of celebrating the Bicentennial, with little if any help to be had, it must be noted, from press, clergy, or the academic world, is sufficient in itself as a commentary on the role of tradition in our society" (Nisbet, 1975:241).

19. Expositions might also reveal some of the less savory aspects of American life, particularly racial and ethnic attitudes and some rather extreme forms of Manifest Destiny, as documented by R. W. Rydell (1980) in his detailed analysis of American international expositions from 1876 to 1916.

20. The literature on this watershed event is justifiably large and detailed (Allwood, 1977:51–57; D. Brown, 1966; Cheney, 1974; Craven, 1956:118–23; Jackson, 1972:231–40; D. Lowenthal, 1977; Maass, 1973; Myers, 1972: 44–45; Pizor, 1970; Post, 1976; Schlereth, 1977, 1980).

21. "Many Americans who visited the exposition or read the reports about it . . . saw what they wanted to see: the emergence of the United States as a world power, the equal of any of the great imperial powers of the Old World. . . . Rather than stimulating a true cosmopolitanism, as Henry Fuller and many others hoped, the Columbian celebrations encouraged more generally a growing spirit of nationalism and were at least partially responsible for the adoption of such patriotic rituals as Columbus Day (instituted originally in the public schools by the National Association of School Superintendents as a special day for reading patriotic essays, singing songs, and similar activities) and the Pledge of Allegiance" (Badger, 1979:114).

22. "The emergence of the world's fair as a symbolic cultural expression during this period [late nineteenth century] is but one of several developments that testify to the self-consciousness of the age. Like the tortured intellectual and literary experiments, the political, theological, and economic debates, and the social and educational movements of the late nineteenth century, the great world's fairs in the broadest sense represented the Victorian era's attempt to both acknowledge the reality of rapid change and to understand and control its direction. Unlike some of these others, the world's fairs operated on a broader and more simplistic level and illustrated more clearly, perhaps, the age's faith that man could have his revolution and control it too. The two elements could not forever be held in balance, however, and when they began to crack the great world's fairs which were their physical manifestation from the first lost their original cultural sig-

nificance. While it lasted, the Victorian faith made the great world's fairs important focal points and sensitive indicators of Western culture" (Badger, 1979:xvi).

23. Also see Benedict (1983:59–60). One likely exception, however, may have been Montreal's brilliant Expo 67, which played a not inconsiderable role in bolstering Canada's self-awareness and greater national unity.

24. In a random sample of 1,290 American museums, 40.8 percent of those founded before 1940 were historical in type (the others being devoted to the sciences, arts, and general and miscellaneous topics), while 48.6 percent of the 1940–79 group were in that category (American Association of Museums, 1979). Michael Kammen (1980) has indicated that the latter-day surge in historical museum creation and attendance is another facet of the nostalgia craze that has gripped the country in recent decades and is also manifest in the vogue for early American antiques. There are many more signs to be found elsewhere, I suspect, as, for example, the recent growing popularity of biblical and other traditional given names for our offspring.

25. The earliest attempt at a national museum, the National Institution of the 1840s, seems to have differed significantly in orientation from our more recent historical museums. "The institution of the United States suggested a national awareness, and even desire to strengthen this awareness by means of a museum, but it was free of all aggressive nationalistic posture, and it was directed to the future in contrast to the emphasis on the history of the past in some of the historical museums of Europe" (Wittlin, 1970:124).

26. Abraham Lincoln Birthplace (BPL) National Historic Site (NHS); Adams NHS; Andrew Johnson NHS; Arlington House, R. E. Lee National Memorial (NMem); Booker T. Washington National Monument (NM); Boston National Historic Park (NHP); Carl Sandburg NHS; Clara Barton NHS; Colonial NHP; Cowpens National Battlefield (NB); Custer Battlefield NM; de Soto NMem; Edgar A. Poe NHS; Edison NHS; Eisenhower NHS; Federal Hall NMem; Ford's Theater NHS; Fort McHenry NM and Historic Site (HS); Fort Necessity NB; Fort Stanwix NM; Fort Washington Park; Frederick Douglass Home; General Grant NMem; George Washington BPL NM; George Rogers Clark NHP; Golden Spike NHS; Guilford Courthouse National Memorial Park (NMP); Hamilton Grange NMem; Harpers Ferry NHP; Herbert Hoover NHS; Home of F. D. Roosevelt NHS; Independence NHP; Jefferson Memorial; John F. Kennedy NHS; Kings Mountain NHP; Lincoln Boyhood NMem; Lincoln Home NHS; Lincoln Memorial; Longfellow NHS; Lyndon B. Johnson NHS; Minute Man NHP; Moores Creek NB; Morristown NHP; Mount Rushmore NMem; National Visitor Center, Perry's Victory and International Peace Memorial (IPMem); Sagamore Hill

NHS; Saint-Gaudens NHS; Saratoga NHP; Statue of Liberty NM; Theodore Roosevelt BPL NHS; Theodore Roosevelt Inaugural NHS; Valley Forge NHP; Washington Monument; White House; William Howard Taft NHS; Wright Brothers NMem.

27. Kammen (1980) has also found some evidence of a falling off in museum patronage after the Bicentennial and following the 1972–76 period, one of "greatest intensity in the contemporary Americana boom." He also hints at the possibility that parallel trends might be found in other countries.

28. In its Planning Report concerning visitors to Washington, the National Capital Planning Commission (1984a) assumed that the upward trend in volume would continue indefinitely. But inspection of a graph entitled "Visits to Selected Facilities Administered by the National Park Service in the Core Area, 1960–1982" (NCPC, 1984a:6) reveals a sharp, possibly persistent decline since 1976. The most benign interpretation of the statistics is that the volume of visitors may have begun to level off around 1980.

29. "In 1980 the District received over 11 million domestic visitors, almost 2 million foreign visitors, and nearly 4 million day visitors (those not staying overnight in the area and/or living within 100 miles of D.C." (District of Columbia, 1981:1).

30. Even allowing for some repeat business at the Air and Space Museum and visits by local residents, one must also grant the fact that not all nonresident tourists to the metropolitan area included this attraction on their itinerary. The total 1982 attendance at the eleven museums operated by the Smithsonian Institution is staggering: 25,314,350 (Greater Washington Board of Trade, n.d.:24). One must assume that the great majority were out-of-towners.

31. "What a profusion of patriotic societies attended popular journalism and schooling, and what propaganda they contributed! In an industrialized country, one had only to get a financial backer (an 'angel') and equip an office with typewriter, telephone, stenographer, mimeograph, and filing cabinet, in order to become organizer and director of some sort of society that in due course would have a big membership and be self-supporting [and possibly profitable?]. There were societies for war veterans, for sons and daughters of veterans, for every conceivable patriotic and national purpose" (Hayes, 1960:88).

32. For the most nearly definitive, annotated listing of fraternal and patriotic organizations in the United States and Canada, see Schmidt (1980).

33. For a general theoretical discussion of the relationships between sport and the state, see Brohm (1978), Gruneau (1982), and Guttmann (1978).

34. "American football has, so far, proven to be the least exportable of the

American spectator sports. . . . Perhaps the reason lies in the emphasis in football on lines—which must be defended, which must be penetrated, which must be moved. Basketball uses some of the peculiarly American imagery and idealism of lines—there are foul lines (as there are in baseball) and court lines which must be crossed—but in football the entire game is built around the frontier, the line, the boundary. Football ritualizes the moving frontier; simultaneously, it also ritualizes the teamwork, cooperation, and individual heroism necessary to resist the moving frontier (football players are pioneers *and* Indians at the same time). Ultimate victory in the game comes from moving the frontier more than the others do, crossing the goal line more frequently. There is little in such a ritual to appeal to the ideals and sensitivities of people who are not American" (Robertson, 1980:256).

35. After nearly forty years, George Orwell's words on international athletic competitions ring truer than ever. "There cannot be much doubt that the whole thing is bound up with the rise of nationalism—that is with the lunatic modern habit of identifying oneself with large power units and seeing everything in terms of comparative prestige. . . . Games are taken seriously in London and New York, and they were taken seriously in Rome and Byzantium; in the Middle Ages they were played, and probably played with much physical brutality, but they were not mixed up with politics nor a cause of group hatreds.

"If you wanted to add to the vast fund of ill-will existing in the world at this moment, you could hardly do it better than by a series of football matches between Jews and Arabs, Germans and Czechs, Indians and British, Russians and Poles, and Italians and Yugoslavs, each match to be watched by a mixed audience of 100,000 spectators. I do not, of course, suggest that sport is one of the main causes of international rivalry; big-scale sport is itself, I think, merely another effect of the causes that have produced nationalism. Still, you do make things worse by sending forth a team of eleven men, labelled as national champions, to do battle against some rival team, and allowing it to be felt on all sides that whichever nation is defeated will 'lose face.'

"I hope, therefore, that we shan't follow up the visit of the Dynamos by sending a British team to the U.S.S.R. If we must do so, then let us send a second-rate team which is sure to be beaten and cannot be claimed to represent Britain as a whole. There are quite enough real causes of trouble already, and we need not add to them by encouraging young men to kick each other on the shins amid the roars of infuriated spectators" (Orwell, 1950:154–55).

36. For example, "in 1844, Burgess, String & Co. of New York, advertised . . . a 'NEW GAME—The National Game of the Star Spangled Banner—or

Geographical Historical Tour Through the United States and Canada,' and two years later a New Orleans firm produced 'The Game of American Story and Glory'" (McClintock and McClintock, 1961:111). We have testimony from a major manufacturer of toys that "warships were more popular during the threat of war or in wartime than in a period of peace" (M. Schwartz, 1975:12).

CHAPTER FOUR

1. "What the eye is to the lover . . . language—whatever language history has made his or her mother-tongue—is to the patriot. Through that language encountered at mother's knee and parted with only at the grave, pasts are restored, fellowships are imagined, and futures dreamed" (Anderson, 1983:140).

2. "There has been little connection between nationalism and language in the United States. Just as there is no concerted and organized movement for the maintenance of Southern speech, so there has never been any strong movement to express nationalism by making its language more different from that of Great Britain. On the contrary, the tendency has generally worked in the other direction. Many of our 'best people' have cultivated some approximation of British usage, and our schools have diligently taught Shakespeare, Milton, and the other great writers of England" (Stewart, 1954:46).

3. Shankle (1941) lists and discusses some three hundred American mottoes and slogans, including all the principal political phrases.

4. A. M. Schlesinger (1941:611–18); Wecter (1941:78–79, 157); Karsten (1978:5–6, 85, 90ff, 207–8); and Stewart (1979:22–23). Many a luminary has been christened in this fashion, for example, Benjamin Franklin Butler, George Washington Cable, George Washington Carver, Andrew Jackson Downing, Lincoln Steffens, Alexander Hamilton Stephens, and Thomas Jefferson Wertenbaker, not to mention Jefferson Davis, Franklin Pierce, or Franklin Delano Roosevelt. However, the practice of naming infants after national notables seems to have declined in recent times (Algeo and Algeo, 1983:110).

5. The adoption of nationalistic names by business enterprises has not received the attention it deserves. Boyd C. Shafer (1972:454) does note the high incidence of corporations listed on the New York Stock Exchange whose names begin with American, National, and United States.

6. No one has yet attempted a comprehensive, worldwide analysis of this toponymic genre—an eminently worthy project. I am confident that such an effort would document the uniqueness of the United States in qualita-

tive as well as quantitative terms. The propensity of heads of state to impose their names on imposing places, or diffidently allowing others to do it on their behalf, is a venerable phenomenon, one that may well antedate the rash of Alexandrias, Caesareas, and their ilk. Although there has never been a dearth of such examples as St. Petersburg, Léopoldville, Stalingrad, Ciudad Trujillo, or the various Latin American localities named after Bolívar, Juárez, or Hidalgo, they have accounted for a miniscule fraction of the total place-name cover of any country until the outbreak of a veritable epidemic in the infant United States. Of course, other revolutionary, or quasi-revolutionary, regimes have emulated this country to some degree, most notably perhaps Mexico, the Soviet Union, and Israel (Cohen and Kliot, 1981). Twentieth-century Iran has experienced two very different spasms of ideologically inspired place-naming or, rather, renaming (P. G. Lewis, 1982). But in those instances and others the veneration of national heroes via place-names has been inhibited by the multiplicity and rootedness of older names. Moreover, such items are handed down from above. In the case of the U.S.S.R., and analogously elsewhere, "this naming is so thoroughly controlled and orchestrated by the Communist Party for political purposes that it lacks true spontaneity and is not a faithful reflection of real hero worship on the part of the people" (C. D. Harris, 1981). In the United States, in contrast, the vast majority of name decisions have been local in character, with little or no guidance or coercion from federal agencies. On the other hand, of course, the names of streets and other items in capital cities bear an especially rich burden of national symbolism (Merriam, 1931:150). The District of Columbia is no exception (Hagner, 1897).

7. Many authors have commented on the deep ideological significance of the classical syndrome in American thought and behavior, including: Nye (1960:270–73); H. M. Jones (1964:227–72); N. Harris (1966:17–18, 41–45); Bellah (1975:22–25); Hitchcock and Seale (1976:76–77, 265–67).

8. For informative discussions of many of these notables and of various commendatory terms that could be characterized as nationalistic, see the alphabetized entries in Stewart (1970).

9. "When Chicago real estate promoter S. E. Warner decided to name the main street of his development in honor of his political hero, Henry Clay, he called it Ashland, in reminiscence of the Whig party leader's home, 'The Ashland,' in Kentucky. Warner left still another marking on the land when he planted both sides of his residential avenue with rows of ash" (Schlereth, 1980:155). Can one imagine any real estate developer of the 1980s paying similar toponymic homage to a political idol?

10. The most comprehensive of available statistical surveys indicates that as of 1964, Smith, Johnson, Jones, and Wilson were, respectively, the first, second, fifth, and tenth most common surnames used by the Ameri-

can population (U.S. Social Security Administration, 1964). It may be interesting to note the rank order of the more important surnames of patriot-heroes and relevant abstract terms among the 152,757,455 account numbers issued by the agency between 1936 and 1964. The computer program used for these tabulations identified only the first six letters of a surname.

Harris(on)	11	Jeffer(son)	354
Jackso(n)	17	Webste(r)	365
Clark	18	Monroe	525
Adams	34	Clay	650
Lee	37	Madiso(n)	1209
Perry	85	Lincol(n)	1906
Washin(gton)	174	Hope	1950
Grant	194	Clinto(n)	2056
Frankl(in)	222		

The names Eden, Joy, Lafayette, and Marion do not appear in the table of the 2,183 most frequent items. Although the Harrisons, Jacksons, Clarks, and Adamses are numerous indeed, my calculations suggest a significantly higher incidence of places so named than would be the case were their occurrence proportional to the representation of these families among the general population.

11. Because her appeal is so primordially mythic as to transcend national boundaries, as is also the case with Joan of Arc, it is doubtful whether the United States can claim exclusive title to the Indian maiden (P. Young, 1962). Concerning the more general question of the weak standing of females amidst the company of American heroes, despite the goodly number of eligible candidates, see Wecter (1941:476–77).

12. The most informative general discussions of Canadian place-names are Orkin (1970:159–90) and Rayburn (1983). One finds relatively few places named after Canadian or British notables (Orkin, 1970:167–68).

13. The graphing of the relative popularity of Washington as a given personal name during the period 1770–1900 produces a pattern parallel to that generated by place-names (Karsten, 1978:91).

14. With the possible exception of John F. Kennedy, even the most revered of twentieth-century presidents and other relatively ephemeral folk- and patriot-heroes, for example, Pershing, Byrd, Lindbergh, MacArthur, Ford, or J. Edgar Hoover, have left only the faintest traces on our place-name cover. Concerning the weak toponymic performance of Woodrow Wilson and the two Roosevelts, see T. A. Bailey (1966:5–8). The Kennedy legacy may be more conspicuous (Wolfe, 1975:395–96, 408–9). Robert I. Alotta (1981) has developed the notion of sequential street-name typologies over time, as has John Algeo (1978). In her study of the names of recent

suburban subdivisions in selected American metropolises, Janet Schwartz (1980) detected only the quietest echoes of patriotic nostalgia amidst the predominantly pastoral nomenclature.

15. Several authors have commented on the powerful Washingtonian imprint upon the American place-name cover: Wecter (1941:136–37), T. A. Bailey (1966:3–4), Boorstin (1965:355–56). Marshall Fishwick (1954:14) offers the strongest statement: "On his two-hundredth birthday there were thousands of 'Washingtons' on the map. The national capital, a state, 33 counties, 121 cities and towns, 257 townships, 1140 streets, and uncounted lakes, schools, mountains, and forts bore his name—a tribute which had been paid to no other man in any country."

16. Jeffersons on the American map are noted in T. A. Bailey (1966:4) and Peterson (1960:273–74). I must not fail to mention Lafayette, another of those remarkable heroes whose name and home (Lagrange) are writ large upon the United States scene, especially after his extraordinary 1824–25 tour (MacIntire, 1967:24).

17. Over much of this territory, the formulaic repetition of a core group of terms—usually Washington, Jefferson, Jackson, and Union, or appropriate variants thereof—in county after county reaches an almost hypnotic, mantralike, regularity. The sheer abundance of nationalistic place-names in portions of Indiana, Ohio, Iowa, and Missouri is impressive. To take one example, in Kosciusko County, Indiana, not only is the county name classifiable as nationalistic but the names of twelve of its seventeen townships fall into the same mold: Clay, Franklin, Harrison, Jackson, Monroe, Scott, Seward, Tippecanoe, Van Buren, Washington, and Wayne.

18. The Illinois State Constitution of 1870 specifically prohibits the legislature from changing the names of persons or places (Seits, 1982). But this stricture came into being after the state had been well settled and nearly all places named. Moreover, as noted above, it is unlikely that more than a small minority of nationalistic place-names supplanted earlier items.

19. Perhaps the most promising line of inquiry is that suggested by the recent work of Forrest McDonald, Grady McWhiney, and their associates at the University of Alabama, namely, that basic cultural differences—and perhaps associated political antagonisms—between the Celtic groups of the British Isles (Scots, Welsh, Irish, and Cornish) and the English have persisted in the United States. In a departure from conventional historical interpretations, their research indicates an American South much more Celtic in ethnic origins and behavioral patterns than the North (McDonald and McWhiney, 1975, 1980; McDonald and McDonald, 1980).

20. If I may cite my personal experience, it was disturbing to realize that it took all of ten years before I noticed the probable origin of the

name Franklin Township in Huntingdon County, Pennsylvania, a locality in which our family acquired some property in 1971.

21. Though somewhat dated now, the best general surveys of American historiography from early Colonial days to the mid-twentieth century are still Kraus (1953) and Van Tassel (1960).

22. American historians were scarcely unique in doing so, for, early and late, their colleagues in other countries have also invoked Clio to build or strengthen the sense of nationhood (B. Lewis, 1975). The publication of local histories and geographies—the starting point for many American authors—need not work against the cause of nationalism so long as such productions are subsumed under the dominant ideology of the great nation or state. In fact, the Japanese authorities have used this strategy to good effect in the early twentieth century (Takeuchi, 1980:242).

23. "For New Englanders, it was easy to extend the tradition of their founding to the founding of all colonies; it was a short step from interpreting their local past as part of a Divine plan to enlarging that scheme to include all of American history" (Shaffer, 1975:57).

24. Although Webster's campaign to establish a specifically American language came to naught, his little blue spellers were extremely influential linguistically as well as ideologically. "No other book, the Bible excepted, played so unifying a part in American culture; it fixed the speech habits of the older English settlers and brought into linguistic harmony with theirs the usage of millions of immigrant children. To Webster's Spelling Book belongs much of the credit that in forty-eight states, each populated with a people of un-English origin numerous enough to destroy the supremacy of the American-English language, a basic pattern of writing and spoken language prevails everywhere" (Warfel, 1936:77–78).

25. "Although there is still much history in America that is as affirmatory as it is annalistic, the situation, even there, is becoming immensely schizophrenic. That image of the past—perhaps one should call it the American image—of America as the land of opportunity, of equality, of men before God, of liberty and personal freedom, hardly buoys up the establishment in the face of both Negro riots and the war in Vietnam. On the other hand, there are aspects of the American past [referring to Manifest Destiny], very appropriate to the present, but no longer usable" (Plumb, 1970:43).

26. The entire passage is memorable, even if the message may be a trifle overwrought. "Nature, as Wilde insists in one of the best of his essays, is always imitating art, is perpetually creating men and things in art's image. How imperfectly did mountains exist before Wordsworth! How dim, before Constable, was English pastoral landscape! Yes, and how dim, for that mat-

ter, before the epoch-making discoveries of Falstaff and the Wife of Bath, were even English men and women!

"Nations are to a very large extent invented by their poets and novelists. The inadequacy of German drama and the German novel perhaps explains the curious uncertainty and artificiality of character displayed by so many of the Germans whom one meets in daily life.

"Thanks to a long succession of admirable dramatists and novelists, Frenchmen and Englishmen know exactly how they ought to behave. Lacking these, the Germans are at a loss. It is good art that makes us natural" (Huxley, 1932:50).

27. One might develop a convincing case that Hollywood and the television studios have become crucial factors in the definition or redefinition of what it is to be an American, by creating the art that life seeks to imitate, and often nearly does (Postman, 1985). But the images so powerfully transmitted and so trustingly absorbed by Americans and foreigners alike are nowadays only marginally concerned with nationalism.

28. An examination of a comprehensive coin catalog (Krause and Mishler, 1973) indicates that Miss Liberty appeared on the face of every single American standard issue during the antebellum period from the half-cent piece up to the twenty-dollar gold coin and that the eagle or a wreath, with or without stars, usually graced the reverse side. Miss Liberty has gradually dropped out of the picture, her farewell bow being the 1947 half-dollar. In her place we have the American Indian, the U.S. shield, fasces, the buffalo, the Liberty Bell, Washington, Jefferson, Franklin, Lincoln, the Lincoln Memorial, F. D. Roosevelt, Eisenhower, and Kennedy. The eagle endures throughout, but the flag does not show up at all.

29. "No other governmental artifact so symbolizes the nation's popular self-image and no single event has been represented more often on these icons of communication than the American Revolution. The postage stamp became a vehicle for impressing on all citizens the reverence of the nation's founders and founding that the federal government felt necessary to create and to maintain a strong national identity" (Skaggs, 1978:198).

30. When philatelist Franklin Delano Roosevelt personally contrived to put Jefferson's face on the three-cent stamp, then the carrier of nearly every first-class letter, there were bellows of outrage from Republicans. "But then the Republicans, in 1929, had relegated Jefferson to the scarce two-dollar bill" (Peterson, 1960:362–63).

31. Skaggs (1978:204) detects a recent trend away from Revolutionary imagery in American stamps, and asks, "Is this because we live in an age without heroes but rather a time with transitory celebrities whose fuzzy images cross our television screens?"

32. The most useful discussion of political iconography, with special attention to campaign and propaganda posters, is Gourévitch (1976).

33. That some posters really did a job is beyond any dispute. James Montgomery Flagg's immortal, mesmerizing painting of a finger-pointing Uncle Sam intoning "I want you" is a case in point. As a probable all-time best-seller, "the poster sold more than 4 million copies during World War I and almost half a million during World War II" (Horwitz, 1976:19), and it still has not been retired from service.

34. It is interesting to note that a similar movement developed some years later with the abortive Southern bid for independence. "It was only when southerners began to think in terms of cultural and then political independence from the North—only when they began to regard the South as a separate nation with a unique nationality—that they began to urge the creation of paintings and statuary that would reflect their own 'Conceptions of excellence in these departments'" (L. B. Miller, 1967:700).

35. In the discussion that follows, I have relied heavily on Michael Kammen's "Revolutionary Iconography in National Tradition," a truly seminal essay (Kammen, 1978:76–109).

36. It is unfortunate that full-size reproductions of statues are more difficult and expensive to turn out than copies of two-dimensional material. Houdon's painstakingly faithful statue of Washington, which stands in the rotunda of Virginia's old capitol in Richmond, is considerably more awe-inspiring than Stuart's portraits or any other canvases.

37. But folk artists have formed emotional attachments to at least two persons. "Paintings and carvings of Theodore Roosevelt and John F. Kennedy, made by self-taught painters and carvers who chose their subjects because of an irrepressible devotion, far exceed the number of portrayals of any other twentieth-century figures" (Horwitz, 1976:107).

38. In writing of the French and Italian artists who were commissioned to do so much of America's monumental sculpture in the late 1800s, Gerdts (1973:50) notes that "their public and their patrons were Americans, but not the same Americans of the pre–Civil War days, and they did not share and enjoy the same youthful ideals. The neoclassic sculptor is as alien to post–Civil War American society, which had cast off the Jeffersonian idealism out of which neoclassicism grew, as he was to the foreign land where he had chosen to live and work."

39. "Few in 1935 escaped the influence of Midwestern 'regionalist' artists like Thomas Hart Benton, Grant Wood, and John Steuart Curry, or the 'social realism' of such artists as Raphael and Moses Soyer, Joe Jones, Ben Shahn, Hugo Gellert, and William Gropper. Regionalists and social realists built their art on American themes and sought to register their message in

the untutored American mind. The roots of these modes lay in the 'country-wide revival of Americanism' Benton once speculated, that followed the defeat of President Woodrow Wilson's universal idealism at the end of World War I. . . . Moreover, a flood of new historical writings during the decade called into question traditional images of America. Artists, flushed from elitist bastions by the depression and caught up in the debate by its dynamism, treated aesthetically what Americans everywhere seemed to be reassessing—the nature of American society" (McKinzie, 1973:106). Although only 1 of the numerous illustrations in Marling's (1982) treatment of the more than 1,100 murals placed on post office walls from 1933 to 1941 incorporates a nationalistic motif, Kammen (1978:90) cites several others that do.

40. "There hasn't been much Revolutionary iconography since World War II. After being documented, illustrated, romanceitized, allegorized, sentimentalized, and mythologized, what was left to be done? Basically, American art went off in other directions—very other" (Kammen, 1978:90).

41. In a substantial contribution to a definitive treatment of the subject, Kammen (1978) deals in some detail with the literary fortunes of Revolutionary themes—assuredly the preeminent cluster of nationalist items—over the course of time in fiction, verse, drama, film, and other media.

42. After lauding the better chronicle plays of the Elizabethan period (those of Marlowe, Chapman, and Shakespeare), Michael Kammen delivers a harsh verdict about the parallel efforts of American dramatists. "It is precisely that mutual understanding of the intimate relationship between past and present that I find missing in most of American historical drama. By and large our playwrights have been historically illiterate: they have known comparatively little about the national narrative, and even less about modes of historic thought. Consequently, they have not served the American Revolution, or their society, well" (Kammen, 1978:142).

43. The Bicentennial does not seem to have helped the situation. On the musical stage, nationalistic projects have been few and futile, at least since the departure of George Cohan. The one apparent exception, *1776* (1969), was cute and folksy rather than reverent. More significantly, when Leonard Bernstein tried his hand with *1600 Pennsylvania Avenue* (1976), the outcome was a critical and box office fiasco.

44. The most useful treatments of the social history and implications of American film may be Buscombe (1979), Jowett (1976), and Sklar (1975). Zimmer (1974) offers a general treatise on the overtly political films of many lands, but largely those of protest and exposé, with little attention to establishmentarian propaganda items.

45. "Even satirical movies like the screwball comedies, or socially aware films like *The Grapes of Wrath*, were carefully constructed to stay within

the bounds of essential American cultural and political myths" (Sklar, 1975:196).

46. Richard MacCann's comment may apply to other modes of promoting the national cause. "But the relative sobriety of wartime film reporting offers a startling contrast with the bravado of World War I. It came partly from the disenchanted attitude of the common soldier (up to and including Eisenhower) who had lived through a decade of depression and anti-war muckraking and simply wanted to get a dirty job done. The honest film people, who had ears to the ground, caught this tonal quality and put it into their sound tracks" (MacCann, 1973:119).

47. "Invented only in 1895, radio made it possible to bypass print and summon into being an aural representation of the imagined community where the printed page scarcely penetrated. Its role in the Vietnamese and Indonesian revolutions, and generally in mid-twentieth-century nationalisms, has been underestimated and understudied" (Anderson, 1983:56).

48. "Haydn is said to have thought of composing a national anthem for Austria because of the influence he saw exercised in England by GOD SAVE THE KING" (A. D. Smith, 1977:111). "Take national anthems ... sung on national holidays. No matter how banal the words and mediocre the tunes, there is in this singing an experience of simultaneity. At precisely such moments, people wholly unknown to each other utter the same verses to the same melody. The image: unisonance. Singing the Marseillaise, Waltzing Matilda, and Indonesia Raya provide occasions for unisonality, for the echoed physical realization of the imagined community. . . . How selfless this unisonance feels! If we are aware that others are singing these songs precisely when and as we are, we have no idea who they may be, or even where, out of earshot, they are singing. Nothing connects us all but imagined sound" (Anderson, 1983:132–33).

49. " 'The Star-Spangled Banner' was not rushed to the front of our national songs until the Civil War. Before that time its progress as a national song had been steady, but comparatively slow. . . . of our 89 school songbooks published in America between 1834 and 1860 and classified as school songbooks in the Library of Congress only 15 include 'The Star-Spangled Banner' " (Sonneck, 1914:83–84).

CHAPTER FIVE

1. Perhaps the best single introduction to recent work and thought in landscape analysis is Meinig (1979), while John Stilgoe (1982) has provided us with an excellent account of the evolution of the "common landscapes" of America from their beginnings until 1845. For specific discussions of

the impact of central authority on the landscape, see Knight (1971) and Whittlesey (1935).

2. Although her volume is concerned primarily with the Upper Midwest, Hildegard Binder Johnson (1976) has given us the best general treatment to date of the history and significance of the U.S. rectangular land survey system.

3. "They mark the new strength of nationalism over localism, the new power of new government. Officially at least, Congress built them well because of their importance and precarious sites. But the federal government may well have understood, if only vaguely, that the towers symbolized its strength and that every man, woman, and child who saw their massiveness might glimpse the permanency and strength of the infant republic" (Stilgoe, 1982:111).

4. The following statement succinctly sums up the astounding amplitude of the U.S. government's physical role in the American scene: "By 1974 the federal government was a property holder with worldwide possessions worth $83 billion plus utility systems, roads, dams, bridges, and harbor and port facilities valued at $39.3 billion. It had gone from the construction of less than a dozen buildings annually in the early years of the Republic to a domestic inventory of over 400,000 buildings containing floor space equivalent to 1,250 Empire State Buildings. It leased properties in another 50,000 locations. . . . On its 200th birthday in 1976 the Corps of Engineers could look back on a record of constructing 4,000 civil works, 25,000 miles of navigable waterways, and 400 man-made lakes" (Craig et al., 1978:440).

5. For discussions of the origin and design of the early city, and the significance thereof see: Bush (1977:39–41); Cosgrove (1984:181–83); C. M. Green (1962–63); Fifer (1981); Gutheim and Washburn (1976); Reps (1967); Thomas (1976); and J. S. Young (1966:1–10).

6. There is not much question of the effectiveness of the Washington, D.C. strategy, even as early as the time of the Civil War. "The Union soldiers themselves were moved by their wartime experience in the city— visited previously only by their political representatives. Their actually seeing it was a fact of immeasurable psychological importance" (Henrikson, 1983:134). And its impact has grown with the years. For a striking comment on the overpowering, but quite this-worldly, character of latter-day architecture in Washington, see Nisbet (1975:35–36). Beyond the immediate physical impact, there are deeper layers of meaning. "It is not entirely farfetched to see in the 'imperial architecture' of the capital city the rudiments of a civic cult. What is one to make of the 'father of his country' when he is commemorated by an outsize phallus dominating the landscape? . . . If the symbolism within the capital which is directed to-

ward Washington and Lincoln respectively suggests the first and second persons of the Christian Godhead, it may not be entirely accidental that the Kennedy memorial evokes the images usually associated with the Holy Spirit; and certainly the eternal flame and the open burial plot permit that construction" (J. F. Wilson, 1971:4).

7. For one of the rare exceptions to this statement and a demonstration of how much historical and geographic meaning can be distilled from a single nationalistic edifice, see D. Harvey (1979).

8. We do have a brief, but useful, essay in the chapter entitled "National Monuments and Monuments to Genius" in Pevsner (1976:11–26), one that emphasizes nineteenth-century Europe. Although it is limited for the most part to funerary items in Western European communities, James Stevens Curl's *A Celebration of Death* (1980) is a major step toward the comprehensive treatment of monuments we so badly need. Much more cursory in nature is Barber (1949).

9. For descriptions of the intense public excitement over the creation and dedication of major monuments, see: Davis (1982:10–13); John Ericsson Memorial Commission (1929); Fairmount Park Art Association (1974:52, 136–37); Goode (1974:25); Riedy (1981:4). And the siting underscores the import of the object: "The apotheosis of the dead [hero] is also evidenced by the memorials in stone and wood erected to them, which from Achilles to Garibaldi have been established not in ordinary cemeteries but on consecrated ground in the midst of cities" (Salomon, 1932:377).

10. "By 1892 . . . there were no fewer than twenty-nine Columbus statues in America alone" (Riedy, 1981:203).

11. But, of course, one can find isolated commemorations for these and other culture heroes, usually in or near the localities with which they were most closely identified. Thus, for example, the many monumental and memorial obeisances to Henry Ford in Detroit, Dearborn, and vicinity (D. L. Lewis, 1976:483–88). Similarly, there are such instances as the Whitman Bridge connecting Philadelphia with Camden, the places dedicated to Samuel Clemens in Hannibal, Hartford, and Elmira, the Melville, Hawthorne, Dickinson, and other house-museums of New England, or the monument to W. C. Handy on Beale Street in Memphis. Conspicuous by their rarity anywhere are monumental remembrances of eminent American females. "Only six of America's historic sites and more than 2,000 landmarks commemorate women—and most of those have been established only in the past five years" (Moynehan, 1980:26).

12. The single apparent exception of a recent figural monument that has captured the imagination of the American public is the Iwo Jima Memorial in Washington (Mergen, 1983). But, interestingly, this sculpture is derived from a (carefully posed) photograph; and, it may be argued, the photograph

is better known and more widely revered than its bronze incarnation. Parallel to the historic trends in monument building are those in other modes of iconography. With the marginal exception of Norman Rockwell's "The Four Freedoms," what has been produced in recent times that bears comparison, in terms of either artistry or general impact, with the better patriotic paintings of our first century of independence? Scarcely any nationalistic art today rises above the level of the cartoon strip or calendar illustration.

13. "More than 1.7 million people visit Presidential Libraries annually; the L. B. J. Library in Austin, Texas and the John F. Kennedy Library in Boston each drew more than half million visitors last year. Fewer than 1 percent of them were scholars interested in combing through the Presidential paperwork; the rest were tourists" (T. Schlesinger, 1981:704).

14. "So the battlefields have had many uses—memorial of the valor and sacrifice of the . . . troops, places for rituals of reconciliation, laboratories for military tactics, and parks which preserve the site of important events pertaining to the preservation of national unity . . . they were sacrificial ground, sanctified by the blood of martyrs. They had the look of sacred space, set apart, marked with monuments, a sacred precinct like those at Delphi or Olympus to honor heroes" (Rainey, 1983:70).

15. "Nostalgia and the attempt to define a national history have created more house-shrines in America than in any other country in the world" (Cohn, 1979:x).

16. "Even a pilgrimage with one's children to Disneyland will teach one much about the American psyche: a sense of universal mission and prettified international relations; an elective system (laissez-faire) of entertainments; a pervasive sense of virtue and uplift in a well-lighted place, where evil, corruption, lust, gambling, misery, power, and oppression have been resolutely swept from view; a place where a Supreme Being is discreetly alluded to and patriotism made the central unifying theme; a place where sanitation is achieved by an efficiency unrivaled anywhere in the world. . . . Shrines of immaculate, innocent perception, as if the American way of life were a design to cleanse all evil from the face of the earth with hygienic thought and determined will. A conspiracy against the dirt and confusion of the older world: *Novus ordo seclorum.* 'In our beginnings, God smiled on us: Annuit coeptis' " (M. Novak, 1974:125).

17. And it may have excited less genuine emotion than the 1876 event. As evidence, consider the fact that in the most definitive catalog of political Americana on textiles we are ever likely to see, the number of Centennial items listed is much greater than that for the Bicentennial (Collins, 1979:188–211, 548–58).

18. It is tempting to speculate that one possible reason for general flag pride in Sweden and Switzerland, as opposed to its visual rarity in other

European lands, may be that these are the only two countries in the region that have not engaged in warfare since the Napoleonic period. But it is equally plausible that coincidence or other factors may have been at work.

19. J. B. Jackson (1982) notes in a personal communication that the usual form of the U.S. shield is "not heraldic in the strict sense." If it were, it would follow the sixteenth-century German or Swiss design. "Why did we deliberately foreswear the feudal or aristocratic shield?"

20. Although it may be a challenging project, especially in view of the fact that color photography and reproduction have only recently come into general use, a determined researcher should be able to measure the changing incidence of the red-white-and-blue motif, at least in rough fashion. Many landscape and genre paintings await analysis; magazine files with color advertisements are available; and we can retrieve records of corporate trademarks and other business iconography.

21. Perhaps even more than contemporary photographs, these delightful drawings offer splendid raw material, as yet almost untouched, to the student who wishes to see how life was being lived, or rather how the privileged imagined it ought to be lived, in the late nineteenth century.

22. Another observation not as readily quantified is that both flags and eagles are entirely absent from houses designed along modernistic or avant-garde, that is, self-consciously sophisticated, lines. Conversely, of course, they are most likely to adorn the most popular vernacular house types of past and present. For example, Grady Clay (1985) reports in a personal communication seeing "a rash of quite new cast-concrete eagles (some painted black) mostly perched on red-brick entrance columns at the driveways to new ranch houses throughout the Commonwealth" during a 1983 traverse across Kentucky. There also appears to be rather more spatial clustering of flags and eagles than would occur randomly. Neighbors emulating neighbors? I regard as debatable James S. Duncan, Jr.'s assertion concerning an elite residential neighborhood in a Westchester County, N.Y. community, namely, that "the American eagle and the carriage lamp-posts which light the driveway are probably meant to convey an image of upper-class prosperity rather than any special attachment to the past" (Duncan, 1973:347), a claim partially contradicted by Allan Jacobs's statement (1985:56) that "eagles, colonial lamp posts, rustic signs, and unique mailboxes are more often displayed by people whose social and economic status have recently risen than by 'old money' families." Eagles—and flags—are associated with residences along the entire socioeconomic spectrum, provided they are built in the folk and popular idioms.

23. Unfortunately, the American flag industry has not formed a trade association, and no hard data on volume of sales over time are available from any source; but the anecdotal evidence does support the argument

advanced in this paper. Journalistic accounts, for example, Eng (1981), indicate a substantial increase in sales since the 1960s, following a temporary surge caused by the introduction of the 50-star flag in 1960. According to an official of Annin & Co., the leading manufacturing firm, demand increased spectacularly in 1975 with the approach of the Bicentennial, and a high level has been maintained ever since (Connors, 1982). Extraordinary events, such as a papal visit or the 1979–81 Iranian hostage crisis, generate extraordinary demand for American (and papal or Iranian!) flags. A disproportionate share of the recent growth in Annin & Co.'s sales has gone to government and corporate customers.

A single national survey of some 8,604 households concerning flag ownership and display habits, carried out in spring 1959, is of some interest, if only for its uniqueness; but the sampling technique and other aspects of its methodology render the results somewhat dubious (National Family Opinion, 1959). Perhaps the most interesting tabulation is one presenting percent of homes, by major geographic region, displaying the flag on nine specified holidays (National Family Opinion, 1959:8). In general, the South scores more poorly than any of the other three regions.

24. "Through its formal qualities contemporary taste was offered an acceptable form and cultural nationalism was appeased. In the eye of the beholder, the Greek temple became the perfect expression of America. For the first time, a style appeared that was celebrated as 'American' and that made previous houses, no matter how elegant and opulent, look old-fashioned" (Cohn, 1979:36).

25. The work of Richard Hunt, Daniel Burnham, and other fashionable architects of the late nineteenth and early twentieth centuries also intensified and prolonged the popularity of classicism in public and commercial buildings, especially after the success of Chicago's 1893 Columbian Exposition.

26. Perhaps a cautionary note is in order. The Colonial and other domestic building styles associated with the American ethos bear cultural messages that are broader and more diffuse than the strictly ideological or quasi-political. They speak to us of ethnicity and that elusive entity, national character, in the most general and comprehensive of terms.

27. A wide variety of evidence bearing upon the evolving character of American nationalism, or nationalism in general, appears piecemeal in numerous studies, each dealing with a single facet of the topic. A full presentation would call for a lengthy essay, but a few authors have sensed and commented upon the broader contours of the phenomenon (Cannadine, 1983; Jackson, 1980; Karp, 1979; Nisbet, 1975).

CHAPTER SIX

1. Although the literature on modernization has reached an enormous size, no one has yet attempted a comprehensive treatment of the phenomenon in its American context. R. D. Brown (1976) offers a useful beginning, but does not carry the story past 1865. The most detailed study for any country, though once again temporally confined (to the 1870–1914 period), is Eugen Weber's (1976) masterly work on the modernization of the French countryside. At a local, personal level, Hélias's (1978) poignant account of the transition to modernity in a Breton village is a classic.

2. "An examination of the morale of the Revolutionary army during 1776 will convince one how near to wreck was the Patriot cause in the crisis. Patriotism of the kind shown in the Civil War, nearly a century later, or of that even higher variety manifested in the Great War (1917–18), was very rare. The 'Spirit of '76' meant in the main enthusiasm for independence, loyalty to a great commander, hate of George III, but not love of country, of a great ideal, of a cause worth more than life itself. Washington rose to that, as did a few others who had the nobility and the vision, but in the masses loyalty to county, province, or section was the ruling motive. Throughout the future of American history, from that day to this, the grander sentiment was to grow. Patriotism was not a plant, like that obedient to the magic of an Indian juggler, to spring at once into full bloom" (Van Tyne, 1929:270–71).

3. "The first general employment of the word [American] in the sense in which we define it seems to have been in this expedition when Englishmen and colonials upon forced association found each other peculiar" (Harkness, 1950:88–89).

4. Other writings on American church history reinforce these sentiments (Bellah, 1978:20–21; Berens, 1978:28; Heimert, 1966; G. Miller, 1976; Strout, 1974:29–30, 48–49). It is also worth noting that "coeval with the Republic, [Methodism] was broadly American in character and was more a cultural instrument of nation-building than of regional formation" (Meinig, 1982:97).

5. The strategy of using war metaphorically to combat depressions, poverty, or whatever has caught on famously in twentieth-century America (Robertson, 1980:331–32). "Anyone who today thinks the American nation in the 1930s did not make use of war symbolism during the largely unsuccessful effort of the New Deal to meet the depression, should go back to illustrated magazines of that time. In terms of frequency of use by the national government not even Hitler's Germany outdid our propagandists" (Nisbet, 1975:185).

6. But the sport of Brit bashing has not totally disappeared. During the

1920s, Chicago's Mayor Thompson made much political hay by tweaking
the British lion's tail (Wecter, 1941:84). The relationship with France has
generally been much smoother. Except for a temporary turn for the worse
during the darker years of the French Revolution and the Napoleonic regime, the record has been one of constant Franco-American friendship (Larson, 1940:25).

7. "Study of the cahiers shows that, in general, national spirit was most
marked in and around Paris and less so as one approached outlying provinces of Brittany, Picardy, Alsace, Provence, and Navarre" (Hayes, 1960:50),
as Weber (1976) has demonstrated in definitive detail.

8. "Even though the United States is one of the most highly urbanized
societies in the world, American men acquire some of their identity
through a shared belief that in some magical fashion they partake of some
of the characteristics of a crude and masculine frontier society where many
of the complexities of European men have no place. In this respect there is
a striking similarity between the Australian national ethos and that of the
United States" (Conway, 1974:76). Do Australian lads play the equivalent
of Cowboys-and-Indians, that ritual reenactment of the winning of the
West that all the urban lads of my generation indulged in (Robertson, 1980:
162)?

9. "They are systems of belief and argument which may be savagely anti-
religious, which may postulate a world without God and may deny an af-
terlife, but whose structure, whose aspirations, whose claims on the be-
liever, are profoundly religious in strategy and in effect" (Steiner, 1974:4).
"A kind of religious void has been created for large numbers of people in
modern Europe and the contemporary world. But . . . any such void is un-
natural, and an urge arises to fill the void with some new faith. Intellectuals have found this in 'scientism,' in 'humanitarianism,' in 'positivism,' in
'freemasonry,' to one or another of which they evince a single-minded and
at least quasi-religious devotion. To be sure, these objects are likely to be
too abstract, too esoteric, for mass adoration. As the masses grow cold
about the historic Christian faith and practice, they have tended, rather, to
accept other and more attractive substitutes offered them by intellectuals,
most notable of which are communism and nationalism. . . . Yet we may
doubt whether Marxian or Leninist communism would have the position
and influence it now has, or threaten to become the world religion of the
future, if it had not latterly exploited and been reinforced by another emotional substitute for traditional supernatural religion: namely, nationalism.
Nationalism has a warmth and a pietistic character which communism
lacks. It is not so coldly and impersonally materialist. It has a spiritual
quality; and, unlike communism, it appreciates the basic religious truth
that man does not live by bread alone. Hence the emotion which national-

ism arouses is likely to be shared to the full not only by an elite but by the mass of common people. Furthermore, nationalism usually gives some satisfaction, which communism scarcely can, to man's craving for immortality and for freedom. At any rate, it relates man to his nation's historic past and identifies him and his descendants with the future life of the nation. And its goal is the assurance of freedom and individuality and autonomy, if not to the person, at least to one's nationality and national state" (Hayes, 1960:15–16). One might add that if nationalism or statism is the high church version of the new dispensation, then sport may be looked upon as its low church manifestation.

10. E. L. Tuveson (1968:133–36) regards the Russian national faith, at least in its pre-Bolshevik version, as being fundamentally different from the American. "The Russian program is static . . . in the Russian version there is no millenial utopia, no confidence that history is moving upward and that the future of the human family on this earth is brilliant" (Tuveson, 1968:35).

11. "If the providential thought of early America could be compressed into one sentence, that sentence would have to be 'Divine Providence is utilizing the United States to achieve universal freedom.' . . . The Americans who made the Revolution, the Constitution, and the new nation were men firmly convinced that they were Heaven's favorites—that they were doing God's republican work in the world" (Berens, 1978:169–70). "What others do, or have done, is sometimes assumed to provide no lessons of experience for America; *sui generis*, it can claim exemption from history" (Nye, 1966:186).

12. American civil religion has received deep and extended treatment in recent years. Among the more notable discussions are Albanese (1976), Bellah (1967), Bellah and Hammond (1980), Berens (1978), Cherry (1970), Gabriel (1956:22–25), Hammond (1976), Mead (1967), M. Novak (1974:105–10), Nye (1966), Richey and Jones (1974), Shaffer (1975:49–50), Tuveson (1968), and Wolfe (1975).

13. "The United States has possessed, for almost two hundred years, a concise statement of its aims, specifically enumerated in writing, periodically re-affirmed, and carefully re-examined. This of course exists in the preamble of the Declaration of Independence, which Archibald MacLeish has called 'the most precisely articulated statement of national purpose in recorded history.' It is probable that only in the United States would a national body, appointed by the head of the state, embark on a study of the national purpose, as President Eisenhower's Commission on National Goals did in 1959" (Nye, 1966:167). Three principal American aims, as noted by the Commission, are worth noting: "that the United States lead others toward a future world-state of freedom and liberty as yet unknown,

and that it serve as surrogate or agent for the rest of mankind in achieving it[;] that the United States serve as an example to the rest of the world of God's plan for mankind, and as proof that man can govern himself in peace and justice[;] that the United States serve as a haven for the oppressed of the world, and as a place of opportunity for the deserving, ambitious, and godly" (Nye, 1966:168). And "Americans . . . are no doubt the only people in the world who blame themselves for not having finally created the perfect society, and who submit themselves to persistent self-examination to determine why they have not" (Nye, 1966:204).

14. In his *Season of Youth*, Michael Kammen (1978) has produced *the* definitive account of the Revolution's image and impact on American thought and creativity, with special emphasis on popular culture. But he also deals with much broader issues, such as political revisionism and the role of tradition in American life. "Insofar as we have had a feeling for tradition at all . . . I am prepared to argue that the American Revolution has been at its core. The Revolution is the one component of our past that we have not, at some point or other, explicitly repudiated" (Kammen, 1978:15).

15. As late as 1850, the supremely articulate and perceptive Herman Melville gave voice to the creed born in the travail of the Revolution in the following molten passage. "Escaped from the house of bondage, Israel of old did not follow after the ways of the Egyptians. To her was given an express dispensation; to her were given new things under the sun. And we Americans are the peculiar, chosen people—the Israel of our time: we bear the ark of the liberties of the world. Seventy years ago we escaped from thrall; and, besides our first birth-right—embracing one continent of earth—God has given to us, for a future inheritance, the broad domains of the political pagans, without bloody hands being lifted. God has predestined, mankind expects, great things from our race; and great things we feel in our souls. The rest of the nations must soon be in our rear. We are the pioneers of the world; the advance-guard, sent on through the wilderness of untried things, to break a new path in the New World that is ours. In our youth is our strength; in our inexperience, our wisdom. At a period when other nations have but lisped, our deep voice is heard afar. Long enough have we been sceptics with regard to ourselves, and doubted whether, indeed, the political Messiah had come. But he has come in *us*, if we would but give utterance to his promptings. And let us always remember that with ourselves, almost for the first time in the history of earth, national selfishness is unbounded philanthropy; for we cannot do a good to America, but we give alms to the world" (Melville, 1850:180–81). Is it too unkind to note that we find considerably more ambivalence concerning America's destiny in Melville's later writings?

16. "The Civil War divided a nation, whereas the American Revolution created and unified it. The Civil War exposed our vilest flaws, whereas the Revolution shaped our character and (we generally assumed) displayed our courage, principles, and highmindedness for all the world to see. What happened in 1776 somehow reflected glory upon us, whereas what happened in 1861, when the polity disintegrated, became an object lesson in the perils of extremism and selfishness. . . . The Revolution's image . . . helped serve to reunite the shattered nation during the quarter century after 1865; but the Civil War Centennial of 1957–65, which took place at a time of domestic tranquillity, turned out to be even more of a fiasco than the Bicentennial activity of the 1970s, which took place under far more troubled circumstances" (Kammen, 1978:258–59).

17. "From the 1870s onward in New England and to a lesser extent in the Middle West, the war became an element of a significant ritual. Its celebration focused on Decoration Day which became an occasion for mobilizing and displaying the unity and solidarity of many communities in their heroic dead. . . . In a nation committed to nonsectarianism, one in which the desire for religious communion was coming to be displaced by nationalism, a ceremony connected with the war was an opportunity for different kinds of people to draw together in the shared recollection of their dead. . . . When there was a conflict between the reality of war and what they wished the symbol to be, the actualities receded and disappeared" (Handlin, 1961: 134–35).

18. There were parallel developments within the regular churches. "We have noted then that the bulk of American Protestantism achieved during this period [following the Civil War] a working ideological harmony with the mode of the modern industrial civilization, the free-enterprise system and the burgeoning imperialism" (Mead, 1963:154).

19. Readers familiar with the work of Carlton Hayes will realize that in the following passage I have shamelessly paraphrased his language (1960: 164–68). An equally persuasive statement of the thoroughly religious character of the fully developed American civil religion is available in Wolfe's (1975) detailed analysis of the Kennedy presidency, and especially the assassination weekend.

20. "No single church evokes the breadth of respect enjoyed by the Supreme Court. The reason, no doubt, is that the Court is a 'vital national seminar' in ways and on issues that churches never have been in the United States." Thus the judicial system is "a religion independent of churches" and "little tied to the ruling regime" (Bellah and Hammond, 1980:75–76). I suspect that if we could chart public esteem for the Supreme Court over time, it would follow much the same trajectory as the presidency. The Congress and its members may weigh lightly on the scale of

popular prestige, for, after all, they are selected by the rabble, they represent limited districts, few senators or representatives trail clouds of glory, and their swearing in is a semiprivate affair, off-camera in a closed chamber. The elaborate, immensely public inauguration of the chief executive instantly transforms the president-elect from being a mere mortal to the stature of a deity. The President appoints (anoints?) federal judges, including justices of the Supreme Court, with the normally automatic amens of the Senate; and what is more natural than that some of the divinity of their progenitor should rub off on the oracular federal judiciary.

21. For the impressive statistics on American foreign missionaries, "native helpers," church members, schools, philanthropic establishments, and contributions in 1906 and 1916, see U.S. Bureau of the Census (1919). Despite the fact that library and archival shelves are groaning under a veritable mountain of printed matter on Christian missions, nearly all was written by or for church people. Remarkably little of it is critical or objective in content. Evidently no historian, geographer, or anthropologist has attempted to describe and analyze the impact of American church missions on foreign populations, a splendid theme that clamors for attention. Incidental facts and comments appear in Neill (1964), Latourette's (1937–45) monumental chronicle of the expansion of Christianity, and the *World Missionary Atlas* (Beech and Fahs, 1925); and in his prescient volume on the Americanization of the world, Stead (1901) offers some passing remarks on the subject. H. B. Johnson's (1967) study of Christian missions in Africa hints at the rich potentialities of this genre for the historical geographer, but hers is a locational analysis involving only European enterprises.

22. At the risk of being tiresome, let me note again how dramatically the Bicentennial celebrations highlighted the great gulf between the ideological worlds of 1776 and 1976. "The two words most muted during the two hundredth year of American independence have been 'people' and 'revolution'" (Morris, 1977:1). And a few years earlier, Edward M. Burns commented sardonically, "today the Revolution of the 1770's is celebrated as if it were about as sedate an event as a meeting of the Presbyterian synod. The ultrarespectable men and women who devote themselves to cherishing its memory would have more in common with Lord North than with Samuel Adams or Thomas Paine. They seem to believe that if America has any lessons to read to the rest of the world, they are lessons of preserving inherited wealth and social privilege" (Burns, 1957:18).

23. "Many Americans are struggling with an ideological credibility gap. They simply cannot believe the patriotic scriptures. Because America's destiny is not manifest, Nathan Hale's storied 'last words' seem hollow or fatuous to many Americans. One explanation is that the Puritan tradition,

which undergirded so many American attitudes, has lost its hold as a system of religious belief" (Ahlstrom, 1975:503).

24. "A variety of evidences, most of them by now obvious to the layman, suggest that confidence and trust have been replaced by opposite sentiments, that government, from being the protector of the lives of its citizens, has become the single greatest source of exploitation in the minds of a growing number of people. Once political government in the United States signified some degree of austerity of life, of commitment to the public weal, of a willingness to forego most of life's luxuries in the name of service that was for a long time closely akin to what one found in the ranks of clergy and teachers. Today, as scores of surveys and polls reveal, government is perceived by large numbers of citizens as the domain of economic luxury, great personal power, high social status, all symbolized perfectly by the pomp and grandeur of public architecture. It is also perceived, we learn from the same surveys and polls, as being possessed of a degree of arrogance that no corporation could today get away with in the business world, that was once regarded as the privilege of hereditary aristocracy" (Nisbet, 1975:4).

25. "National boundaries defined by vernaculars are as defenseless against information moving with the speed of light as against the intercontinental ballistic missile. The attempt to cram nationalism as content into the new media tends to produce the barbarous and the ludicrous— 'Canadian content' rules being a case in point. TV relieved radio of its national burden to show the flag, and freed it to go local and universal; the communication satellite promises to internationalize TV and, in the process, leave national content with nowhere to go" (Watkins, 1966:290–91).

26. "It is doubtful that any national state in the Western world at the present time, not even the United States, is really capable of restraining the huge conglomerates which, wherever they initiate, reach out to invade dozens of countries for purposes of consumer-capture and, in the process, necessarily become like those feudal-military powers which by the sixth century in the West had made chaos of the once-sovereign Roman Empire in the West. The seeming incapacity of any national government to contain or restrain the huge multinational corporations is only in part, of course, the result of the potency of these economic leviathans. Far more does this incapacity result from the immensely diminished role of the political state, of government no matter in whose hands, to enlist any longer the confidence of substantial numbers of its citizens" (Nisbet, 1975:12–13).

27. The most logical and, in my opinion, desirable alternative to our present nexus of nation-state and market economy (whether under capitalist or ostensibly socialist auspices) has been with us for some generations,

but largely as a tradition within the intellectual underground or in quite localized practice. It goes by several names or forms: the communal (or communitarian) movement, the counterculture, the cooperative movement, anarchism, syndicalism, utopian organizations, libertarianism. But the guiding principle is constant: that the world of humankind should be organized from the bottom up, not from top down, by locally based, voluntary associations of free individuals determining their own social, economic, and cultural existences and interacting peacefully with other such associations. Perhaps still the most eloquent and persuasive spokesperson for such a world, though writing several decades ago, has been the geographer Peter Kropotkin (1968; Capouya and Tompkins, 1975); but his work has been updated by a number of other scholars cognizant of the changing conditions of the twentieth century, for example, Murray Bookchin (1971) and Karl Hess (1975). The great difficulty, of course, is how to get from here to there, how—barring a military or ecological catastrophe of unimaginable severity—to alter radically the mind-sets of enough persons as well as our complex existing institutional framework. Recent advances in the technologies of production and communication offer both greater opportunities and greater obstacles to the realization of such a transformation. The history of the ill-fated attempts to establish such utopian societies in the United States and elsewhere is long, interesting, and both inspiring and discouraging (Case and Taylor, 1979; Veysey, 1973). However, there is a glimmer of hope in the fact that, after decades of agitation, libertarian communes came into being in Catalonia and other parts of Spain on a local and regional basis; and, despite incredibly difficult external political and military pressures, they demonstrated for a few glorious months in 1936 that their revolutionary system was indeed workable and highly acceptable in human terms (Dolgoff, 1974; Orwell, 1938).

BIBLIOGRAPHY ★ ★ ★ ★ ★

Asterisks indicate publications of outstanding value to the student of nationalism in the United States and elsewhere.

Abler, Ronald F. (1983). Personal communication, Nov. 2.

Adam, Thomas R. (1937). *The Civic Value of Museums*. New York: American Association for Adult Education.

Adams, James N. (1969). *Illinois Place Names*. Occasional Publication no. 54. Springfield: Illinois State Historical Society.

Ageron, Charles-Robert (1984). "L'Exposition Coloniale de 1931." Pp. 561–91 in Pierre Nora, ed., *Les lieux de mémoire*. Vol. 1, *La République*. Paris: Gallimard.

Agulhon, Maurice (1979a). *Marianne au combat: L'imagerie et la symbolique républicaine de 1789 à 1880*. Paris: Flammarion.

———— (1979b). "Propos sur l'allégorie politique (en réponse à Eric Hobsbawm)." *Actes de la Recherche en Sciences Sociales*, no. 28:27–32, 85."

Ahlstrom, Sidney E. (1975). "Religion, Revolution, and the Rise of Modern Nationalism." *Church History* 44(4):492–504.

Albanese, Catherine (1974). "Requiem for Memorial Day: Dissent in the Redeemer Nation." *American Quarterly* 26:386–98.

*———— (1976). *Sons of the Fathers: The Civil Religion of the American Revolution*. Philadelphia: Temple University Press.

———— (1978). "Citizen Crockett: Myth, History, and Nature Religion." *Soundings: An Interdisciplinary Journal* 61(1):87–104.

———— (1979). "King Crockett: Nature and Civility on the American Frontier." *Proceedings of the American Antiquarian Society* 88(2):225–49.

Albinski, Henry S. (1985). Personal communication, May 10.

Alderson, William T., and Shirley Payne Low (1976). *Interpretation of Historic Sites*. Nashville: American Association for State and Local History.

Alexander, Charles C. (1980). *Here the Country Lies: Nationalism and the Arts in Twentieth-Century America*. Bloomington: Indiana University Press.

Alexander, Edward P. (1979). *Museums in Motion: An Introduction to the History and Functions of Museums.* Nashville: American Association for State and Local History.

Algeo, John (1978). "From Classic to Classy: Changing Fashions in Street Names." *Names* 26:80–95.

Algeo, John, and Adele Algeo (1983). "Bible Belt Onomastics Revisited." *Names* 31(2):103–16.

Allen, Sister Christine Hope (1983). "Public Celebrations and Private Grieving: The Public Healing Process after Death." Paper presented at Biennial Meeting of American Studies Association, Philadelphia.

Alley, Robert S. (1972). *So Help Me God: Religion and the Presidency, Wilson to Nixon.* Richmond: John Knox Press.

Allwood, John (1977). *The Great Exhibitions.* London: Studio Vista.

Alotta, Robert I. (1981). "Popularity: The Street Names of Philadelphia." Paper presented at the fourteenth International Congress of Onomastic Sciences, Ann Arbor, Mich.

Amalvi, Christian (1984). "Le 14-Juillet." Pp. 421–72 in Pierre Nora, ed., *Les lieux de mémoire.* Vol. 1, *La République.* Paris: Gallimard.

American Association of Museums (1979). *The Official Museum Directory 1980: United States, Canada.* Washington, D.C., and Skokie, Ill.: AAM and National Register Publishing Co.

American Revolution Bicentennial Administration (1977). *The Bicentennial of the United States of America: A Final Report to the People.* 5 vols. Washington, D.C.: Government Printing Office.

Ames, Kenneth L. (1985). "Introduction." Pp. 1–14 in Alan Axelrod, ed., *The Colonial Revival in America.* New York: W. W. Norton.

*Anderson, Benedict (1983). *Imagined Communities: Reflection on the Origin and Spread of Nationalism.* London: Verso.

Antrim History Committee (1977). *Parades and Promenades. Antrim, New Hampshire . . . the Second Hundred Years.* Canaan, N.H.: Phoenix Publishing.

Arieli, Yehoshua (1964). *Individualism and Nationalism in American Ideology.* Cambridge: Harvard University Press.

Asher, Herbert B. (1980). *Presidential Elections and American Politics.* Rev. ed. Homewood, Ill.: Dorsey Press.

Atwan, Robert, Donald McQuade, and John W. Wright (1979). *Edsels, Luckies and Frigidaires: Advertising the American Way.* New York: Dell.

Badger, Reid (1979). *The Great American Fair: The World's Columbian Exposition and American Culture.* Chicago: Nelson Hall.

Bailey, Alfred Goldsworthy (1972). *Culture and Nationality: Essays by Alfred Goldsworthy Bailey.* Toronto: McClelland and Stewart.

Bailey, Thomas A. (1966). *Presidential Greatness: The Image and the Man from George Washington to the Present.* New York: Appleton-Century-Crofts.

———— (1968). "The Mythmakers of American History." *Journal of American History* 55:5–21.

Bailyn, Bernard (1967). *The Ideological Origins of the American Revolution.* Cambridge: Harvard University Press.

Balch, George (1890). *Methods of Teaching Patriotism in the Public Schools.* New York: Van Nostrand.

Barber, Bernard (1949). "Place, Symbol, and Utilitarian Function in War Memorials." *Social Forces* 28:64–68.

Barnet, Richard J. (1980). *The Lean Years: Politics in the Age of Scarcity.* New York: Simon & Schuster.

Barnet, Richard J., and Ronald E. Müller (1974). *Global Reach: The Power of the Multinationals.* New York: Simon & Schuster.

Barthes, Roland (1972). *Mythologies.* New York: Hill & Wang.

Baruch, Mildred C., and Ellen J. Beckman (1978). *Civil War Monuments: A List of Union Monuments, Markers and Memorials of the American Civil War, 1861–1865.* Washington, D.C.: Daughters of Union Veterans of the Civil War, 1861–1865.

Basler, Roy P. (1935). *The Lincoln Legend.* Boston: Houghton Mifflin.

Beale, Howard K. (1936). *Are American Teachers Free?* New York: Scribner's.

Beard, Charles A. (1934). "Nationalism in American History." Pp. 39–51 in Waldo G. Leland, ed., *Nationalism: Papers Presented at the Fourth Chicago Meeting of the American Association for the Advancement of Science.* Bloomington, Ind.: American Association for the Advancement of Science.

Beck, Horace P. (1971). "The Making of the Popular Legendary Hero." Pp. 121–32 in Wayland D. Hand, ed., *American Folk Legend: A Symposium.* Berkeley: University of California Press.

Beech, H. P., and C. H. Fahs, eds. (1925). *World Missionary Atlas.* New York: Institute of Social and Religious Research.

Bell, Daniel (1975). "The End of American Exceptionalism." *The Public Interest* 41:193–224.

Bellah, Robert N. (1967). "Civil Religion in America." *Daedalus* 96(1):1–21.

*———— (1975). *The Broken Covenant: American Civil Religion in Time of Trial.* New York: Seabury Press.

———— (1978). "Religion and the Legitimation of the American Republic." *Society* 15(4):16–23.

Bellah, Robert N., and Phillip E. Hammond (1980). *Varieties of Civil Reli-

gion. San Francisco: Harper & Row.

Benedict, Burton (1983). *The Anthropology of World's Fairs: San Francisco's Panama Pacific International Exposition of 1915.* London and Berkeley: Lowie Museum of Anthropology and Scolar Press.

*Bercovitch, Sacvan (1978). *The American Jeremiad.* Madison: University of Wisconsin Press.

Berens, John F. (1978). *Providence and Patriotism in Early America, 1640–1815.* Charlottesville: University Press of Virginia.

Berger, Peter L., and Thomas Luckman (1966). *The Social Construction of Reality: A Treatise in the Sociology of Knowledge.* Garden City, N.Y.: Doubleday.

Berry, Christopher J. (1981). "Nations and Norms." *The Review of Politics* 43:75–87.

Binkley, Wilfred E. (1952). "The President as a National Symbol." *Annals of the American Academy of Political and Social Science* 283:86–93.

———— (1958). *The Man in the White House: His Powers and Duties.* Baltimore: Johns Hopkins University Press.

Birnbaum, N. (1955). "Monarchs and Sociologists: A Reply to Professor Shils and Mr. Young." *Sociological Review* 3(1):1–23.

Black, Mary (1976). *American Advertising Posters of the Nineteenth Century from the Bella C. Landauer Collection of the New York Historical Society.* New York: Dover.

Black, Percy (1953). *The Mystique of Modern Monarchy.* London: Watts.

Blaut, J. M. (1980). "Nairn on Nationalism." *Antipode* 12(3):1–17.

———— (1982). "Nationalism as an Autonomous Force." *Science and Society* 46(1):1–23.

Boatner, Mark M., III (1973). *Landmarks of the American Revolution.* Harrisburg: Stackpole Books.

Boehm, Max Hildebert (1933). "Nationalism: Theoretical Aspects." Vol. 11, pp. 231–40, in *Encyclopedia of the Social Sciences.* New York: Macmillan.

Bohn, Thomas William (1968). *An Historical and Descriptive Analysis of the "Why We Fight" Series.* Ph.D. dissertation, University of Wisconsin.

Boller, Paul F., Jr. (1984). *Presidential Campaigns.* New York: Oxford University Press.

Bolwell, Robert Whitney (1939). "Concerning the Study of Nationalism in American Literature." *American Literature* 10:405–16.

Bookchin, Murray (1971). *Post-Scarcity Anarchism.* Berkeley: Ramparts Press.

———— (1987). *The Rise of Urbanization and the Decline of Citizenship.* San Francisco: Sierra Club Books.

*Boorstin, Daniel J. (1965). *The Americans: The National Experience.* New York: Random House.

Borza, Eugene N. (1973). "Sentimental Philhellenism and the Image of Greece." Pp. 5–25 in Eugene N. Borza and Robert W. Carrubba, eds., *Classics and the Classical Tradition.* University Park: Pennsylvania State University Press.

Bostick, Virginia L. (1978). *The History of the Public Monuments and Sculpture of Morris County, New Jersey.* Morristown: Morris County Free Library.

Boyd, Malcolm (1980). "National Anthems." Vol. 13, pp. 46–75, in Stanley Sadie, ed., *The New Grove Dictionary of Music and Musicians.* London: Macmillan.

Boynton, Percy H. (1936). *Changing Ideas on American Patriotism.* Chicago: University of Chicago Press.

Bradsher, Earl L. (1940). "The Rise of Nationalism in American Literature." Pp. 269–87 in Nathaniel Caffee and Thomas A. Kirby, eds., *Studies for William Alexander Read.* Baton Rouge: Louisiana State University Press.

Brandon, Edgar Ewing, comp. (1950–57). *Lafayette, Guest of the Nation: A Contemporary Account of the Triumphal Tour of General Lafayette.* 3 vols. Oxford, Ohio: Oxford Historical Press.

Brandt, Nat (1971). "To the Flag." *American Heritage* 22(4):72–75, 104.

Brauer, Jerald C., ed. (1976). *Religion and the American Revolution.* Philadelphia: Fortress Press.

Briggs, Rose T. (1968). *Plymouth Rock: History and Significance.* Boston: Pilgrim Society.

Bristow, Dick (1971). *The Illustrated Political Button Book.* Santa Cruz, Calif.: Dick Bristow.

———— (1973). *Presidential Campaign Items, 1789–1892.* Santa Cruz, Calif.: Dick Bristow.

Brock, William (1971). "The Image of England and American Nationalism." *Journal of American Studies* 5(3):225–45.

Brody, M. Kenneth (1977). *Sociological Theories of Symbolic Activity: A Case Study Application to the Bicentennial Observance.* Ph.D. dissertation, University of Iowa.

Brohm, Jean-Marie (1978). *Sport—A Prison of Measured Time.* London: Ink Links.

Brophy, Donald (1975). *American Bread: A Calendar of American Heroes and Villains.* Paramus, N.J.: Paulist Press.

Brown, Dee (1966). *The Year of the Century: 1876.* New York: Scribner's.

Brown, Richard D. (1976). *Modernization: The Transformation of Ameri-*

can Life. New York: Hill & Wang.

Browne, Ray B., and Marshall W. Fishwick, eds. (1983). *The Hero in Transition*. Bowling Green: Bowling Green University Popular Press.

Brownlow, Kevin (1979). *The War, the West and the Wilderness*. New York: Knopf.

Bryan, William Alfred (1952). *George Washington in American Literature, 1775–1865*. New York: Columbia University Press.

Bullard, F. Lauriston (1952). *Lincoln in Marble and Bronze*. New Brunswick: Rutgers University Press.

Burg, David F. (1976). *Chicago's White City of 1893*. Lexington: University of Kentucky Press.

Burnham, Irene (1982). "Making History Out of Artifacts: An Interpretive Exhibit at the Valley Forge Museum." *Valley Forge Journal* 1(1):82–96.

Burns, Edward McNall (1957). *The American Idea of Mission: Concepts of National Purpose and Destiny*. New Brunswick: Rutgers University Press.

Burrows, Edwin G., and Michael Wallace (1972). "The American Revolution: The Ideology and Psychology of National Liberation." *Perspectives in American History* 6:167–306.

Buscombe, Edward (1979). "America on Screen?: Hollywood Feature Films as Social and Political Evidence." Pp. 25–29 in M. J. Clark, ed., *Politics and the Media: Film and Television for the Political Scientist and Historian*. Oxford: Pergamon.

Bush, Clive (1977). *The Dream of Reason: American Consciousness and Cultural Achievement from Independence to the Civil War*. New York: St. Martin's Press.

Butterfield, L. H. (1953). "The Jubilee of Independence: July 4, 1826." *Virginia Magazine of History and Biography* 61(2):119–40.

Bynack, V. B. (1984). "Noah Webster, Linguistic Thought and the Idea of an American National Culture: The Pathology of Epistemology." *Journal of the History of Ideas* 45(1):99–114.

Cahill, Holger (1942). *Emblems of Unity and Freedom*. New York: Metropolitan Museum of Art.

Calkin, Homer L. (1976). "The Centennial of American Independence 'Round the World." *The Historian* 38:613–28.

Campbell, J. Duncan, and Edgar M. Howell (1963). *American Military Insignia, 1800–1851*. Washington, D.C.: Smithsonian Institution.

Campbell, Joseph (1949). *The Hero with a Thousand Faces*. Princeton: Princeton University Press.

*Cannadine, David (1983). "The Context, Performance and Meaning of Ritual: The British Monarchy and the 'Invention of Tradition', c. 1820–

1977." Pp. 101–64 in Eric Hobsbawm and Terence Ranger, eds., *The Invention of Tradition*. Cambridge: Cambridge University Press.

Capouya, Emile, and Keith Tompkins, eds. (1975). *The Essential Kropotkin*. New York: Liveright.

Carlson, Robert A. (1975). *The Quest for Conformity: Americanization through Education*. New York: Wiley.

Carpenter, Charles (1963). *History of American Schoolbooks*. Philadelphia: University of Pennsylvania Press.

Carson, Cary (1981). "Living Museums of Everyman's History." *Harvard Magazine* 83:22–32.

Cary, Norman Miller, Jr. (1975). *Guide to U.S. Army Museums and Historic Sites*. Washington, D.C.: Department of the Army, Center of Military History.

Case, John, and Rosemary C. R. Taylor, eds. (1979). *Co-ops, Communes and Collectives: Experiments in Social Change in the 1960s and 1970s*. New York: Pantheon.

Cassinelli, C. W. (1969). "The National Community." *Polity* 2:14–31.

Cassirer, Ernst (1946). *The Myth of the State*. New Haven: Yale University Press.

Castells, Manuel (1983). *The City and the Grassroots: A Cross-Cultural Theory of Urban Social Movements*. Berkeley: University of California Press.

Cawelti, John G. (1976). "The Frontier and the Native American." Pp. 133–83 in Joshua C. Taylor, ed., *America as Art*. New York: Harper & Row.

Cheney, Lynne Vincent (1974). "1876: The Eagle Screams." *American Heritage* 25(3):15–17, 32–35, 98–99.

Cherry, Conrad (1970). "American Sacred Ceremonies." Pp. 303–16 in Phillip E. Hammond and Benton Johnson, eds., *American Mosaic: Social Patterns of Religion in the United States*. New York: Random House.

Clark, Gordon L., and Michael Dear (1984). *State Apparatus: Structures and Language of Legitimacy*. Boston: Allen & Unwin.

Clay, Grady (1985a). Personal communication, May 10.

―――― (1985b). "The Vietnam Veterans Memorial Competition." *Harvard Magazine* 87(6):56a–h.

Cobb, Lawrence Wells (1978). *Patriotic Themes in American National Magazine Advertising, 1898–1948*. Ph.D. dissertation, Emory University.

Coblenz, William A. (1967). *Ceremonies and Reenactment of the One Hundredth Anniversary of the Second Inauguration of Abraham Lin-*

coln, *1865–1965 . . . March 4, 1965.* Washington, D.C.: Government
Printing Office.

Cochran, Thomas C. (1981). *Frontiers of Change: Early Industrialism in
America.* New York: Oxford University Press.

Coffey, John W., II (1978). *American Posters of World War One: Catalogue
and Exhibition.* Williamstown, Mass.: Williams College Museum of Art.

Cohen, Abner (1979). "Political Symbolism." *Annual Review of Anthropology* 8:87–113.

Cohen, Morris R. (1946). "Baseball as a National Religion." Pp. 334–36 in
The Faith of a Liberal. New York: Holt.

Cohen, Saul B., and Nurit Kliot (1981). "Israel's Place-Names as a Reflection of Continuity and Change in Nation-Building." *Names* 29(3):227–
48.

Cohn, Jan (1979). *The Palace or the Poorhouse: The American House as a
Cultural Symbol.* East Lansing: Michigan State University Press.

Coker, Francis W. (1934). "Patriotism." Vol. 12, pp. 26–29, in *Encyclopedia
of the Social Sciences.* New York: Macmillan.

Cole, Charles William (1937). "Jeremy Belknap: Pioneer Nationalist." *New
England Quarterly* 10:743–51.

Coleman, John A. (1970). "Civil Religion." *Sociological Analysis* 31:67–77.

Coleman, Laurence Vail (1933). *Historic House Museums.* Washington,
D.C.: American Association of Museums.

Collins, Herbert Ridgeway (1979). *Threads of History: American History
Recorded on Cloth 1775 to the Present.* Washington, D.C.: Smithsonian
Institution Press.

*Commager, Henry Steele (1975). "The Origins and Nature of American
Nationalism." Pp. 157–96 in *Jefferson, Nationalism, and the Enlightenment.* New York: Braziller.

Connelly, Thomas L. (1977). *The Marble Man: Robert E. Lee and His Image in American Society.* New York: Knopf.

Connors, Daniel (1982). Personal communication, Aug.

Contreras, Belisario R. (1983). *Tradition and Innovation in New Deal Art.*
Lewisburg: Bucknell University Press.

Conway, Jill (1974). "Culture and National Identity." Pp. 71–81 in Geoffrey
Milburn and John Herbert, eds., *National Consciousness and the Cur-
riculum: The Canadian Case.* Toronto: Ontario Institute for Studies in
Education.

Cosgrove, Denis E. (1984). *Social Formation and Symbolic Landscape.*
London: Croom Helm.

Cox, William V. (1901). *Celebration of the One Hundredth Anniversary of
the Establishment of the Seat of Government in the District of Colum-*

bia. Washington, D.C.: Government Printing Office.

Craig, Lois, et al. (1978). *The Federal Presence: Architecture, Politics, and Symbols in United States Government Buildings*. Cambridge: MIT Press.

Cramer, M. Richard (1981). "Social Science and the American Bicentennial." Paper presented at the 1981 meeting of the Mid-South Sociological Association.

Crapol, Edward P. (1973). *America for Americans*. Westport, Conn.: Greenwood.

Craven, Wesley Frank (1956). *The Legend of the Founding Fathers*. New York: New York University Press.

Crawford, Anthony R. (1979). *Posters of World War I and World War II in the George C. Marshall Research Foundation*. Charlottesville: University Press of Virginia.

Creighton, Thomas H. (1962). *The Architecture of Monuments: The Franklin Delano Roosevelt Memorial Competition*. New York: Reinhold.

Crepeau, Richard C. (1980). *Baseball: America's Diamond Mind 1919–1941*. Gainesville: University Presses of Florida.

Cresswell, Donald H., comp. (1975). *The American Revolution in Drawings and Prints*. Washington, D.C.: Library of Congress.

Cromie, Alice H. (1975). *A Tour Guide to the Civil War*. 2d ed. New York: E. P. Dutton.

Cunliffe, Marcus (1958). *George Washington: Man and Monument*. Boston: Little, Brown.

——— (1968). *Soldiers and Civilians: The Martial Spirit in America, 1775–1865*. Boston: Little, Brown.

Curl, James Stevens (1980). *A Celebration of Death: An Introduction to Some of the Buildings, Monuments, and Settings of Funerary Architecture in the Western European Tradition*. London: Constable.

Curti, Merle (1937). "The Dime Novel and the American Tradition." *Yale Review* 26:761–78.

*——— (1946). *The Roots of American Loyalty*. New York: Russell & Russell.

——— (1950). "America at World's Fairs: 1851–1893." *American Historical Review* 55:833–56.

——— (1963). *American Philanthropy Abroad: A History*. New Brunswick: Rutgers University Press.

Cutler, Phoebe (1985). *The Public Landscape of the New Deal*. New Haven: Yale University Press.

Cybriwsky, Roman A. (1972). *Social Relations and the Spatial Order in the Urban Environment: A Study of Life in a Neighborhood in Central*

Philadelphia. Ph.D. dissertation, Pennsylvania State University.

Darracott, Joseph, and Belinda Loftus (1972). *First World War Posters.* London: Imperial War Museum.

Davies, William Evans (1955). *Patriotism on Parade: The Story of Veterans' and Hereditary Organizations in America, 1783–1900.* Cambridge: Harvard University Press.

Davis, Stephen (1982). "Empty Eyes, Marble Hand: The Confederate Monument and the South." *Journal of Popular Culture* 16(3):2–21.

Dearing, Mary R. (1952). *Veterans in Politics: The Story of the G.A.R.* Baton Rouge: Louisiana State University Press.

Deetz, James (1977). *In Small Things Forgotten: The Archaeology of Early American Life.* Garden City, N.Y.: Doubleday.

Delaplaine, Edward S. (1947). *Francis Scott Key and the National Anthem.* Washington, D.C.: Wilson-Epes Press.

Deutsch, Karl W. (1966). *Nationalism and Social Communication: An Inquiry into the Foundations of Nationality.* Cambridge: MIT Press.

Deutsch, Karl W. and R. L. Merritt (1970). *Nationalism and National Development: An Interdisciplinary Bibliography.* Cambridge: MIT Press.

Deutsch, Monroe (1923). "E Pluribus Unum." *Classical Journal* 18:387–407.

——— (1955). "Our National Motto." *Pacific Spectator* 9:120–25.

Dikshit, R. D. (1976). *The Political Geography of Federalism: An Inquiry into Origins and Stability.* New York: Wiley.

Dippie, Brian W. (1976). *Custer's Last Stand: The Anatomy of an American Myth.* University of Montana Publications in History. Missoula: University of Montana.

District of Columbia, Office of Business and Economic Development (1981). *District of Columbia Tourism Development Policy Study.* Washington, D.C.: District of Columbia, Office of Business and Economic Development.

Doezema, Marianne (1977). "The Public Monument in Tradition and Transition." Pp. 8–21 in *The Public Monument and Its Audience.* Cleveland and Kent: Cleveland Museum of Art and Kent State University Press.

Dohen, Dorothy (1967). *Nationalism and American Catholicism.* New York: Sheed & Ward.

Dolgoff, Sam, ed. (1974). *The Anarchist Collectives: Workers' Self-Management in the Spanish Revolution, 1936–1939.* New York: Free Life Editions.

Donald, David (1959). "Getting Right with Lincoln." Pp. 3–18 in David Donald, *Lincoln Reconsidered: Essays on the Civil War.* New York: Knopf.

Doob, Leonard W. (1964). *Patriotism and Nationalism: Their Psychological Foundations.* New Haven: Yale University Press.

Duchacek, Ivo D. (1970). *Comparative Federalism: The Territorial Dimension of Politics.* New York: Holt, Rinehart & Winston.

Dudden, Arthur P. (1961). "Nostalgia and the American." *Journal of the History of Ideas* 22:515–30.

Duncan, James S., Jr. (1973). "Landscape Taste as a Symbol of Group Identity: A Westchester County Village." *Geographical Review* 63:334–55.

Dupuy, Trevor Nevitt, ed. (1965). *Holidays: Days of Significance for Americans.* New York: Franklin Watts.

Durbin, Louise (1971). *Inaugural Cavalcade.* New York: Dodd, Mead.

Dusterberg, Richard B. (1976). *The Official Inaugural Medals of the Presidents of the United States.* Cincinnati: Medallion Press.

Edelman, Murray (1967). *The Symbolic Uses of Politics.* Urbana: University of Illinois Press.

Edelman, Murray, and Rita James Simon (1969). "Presidential Assassinations: Their Meaning and Impact on American Society." *Ethics* 79:191–221.

Eisen, Gustavus A. (1932). *Portraits of Washington.* 3 vols. New York: Robert Hamilton.

Eisenstadt, S. N. (1978). *Revolution and the Transformation of Societies: A Comparative Study of Civilizations.* New York: Free Press.

Elazar, Daniel J. (1972). *American Federalism: A View from the States.* 2d ed. New York: Crowell.

Eliot, George (1979). *Daniel Deronda.* New York: New American Library. First published in 1876.

Elkins, Stanley, and Eric McKitrick (1961). "The Founding Fathers, Young Men of the Revolution." *Political Science Quarterly* 76:181–216.

Ellis, G. Edward (1843). *Sketches of Bunker Hill Battle and Monument.* 2d ed. Charlestown, Mass.: C. P. Emmons.

Ellul, Jacques (1975). *The New Demons.* New York: Seabury Press.

Elson, Ruth Miller (1964). *Guardians of Tradition, American Textbooks of the Nineteenth Century.* Lincoln: University of Nebraska Press.

Emerson, Mrs. Bettie Alder Calhoun (1911). *Historic Southern Monuments: Representative Memorials of the Heroic Dead of the Southern Confederacy.* New York and Washington, D.C.: Neale Publishing Co.

Eng, Peter (1981). "American Flags Are Flying High Again across U.S." *Washington Post,* July 3, B1, B7.

Evans, James Matthew (1981). *The Landscape Architecture of Washington, D.C.: A Comprehensive Guide.* Washington, D.C.: Landscape Architecture Foundation.

Everett, Lou Ann (1958). "Myth on the Map." *American Heritage*
10(1):62–64.

Fairman, Charles E. (1927). *Art and Artists of the Capitol.* Washington,
D.C.: Government Printing Office.

Fairmount Park Art Association (1974). *Sculpture of a City: Philadelphia's
Treasures in Bronze and Stone.* New York: Walker Publishing Co.

Federal Writers' Project (1937). *Washington: City and Capital.* Washington, D.C.: Government Printing Office.

Feeley, Stephen V. (1957). *The Story of the Capitol.* Buffalo: Henry Stewart.

Fellman, Michael (1971). "The Earthbound Eagle: Andrew Jackson and the
American Pantheon." *Midcontinent American Studies Journal* 12:67–76.

Ferguson, Charles A., and Shirley Brice Heath, eds. (1981). *Language in
the USA.* Cambridge: Cambridge University Press.

Fersh, Seymour H. (1961). *The View from the White House: A Study of
the Presidential State of the Union Messages.* Washington, D.C.: Public
Affairs Press.

Feutl, Rita (1984). "The Do's and Don'ts of Flying the Flag." *Toronto Globe
and Mail,* Aug. 30, 11.

*Field, James A., Jr. (1971). "Transnationalism and the New Tribe." *Inter-
national Organization* 25:353–72.

Fifer, J. Valerie (1976). "Unity by Inclusion: Core Area and Federal State at
American Independence." *Geographical Journal* 142:462–70.

———— (1981). "Washington, D.C.: The Political Geography of a Federal
Capital." *Journal of American Studies* 15(1):5–26.

Firth, Raymond (1973). *Symbols: Public and Private.* Ithaca: Cornell University Press.

Fischer, Roger A. (1980). "1896 Campaign Artifacts: A Study in Inferential
Reconstruction." *Journal of American Culture* 3:706–21.

Fisher, Sydney G. (1912). "The Legendary and Myth-Making Process in
Histories of the American Revolution." *Proceedings of the American
Philosophical Society* 51:53–75.

Fishwick, Marshall W. (1950). *A Bibliography of the American Hero.* Charlottesville: Bibliographical Society of America.

———— (1954). *American Heroes: Myth and Reality.* Washington, D.C.:
Public Affairs Press.

———— (1969). *The Hero, American Style.* New York: David McKay.

Fite, Gilbert C. (1952). *Mount Rushmore.* Norman: University of Oklahoma Press.

FitzGerald, Frances (1979). *America Revised: History Schoolbooks in the
Twentieth Century.* Boston: Little, Brown.

Fleming, E. McClung (1968). "Symbols of the United States: From Indian
Queen to Uncle Sam." Pp. 1–24 in Ray B. Browne, Richard H. Crowder,

Virgil L. Lokke, and William T. Stafford, eds., *Frontiers of American Culture.* Lafayette: Purdue University Studies.

―――― (1982). "The Great Seal." *American Heritage* 33(4):70–73.

Ford, Henry J. (1924), "The Liberty Bell." *American Mercury* 3:279–84.

Forgie, George B. (1979). *Patricide in the House Divided: A Psychological Interpretation of Lincoln and His Age.* New York: W. W. Norton.

Fox, Frederic (1972). "The National Day of Prayer." *Theology Today* 29(3):258–80.

Freitag, Ruth S., comp. (1969). *Presidential Inaugurations: A Selected List of References.* 3d ed. Washington, D.C.: Library of Congress.

Fresno Mall Art Committee (1973). *Publicly Owned Art in Fresno.* Fresno: Fresno County and City Chamber of Commerce.

Fried, Frederick (1964). *A Pictorial History of the Carousel.* New York: A. S. Barnes & Co.

Fried, Frederick, and Edmund V. Gillon, Jr. (1976). *New York Civic Sculpture: A Pictorial Guide.* New York: Dover.

Fried, Morton (1967). *The Evolution of Political Society.* New York: Random House.

Friedlander, Lee (1976). *The American Monument.* New York: Eakins.

Friedman, Lawrence J. (1975). *Inventors of the Promised Land.* New York: Knopf.

Frisch, Michael H. (1983). "The Unshakable Ikons of Grade-School History: An Empirical Inquiry." Paper presented at Biennial Meeting of the American Studies Association, Philadelphia.

Gabriel, Ralph Henry (1956). *The Course of American Democratic Thoughts.* 2d ed. New York: Ronald Press.

Galtung, Johan (1980). *The True Worlds: A Transnational Perspective.* New York: Free Press.

Gay, Vernon, and Marilyn Evert (1983). *Discovering Pittsburgh's Sculpture.* Pittsburgh: University of Pittsburgh Press.

Geist, Christopher D. (1978). "Historic Sites and Monuments as Icons." Pp. 57–66 in Ray B. Browne and Marshall Fishwick, eds., *Icons of America.* Bowling Green: Popular Press.

*Gellner, Ernest (1983). *Nations and Nationalism.* Ithaca: Cornell University Press.

Gerdts, William H. (1973). *American Neo-Classic Sculpture: The Marble Resurrection.* New York: Viking.

Gerth, Hans, and C. Wright Mills (1954). *Character and Social Structure: The Psychology of Social Institutions.* London: Routledge & Kegan Paul.

Gifford, Carey Jerome (1980). *Space and Time as Religious Symbols in Ante-Bellum America.* Ph.D. dissertation, Claremont Graduate School.

Ginsburg, Isidor (1933). "National Symbolism." Pp. 292–324 in Paul

Kosok, ed., *Modern Germany: A Study of Conflicting Loyalties.* Chicago: University of Chicago Press.

Glassie, Henry (1975). *Folk Housing in Middle Virginia.* Knoxville: University of Tennessee Press.

Goethals, Gregor T. (1981). *The TV Ritual: Worship at the Video Altar.* Boston: Beacon Press.

Goode, James M. (1974). *The Outdoor Sculpture of Washington.* Washington, D.C.: Smithsonian Institution Press.

Goodman, Paul (1969). *Growing Up Absurd.* New York: Random House.

Goodsell, Charles T. (1984). "The City Council Chamber: From Distance to Intimacy." *The Public Interest* 74:116–31.

Gottmann, Jean (1973). *The Significance of Territory.* Charlottesville: University Press of Virginia.

Gottschalk, Louis (1935). *Lafayette Comes to America.* Chicago: University of Chicago Press.

Gourévitch, Jean-Paul (1976). *L'Image politique.* Paris: Ligue Française de l'Enseignement et de l'Éducation Permanente.

Gowans, Alan (1964). *Images of American Living: Four Centuries of Architecture and Furniture as Cultural Expression.* Philadelphia: Lippincott.

———— (1966). *Building Canada: An Architectural History of Canadian Life.* Toronto: Oxford University Press.

———— (1968). "The Canadian National Style." Pp. 208–19 in W. L. Morton, ed., *The Shield of Achilles: Aspects of Canada in the Victorian Age.* Toronto and Montreal: McClelland & Stewart.

———— (1981). *Learning to See: Historical Perspectives on Modern Popular/Commercial Arts.* Bowling Green: Bowling Green University Popular Press.

———— (1982). Personal communication, May 2.

———— (1986). *The Comfortable House: North American Suburban Architecture, 1890–1930.* Cambridge: MIT Press.

Graebner, Oliver E. (1967). "Pastor and People at Kennedy's Casket." Pp. 315–25 in Richard D. Knudten, comp., *The Sociology of Religion: An Anthology.* New York: Appleton-Century-Crofts.

Greater Washington Board of Trade (n.d.). *The Case for Washington: Our Resources.* Washington, D.C.: Greater Washington Board of Trade.

Greeley, Andrew M. (1974). *Ethnicity in the United States: A Preliminary Reconnaissance.* New York: Wiley.

Green, Constance McLaughlin (1962–63). *Washington: Village and Capital, 1800–1878.* 2 vols. Princeton: Princeton University Press.

Green, Fletcher M. (1969). "Listen to the Eagle Scream: One Hundred Years of the Fourth of July in North Carolina, 1776–1876." Pp. 111–56 in

J. Isaac Copeland, ed., *Democracy in the Old South, and Other Essays by Fletcher Melvin Green*. Nashville: Vanderbilt University Press.

Greene, Jack P. (1969). "Search for Identity: An Interpretation of the Meaning of Selected Patterns of Social Response in Eighteenth-Century America." *Journal of Social History* 3:189–224.

Greene, Theodore P. (1970). *America's Heroes: The Changing Models of Success in American Magazines*. New York: Oxford University Press.

Greenstein, Fred I. (1965). *Children and Politics*. New Haven: Yale University Press.

Gruneau, Richard (1982). "Sport and the Debate on the State." Pp. 1–38 in Hart Cantelon and Richard Gruneau, eds., *Sport, Culture and the Modern State*. Toronto: University of Toronto Press.

Gulliford, Andrew (1981). *Country School Legacy: Humanities on the Frontier*. Silt, Colo.: Country School Legacy.

Gunderson, Robert Gray (1957). *The Log-Cabin Campaign*. Lexington: University of Kentucky Press.

Gutheim, Frederick, and Wilcomb E. Washburn (1976). *The Federal City: Plans and Realities*. Washington, D.C.: Smithsonian Institution Press.

Guttmann, Allen (1978). *From Ritual to Record: The Nature of Modern Sports*. New York: Columbia University Press.

Haas, Irvin (1974). *America's Historic Villages and Restorations*. New York: Arco.

———— (1976). *Historic Homes of the American Presidents*. New York: David McKay.

———— (1979). *Citadels, Ramparts and Stockades: America's Historic Forts*. New York: Everest House.

Hägerstrand, Torsten (1984). Personal communication, Dec.

Hagner, Alexander B. (1897). *Street Nomenclature of Washington City*. Address before Columbia Historical Society delivered May 3, 1897. Washington, D.C.: Alexander B. Hagner.

Halberstam, David (1970). "Baseball and the National Mythology." *Harper's* 241:22–25.

Hale, Edward Everett (1865). *The Man Without a Country*. Boston: Ticknor & Fields.

Hamlin, Talbot F. (1964). *Greek Revival Architecture*. New York: Dover.

Hammond, Phillip E. (1976). "The Sociology of American Civil Religion: A Bibliographic Essay." *Sociological Analysis* 2:169–82.

Hampton, William Judson (1928). *Presidential Shrines from Washington to Coolidge*. Boston: Christopher Publishing House.

Handlin, Oscar (1961). "The Civil War as Symbol and as Actuality." *Massachusetts Review* 3:133–43.

———— (1971). *Statue of Liberty*. New York: Newsweek.

Hapgood, David, and Meridan Bennett (1968). *Agents of Change: A Close Look at the Peace Corps.* Boston: Little, Brown.

Hargrove, June (1977). "A Social History of the Public Monument in Ohio." Pp. 22–64 in *The Public Monument and Its Audience.* Cleveland and Kent: Cleveland Museum of Art and Kent State University Press.

Harkness, Albert J. (1950). "Americanism and Jenkins's Ear." *Mississippi Valley Historical Review* 37:61–90.

Harper, Herbert L. (1971). "The Antebellum Courthouses of Tennessee." *Tennessee Historical Quarterly* 30:3–25.

Harris, Chauncy D. (1981). Personal communication, Aug. 24.

Harris, Louise (1971). *The Flag over the Schoolhouse.* Providence: Brown University.

Harris, Neil (1966). *The Artist in American Society: The Formative Years, 1790–1860.* New York: Braziller.

———— (1979). "Iconography and Intellectual History: The Half-Tone Effect." Pp. 196–211 in John Higham and Paul Conkin, eds., *New Directions in American Intellectual History.* Baltimore: Johns Hopkins University Press.

———— (1983). "John Philip Sousa and the Culture of Reassurance." Pp. 11–40 in Jon Newsom, ed., *Perspectives on John Philip Sousa.* Washington, D.C.: Library of Congress.

Harrison, Helen A., ed. (1980). *Dawn of a New Day: The New York World's Fair, 1939/40.* New York: New York University Press and Queens Museum.

———— (1983). "The Usable Past Meets the Usable Future: The 1939/40 New York World's Fair." Paper presented at the Biennial Meeting of the American Studies Association, Philadelphia.

Hartje, Robert G. (1973). *Bicentennial USA: Pathways to Celebration.* Nashville: American Association for State and Local History.

Hartmann, Edward George (1948). *The Movement to Americanize the Immigrant.* New York: Columbia University Press.

Hartz, Louis (1964). *The Founding of New Societies: Studies in the History of the United States, Latin America, South Africa, Canada, and Australia.* New York: Harcourt, Brace & World.

Harvey, David (1979). "Monument and Myth." *Annals of the Association of American Geographers* 69:362–81.

Harvey, Frederick L. (1903). *History of the Washington National Monument and Washington National Monument Society.* Washington, D.C.: Government Printing Office.

Hatch, Jane M., ed. (1978). *The American Book of Days.* 3d ed. New York: H. W. Wilson.

Hatch, Nathan O. (1977). *The Sacred Cause of Liberty: Republican Thought and the Millennium in Revolutionary New England.* New Haven: Yale University Press.

Hauptman, Laurence M. (1978). "Westward the Course of Empire: Geography Schoolbooks and Manifest Destiny, 1783–1893." *The Historian* 40:423–40.

Hay, Robert Pettus (1967). *Freedom's Jubilee: One Hundred Years of the Fourth of July, 1776–1876.* Ph.D. dissertation, University of Kentucky.

———— (1969a). "George Washington: American Moses." *American Quarterly* 21:780–91.

———— (1969b). "Providence and the American Past." *Indiana Magazine of History* 65(2):79–101.

*Hayes, Carlton J. H. (1926). *Essays on Nationalism.* New York: Russell.

———— (1931). *The Historical Evolution of Modern Nationalism.* New York: Richard R. Smith.

* ———— (1960). *Nationalism: A Religion.* New York: Macmillan.

Hazleton, John H. (1906). *The Declaration of Independence: Its History.* New York: Dodd, Mead.

Hébert, Bruno (1980). *Monuments et patrie: Une réflexion philosophique sur un fait historique: La célébration commémorative au Québec de 1881 à 1929.* Québec: Les Éditions Pleins Bords.

Hechter, Michael (1973). "The Persistence of Regionalism in the British Isles, 1885–1966." *American Journal of Sociology* 79(2):319–42.

Heilbroner, Robert L. (1974). *An Inquiry into the Human Prospect.* New York: W. W. Norton.

———— (1983). "Reflections: Economic Prospects." *The New Yorker* 59 (Aug. 29): 66–78.

Heimert, Alan (1966). *Religion and the American Mind: From the Great Awakening to the Revolution.* Cambridge: Harvard University Press.

Held, Daniel, and Joel Krieger (1984). "Theories of the State: Some Competing Claims." Pp. 1–20 in Stephen Bornstein, David Held, and Joel Krieger, eds., *The State in Capitalist Europe: A Casebook.* London: George Allen & Unwin.

Hélias, Pierre-Jakez (1978). *The Horse of Pride: Life in a Breton Village.* New Haven: Yale University Press.

Henrikson, Alan K. (1983). " 'A Small, Cozy Town, Global in Scope': Washington, D.C." *Ekistics* 50(299):123–45.

Herberg, Will (1960). *Protestant, Catholic, Jew: An Essay in American Religious Sociology.* Rev. ed. Garden City, N.Y.: Doubleday.

Herrick, Francis Hobart (1934). *The American Eagle.* New York: Appleton-Century.

Hess, Karl (1975). *Dear America.* New York: Wm. Morrow.

Hess, Stephen, and Milton Kaplan (1975). *The Ungentlemanly Art: A History of American Political Cartoons.* New York: Macmillan.

Higham, John (1984). "The Transformation of the Statue of Liberty." Pp. 71–80 in *Send These to Me: Immigrants in Urban America.* Rev. ed. Baltimore: Johns Hopkins University Press.

Hine, Thomas (1982). "The Roll is Written in Granite." *Philadelphia Inquirer.* Nov. 12, C-1, C-6.

Hinkel, John Vincent (1970). *Arlington: Monument to Heroes.* Rev. ed. Englewood Cliffs, N.J.: Prentice-Hall.

Hitchcock, Henry-Russell, and William Seale (1976). *Temples of Democracy: The State Capitols of the USA.* New York: Harcourt Brace Jovanovich.

Hobsbawm, Eric (1983a). "Introduction: Inventing Traditions." Pp. 1–14 in Eric Hobsbawm and Terence Ranger, eds., *The Invention of Tradition.* Cambridge: Cambridge University Press.

––––––– (1983b). "Mass-Producing Traditions: Europe, 1870–1914." Pp. 263–307 in Eric Hobsbawm and Terence Ranger, eds., *The Invention of Tradition.* Cambridge: Cambridge University Press.

Hoff, Carol (1967). *Holidays and History.* Austin, Tex.: Steck-Vaughn.

Hoffman, Daniel G. (1961). "Deaths and Three Resurrections of Davy Crockett." *Antioch Review* 21:5–13.

Hook, Sidney (1943). *The Hero in History: A Study in Limitation and Possibility.* Boston: Beacon Press.

Hoover Institution on War, Revolution, and Peace (1972). *War, Revolution, and Peace: Propaganda Posters from the Hoover Institution Archives.* Stanford: Hoover Institution on War, Revolution, and Peace.

Hope, Ashley Guy (1973). *Symbols of the Nations.* Washington, D.C.: Public Affairs Press.

Hornung, Clarence (1941). "The American Eagle, Symbol of Freedom." *American Artist* 5:10–13.

*Horwitz, Elinor Lander (1976). *The Bird, the Banner, and Uncle Sam: Images of America in Folk and Popular Art.* Philadelphia: Lippincott.

Hosmer, Charles B., Jr. (1965). *Presence of the Past: A History of the Preservation Movement in the United States before Williamsburg.* New York: Putnam's.

Howlett, Catherine M. (1985). "The Vietnam Veterans Memorial: Public Art and Politics." *Landscape* 28(2):1–9.

Hubbard, William (1984). "A Meaning for Monuments." *The Public Interest* 74:17–30.

Hudson, Winthrop S. (1971). "Fast Days and Civil Religion." Pp. 1–17 in

Winthrop S. Hudson and Leonard J. Trinterud, *Theology in Sixteenth and Seventeenth Century England*. Los Angeles: William Andrews Clark Memorial Library.

Huff, A. V., Jr. (1974). "The Eagle and the Vulture: Changing Attitudes toward Nationalism in Fourth of July Orations Delivered in Charleston 1778–1860." *South Atlantic Quarterly* 73:10–22.

Huizinga, Johan (1959). "Patriotism and Nationalism in European History." Pp. 97–155 in *Men and Ideas*. London: Eyre & Spottiswoode.

Humphrey, Edward Frank (1924). *Nationalism and Religion in America, 1774–1789*. Boston: Chapman Law Publishing Co.

Hunt, Gaillard (1909). *The History of the Seal of the United States*. Washington, D.C.: Department of State.

Hutton, Ann Hawkes (1959). *Portrait of Patriotism: "Washington Crossing the Delaware."* Philadelphia: Chilton.

Huxley, Aldous (1932). *Texts & Pretexts: An Anthology with Commentaries*. London: Chatto & Windus.

Hymans, Harold M. (1960). *To Try Men's Souls: Loyalty Tests in American History*. Berkeley: University of California Press.

Inkeles, Alex (1980). "The Emerging Social Structure of the World." Pp. 482–515 in Harold D. Lasswell, Daniel Lerner, and Hans Speier, eds., *Propaganda and Communication in World History*. Vol. 3, *A Pluralizing World in Formation*. Honolulu: University Press of Hawaii.

*Isaacs, Harold R. (1975). *Idols of the Tribes: Group Identity and Political Change*. New York: Harper & Row.

Isaacson, Philip M. (1975). *The American Eagle*. Boston: New York Graphic Society.

Jackson, J. B. (1972). *American Space: The Centennial Years 1865–1876*. New York: W. W. Norton.

――― (1980). "The Necessity for Ruins." Pp. 89–102 in J. B. Jackson, *The Necessity for Ruins and Other Topics*. Amherst: University of Massachusetts Press.

――― (1982). Personal communication, Nov. 20.

Jacobs, Allan B. (1985). *Looking at Cities*. Cambridge: Harvard University Press.

Jaffe, Irma B. (1976). *Trumbull: The Declaration of Independence*. New York: Viking.

Jessop, Bob (1982). *The Capitalist State: Marxist Theories and Methods*. Oxford: Martin Robertson.

Jewett, Robert, and John Shelton Lawrence (1977). *The American Monomyth*. Garden City, N.Y.: Doubleday.

John Ericsson Memorial Commission (1929). *Proceedings at the Unveiling of the Statue of John Ericsson in Potomac Park, Washington, D.C., under the Auspices of the John Ericsson Memorial Commission.* Washington, D.C.: Government Printing Office.

Johnson, Gerald W. (1953). *Mount Vernon: The Story of a Shrine.* New York: Random House.

Johnson, Hildegard Binder (1967). "The Location of Christian Missions in Africa." *Geographical Review* 57:168–202.

_____ (1976). *Order upon the Land: The U.S. Rectangular Land Survey and the Upper Mississippi Country.* New York: Oxford University Press.

_____ (1982). Personal communication, Aug. 24.

Johnson, Philip C. (1945). "War Memorials: What Aesthetic Price Glory?" *Art News* 44:9–10, 24–25.

Jones, Alfred Haworth (1974). *Roosevelt's Image Brokers: Poets, Playwrights, and the Use of the Lincoln Symbol.* Port Washington, N.Y.: Kennikat Press.

Jones, Cranston (1962). *Homes of the American Presidents.* New York: Bonanza Books.

Jones, E. L. (1981). *The European Miracle: Environments, Economies, and Geopolitics in the History of Europe and Asia.* Cambridge: Cambridge University Press.

Jones, H. G. (1969). *The Records of a Nation: Their Management, Preservation, and Use.* New York: Atheneum.

*Jones, Howard Mumford (1964). *O Strange New World. American Culture: The Formative Years.* New York: Viking.

Jones, Louis C. (1975). *Outward Signs of Inner Beliefs: Symbols of American Patriotism: A Bicentennial Exhibit.* Cooperstown: New York State Historical Association.

Jones, Thomas C., ed. (1977). *The Halls of Fame: Featuring Specialized Museums of Sports, Agronomy, Entertainment and the Humanities.* Chicago: J. G. Ferguson Publishing Co.

Jowett, Garth (1976). *Film: The Democratic Art.* Boston: Little, Brown.

Judd, Denis (1972). *Posters of World War Two.* London: Wayland.

Kamenka, Eugene (1976). "Political Nationalism—the Evolution of the Idea." Pp. 2–20 in Eugene Kamenka, ed., *Nationalism: The Nature and Evolution of an Idea.* New York: St. Martin's.

*Kammen, Michael (1978). *A Season of Youth: The American Revolution and the Historical Imagination.* New York: Knopf.

_____ (1980). "In Search of America." *Historic Preservation* 32:30–39.

_____ (1986a). *The Machine That Would Go of Itself: The Constitution in American Culture.* New York: Knopf.

_____ (1986b). *Spheres of Liberty: Changing Perceptions of Liberty in*

American Culture. Madison: University of Wisconsin Press.

Kane, Joseph Nathan (1960). *The American Counties.* New York: Scarecrow Press.

Karp, Walter (1979). *The Politics of War: The Story of Two Wars Which Altered Forever the Political Life of the American Republic (1890–1920).* New York: Harper & Row.

*Karsten, Peter (1978). *Patriot-Heroes in England and America: Political Symbolism and Changing Values over Three Centuries.* Madison: University of Wisconsin Press.

Keay, Carolyn (1975). *American Posters of the Turn of the Century.* New York: St. Martin's.

Kedourie, Elie (1961). *Nationalism.* 2d ed. London: Hutchinson.

Kennedy, P. M. (1973). "The Decline of Nationalistic History in the West, 1900–1970." *Journal of Contemporary History* 8:77–100.

Ketcham, Ralph (1974). *From Colony to Country: The Revolution in American Thought, 1750–1820.* New York: Macmillan.

Ketchum, Alton (1959). *Uncle Sam: The Man and the Legend.* New York: Hill & Wang.

Killian, Lewis M. (1970). *White Southerners.* New York: Random House.

King, James Clement (1935). *Some Elements of National Solidarity.* Dissertation abstract. Chicago: University of Chicago Libraries.

Klamkin, Marian (1973). *American Patriotic and Political China.* New York: Scribner's.

Klapp, Orrin E. (1949). "Hero Worship in America." *American Sociological Review* 14:53–62.

——— (1962). *Heroes, Villains, and Fools: The Changing American Character.* Englewood Cliffs, N.J.: Prentice-Hall.

Knight, David B. (1971). "Impress of Authority and Ideology on Landscape: A Review of Some Unanswered Questions." *Tijdschrift voor Economische en Sociale Geographie* 63:383–87.

——— (1982). "Identity and Territory: Geographical Perspectives on Nationalism and Regionalism." *Annals of the Association of American Geographers* 72:514–31.

Knittle, Rhea Mansfield (1927). *Early American Glass.* New York: Century.

Knock, Thomas J. (1978). " 'History with Lightning': The Forgotten Film *Wilson.*" Pp. 95–115 in Leila Zenderland, ed., *Recycling the Past: Popular Uses of American History.* Philadelphia: University of Pennsylvania Press.

Koch, Koen (1980). "The New Marxist Theory of the State or the Rediscovery of the Limitations of a Structural-Functionalist Paradigm." *Neth-*

erlands Journal of Sociology 19:1–19.

Kohn, Hans (1944). *The Idea of Nationalism: A Study in Its Origins and Background.* New York: Macmillan.

——— (1957). *American Nationalism: An Interpretative Essay.* New York: Macmillan.

——— (1962). *The Age of Nationalism: The First Era of Global History.* New York: Harper.

Kosiński, Leszek A. (1980). *Yugoslavs in Canada.* Occasional Paper 2. Edmonton: University of Alberta, Division of East European Studies.

Kouwenhoven, John Atlee, and Lawton M. Patten (1937). "New Light on 'The Star-Spangled Banner.'" *Musical Quarterly* 22:198–200.

Kraske, Robert (1972). *America the Beautiful: Stories of Patriotic Songs.* Champaign, Ill.: Garrard.

Kraus, Michael (1928). *Intercolonial Aspects of American Culture on the Eve of Revolution, with Special Reference to the Northern Towns.* New York: Columbia University Press.

——— (1953). *The Writing of American History.* Norman: University of Oklahoma Press.

Krause, Chester L., and Clifford Mishler (1973). *Standard Catalog of World Coins.* 2d ed. Iola, Wisc.: Krause Publications.

Kropotkin, Peter (1968). *Fields, Factories and Workshops.* New York and London: Benjamin Blom. First published 1913.

Krout, John Allen, and Dixon Ryan Fox (1944). *The Completion of American Independence, 1790–1830.* New York: Macmillan.

Krythe, Maymie Richardson (1968). *What So Proudly We Hail.* New York: Harper & Row.

Kumar, Martha Joynt (1983). "Presidential Libraries: Gold Mine, Booby Trap, or Both?" Pp. 199–224 in George C. Edwards III and Stephen J. Wayne, eds., *Studying the Presidency.* Knoxville: University of Tennessee Press.

Laas, William (1972). *Monuments in Your History.* New York: Popular Library.

Laird, Archibald (1971). *Monuments Marking the Graves of the Presidents.* North Quincy, Mass.: Christopher Publishing House.

——— (1980). *The Near Great—Chronicle of the Vice Presidents.* North Quincy, Mass.: Christopher Publishing House.

Lambert, Phyllis (1978). "The Record of Buildings as Evidence." Pp. 10–13 in Richard Pare, ed., *Court House: A Photographic Document.* New York: Horizon.

Lang, Kurt, and Gladys Engel (1968). "MacArthur Day in Chicago." Pp. 36–77 in Kurt Lang and Gladys Engel, *Politics and Television.* Chicago: Quadrangle Books.

Larson, Cedric (1940). "Patriotism in Carmine: 162 Years of July 4th Oratory." *Quarterly Journal of Speech* 26(1):12–25.

Larson, Gary O. (1983). *The Reluctant Patron: The United States Government and the Arts, 1943–1965*. Philadelphia: University of Pennsylvania Press.

Lassen, Harry C. (1985). Personal communication, May 10.

Lasswell, Harold D. (1966). "Nations and Classes: The Symbols of Identification." Pp. 27–42 in Bernard Berelson and Morris Janowitz, eds., *Reader in Public Opinion and Communication*. 2d ed. New York: Free Press. First published 1935.

Latourette, Kenneth Scott (1937–45). *A History of the Expansion of Christianity*. 7 vols. New York: Harper & Brothers.

Lawrence, Vera Brodsky (1975). *Music for Patriots, Politicians, and Presidents: Harmonies and Discords of the First Hundred Years*. New York: Macmillan.

Lebovich, William L. (1984). *America's City Hall*. Washington: Preservation Press.

Leclercq, Jean-Michel (1979). *La nation et son idéologie*. Paris: Éditions Anthropos.

Lee, Antoinette J. (1982). "From Patriotism to Profits: Historic Preservation in the United States." Paper presented at Annual Meeting of the Association of American Geographers, San Antonio.

Leighly, John B. (1985). Personal communication, May 7.

Lemberg, Eugen (1964). *Der Nationalismus: Psychologie und Geschichte*. Munich: Rowohlt.

Lemisch, Jesse (1976). "Bicentennial Schlock." *New Republic* 175 (Nov. 6): 21–23.

Lenggenhager, Werner (1967–70). *Historical Markers and Monuments of the State of Washington*. 2 vols. Seattle: Werner Lenggenhager.

Leopold-Sharp, Lynne A. (1980). "The Emergence of American Identity: Words and Images on Paper." Pp. 26–53 in John C. Milley, ed., *Treasures of Independence: Independence National Historical Park and Its Collections*. New York: Mayflower Books.

Lerner, Max (1937). "The Constitution and the Court as Symbols." *Yale Law Journal* 46:1290–1319.

Lever, Janet (1969). "Soccer: Opium of the Brazilian People." *Transaction* 7 (Dec.): 36–43.

Lewis, Bernard (1975). *History Remembered, Recovered, Invented*. Princeton: Princeton University Press.

Lewis, David L. (1976). *The Public Image of Henry Ford: An American Folk Hero and His Company*. Detroit: Wayne State University Press.

Lewis, Lloyd (1929). *Myths after Lincoln*. New York: Harcourt, Brace.

Lewis, Peter G. (1982). "The Politics of Iranian Place-Names." *Geographical Review* 72:99–102.

Lewis, Read (1930). "Americanization." Vol. 2, pp. 31–33, in *Encyclopedia of the Social Sciences*. New York: Macmillan.

*Liebman, Charles S., and Eliezer Don-Yehiya (1983). *Civil Religion in Israel: Traditional Judaism and Political Culture in the Jewish State*. Berkeley: University of California Press.

Lindsey, Bessie M. (1967). *American Historical Glass*. Rutland, Vt.: Charles E. Tuttle.

Lipset, Seymour Martin (1963). *The First New Nation: The United States in Historical and Comparative Perspective*. New York: Basic Books.

———— (1965). "Revolution and Counter-Revolution—the United States and Canada." Pp. 21–64 in Thomas R. Ford, ed., *The Revolutionary Theme in Contemporary America*. Lexington: University of Kentucky Press.

Little, David B. (1961). *America's First Centennial Celebration: The Nineteenth of April 1875 at Lexington and Concord, Massachusetts*. Boston: Club of Odd Volumes.

Lofaro, Michael A., ed. (1985). *Davy Crockett: The Man, the Legend, the Legacy*. Knoxville: University of Tennessee Press.

Longstreet, Donna M., and Sandra J. Lamprecht (1975). "Spirit of '76. U.S. Government Documents and the Bicentennial: A Selected Bibliography." *California Librarian* 36 (Oct.): 13–30.

Lott, Albert J., and Bernice E. Lott (1963). "Ethnocentrism and Space Superiority Judgments Following Cosmonaut and Astronaut Flights." *Public Opinion Quarterly* 27:604–11.

Loubat, J. F. (1878). *The Medallic History of the United States of America, 1776–1876*. New York: J. F. Loubat.

Love, W. DeLoss (1895). *The Fast and Thanksgiving Days of New England*. Boston: Houghton Mifflin.

———— (1904). "The Day We Celebrate: From the Journal of a Country Parson, 1836–1860, Being a Record of Fourth of July from 1836 to 1860." *Atlantic Monthly* 94 (July): 108–13.

Loveland, Anne C. (1971). *Emblem of Liberty: The Image of Lafayette in the American Mind*. Baton Rouge: Louisiana State University Press.

Lowenthal, David (1966). "The American Way of History." *Columbia University Forum* 9(3):27–32.

———— (1976). "The Place of the Past in the American Landscape." Pp. 89–117 in David Lowenthal and Martyn J. Bowden, eds., *Geographies of the Mind*. New York: Oxford University Press.

———— (1977). "The Bicentennial Landscape: A Mirror Held Up to the Past." *Geographical Review* 67:253–67.

———— (1985). *The Past Is a Foreign Country.* Cambridge: Cambridge University Press.

Lowenthal, Leo (1956). "Biographies in Popular Magazines." Pp. 63–118 in William Peterson, ed., *American Social Patterns.* Garden City, N.Y.: Doubleday.

Lucas, John A. (1973). "The Modern Olympic Games: Fanfare and Philosophy." *Maryland Historian* 4(2):71–87.

Lynch, Kenneth (1979). *The Book of Garden Ornament.* Canterbury, Conn.: Canterbury Publishing Co.

Lynn, Robert Wood (1973). "Civil Catechetics in Mid-Victorian America: Some Notes about American Civil Religion, Past and Present." *Religious Education* 68:5–27.

Maass, John (1970). "Architecture and Americanism or Pastiches of Independence Hall." *Historic Preservation* 22 (April–June): 17–25.

———— (1973). *The Glorious Enterprise: The Centennial Exhibition of 1876 and H. J. Schwarsmann, Architect-in-Chief.* Watkins Glen, N.Y.: American Life Foundation.

———— (1976a). "The Declaration of Independence." *Antiques* 110(1):106–10.

———— (1976b). "Historic Preservation and the National Mythology." *Monumentum* 13:35–44.

MacCann, Richard Dyer (1973). *The People's Films: A Political History of U.S. Government Motion Pictures.* New York: Hastings House.

McCardell, John (1979). *The Idea of a Southern Nation: Southern Nationalists and Southern Nationalism, 1830–1860.* New York: W. W. Norton.

McClintock, Inez, and Marshall McClintock (1961). *Toys in America.* Washington, D.C.: Public Affairs Press.

McCoy, Donald R. (1978). *The National Archives: America's Ministry of Documents, 1934–1968.* Chapel Hill: University of North Carolina Press.

McDonald, Forrest, and Ellen Shapiro McDonald (1980), "Ethnic Origins of the American People, 1790." *William and Mary Quarterly,* 3d series 38(2):179–99.

McDonald, Forrest, and Grady McWhiney (1975). "The Antebellum Herdsman: A Re-Interpretation." *Journal of Southern History* 41:147–66.

———— (1980). "The Celtic South." *History Today* 30 (July): 11–15.

McDowell, Jennifer (1974). "Soviet Civil Ceremonies." *Journal for the Scientific Study of Religion* 13:265–79.

MacIntire, Jane Bacon (1967). *Lafayette, the Guest of the Nation: The Tracing of the Route of Lafayette's Tour of the United States in 1824–25.* Newton, Mass.: Anthony J. Simone.

McKinzie, Richard D. (1973). *The New Deal for Artists.* Princeton: Princeton University Press.

MacLeod, Anne Scott (1975). *A Moral Tale: Children's Fiction and American Culture, 1820–1860*. Hamden, Conn.: Archon Books.

MacRae, Marion, and Anthony Adamson (1983). *Cornerstone of Order: Courthouses and Town Halls of Ontario, 1784–1914*. Toronto: Clarke Irwin.

McWhiney, Grady, and Forrest McDonald (1983). "Celtic Names in the Antebellum Southern United States." *Names* 31:89–102.

Madsen, David (1966). *The National University: Enduring Dream of the USA*. Detroit: Wayne State University Press.

Malone, Dumas (1954). *The Story of the Declaration of Independence*. New York: Oxford University Press.

Malone, Kemp (1925). "A Linguistic Patriot." *American Speech* 1(1):26–31.

Manson, George J. (1900). "A Renaissance of Patriotism." *The Independent* 52:1612–15.

Manwaring, David (1962). *Render unto Caesar, The Flag Salute Controversy*. Chicago: University of Chicago Press.

Marienstras, Elise (1976). *Les mythes fondateurs de la nation Américaine: Essai sur le discours idéologique aux États-Unis à l'époque de l'indépendance (1763–1800)*. Paris: François Maspero.

Markoff, John, and Daniel Regan (1981). "The Rise and Fall of Civil Religion: Comparative Perspectives." *Sociological Analysis* 42:333–52.

Marling, Karal Ann (1982). *Wall-To-Wall America: A Cultural History of Post-Office Murals in the Great Depression*. Minneapolis: University of Minnesota Press.

Marling, Karal Ann, and Robert Silberman (1985), "Abstraction or Realism: Vietnam Remembered." Paper presented at Tenth Biennial Convention of American Studies, San Diego.

Martin, Howard H. (1958). "The Fourth of July Oration." *Quarterly Journal of Speech* 44(4):393–401.

Martin, Kingsley (1962). *The Magic of the British Monarchy*. Boston: Little, Brown.

Marx, Leo (1964). *The Machine in the Garden: Technology and the Pastoral Ideal in America*. New York: Oxford University Press.

Mason, Philip (1970). *Patterns of Dominance*. London: Oxford University Press.

*Mastai, Boleslaw, and Marie-Louise D'Otrange (1973). *The Stars and the Stripes: The American Flag as Art and as History from the Birth of the Republic to the Present*. New York: Knopf.

Mathews, Albert (1901). "Brother Jonathan." *Transactions, Colonial Society of Massachusetts* 7:94–119.

———— (1906). "Celebrations of Washington's Birthday." *Publications of the Colonial Society of Massachusetts* 10:252–58.

———— (1908). "Uncle Sam." *American Antiquarian Society Proceedings,* n.s. 19:21–65.

———— (1926). "Centennial Celebrations." *Publications of the Colonial Society of Massachusetts* 26:402–26.

Mathews, Donald G. (1969). "The Second Great Awakening as an Organizing Process, 1780–1830: An Hypothesis." *American Quarterly* 21:23–43.

Mathews, M. M., ed. (1931). *The Beginnings of American English.* Chicago: University of Chicago Press.

Mathisen, James A. (1986). "From Civil Religion to Folk Religion: The Case of American Sport." Paper presented at the meeting of the Society for the Scientific Study of Religion, Washington, D.C.

Mayo, Bernard (1959). *Myths and Men: Patrick Henry, George Washington, Thomas Jefferson.* Athens: University of Georgia Press.

Mead, Sidney E. (1963). *The Lively Experiment.* New York: Harper & Row.

———— (1967). "The Nation with the Soul of a Church." *Church History* 36(3):262–83.

———— (1977). *The Old Religion in the Brave New World: Reflections on the Relation between Christendom and the Republic.* Berkeley: University of California Press.

Meade, Robert D. (1957). *Patrick Henry, Patriot in the Making.* Philadelphia: Lippincott.

Meadows, Paul (1945). "Some Notes on the Social Psychology of the Hero." *Southwestern Social Science Quarterly* 26:239–47.

Meinig, Donald W. (1982). "New York and Its Neighbors: Some Problems of Regional Interpretation." Pp. 69–108 in Manfred Jonas and Robert V. Wells, eds., *New Opportunities in a New Nation: The Development of New York after the Revolution.* Syracuse: Syracuse University Press.

———— (1986). *The Shaping of America: A Geographical Perspective on 500 Years of History.* Vol. 1, *Atlantic America, 1492–1800.* New Haven: Yale University Press.

————, ed. (1979). *The Interpretation of Ordinary Landscapes: Geographical Essays.* New York: Oxford University Press.

Melder, Keith E. (1976). *The Village and the Nation.* Sturbridge, Mass.: Old Sturbridge Village.

Melville, Herman (1850). *White-Jacket or the World in a Man-of-War.* New York: Harper & Brothers.

Mergen, Bernard (1983). "Artifacts as Historical Documents: The Aesthetics and Politics of the Marine Corps War Memorial and the Vietnam

Veterans Memorial." Paper presented at the Biennial Meeting of American Studies Association, Philadelphia.

Merk, Frederick (1963). *Manifest Destiny and Mission in American History: A Reinterpretation.* New York: Knopf.

*Merriam, Charles Edward (1931). *The Making of Citizens: A Comparative Study of Methods of Civic Training.* Chicago: University of Chicago Press.

Merritt, Richard L. (1966a). "Nation-Building in America: The Colonial Years." Pp. 56–72 in Karl Deutsch and William Foltz, eds., *Nation-Building.* New York: Atherton.

———— (1966b). *Symbols of American Community, 1735–1775.* New Haven: Yale University Press.

Meyrowitz, Joshua (1985). *No Sense of Place: The Impact of Electronic Media on Social Behavior.* New York: Oxford University Press.

Michaelsen, Robert (1970). *Piety in the Public Schools.* New York: Macmillan.

Mickelson, Peter (1968). "Nationalism in Minnesota during the Spanish-American War." *Minnesota History* 41:1–12.

Middelkauff, Robert (1970). "The Ritualization of the American Revolution." Pp. 31–43 in Stanley Coben and Lorman Ratner, eds., *The Development of an American Culture.* Englewood Cliffs, N.J.: Prentice-Hall.

Miles, Edwin A. (1974). "The Young American Nation and the Classical World." *Journal of the History of Ideas* 35:259–74.

Miliband, Ralph (1969). *The State in Capitalist Society.* New York: Basic Books.

Miller, Glenn (1976). "The American Revolution as a Religious Event: An Essay in Political Theology." *Foundations: A Baptist Journal of History and Theology,* no. 2:111–20.

Miller, Lillian B. (1966). *Patrons and Patriotism: The Encouragement of the Fine Arts in the United States, 1790–1860.* Chicago: University of Chicago Press.

———— (1967). "Paintings, Sculpture, and the National Character, 1815–1860." *Journal of American History* 53:696–707.

Milley, John C. (1980). *Treasures of Independence: Independence National Historical Park and Its Collections.* New York: Mayflower Books.

Milton, Brian Gerard (1972). *Sport as a Functional Equivalent of Religion.* Master's thesis, University of Wisconsin.

Minnich, Harvey C. (1936). *William Holmes McGuffey and His Readers.* New York: American Book Co.

Minott, Rodney G. (1962). *Peerless Patriots: Organized Veterans and the Spirit of Americanism.* Washington, D.C.: Public Affairs Press.

Mollenhoff, Gjore (1983). "VA National Cemeteries: America's Military

Dead and Military Culture." Paper presented at the Biennial Meeting of American Studies Association, Philadelphia.

Moore, Frank (1846). *Songs and Ballads of the American Revolution*. New York: Appleton.

Morris, Richard B. (1970). *The Emerging Nations and the American Revolution*. New York: Harper & Row.

———— (1977). " 'We the People of the United States': The Bicentennial of a People's Revolution." *American Historical Review* 82:1–19.

Mosse, George L. (1975). *The Nationalization of the Masses*. New York: Fertig.

———— (1976). "Mass Politics and the Political Liturgy of Nationalism." Pp. 38–54 in Eugene Kamenka, ed., *Nationalism: The Nature and Evolution of an Idea*. New York: St. Martin's.

———— (1979). "National Cemeteries and National Revival: The Cult of the Fallen Soldiers in Germany." *Journal of Contemporary History* 14:1–20.

Moynehan, B. (1980). "Seneca Falls Rises: From Laundromat to Women's Rights National Park." *Ms. Magazine* 8 (Jan.): 26.

Mrozek, Donald J. (1983). *Sport and American Mentality, 1880–1910*. Knoxville: University of Tennessee Press.

Murray, Robert K., and Tim H. Blessing (1983). "The Presidential Performance Study—a Progress Report." *Journal of American History* 70:535–55.

Myers, Robert J. (1972). *Celebrations: The Complete Book of American Holidays*. Garden City, N.Y.: Doubleday.

Nagel, Paul C. (1964). *One Nation Indivisible: The Union in American Thought, 1776–1861*. New York: Oxford University Press.

———— (1971). *This Sacred Trust: American Nationality, 1798–1898*. New York: Oxford University Press.

———— (1975). "Historiography and American Nationalism: Some Difficulties." *Canadian Review of Studies in Nationalism* 2(2):225–37.

Nairn, Tom (1977). *The Break-Up of Britain: Crisis and Neo-Nationalism*. London: New Left Books.

Namenwirth, J. Zvi, and Harold D. Lasswell (1970). *The Changing Language of American Values: A Computer Study of Selected Party Platforms*. Comparative Politics Series, vol. 1. Beverly Hills: Sage Publications.

Nash, Roderick (1970). "The American Invention of National Parks." *American Quarterly* 22:726–35.

National Capital Planning Commission (1978). *Tourist, Business Visitor and Convention Activities, 1976. Phase I*. Washington, D.C.: National Capital Planning Commission.

—— (1984a). *Comprehensive Plan for the National Capital. Visitors to the National Capital. Planning Report.* Washington, D.C.: National Capital Planning Commission.

—— (1984b). *Comprehensive Plan for the National Capital. Visitors to the National Capital. Proposed Federal Element.* Washington, D.C.: National Capital Planning Commission.

National Family Opinion (1959). *We Asked 10,000 Families about the American Flag.* Toledo: National Family Opinion.

Nawrocki, Dennis Alan (1980). *Art in Detroit Public Places.* Detroit: Wayne State University Press.

Neil, J. Meredith (1975). *Toward a National Taste: America's Quest for Aesthetic Independence.* Honolulu: University of Hawaii Press.

Neill, Stephen (1964). *Christian Missions.* Grand Rapids: Wm. B. Eerdmans Publishing Co.

Nelson, Mary Anne (1975). *Toponyms of Rural Schools in McLean County, Illinois: A Study in Cultural Processes.* Master's thesis, Illinois State Normal University.

Nettl, Bruno (1967). *National Anthems.* 2d ed. New York: Frederick Ungar.

Nevitte, Neil (1979). "Nationalism, States and Nations." Pp. 343–59 in Elliot J. Feldman and Neil Nevitte, eds., *The Future of North America.* Harvard Studies in International Affairs, no. 42. Cambridge: Center for International Affairs.

New York State Historical Association (1975). *Outward Signs of Inner Beliefs: Symbols of American Patriotism: A Bicentennial Exhibit.* Cooperstown, N.Y.: New York State Historical Association.

Nicolaisen, W. F. H. (1976). "Words as Names." *Onoma* 20:142–63.

—— (1979). " 'Distorted Function' in Material Aspects of Culture." *Folklore Forum* 12(2/3):223–35.

Nietz, John A. (1961). *Old Textbooks.* Pittsburgh: University of Pittsburgh Press.

Nisbet, Robert (1974). "The Decline of Academic Nationalism." *Change* 6(6):26–31.

*—— (1975). *Twilight of Authority.* New York: Oxford University Press.

Noah, Harold J., Carl E. Prince, and C. Russell Riggs (1962). "History in High School Texts: A Note." *School Review* 70:415–36.

Nora, Pierre (1984a). "Entre mémoire et histoire: La problématique des lieux." Pp. xvii–xlii in Pierre Nora, ed., *Les lieux de mémoire.* Vol. 1, *La République.* Paris: Gallimard.

——, ed. (1984b). *Les lieux de mémoire.* Vol. 1, *La République.* Paris: Gallimard.

Novak, Barbara (1980). *Nature and Culture: American Landscape and*

Painting, 1825–1876. New York: Oxford University Press.

Novak, Michael (1974). *Choosing Our King: Powerful Symbols in Presidential Politics.* New York: Macmillan.

*———— (1976). *The Joy of Sports: End Zones, Bases, Baskets, Balls, and the Consecration of the American Spirit.* New York: Basic Books.

Noverr, Douglas A., and Lawrence E. Ziewacz (1983). *The Games They Played: Sports in American History, 1865–1980.* Chicago: Nelson-Hall.

Nugent, Walter (1979). "The American People and the Centennial of 1876." *Indiana Magazine of History* 75:53–69.

Nye, Russel Blaine (1960). *The Cultural Life of the New Nation, 1776–1830.* London: Hamish Hamilton.

*———— (1966). *This Almost Chosen People: Essays in the History of American Ideas.* East Lansing: Michigan State University Press.

Ohman, Marian M. (1985). *A History of Missouri's Counties, County Seats, and Courthouse Squares.* Columbia: University of Missouri, Columbia Extension Division.

Orkin, Mark H. (1970). *Speaking Canadian English: An Informal Account of the English Language in Canada.* Toronto: General Publishing.

Orlansky, Harold (1947). "Reactions to the Death of President Roosevelt." *Journal of Social Psychology* 26:235–66.

Orwell, George (1938). *Homage to Catalonia.* London: Secker & Warburg.

———— (1950). "The Sporting Spirit." Pp. 151–55 in *Shooting an Elephant, and Other Essays.* New York: Harcourt, Brace & World.

———— (1953). *England Your England, and Other Essays.* London: Secker & Warburg.

Ozouf, Mona (1976). *La fête révolutionnaire, 1789–1799.* Paris: Gallimard.

Palmer, Robert R. (1940). "The National Idea in France before the Revolution." *Journal of the History of Ideas* 1:95–111.

———— (1976). "The Impact of the American Revolution Abroad." Pp. 5–19 in *The Impact of the American Revolution Abroad.* Washington, D.C.: Library of Congress.

Pare, Richard, ed. (1978). *Court House: A Photographic Document.* New York: Horizon.

Patterson, John S. (1974). "Zapped at the Map: The Battlefield at Gettysburg." *Journal of Popular Culture* 7(4):825–37.

———— (1982). "A Patriotic Landscape: Gettysburg, 1863–1913." Vol. 7, pp. 315–33, in Jack Salzman, ed., *Prospects: The Annual of American Cultural Studies.* New York: Burt Franklin & Co.

Patterson, Richard S., and Richardson Dougall (1976). *The Eagle and the Shield: A History of the Great Seal of the United States.* Washington, D.C.: Department of State.

Pattison, William D. (1967). *Beginnings of the American Rectangular Sur-*

vey System, 1784–1800. Research Paper no. 50. Chicago: University of Chicago, Department of Geography.

Pauli, Hertha, and E. B. Ashton (1969). *I Lift My Lamp, the Way of a Symbol.* Port Washington, N.Y.: Ira J. Friedman. First published in 1948.

Pauly, Thomas H. (1978). "In Search of 'The Spirit of '76.'" Pp. 29–49 in Leila Zenderland, ed., *Recycling the Past: Popular Uses of American History.* Philadelphia: University of Pennsylvania Press.

*Peterson, Merrill D. (1960). *The Jefferson Image in the American Mind.* New York: Oxford University Press.

Pevsner, Nikolaus (1976). *A History of Building Types.* Bollingen Series 35. Vol. 19 of the Mellon Lectures in the Fine Arts. Princeton: Princeton University Press.

Phelps, David (1985). "Controversy Dogs Korean War Memorial Booster." *Minneapolis Star and Tribune,* Oct. 20.

Piaget, J., and Anne-Marie Weil (1951). "The Development in Children of the Idea of the Homeland and of Relations with Other Countries." *International Social Science Bulletin* 3:561–78.

Pierce, Bessie Louise (1930). *Civic Attitudes in American School Textbooks.* Chicago: University of Chicago Press.

––––– (1933). *Citizens' Organizations and the Civic Training of Youth.* New York: Scribner's.

Pinckney, Pauline A. (1940). *American Figureheads and Their Carvers.* New York: W. W. Norton.

Pious, Richard M. (1979). *The American Presidency.* New York: Basic Books.

Pisney, Raymond F. (1977). *Historical Markers: A Bibliography.* Verona, Va.: McClure Press.

Pizor, Faith K. (1970). "Preparations for the Centennial Exhibition of 1876." *Pennsylvania Magazine of History and Biography* 94:213–32.

Plongeron, Bernard (1982). "Religion et nationalisme aux États-Unis au cours de l'indépendance." *Annales Historiques de la Révolution Française,* no. 249:416–39.

Plumb, J. H. (1970). *The Death of the Past.* Boston: Houghton Mifflin.

Polanyi, Karl (1944). *The Great Transformation.* New York: Rinehart.

Porter, Philip W., and Fred E. Lukermann (1975). "The Geography of Utopia." Pp. 197–233 in David Lowenthal and Martyn J. Bowden, eds., *Geographies of the Mind.* New York: Oxford University Press.

Post, Robert C., ed. (1976). *1876: A Centennial Exhibition.* Washington: Smithsonian Institution.

Postman, Neil (1985). *Amusing Ourselves to Death: Public Discourse in the Age of Show Business.* New York: Viking.

Potok, Chaim (1973). "Heroes for an Ordinary World." Pp. 71–76 in Robert

M. Hutchins and Mortimer J. Adler, eds., *The Great Ideas Today.* Chicago: Encyclopedia Britannica.

Potter, David M. (1954). "Nathan Hale and the Ideal of American Union." *Connecticut Antiquarian* 6:20–26.

Poulsen, Thomas M. (1986). "A Nation Is Not a State—and Vice Versa." *The American Philatelist* 100(1):59–62.

Powell, Barbara MacDonald (1983). *The Most Celebrated Encampment: Valley Forge in American Culture, 1777–1983.* Ph.D. dissertation, Cornell University.

Prebish, Charles S. (1982). "Sport Religion: The New Nirvana." *Women's Sports* 4 (Sept.): 58, 60.

―――― (n.d.). "Religion and Sport: Convergence or Identity?" Unpublished paper. University Park, Pa.

Prince, Hugh (1981). Personal communication, Sept. 1.

Prost, Antoine (1984). "Les monuments aux morts." Pp. 195–225 in Pierre Nora, ed., *Les lieux de mémoire.* Vol. 1, *La République.* Paris: Gallimard.

Pullen, John J. (1971). *Patriotism in America: A Study of Changing Devotion.* New York: American Heritage Press.

Quaife, Milo Milton (1942). *The Flag of the United States.* New York: Grosset & Dunlap.

Quaife, Milo Milton, Melvin J. Weig, and Roy E. Appleman (1961). *The History of the United States Flag.* New York: Harper.

Rabbow, Arnold (1970). *Lexicon Politischer Symbole.* Munich: Deutscher Taschenbuch Verlag.

―――― (1980). "A New Constellation—Wie sah das erste Sternbanner aus? (What Did the First Stars and Stripes Look Like?)." 2d Special Edition of the *Flag Plaza Standard.* Pittsburgh: National Flag Foundation.

Rabinowitz, Howard N. (1978). "George Washington as Icon, 1865–1900." Pp. 67–86 in Ray B. Browne and Marshall Fishwick, eds., *Icons of America.* Bowling Green: Popular Press.

Raglan, Lord (1949). *The Hero: A Study in Tradition, Myth, and Drama.* London: Watts & Co.

Rainey, Reuben M. (1983). "The Memory of War: Reflections on Battlefield Preservation." Vol. 1, pp. 69–89, in *Yearbook of Landscape Architecture.* New York: Van Nostrand Reinhold.

Rand McNally & Co. (1982). *1982 Commercial Atlas and Marketing Guide.* 113th ed. Chicago: Rand McNally & Co.

Randall, John C. (1969). "Patriotism and Humanitarian Reform in Children's Literature, 1825–1860." *American Quarterly* 21:3–22.

Rayburn, Alan (1983). "Nationalism in Canada's Geographical Names." Paper presented at the Annual Meeting of American Name Society.

Reed, John Shelton (1972). *The Enduring South: Subcultural Persistence in Mass Society.* Lexington, Mass.: Lexington Books.

Rees, Ronald (1978). "Landscape in Art." Pp. 48–68 in Karl W. Butzer, ed., *Dimensions of Human Geography.* Research Paper 186. Chicago: University of Chicago, Department of Geography.

Reiff, Henry (1940). "We Live by Symbols." *The Social Studies* 31:99–103.

Reps, John W. (1967). *Monumental Washington: The Planning and Development of the Capitol Center.* Princeton: Princeton University Press.

Rhoads, William B. (1976). "The Colonial Revival and American Nationalism." *Journal of the Society of Architectural Historians* 35:239–54.

———— (1977). *The Colonial Revival in America.* 2 vols. New York: Garland.

Richards, Maurice (1968). *Posters of the First World War.* New York: Walker & Co.

Richey, Russell E., and Donald G. Jones, eds. (1974). *American Civil Religion.* New York: Harper & Row.

Riedy, James L. (1981). *Chicago Sculpture.* Urbana: University of Illinois Press.

Robertson, James Oliver (1980). *American Myth, American Reality.* New York: Hill & Wang.

Rocker, Rudolf (1978). *Nationalism and Culture.* Stillwater, Minn.: Croixside Press. First published in 1937.

Roe, Alfred Seelye (1910). *Monuments, Tablets and Other Memorials Erected in Massachusetts to Commemorate the Services of Her Sons in the War of the Rebellion, 1861–1865.* Boston: Wright & Potter Printing Co.

Roelofs, H. Mark (1976). *Ideology and Myth in American Politics: A Critique of a National Political Mind.* Boston: Little, Brown.

Rokkan, S., Kirstl Soden, and Joan Warmbrunn (1973). "Building States and Nations: A Selected Bibliography of the Research Literature by Theme and Country." Pp. 277–397 in S. N. Eisenstadt and Stein Rokkans, eds., *Building States and Nations.* Vol. 1, *Models and Data Resources.* Beverly Hills: Sage Publications.

Rollins, Richard M. (1976). "Words as Social Control: Noah Webster and the Creation of the American Dictionary." *American Quarterly* 28:415–30.

———— (1980). *The Long Journey of Noah Webster.* Philadelphia: University of Pennsylvania Press.

Roorbach, Agnew D. (1937). *The Development of Social Studies in American Secondary Studies before 1861.* Ph.D. dissertation, University of Pennsylvania.

Rosenberg, Bruce A. (1974). *Custer and the Epic of Defeat*. University Park: Pennsylvania State University Press.

Rosenthal, Michael (1986). *The Character Factory: Baden-Powell's Boy Scouts and the Imperatives of Empire*. New York: Pantheon.

Rosewater, Victor (1926). *The Liberty Bell: Its History and Significance*. New York: Appleton-Century.

Rossiter, Clinton (1960). *The American Presidency*. 2d ed. New York: New American Library.

––––––– (1971). *The American Quest, 1790–1860: An Emerging Nation in Search of Identity, Unity, and Modernity*. New York: Harcourt Brace Jovanovich.

Roy, Pierre-George (1923). *Les monuments commémoratifs de la province de Québec*. 2 vols. Québec: Proulx.

Royce, Josiah (1908). "Provincialism." Pp. 55–108 in *Race Questions, Provincialism and Other American Problems*. New York: Macmillan.

Rubinoff, Lionel (1975). "Nationalism and Celebration: Reflections on the Sources of Canadian Identity." *Queen's Quarterly* 82:1–13.

Runte, Alfred (1979). *National Parks: The American Experience*. Lincoln: University of Nebraska Press.

Rydell, Robert William, II (1980). *All the World's a Fair: America's International Expositions, 1876–1916*. Ph.D. dissertation, University of California.

Sack, Robert David (1978). "Geographic and Other Views of Space." Pp. 166–84 in Karl W. Butzer, ed., *Dimensions of Human Geography*. Research Paper 186. Chicago: University of Chicago, Department of Geography.

Sacks, William S. (1955). "Interurban Correspondents and the Development of a National Economy before the Revolution: New York as a Case Study." *New York History* 36:320–35.

Salomon, Gottfried (1932). "Hero Worship." Vol. 7, pp. 336–38 in *Encyclopedia of the Social Sciences*. New York: Macmillan.

Saltus, J. Sanford, and Walter E. Tisné (1923). *Statues of New York*. New York: G. P. Putnam's Sons.

Sanford, Charles L. (1961). *The Quest for Paradise: Europe and the American Moral Imagination*. Urbana: University of Illinois Press.

Sarles, Frank B., Jr., and Charles E. Shedd (1964). *Colonials and Patriots: Historic Places Commemorating Our Forebears, 1700–1783*. Washington, D.C.: National Park Service.

Savelle, Max (1962). "Nationalism and Other Loyalties in the American Revolution." *American Historical Review* 67:901–23.

Schauffler, Robert Haven, ed. (1916). *Washington's Birthday: Its History,*

Observance, Spirit and Significance as Related in Prose and Verse, with a Selection from Washington's Speeches and Writings. New York: Moffat, Yard.

Schechter, Frank I. (1915). "The Early History of the Tradition of the Constitution." *American Political Science Review* 9:707–34.

Schein, Richard H. (1983). *A Geographical and Historical Account of the American Benevolent Fraternal Order.* Master's thesis, Pennsylvania State University.

Schiller, Beatriz (1982). Personal communication, Nov. 14.

Schlereth, Thomas J. (1977). "The Philadelphia Centennial as a Teaching Model." *Hayes Historical Journal* 1(3):201–10.

_____ (1980). *Artifacts and the American Past.* Nashville: American Association for State and Local History.

_____ (1981). "History Outside the History Museum: The Past on the American Landscape." Pp. 87–101 in Fred E. H. Schroeder, ed., *Twentieth-Century Popular Culture in Museums and Libraries.* Bowling Green: Bowling Green University Popular Press.

_____ (1982). Personal communication, Dec. 21.

_____ (1985). *U.S. 40: A Roadscape of the American Experience.* Indianapolis: Indiana Historical Society.

Schlesinger, Arthur M. (1941). "Patriotism Names the Baby." *New England Quarterly* 14:611–18.

_____ (1952). "Liberty Tree: A Genealogy." *New England Quarterly* 25:435–58.

Schlesinger, Tom (1981). "Why the Nixon Library Is Good for Duke." *The Nation* 233(22):704–7.

Schmidt, Alvin J. (1980). *Fraternal Organizations.* Westport, Conn.: Greenwood Press.

Schroeder, Fred E. H. (1977). *Outlaw Aesthetics: Arts and the Public Mind.* Bowling Green: Bowling Green University Popular Press.

Schwartz, Barry (1982). "The Social Context of Commemoration: A Study in Collective Memory." *Social Forces* 61:374–402.

Schwartz, Barry, Yael Zerubavel, and Bernice M. Barrett (1986). "The Recovery of Masada: A Study in Collective Memory." *Sociological Quarterly* 27(2):147–64.

Schwartz, Janet (1980). "The Poet and the Pastoral in the Naming of Suburbia." *Names* 28:231–54.

Schwartz, Marvin (1975). *F.A.O. Schwartz Toys through the Years.* Garden City, N.Y.: Doubleday.

Scott, Jonathan French (1916). *Patriots in the Making: What America Can Learn from France and Germany.* New York: Appleton.

Scully, Michael A. (1984). "The Triumph of the Capitol." *The Public Interest* 74:99–115.

Scully, Vincent J., Jr. (1971). *The Shingle Style and the Stick Style: Architectural Theory and Design from Richardson to the Origins of Wright.* New Haven: Yale University Press.

Searcher, Victor (1965). *The Farewell to Lincoln.* Nashville: Abingdon Press.

Sebba, Gregor (1962). "Symbol and Myth in Modern Rationalistic Society." Pp. 141–68 in Thomas J. J. Altizer, William D. Beardslee, and J. Harvey Young, eds., *Truth, Myth, and Symbol.* Englewood Cliffs, N.J.: Prentice-Hall.

Seits, Laurence (1982). Personal communication, May 26.

Sellers, Charles Coleman (1962). *Benjamin Franklin in Portraiture.* New Haven: Yale University Press.

Seton-Watson, Hugh (1977). *Nations and States: An Enquiry into the Origins of Nations and the Politics of Nationalism.* London: Methuen.

Shackford, James A. (1956). *David Crockett: The Man and the Legend.* Chapel Hill: University of North Carolina Press. Reprint (1986). Chapel Hill: University of North Carolina Press.

*Shafer, Boyd C. (1972). *Faces of Nationalism: New Realities and Old Myths.* New York: Harcourt Brace Jovanovich.

Shaffer, Arthur H. (1975). *The Politics of History: Writing the History of the American Revolution, 1783–1815.* Chicago: Precedent Publishing.

Shankle, George Earlie (1941). *American Mottoes and Slogans.* New York: H. W. Wilson.

Sharp, Lewis I. (1974). *New York City Public Sculpture by 19th-Century Artists.* New York: Metropolitan Museum of Art.

Sheatsley, Paul B., and Jacob B. Feldman (1965). "A National Survey of Public Reactions and Behavior." Pp. 149–77 in Bradley S. Greenberg and Edwin B. Parker, eds., *The Kennedy Assassination and the American Public: Social Communication in Crisis.* Stanford: Stanford University Press.

Shils, Edward, and Michael Young (1975). "The Meaning of the Coronation." Pp. 135–52 in Edward Shils, ed., *Center and Periphery: Essays in Macrosociology.* Chicago: University of Chicago Press.

Shinn, Roger L. (1969). "Apollo as Ritual." *Christianity and Crisis* 29:223.

Shurtleff, Harold R. (1939). *The Log Cabin Myth.* Cambridge: Harvard University Press.

Silber, Irwin (1971). *Songs America Voted By.* Harrisburg: Stackpole Books.

Silverman, Kenneth (1976). *A Cultural History of the American Revolution . . . 1763–1789.* New York: Crowell.

Silvert, K. H., ed. (1963). *Expectant Peoples: Nationalism and Development.* New York: Random House.

Skaggs, David Curtis (1978). "Postage Stamps as Icons." Pp. 198–208 in Ray B. Browne and Marshall Fishwick, eds., *Icons of America.* Bowling Green: Popular Press.

Skjelsbaek, Kjell (1971). "The Growth of Nongovernmental Organizations in the Twentieth Century." *International Organization* 25:420–43.

Sklar, Robert (1975). *Movie-Made America: A Social History of American Movies.* New York: Random House.

Smith, Allan (1970). "Metaphor and Nationality in North America." *Canadian Historical Review* 51:247–75.

———— (1971). "American Culture and the English Canadian Mind at the End of the Nineteenth Century." *Journal of Popular Culture* 4:1045–51.

*Smith, Anthony D. (1977). *Nationalist Movements.* New York: St. Martin's Press.

———— (1979). *Nationalism in the Twentieth Century.* New York: New York University Press.

* ———— (1981). *The Ethnic Revival.* Cambridge: Cambridge University Press.

Smith, Henry Nash (1950). *Virgin Land: The American West as Symbol and Myth.* Cambridge: Harvard University Press.

Smith, Neil (1977). "Symbol, Space, and the Bicentennial." *Antipode* 9(2):76–83.

Smith, Whitney (1975). *The Flag Book of the United States.* Rev. ed. New York: Wm. Morrow.

Smith, William Raymond (1966). *History as Argument: Three Patriot Historians of the American Revolution.* The Hague: Mouton.

Smithsonian Institution, National Museum of History and Technology (1975). *We the People: The American People and Their Government.* Washington, D.C.: Smithsonian Institution Press.

Smylie, James H. (1976). "The President as Republican Prophet and King: Clerical Reflections on the Death of Washington." *Journal of Church and State* 18:233–52.

Smylie, John Edwin (1963). "National Ethos and the Church." *Theology Today* 20:313–21.

Snipper, Martin (1975). *A Survey of Artwork in the City and County of San Francisco.* San Francisco: Art Commission, City and County of San Francisco.

Snyder, Louis L. (1959). *The Meaning of Nationalism.* New Brunswick: Rutgers University Press.

———— (1976). *Varieties of Nationalism: A Comparative Study.* New York: Holt, Rinehart & Winston.

Soderberg, Paul, and Helen Washington (1977). *The Big Book of Halls of Fame in the United States and Canada*. New York: R. R. Bowker.

Somerville, Mollie D. (1979). *Historic and Memorial Buildings of the Daughters of the American Revolution*. Washington, D.C.: National Society, Daughters of the American Revolution.

Somkin, Fred (1967). *Unquiet Eagle: Memory and Desire in the Idea of American Freedom, 1815–1860*. Ithaca: Cornell University Press.

Sonneck, Oscar George Theodore (1914). *The Star Spangled Banner*. Washington, D.C.: Government Printing Office.

Soule, George (1931). "Heroes for America." *Virginia Quarterly Review* 7:261–70.

———— (1937). "New American Heroes." *Virginia Quarterly Review* 13:513–22.

Spencer, Benjamin T. (1936). "A National Literature, 1837–1855." *American Literature* 8:125–59.

———— (1957). *The Quest for Nationality: An American Literary Campaign*. Syracuse: Syracuse University Press.

*Stahl, William A. (1981). *Symbols of Canada: Civil Religion, Nationality, and the Search for Meaning*. Ph.D. dissertation, Graduate Theological Union, Berkeley.

Starbuck, James C. (1976). *Theme Parks: A Partially Annotated Bibliography of Articles about Modern Amusement Parks*. Council of Planning Librarians Exchange, Bibliography 953. Monticello, Ill.: Council of Planning Librarians Exchange.

Stead, W. T. (1901). *The Americanization of the World: Or the Trend of the Twentieth Century*. New York: Horace Markley.

Steckmesser, Kent Ladd (1965). *The Western Hero in History and Legend*. Norman: University of Oklahoma Press.

Steere, Edward (1953–54a). "Expansion of the National Cemetery System, 1880–1900." *Quartermaster Review* 33(2):20–21, 131–37.

———— (1953–54b). "National Cemeteries and Memorials in Global Conflict." *Quartermaster Review* 33(3):18–19, 130–36.

———— (1953–54c). "National Cemeteries and Public Policy." *Quartermaster Review* 33(4):18–19, 142–54.

Steiner, George (1967). *Language and Silence: Essays on Language, Literature, and the Inhuman*. New York: Atheneum.

———— (1974). *Nostalgia for the Absolute*. C.B.C. Massey Lectures. Toronto: Canadian Broadcasting Corporation.

Stephens, H. Morse (1916). "Nationality and History." *American Historical Review* 21:225–36.

Stevens, Ruth Davis, and David Harrison Stevens, eds. (1917). *American Patriotic Prose and Verse*. Chicago: A. C. McClurg.

Stewart, George R. (1953). *U.S. 40: Cross Section of the United States of America.* Boston: Houghton Mifflin.

—— (1954). *American Ways of Life.* Garden City, N.Y.: Doubleday.

—— (1958). *Names on the Land.* Rev. ed. Boston: Houghton Mifflin.

—— (1970). *American Place-Names: A Concise and Selective Dictionary for the Continental United States of America.* New York: Oxford University Press.

—— (1979). *American Given Names.* New York: Oxford University Press.

Stiffler, Stuart A. (1957). "Davy Crockett: The Genesis of Heroic Myth." *Tennessee Historical Quarterly* 16:134–40.

*Stilgoe, John R. (1982). *Common Landscape of America, 1580 to 1845.* New Haven: Yale University Press.

Stone, James (1941). "War Music and War Psychology in the Civil War." *Journal of Abnormal and Social Psychology* 36:543–60.

Strayer, Martha (1958). *The D.A.R.: An Informal History.* Washington, D.C.: Public Affairs Press.

Strout, Cushing (1974). *The New Heavens and New Earth: Political Religion in America.* New York: Harper & Row.

Stump, Roger (1981). "The Dutch Colonial House and the Colonial Revival." *Journal of Cultural Geography* 1(2):44–55.

—— (1985). "Toward a Geography of American Civil Religion." *Journal of Cultural Geography* 5(2):87–95.

Sulzbach, Walter (1943). *National Consciousness.* Washington, D.C.: American Council on Public Affairs.

Sward, Keith (1948). *The Legend of Henry Ford.* New York: Rinehart.

Symmons-Symonolewics, Konstantin (1980). "National Consciousness and Social Theory." *Canadian Review of Studies in Nationalism* 7:386–90.

Takeuchi, Keiichi (1980). "Some Remarks on the History of Regional Description and the Tradition of Regionalism in Modern Japan." *Progress in Human Geography* 4:238–48.

Taylor, Joe Gray (1982). *Eating, Drinking, and Visiting in the South: An Informal History.* Baton Rouge: Louisiana State University Press.

Taylor, Joshua C. (1976). *America as Art.* New York: Harper & Row.

Textor, Robert B., ed. (1966). *Cultural Frontiers of the Peace Corps.* Cambridge: MIT Press.

Thane, Elswyth (1966). *Mount Vernon Is Ours. The Story of Its Preservation.* New York: Duell, Sloan & Pearce.

—— (1967). *Mount Vernon: The Legacy. The Story of Its Preservation and Care since 1885.* Philadelphia: Lippincott.

Thieme, Otto Charles (1980). " 'Wave High the Red Bandanna': Some

Handkerchiefs of the 1888 Presidential Campaign." *Journal of American Culture* 3:686–705.

Thomas, Jean-Claude Marceau (1976). "Washington." Pp. 297–344 in John S. Adams, ed., *Contemporary Metropolitan America.* Vol. 4, *Twentieth Century Cities.* Cambridge: Ballinger.

Thomas, Michael C., and Charles C. Flippen (1972). "American Civil Religion: An Empirical Study." *Social Forces* 51:218–25.

Thompson, E. P. (1983). "On Peace, Power and Parochialism." *The Nation* 237(8):225, 238–44.

Thompson, William Irwin (1976). *Evil and World Order.* New York: Harper & Row.

Thrower, Norman J. W. (1972). "Cadastral Survey and County Atlases of the United States." *Cartographic Journal* 9:1–9.

Thurlow, Fearn (1975). "Newark's Sculpture." *Newark Museum Quarterly* 26:1–32.

Tocqueville, Alexis de (1947). *Democracy in America.* Edited by Henry Steele Commager. New York: Oxford University Press. First published in 1835.

Toffler, Alvin (1980). *The Third Wave.* New York: William Morrow.

Trachtenberg, Marvin (1976). *The Statue of Liberty.* New York: Viking.

Trimmer, Joseph F. (1976). "Monuments and Myths: Three American Arches." *English News,* pp. 1, 6–7. Reprint (1982). Pp. 269–77 in Thomas J. Schlereth, ed., *Material Culture Studies in America.* Nashville: American Association for State and Local History.

Tripp, William R. (1976). *Presidential Campaign Posters.* New York: Drake.

Tuan, Yi-Fu (1974). *Topophilia: A Study of Environmental Perception, Attitudes, and Values.* Englewood Cliffs, N.J.: Prentice-Hall.

——— (1978). "Sacred Space: Exploration of an Idea." Pp. 84–99 in Karl W. Butzer, ed., *Dimensions of Human Geography.* Research Paper 186. Chicago: University of Chicago, Department of Geography.

Tudor, Henry (1972). *Political Myth.* New York: Praeger.

*Tuveson, Ernest Lee (1968). *Redeemer Nation: The Idea of America's Millennial Role.* Chicago: University of Chicago Press.

U.S. Bureau of the Census (1919). *Religious Bodies, 1916. Part I. Summary and General Tables.* Washington, D.C.: Government Printing Office.

U.S. National Park Service (1974). *Public Use of the National Park System. Calendar Year Report—1973.* Washington, D.C.: U.S. National Park Service.

——— (1977). *The Presidents from the Inauguration of George Washington to the Inauguration of Jimmy Carter: Historic Places Commemorating the Chief Executive of the United States.* Washington, D.C.: U.S.

National Park Service.

U.S. Post Office Department (1908). *Street Directory of the Principal Cities of the United States, Embracing Letter-Carrier Offices Established to April 30, 1908.* New York: Manhattan Press.

U.S. Social Security Administration (1964). *Report of Distribution of Surnames in the Social Security Account Number File.* Washington, D.C.: U.S. Social Security Administration.

Van Alstyne, Richard W. (1958). "American Nationalism and Its Mythology." *Queens Quarterly* 65:423–36.

———— (1970). *Genesis of American Nationalism.* Waltham, Mass.: Blaisdell.

Van Doren, Carl (1919). "The Poetical Cult of Lincoln." *The Nation* 106(2811):777.

Van Tassel, David D. (1960). *Recording America's Past: An Interpretation of the Development of Historical Studies in America, 1607–1884.* Chicago: University of Chicago Press.

Van Tyne, Claude H. (1929). *The War of Independence: American Phase.* Boston: Houghton Mifflin.

Varg, Paul A. (1964). "The Advent of Nationalism, 1758–1776." *American Quarterly* 16:169–81.

Verba, Sidney (1965). "The Kennedy Assassination and the Nature of Political Commitment." Pp. 349–60 in Bradley S. Greenberg and Edwin B. Parker, eds., *The Kennedy Assassination and the American Public.* Stanford: Stanford University Press.

Veysey, Laurence (1973). *The Communal Experience: Anarchist and Mystical Counter-Cultures in America.* New York: Harper & Row.

———— (1979). "The Autonomy of American History Reconsidered." *American Quarterly* 31:455–77.

Voigt, David Q. (1976). *America through Baseball.* Chicago: Nelson-Hall.

Vovelle, Michel (1984). "La Marsellaise." Pp. 85–136 in Pierre Nora, ed., *Les lieux de mémoire.* Vol. 1, *La République.* Paris: Gallimard.

*Wachhorst, Wyn (1981). *Thomas Alva Edison: An American Myth.* Cambridge: MIT Press.

Wakeling, Donald R. (1954). "National Anthems." Vol. 6, pp. 14–29, in Eric Blom, ed., *Grove's Dictionary of Music and Musicians.* 5th ed. New York: St. Martin's.

Walden, Daniel (1986). "Where Have All Our Heroes Gone?" *USA Today* 114:20–25.

Walker, Francis A. (1895). "The Growth of American Nationality." *Forum* 19:385–400.

Wallace, Michael (1981). "Visiting the Past: History Museums in the United States." *Radical History Review* 25:63–96.

Wallach, Bret (1982). "The Facsimile Fallacy." *American Review of Canadian Studies* 12(2):82–86.

Walzer, Michael (1967). "On the Role of Symbolism in Political Thought." *Political Science Quarterly* 82:191–204.

Ward, John William (1955). *Andrew Jackson: Symbol for an Age.* New York: Oxford University Press.

———— (1958). "The Meaning of Lindbergh's Flight." *American Quarterly* 10:3–16.

Warfel, Harry R. (1936). *Noah Webster, Schoolmaster to America.* New York: Macmillan.

*Warner, W. Lloyd (1959). *The Living and the Dead: A Study of the Symbolic Life of Americans.* New Haven: Yale University Press.

Warren, Charles (1932). "How Politics Intruded into the Washington Centenary of 1832." *Proceedings of the Massachusetts Historical Society* 65:37–62.

———— (1945). "Fourth of July Myths." *William and Mary Quarterly* 3d ser. 2:237–72.

Washburn, Wilcomb E. (1963). "The Great Autumnal Madness: Political Symbolism in Mid-Nineteenth Century America." *Quarterly Journal of Speech* 49:417–31.

Washington Convention and Visitors Association (1981). *50th Anniversary Annual Report.* Washington, D.C.: Washington Convention and Visitors Association.

Watkins, Melville (1966). "Technology and Nationalism." Pp. 284–302 in Peter Russell, ed., *Nationalism in Canada.* Toronto: McGraw-Hill.

*Weber, Eugen (1976). *Peasants into Frenchmen: The Modernization of Rural France, 1870–1914.* Stanford: Stanford University Press.

*Wecter, Dixon (1941). *The Hero in America: A Chronicle of Hero-Worship.* New York: Scribner's.

Weinberg, Albert K. (1935). *Manifest Destiny: A Study of Nationalist Expansionism in American History.* Baltimore: Johns Hopkins University Press.

Weitenkampf, Frank (1952). "Our Political Symbols." *New York History* 33:371–78.

Weld, Isaac (1807). *Travels through the States of North America, and the Provinces of Upper and Lower Canada during the Years 1795, 1796, and 1797.* 2 vols. London: J. Stockdale.

Werner, Dorothy Leeds (1932). *The Idea of Union in American Verse, 1776–1876.* Ph.D. dissertation, University of Pennsylvania.

White, Richard Grant (1861). *National Hymns.* New York: Rudd & Carleton.

Whitehill, Walter Muir (1962). *Independent Historical Societies.* Boston:

Boston Atheneum and Harvard University Press.

———— (1970). *Boston Statues*. Barre, Mass.: Barre Publishers.

Whittemore, Frances Davis (1933). *George Washington in Sculpture*. Boston: Marshall Jones.

Whittlesey, Derwent (1935). "The Impress of Effective Central Authority upon the Landscape." *Annals of the Association of American Geographers* 25:85–97.

"Who Owns the Stars and Stripes?" (1976). *Time* 96 (July 6): 8–15.

Widener, Ralph W., Jr. (1982). *Confederate Monuments*. Washington, D.C.: Andromeda Associates.

Wiggin, Gladys Anna (1962). *Education and Nationalism: An Historical Interpretation of American Education*. New York: McGraw-Hill.

Wilbur, W. Allan (1973). *The Western Hero: A Study in Myth and American Values*. Menlo Park, Calif.: Addison-Wesley.

Williams, Colin H. (1981). "Nationalism: An Enigma for Geography." Unpublished paper.

———— (1982). "Social Mobilization and Nationalism in Multicultural Societies." *Ethnic and Racial Studies* 5:349–65.

———— (1984). "Ideology and the Interpretation of Minority Cultures." *Political Geography Quarterly* 3(2):105–25.

•Wills, Garry (1978). *Inventing America: Jefferson's Declaration of Independence*. Garden City, N.Y.: Doubleday.

———— (1984). *Cincinnatus: George Washington and the Enlightenment*. Garden City, N.Y.: Doubleday.

Wilson, Edmund (1954). "Abraham Lincoln: The Union as Religious Mysticism." Pp. 181–202 in *Eight Essays*. Garden City, N.Y.: Doubleday.

Wilson, John F. (1971). "The Status of 'Civil Religion' in America." Pp. 1–21 in Elwyn A. Smith, ed., *The Religion of the Republic*. Philadelphia: Fortress Press.

———— (1979). *Public Religion in American Culture*. Philadelphia: Temple University Press.

Winberry, John J. (1982). "Symbols in the Landscape: The Confederate Memorial." *Pioneer America Transactions, 1982*, pp. 9–15.

———— (1983). " 'Lest We Forget': The Confederate Monument and the Southern Townscape." *Southeastern Geographer* 23(2):107–21.

Windmiller, Marshall (1970). *The Peace Corps and Pax Americana*. Washington, D.C.: Public Affairs Press.

Windrow, Martin C., and Gerry Embleton (1973). *Military Dress of North America, 1665–1970*. New York: Scribner's.

Winks, Robin (1976). "Conservation in America: National Character as Revealed by Preservation." Pp. 141–49 in Jane Fawcett, ed., *The Future* of the Past: Attitudes to Conservation, 1174–1974. New York: Whitney Library of Design.

Wittlin, Alma S. (1970). *Museums: In Search of a Usable Future.* Cambridge: MIT Press.

Woelfly, S. J. (1914). *Under the Flag: History of the Stars and Stripes.* Harrisburg: United Evangelical Press.

*Wolfe, James Snow (1975). *The Kennedy Myth: American Civil Religion in the Sixties.* Ph.D. dissertation, Graduate Theological Union, Berkeley.

Wolfenstein, Martha, and Gilbert Kliman, eds. (1965). *Children and the Death of a President: Multi-Disciplinary Studies.* Garden City, N.Y.: Doubleday.

Wood, James Edward, Jr. (1977). *Nationhood and the Kingdom.* Nashville: Broadman Press.

Woodward, C. Vann (1977). "Aging of America." *American Historical Review* 82:583–94.

Wright, Nathalia (1953). "The Monument that Jonathan Built." *American Quarterly* 5:166–74.

Yanker, Gary (1972). *Prop Art: Over 1000 Contemporary Political Posters.* New York: Darien House.

Young, James Sterling (1966). *The Washington Community, 1800–1828.* New York: Columbia University Press.

Young, Philip (1962). "The Mother of Us All: Pocahontas Reconsidered." *Kenyon Review* 24:391–415.

Zangrando, Joanna Schneider (1974). *Monumental Bridge Design in Washington, D.C., as a Reflection of American Culture, 1886 to 1932.* Ph.D. dissertation, George Washington University.

Zeldin, Mary-Barbara (1969). "The Religious Nature of Russian Marxism." *Journal of the Society of Architectural Historians* 13:9–12.

Zelinsky, Wilbur (1954). "The Greek Revival House in Georgia." *Journal for the Scientific Study of Religion* 8:100–111

———— (1967). "Classical Town Names in the United States: The Historical Geography of an American Idea." *Geographical Review* 57:463–95.

———— (1973). *The Cultural Geography of the United States.* Englewood Cliffs, N.J.: Prentice-Hall.

———— (1975). "The Demigod's Dilemma." *Annals of the Association of American Geographers* 65:123–43.

———— (1983). "Nationalism in the American Place-Name Cover." *Names* 30:1–28.

———— (1984a). *The Historical Geography of Season of Marriage: North America, 1844–1974.* Population Issues Research Center. Working Paper no. 1984-15. University Park, Pa.

_____ (1984b). "O Say, Can You See? Nationalist Emblems in the Landscape." *Winterthur Portfolio* 19(4):77–86.

Zeman, Zbynek (1978). *Selling the War: Art and Propaganda in World War II.* London: Orbis.

Zenderland, Leila, ed. (1978). *Recycling the Past: Popular Uses of American History.* Philadelphia: University of Pennsylvania Press.

Zikmund, Joseph, II (1969). "National Anthems as Political Symbols." *Australian Journal of Politics and History* 15(3):73–80.

Zimmer, Christian (1974). *Cinema et politique.* Paris: Éditions Seghers.

Zook, Nicholas (1971). *Museum Villages USA.* Barre, Mass.: Barre Publishers.

Zuckerman, Michael (1978). "The Irrelevant Revolution: 1776 and Since." *American Quarterly* 30:224–42.

Zurier, Rebecca (1982). *The American Firehouse: An Architectural and Social History.* New York: Abbeville Press.

INDEX ★ ★ ★ ★ ★ ★ ★ ★

Greenough, Horatio, 186
Griffith, D. W., 168

Hail Columbia, 171
Halberstam, David, 110
Hale, Nathan, 41–42, 44, 66
Hall of Fame, 193
Hamilton, Alexander, 35, 166; post-
humous reputation, 36, 38; sym-
bolic significance, 38; iconogra-
phy, 185
Hampden, John, 29, 39
Hancock, John, 35
Harding, Warren G., 60, 91
Harkness, Albert, 225
Harper, William Rainey, 56
Harris, Neil, 152, 181
Harrison, Benjamin, 82
Harrison, William Henry, 43, 60,
77, 91
Hasbrouck House, 186
Hawthorne, Nathaniel, 157, 247
Hay, R. P., 73, 240
Hayes, Carlton, 1, 233–34, 287
(n. 19)
Hélias, Pierre-Jakez, 283 (n. 1)
Henry, Patrick, 42, 44, 127, 229
Heroes: folk, 21, 28, 44, 66; universal, 21, 66; theory of, 27; frontier,
27, 43–44, 51; Revolutionary War,
31–41; children's and adolescents' choice as exemplars, 37;
culture heroes, 39, 68; military,
43, 50; segmental, 44, 51, 65;
generalized, anonymous, 50, 55–
56, 66; criminal, 51; technological wizard, 51, 52–55, 68; business tycoon, 51, 54, 55; athletic,
51–52, 64; decline of, 62–68; female, 68, 121–22, 271 (n. 11), 279
(n. 11); geography of, 261 (n. 12)
Hero-worship, 27, 259 (n. 3)

Hickok, Wild Bill, 44
Hill, James J., 51
Historical markers, 180–81
Historical societies, 144
Historic preservation, 93, 105, 107,
186, 191–94
Historic sites, 96–104, 244. *See also*
Historic preservation
Historiography, 17, 144–52; de-
bunking mode, 147; school texts,
147–50; local, 273 (n. 22)
Hobsbawm, Eric, 213
Holidays, national, 33, 69–75, 261–
62 (n. 2), 262 (n. 30)
Honor rolls, 183
Hook, Sidney, 27
Hooker, Thomas, 30
Hoover, Herbert, 60, 192, 271
(n. 14)
Hoover, J. Edgar, 51, 59
Horatio Alger hero, 27
Horwitz, Elinor, 157
Houdon, J. A., 157, 275 (n. 36)
Houston, Sam, 30, 44
Howe, Elias, 52
Hudson River School, 162
Hughes, Howard, 51
Humboldt, Alexander von, 68, 121
Hume, David, 10
Hutchins, Robert Maynard, 56
Huxley, Aldous, 152, 246

Iconography, 32–33, 152–65
Idealized national figures, 22–27
Ideology, 14
Illinois, scarcity of nationalistic
names, 141
Inaugural addresses, 79
Inaugurations, 76, 78–80, 263–64
(n. 4)
Independence, as concept in names,
121

significance of death, 60; as transnational figure, 66; bicentennial, 82; inaugural journey, 87, 185; funeral sermons, 117; in music, 171; design of D.C., 179
Washington, Martha, 43
Washington, D.C., 101, 104, 176, 179–80, 278–79 (n. 6)
Washington Crossing the Delaware, 95, 159–60
Washington Monument, 96, 182, 183, 186, 213
Washington's Birthday, 33, 70, 72, 117, 262–63 (n. 7)
Watkins, C. E., 162
Watkins, Melville, 251
Wayne, Anthony, 35
Weber, Eugen, 283 (n. 1)
Webster, Daniel, 43, 117, 145
Webster, Noah, 116, 148–49, 167, 271 (n. 24)
Wecter, Dixon, 27, 36
Weems, Mason Locke, 34, 145, 146
Welcoming festivities, 90
Weld, Isaac, 231
West, Benjamin, 158
West, as symbol, 167, 232
Wheeler, Benjamin Ide, 56
Whitehill, Walter M., 188
White House, 101
White paint, 210
Whitman, Walt, 157, 184

Whitney, Eli, 52
Why We Fight, 169
Willard, Archibald, 160
Williams, Roger, 30
Williamsburg, Colonial, 93, 94, 95, 96, 192, 194, 214
Wilson, J. F., 45
Wilson, John, 239
Wilson, Samuel, 24
Wilson, Woodrow, 48, 121, 169, 271 (n. 14)
Wilson (film), 48, 169
Winthrop, John, 30
Wolfe, James S., 60–62, 78–79
Wood, Grant, 275 (n. 39)
Works Progress Administration, 164, 177
World's fairs, 85–89, 90, 265 (n. 22)
World War I, 75, 154, 171, 190, 248
World War II, 154–55, 165, 169, 171, 190, 248
Wright, Orville and Wilbur, 52

Xenophobia, 4

Yankee Doodle, 24, 171
York, Alvin C., 50
Youth's Companion, 203

Zanuck, Darryl, 48, 169
Zook, Nicholas, 192
Zuckerman, Michael, 84

CPSIA information can be obtained at www.ICGtesting.com
Printed in the USA
LVOW062028281212

313670LV00001B/37/P